500 Events That Shaped the History of Money

500 Events
That Shaped the
History of Money

Alexander Paris-Callahan

KB

Kingman Books
Los Angeles, California

ISBN (paperback): 979-8-9997559-2-6
ISBN (hardcover): 979-8-9997559-1-9

Published by Kingman Books
Los Angeles, California

Layout design by Alexander Paris-Callahan
Edited by Tristin Milazzo and Michael Stroup, PhD
Cover design by Shoib Brohi

Contents

Introduction

Today, trillions of dollars in financial transactions are processed daily worldwide at lightning speeds. Complex algorithms dictate the prices of stocks and bonds. Giant banks and investment firms serve hundreds of millions of customers, while ordinary people, even in the poorest countries, can send and receive money from their phones. And new forms of cryptocurrency keep emerging.

Yet the current era of financial innovation is hardly unique.

Five thousand years ago, banking and taxation were developed in Mesopotamia and Egypt, followed by the invention of coinage and the rise of more complicated financial systems in Ancient Greece and Rome. The Renaissance, Age of Exploration, and industrialization also spurred financial innovations, and by the mid-20th century, finance itself was becoming one of the dominant forces shaping the world. Financial innovation continues in the early 21st century, powered by new technologies.

This book takes a new approach to telling the story of money. Organized into 500 key events, it offers a sweeping global look at money's evolution across different societies.

Chapters one and two chronicle the birth of money, from the barter and gift systems of prehistory to economies in the first states. Mesopotamia's rudimentary financial systems are the foundations for many important financial tools we use today. Ancient people invented the basis for banking, lending, and exchanging, as well as laws that continue to govern how people interact with money.

Chapters three, four, and five look at the evolution of finance from the Middle Ages to the creation of new institutions for lending, borrowing, and investing that emerged by the 19th century. Powerful banks in Italy, most famously the Medici

Bank, helped fuel economic growth during the Renaissance, along with improvements in accounting. Spain's conquests in the New World brought an influx of gold and silver to the continent. Amsterdam became a financial powerhouse, home to both the world's first stock market and modern joint-stock corporation. Not all innovation was in Europe, though. China, India, the Muslim world, and the empires of the Americas were also key grounds for financial development. Paper money was first put to widespread use in China, while the Muslim world developed early nonprofit endowments. The Incas didn't have money in the traditional sense or a true capitalist economy. They kept accounts with knotted strings.

Chapters six and seven tell of the accelerating pace of financial innovation in the 19th and 20th centuries as industrialization transformed societies and turbocharged wealth creation. Booms and busts were a defining feature of this period, as ever more complex systems for managing money created new systemic risks. Millions of people benefited from surging economic prosperity. Many also suffered when speculation led to financial panics, which punctuated the 19th century.

Societies coped with these instabilities by creating new structures to reduce financial risks and protect their citizens. Many countries opened central banks, as did the United States with the Federal Reserve in 1913. Modern welfare states appeared as well, providing payments to the unemployed and aged. Meanwhile, financial innovation increasingly transformed how people lived, allowing them to borrow money more easily to purchase an expanding array of consumer goods through installment loans.

The events of chapters eight and nine take us into the age of financialization, which began in the 1970s. As advanced capitalism created vast new wealth, the systems for lending, investing, and moving money around globally became ever more sophisticated. The financial sector grew in size and influence. Massive banks and investment firms came to manage trillions of dollars in assets, including huge sums in retirement accounts held by ordinary people. This era, too, saw spectacular crashes, including the 2008 financial crisis.

In recent years, new technologies have further transformed finance, with cryptocurrency moving from the fringes of the economy to play an increasingly large role. At the same time, the spread of smartphones enabled people worldwide to access banking and engage in financial transactions.

These financial developments do not just make money easier to use. They make our modern society possible. Most key markers of modernity such as cars, large universities, and skyscrapers are not only expensive to build but also require many complex parts. The financial system offers a means for people to pool large sums of money to invest in these kinds of projects and allows for an efficient way to gain access to the labor of specialists. In the Middle Ages a cathedral could be built over decades or centuries with contributions from monarchs or wealthy patrons. Today, skyscrapers that cost billions can be put up in a few years. Virtually no one has billions in ready cash to build a skyscraper; but with modern banking, corporations can finance construction as well as raise money from their base of shareholders, none of whom are risking their own livelihoods by participating in the project.

By breaking the history of money into 500 events, this book takes a broad yet also nuanced look at how money and finance have evolved over thousands of years, making today's society possible. Many of the events are well-known; a number are quite obscure. But they have all pushed history forward and helped create the world we live in today. Money is an integral part of the human experience. It says a lot about who we are and the societies in which we live. To understand the history of money is to understand the history of civilization.

What is Money?

Economics traditionally defines money as either a physical medium or concept that fulfills the following uses:

- A means of exchange
- A store of value
- A unit of account
- A standard of deferred payment

First, a means of exchange means that money is a physical token that can be used to exchange. Second, a store of value means that the token has and keeps value, either because it is accepted at its face-value, as in the case of fiat money, or because it is made of a precious metal that continues to be valuable. Third, a unit of account means that a currency represents a standard unit that can be used for bookkeeping—even if there is no physical token associated with it. Finally, money can be a standard of deferred payment, meaning that it is accepted as the value of debt and for a good bought now and paid for later.

Not all money fulfills all four purposes, but at least one of these four definitions applies to every type of money. The definitions themselves have evolved. Before coinage was invented, money was no more than a unit of account (and maybe a store of value). Overall, though, what money is has stayed the same, even though how it is represented—be it grain, coins, notes, or bonds—has changed.

I

The Birth of Money:
Prehistory – 650 BC

Trade has existed for as long as humans have. Early humans used barter and the gift economy to acquire items they did not produce themselves. These systems worked well for small bands of people trading among themselves or for trade with other small bands when there were not many things to trade. Barter is efficient when both sides of an exchange desire what the other side has to offer. Goods that have near-universal demand, are easily transported, and retain value for future trades are ideal for barter. Soon, commodities like grain, seed, and rare metals useful for production or decoration became popular items with which to trade as a form of early commodity money.

Starting in around the fifth or fourth millennia BC, the first states emerged. They were larger and more impersonal administrative and cultural bodies resembling governments. Economically, one of the most important features of states was taxes. Taxes allowed one class of people to be supported by the production of another. This meant that some did not have to farm for themselves and could instead govern, plan, build infrastructure, and run a system to promote the general welfare, as well as wage war. Some of today's most important types of financial institutions arose during this time. Temples in Mesopotamia acted as banks by taking deposits and making loans. Some banks facilitated fund transfer systems between borrowers and lenders. Societies developed laws and moral codes to address this practice, such as the Bible of the Israelites and the Code of Hammurabi in Babylonia, that continue to influence our society and perceptions of money today.

Formally minted coinage had yet to appear on the scene, even though barter was phased out in ever-growing societies. Banking and taxes existed without it. The non-existence of convenient coinage forced societies to develop intra-bank transactions, which made it easier to transfer otherwise burdensome commodities. The record-keeping required for these institutions was the impetus for the invention of writing. There are literally hundreds of thousands of written records remaining from ancient Mesopotamia. Many of them are receipts for transactions, lists of goods, and contracts.

Mesopotamia's rudimentary financial systems, developed thousands of years ago, are the foundations for many important financial tools we use today. Ancient people invented the basis for banking, lending, and exchanging, as well as the laws that continue to govern how people interact with money.

First Trade: Barter and the Gift Economy

1 200,000 BC Since the dawn of man, people have needed the functions that money provides; however, early on, there was no technology advanced enough to create a physical object to carry out those functions. Aristotle and Adam Smith both claimed that prehistoric men and women made logical, clear, and fair transactions through barter. If John had a cow but needed some apples, and Sam was an orchardman but needed a cow, the two could make a fair trade.

Barter, however, requires a "double coincidence of wants." Each person needs to want what the other offers—an often unlikely scenario. Additionally, barter assumes that the price of every single commodity can be denominated in every other commodity. This would mean that there would be too many different price combinations to easily keep track of. These problems made widespread barter unlikely.

In his book *Debt: The First 5000 Years*, David Graeber proposes that pre-money societies used a gift economy. He points out that economics textbooks imagine some fantasy land where people who used barter had "a tendency to shift from imaginary savages to small-town shopkeepers." According to Graeber, in the gift economy, if John needed some apples, Sam gifted them to him, and maybe in the future John would reciprocate by giving Sam some milk.

Accountants Invent Writing

2 ca. 32nd c. BC Finance, including its terms and obligations, was the first motivator to invent writing. Many of the oldest surviving written documents—cuneiform tablets from Mesopotamia as early as 3100 BC—are lists and quantities of agricultural products, banking contracts, and account information. The system for numbers started simply with a stroke for single units and a circle to represent 10. Later, the base-60 system developed, using units of 60 rather than 10. This evolved into a more complex system of characters called cuneiform, meaning "wedge-shaped," as the characters are composed of wedges. In cuneiform, each character represents a syllable, rather than a single sound as in English.

Hundreds of thousands of these tablets have been dug up, and many are now on display in museums. One such tablet is an agreement that, after a slave was sold, his previous owners would make no claim on him. It reads: "Sini-Ishtar has bought a slave, Ea-tappi by name, from Ilu-elatti, and Akhia, his son, and has paid ten shekels of Silver, the price agreed. Ilu-elatti, and Akhia, his son, will not set up a future claim on the slave." Writing turned what were previously oral agreements into clear, legally binding contracts. Credible contracts made transactions reliable and thus more valuable.

First Tax in Egypt

3 ca. 27th c. BC Egypt instituted the world's first taxes during the Old Kingdom period. The taxes were charged, usually annually, in the form of money used at the time: cattle, grain, and human labor. There is some evidence to suggest that censuses were taken to aid in the collection of taxes. A novel system known as writing was developed for documentation, though not very widely.

In general, tax rates were set rather precisely (although, the pharaoh would sometimes tack on discretionary taxes to subsidize the standard tax). The annual Nile flood was the biggest determiner of the amount of agricultural production in Egypt, and thus tax rates were set based on the predicted amount of flooding. These rates were then revised after the government sent surveyors out after the flood receded to measure how large the flood turned out to be.

The money collected went to projects such as the construction of the Pyramids of Giza. The exemption of the clergy from paying taxes, however, cut into the size of Egypt's tax-base substantially, which, along with high government spending, eventually bankrupted the Old Kingdom treasury.

This economic document from about 2500 BC is written in Sumerian cuneiform. Scribes often wrote cuneiform characters smaller than modern type

Rise of Mesopotamia's Monetary System

4 **24th c. BC** The ancient Mesopotamian monetary system was based on commodity weights and continued for at least a few centuries after the first coins stamped with a face-value were issued. In ascending order of value, the materials that usually functioned as money were barley, lead, copper or bronze, tin, silver, and gold. Other goods, such as animals, slaves, utensils, and other one-off objects, could also fill in for trade. Interestingly, around 2400 BC, a duck-shaped basalt figure inscribed with its weight came to be used as a sort of rudimentary coin in Sumeria. This system was not fixed, and the value of commodities fluctuated based on time and place. This is why interest on barley loans—a good which is subject to seasonal fluctuation—was often as much as one-third of the principal, while that for silver was only one-fifth.

Weights became standardized to some extent with the system of shekels, minae, and talents, though the exact weight of each of these units differed by time and place.

In general, one mina was worth 60 shekels, each of which weighed about eight grams; one talent was 60 minae. These names are English versions—the Sumerian term for shekel was "gin," and mina was "mana."

Taxation Invented in Mesopotamia

5 21st c. BC The earliest known tax system, the *bala*, meaning "rotation," was introduced as early as 6,000 BC in Mesopotamia. Its form was finalized under King Shulgi of Mesopotamia's Ur III dynasty, who ruled in the last century of the third millennium BC. Under the tax system, provinces sent labor, livestock, and commodities—usually those in which each province specialized—to a central collection point on a rotating schedule. Provinces paid in during a certain period of time, which was determined by the central government. The term *bala* technically referred to the period of time that a province needed to pay the tax. The *bala* period was usually one month a year.

The provincial administrators were the people who physically handed over the money for the tax, and the accounts were in their names. Some larger provinces paid the tax for up to three months, while smaller ones needed to work together to pay their tax burden in full. The collected revenue was then used to maintain temples and other government works that Mesopotamia's central government deemed important.

Banking Invented

6 ca. 20th c. BC It would be a little odd today to go to your priest and ask him to hold onto your grain for you, but that is how the earliest banking worked in Mesopotamia. Banking began in temples and royal houses because they were safer than private residences. Thus, temple and royal officials became bankers. Early on, only grain was deposited, but other commodities came to be accepted over time. Temple-banks eventually started taking precious metals, which soon became the standard medium for making money.

Depositors were given a receipt of their deposit written on clay in cuneiform, which could be traded with a third party, thus becoming a sort of debt receipt. The thousands of remaining banking-related cuneiform tablets show that banking was an everyday affair and important enough to be regulated by the Code of Hammurabi. In addition to taking deposits, some later private banks acted as pawnbrokers, tax agents, or jewelers. Private banks also financed public works. These private banks, such as the House of Egibi, one of the earliest on record, started vying with temple banks likely around the sixth century BC [see: 22].

Loans in Mesopotamia

7 ca. 20th c. BC The earliest recorded evidence of loan making was from Mesopotamia during the Ur III period, though it possibly started even earlier. Both individuals and institutions acted as creditors. There were three types of loans during this period: customary loans, interest-free loans, and antichretic loans.

Customary loans were paid in-kind or in precious metal, including barley, gold, and silver, and interest was charged on the loan. The time by which the loan had to be repaid was not always specified. Interest-free loans were often given for short durations, sometimes less than a month. These loans were sometimes used to remedy emergencies when money was quickly needed. The interest for antichretic loans was paid in labor. The specific terms of these loans varied, as different people were assigned to do the labor in different cases.

At times, an advance of silver and barley was accorded for a loan. In some cases, loans could be transferred or sold—key part of modern loan-making. Thus, the Fertile Crescent, the birthplace of civilization, was also the birthplace of finance.

Babylonian Tapputum Companies

8 18th c. BC The structure of a corporation allows money from multiple sources to be channeled to productive projects more effectively than a sole proprietorship. One of the first corporation-like agreements was the *tapputum* contract in Ancient Babylonia. This type of contract was not a true corporation in the modern sense, but it did feature key characteristics of its modern counterpart. The *tapputum* was a type of loan that came into use at least before the 18th century BC. One or more parties, all of whom bore joint liability, loaned money to another party. The borrower used the money for a trading venture or expedition, such as buying and selling gold or corn. The partnership ended with the end of the venture—usually after a few months.

After the contract ended, the lenders and debtor took proportional shares in the profit, based on their stake, much like a rudimentary stock dividend. The Code of Hammurabi later regulated *tapputum* agreements to prevent fraud and ensure fairness. The *tapputum* may have been unknown to the inventors of the modern corporation, but it is significant as an early attempt to let investors with a joint vision put their money to its most efficient uses.

First Financial Regulation, Code of Hammurabi

9 18th c. BC King Hammurabi ruled the old Babylonian Empire from about 1792 BC until his death in 1750. He produced the world's first written set of laws, the Code of Hammurabi, which was inscribed on a seven-foot-tall block of diorite and is now on display at the Louvre. The laws in the Code addressed all areas of ancient Babylonian life, including financial transactions. The discussion of loans in the Code showed what the thousands of remaining loan-related cuneiform tablets suggest: the number of Babylonia's wealthy became great enough that standardized laws for them were deemed necessary, and financial transactions such as loans became common in Mesopotamian life.

Relating to loans, section 102 reads: "If a merchant entrusts money to an agent (broker) for some investment, and the broker suffers a loss in the place to which he goes, he shall make good the capital to the merchant." Section 108 addresses commodity payments: "If a tavern-keeper does not accept corn according to gross weight in payment of drink, but takes money, and the price of the drink is less than that of the corn, she shall be convicted and thrown into the water." These detailed provisions show clear economic development by demonstrating standardization of somewhat advanced financial concepts.

Criticisms of Usury

10 Usury was forbidden in most of the world until the Renaissance. Today, usury means lending at excessive interest. In the past, however, charging any interest was prohibited as usury. Key early works in the West ban usury, such as the Code of Hammurabi and the Bible. In Classical times, Plato argued that usury is unjust, as it increases the gap between the rich and poor and creates tensions between people. Islam prohibited usury for many of the same reasons as Plato, who saw charging interest as exploitation and the pursuit of profits as a distraction from religious duties. In the East, usury was prohibited by Hinduism.

Medieval thinkers developed justifications for the prohibition of usury, based on Aristotle and Aquinas. According to Aristotle, two animals may breed, thereby increasing their numbers on their own, which is natural. Money, however, is "sterile," meaning that it cannot increase or decrease on its own. Thus, interest, which increases money on its own, is unnatural [see: 35].

Aquinas added to the theory of the sterility of money by differentiating two categories of goods: fungible and non-fungible. Non-fungible goods can be employed productively without necessarily being consumed. For example, a farmer can work farmland without the land losing value. Conversely, fungible goods, like wine or food, can be consumed and lose value when they are consumed.

Aquinas saw money as fungible. The value of the use of a fungible good and the value of the good itself are the same because fungible goods are meant to be consumed. Therefore you cannot charge for both. You cannot sell a cake and sell the permission to eat it too. You cannot lend money and charge for the permission to borrow (interest). Additionally, paying back a loan with interest is repaying more than was initially taken. The lender is getting more than he gave, which is unfair. While Aquinas ignored the lender's lost opportunity to use the money while it's loaned, his perspective informed finance law on usury until the Renaissance.

Old Testament Regulates Usury

11 14th c. BC The Old Testament prohibits charging interest on loans, particularly within the Jewish community. Exodus states, "If you lend money to one of my people among you who is needy, do not treat it like a business deal; charge no interest." Deuteronomy clarifies this restriction, adding, "Do not charge a fellow Israelite interest. . . . You may charge a foreigner interest, but not a fellow Israelite." Ezekiel goes even further: "He lends at interest and takes a profit. Will such a man live? He will not! Because he has done all these detestable things, he is to be put to death." The prohibition was rooted in the Jewish social context, where lending was often seen as a duty to help those in need rather than a commercial transaction.

The New Testament does not explicitly ban interest but emphasizes generosity in lending. In Luke, Jesus teaches: "And if you lend to those from whom you expect repayment, what credit is that to you? Even sinners lend to sinners, expecting to be repaid in full. But love your enemies, [...] lend to them without expecting to get anything back." While the prohibition of usury originated in a limited context, it later, through evolving Christian doctrine, was interpreted to mean that charging any interest at all was a sin.

Tool Money in China

12 ca. 12th c. BC The first coins in China were not round discs. They were shaped like tools—knives, spades, and hoes. They were issued and authenticated by the state, bearing inscriptions attesting to their authenticity. Accepted based on face value and generally identical, the coins thus represent standardized values. They were coins in

The Code of Hammurabi is over seven feet tall, and is presently on display at the Louvre. French archaeologists found it in the city of Susa, Iran in 1901.

every respect of the word, except they weren't round like later coins. The early Chinese tool money coins beg the question of if is it fair to call those seventh century BC coin strikings of Lydia the world's first coins [see: 17].

This tool-shaped money first appeared around the end of the second millennium BC and was in use by the time of the Zhou Dynasty, mostly north of the Yellow River. During the Warring States period, each state issued its own tool money, which propagated around much of East Asia. Made of bronze, tool money made the use of base metal standard, which continued to be the metal of choice for indigenous Chinese coinage until the introduction of Western coinage. Tool money started to be replaced with circular coins during the Warring States period and was fully phased out by the Qin Dynasty.

Shells Used as Money

13 **late 2nd mil. BC** It is unclear when or where cowrie shells were first used as money. It was likely sometime about a millennium BC. The cowrie shell is a mollusk shell usually about one inch long. Cowries are durable, are easily counted, difficult to counterfeit, and easier to come by than proper coinage. You can find them on the beach (which also makes them a poor choice for money, as they aren't scarce).

Dotted around the Indian and Pacific oceans, cowries were used as money in China—possibly as early as the Shang Dynasty—India, and Southeast Asia. They also made it to the Middle East and Africa. Cowries were usually used as small denominations. Much later, they may have been used on the Silk Road, and from the 15th through the 19th centuries, European traders brought cowries from the Indian Ocean to West Africa in large quantities, damaging the local money system. While coin money soon usurped cowries' role in much of the world, parts of Africa continued using cowries until only the last few centuries. In the late 18th century, you could purchase a woman for two cowries in remote parts of Uganda. Inflation set in, and by 1860 a woman cost one thousand cowries. You could pay taxes with cowries until the twentieth century.

*Cowries are a family of small sea snails. They are
often found on rocky parts of the sea bed.*

China "Prints" Money by Making Shells

14 **1st mil. BC** When there is a shortage of money today, a country's central bank can simply print more. Increasing the money supply was somewhat more difficult for the people of Ancient China, as they used cowrie shells that were found on the beach. So, when shells ran short, the Chinese used imitation cowrie shells as substitutes for real ones. These imitations were made of a wide range of materials, like marble, bronze, jade, clay, iron, quartz, ivory, mother-of-pearl, and bone.

This diversity of materials posed a problem from an economic perspective. Imitations made of different materials and with different qualities of craftsmanship were likely perceived as worth different amounts. Trying to keep the values of the different imitation cowries equal relative to each other would prove futile, and this inconsistency would likely have led to Gresham's Law becoming an issue [see: 230].

Cowrie shells were used not only as trade money but also as ornaments, magical objects, and burial money. It is possible that people used the cheaper imitations for these non-monetary purposes, while only the real shells were circulated as money. Another hypothesis suggests that different substitutes circulated during different time periods. Regardless, the use of cowrie shells may be one of the first instances of the intentional expansion of the money supply.

Hacksilver Viking Money

15 10th c. BC Hacksilver is fragments of silver that were used as money around Europe and the Mediterranean, especially by the Vikings. In general, while a powerful government can force its citizens to take and use its coins at face value, weight is used to determine value when such a government does not exist. Thus, hacksilver fragments, found in hoards that also included coins and ornaments, were weighed and used as a form of money. Weighing technology, which had little use outside of accounting, became widespread in the 14th and 13th centuries BC, suggesting a likely start-date for the use of hacksilver.

Two thousand years later, the Viking raids on England in the AD ninth through 11th centuries put Scandinavians in contact with the superior coinage system of the Anglo-Saxon kingdoms. Scandinavians started minting coins modeled on those of the Anglo-Saxon kingdoms. Subsequent hoards dated to the 11th and 12th centuries in Scandinavia were found to lack hacksilver and foreign coinage, implying that by then Scandinavian coinage had replaced hacksilver.

Well-Field System in China

16 9th c. BC The well-field system emerged in Zhou China in the ninth century BC. This system dictated how much land peasant farmers worked for themselves and how much land they worked for the government. Square parcels of land were broken into nine pieces, similar to the grid of the # symbol. Each of eight farmer families cultivated one of the eight outer parcels while all the families cultivated the central parcel communally, either for themselves or for the land's lord.

The socialistic nature of the well-field arrangement has led historians to make two generalizations. Some see the system as a balance between the need to support oneself and to help one's neighbors. The well-field system aligns with Confucian values as a middle-ground between excessive altruism and self-focus. On the other hand, Marxist scholars claim that the system was designed to exploit the people working on the eight private plots, who were serfs by Marxist definition.

The well-field system flourished during the Western Zhou period (11th to eighth centuries BC). It started declining during the Spring and Autumn Period and ultimately died out during the Warring States Period. It was briefly resuscitated by Wang Mang, who sought to bring back old virtues [see: 57].

II

Coinage and Early Finance: 7th c. BC – 5th c. AD

The invention of coinage marked a change in what money was perceived to be. Before coinage, money referred to a unit of value that existed as a number of rudimentary bank account books. After the invention of coinage around 650 BC, money broadly came to be understood as precious metal coinage. This doesn't mean in only *was* precious metal coinage. Bank money continued to exist, but was generally only used for more specialized purposes. Coinage was first invented in the kingdom of Lydia in modern-day Turkey, and from there spread to Greece and around the Mediterranean. Coinage was nearly simultaneously introduced in China and India. Even though the three regions had no connection, they chose to make coins out of the same precious metals: gold, silver, and bronze.

Coinage allowed transactions to become more impersonal and efficient, as people weren't bartering in grain. Coinage also acted as political propaganda. Rulers realized that the hundreds of tokens circulating around a kingdom could be used to spread any message that could be struck on a small disk. Julius Caesar was the first Roman to reinforce his power by minting an image of himself on Rome's coinage. All later emperors of Rome followed suit.

Coinage also likely aided in economic expansion that necessitated the development of more advanced financial tools, like banking. The *trapeza* bankers emerged in Ancient Greece, while separate types of banks later emerged in Rome. Early corporate organizations assisted in economic development in Rome. *Societates*—Rome's main corporate structure—allowed over a dozen partners to work jointly on a venture. Other financial tools were developed, such as annuities, while culture around economics developed through the writings of men like Aristotle and Confucius.

While the roots of most fundamental institutions in the financial system were developed in the era covered in the last chapter, in this period those institutions become more advanced. Coinage played an important role in developing new uses of money. Monetization and impersonalization were characteristics of the period. Impersonalization made financial transactions more efficient, which was necessary to manage a society as large as Rome and Greece. One of the key jobs of those *societates* corporations was to build public infrastructure and manage other government affairs, something that required corporation-like joint organization. This period saw the emergence of a more widespread financial system.

World's First Coins

17 7th c. BC Lydia, a wealthy kingdom in modern-day western Turkey, is where coinage originated. The precious metal of choice at the time was electrum, a naturally occurring light-yellow alloy of gold and silver, usually found by panning in rivers. At first, around the end of the eighth and the beginning of the seventh centuries, the metal was fashioned into irregularly shaped blobs. By about 650 BC, the blobs became circular and punch-marked or scratched. Primarily used to guarantee purity, the scratches became a mark of authenticity. The earlier coins were also stamped by merchants as another symbol of authenticity. Lydia narrowly beat its neighbor, Ionia, to the invention of coinage. We do not know what these specific marks represented and cannot determine if Lydian coins were valued by face-value or weight.

The invention itself was quite simple. Tokens of sorts existed for a long time, and it was no great task making them standardized and marked. Why in Lydia? Herodotus said that the Lydians had a highly commercialized society and were first to establish permanent stores. This type of commercialization along with the growing size of society necessitated standardized and impersonal means of exchange.

Lydia's first coins, produced in the late seventh to mid-sixth centuries, featured a roaring lion on the obverse.

Coin Minting Technologies Develop

18 7th c. BC There are three methods of minting coins: hammering, casting, and milling. Hammered coinage was the most common type from the invention of coinage in the seventh century BC to the 17th century AD. These coins were minted by first putting a blank piece of metal called a planchet or flan on top of one die. This usually corresponded with the reverse side of the coin. The other side of the coin, known as the obverse side, was then struck with a hammer. The hammer put an engraved image on both sides of the blank coin. Dies normally lasted about 10,000 strikes before becoming excessively worn. Reverse-side dies generally wore more slowly. Nine obverse dies found at Delphi, Greece, for example, seem to have struck some 23,000–47,000 coins.

Cast coinage is as old as hammered coinage. This form of coinage was generally used only by forgers, except for in Asia, where governments produced coinage by casting. As the name suggests, precious metal (or bronze in Asia) was poured into molds to cast coins. It is not difficult to tell if a coin is cast, as such coins often show a seam where the molds joined, and have more irregular weights than their more precise hammered counterparts. Additionally, the process of cooling leaves cast coinage with a different molecular pattern than hammered coins have—a difference that can be identified under a microscope.

Milled coinage is a broad category of coin produced by machine. With the inflow of precious metal discovered in the Americas in the 16th century, European mints became overworked and started producing inferior products. To remedy this problem, an automatic striking machine was invented in Germany in the 1550s [see: 131].

First Coins in India

19 6th c. BC India invented coinage independently from Lydia and China, and its early coins display several unique characteristics that set them apart. The first Indian coins, which emerged around the sixth century BC, were initially disk-shaped but later evolved into bar-like forms. This change may have resulted from the minting process, where silver sheets were cast and then cut into rectangular segments, producing a bar shape. Rather than being struck with standardized images on both faces—as was typical in Western mints—Indian coins featured multiple small symbols, known as punch-marks, scattered across one side.

These punch-marks were applied while the silver was still hot and may have served several purposes. They could have demonstrated the coin's integrity, proving it was solid silver throughout. They might also have functioned as marks of authenticity, signifying approval by the powerful authorities or guilds. In addition to the numerous small symbols, each coin bore one larger punch-mark featuring a number between one and five. These numbers may have identified who minted or issued the coin. As was standard across much of the ancient world, the value of these coins was determined by their silver weight rather than their face value.

Persia Introduces Coinage

20 late 6th c. BC Cyrus the Great's conquest of Lydia in the 540s BC put the Achaemenid Empire in charge of Lydia's coinage system, which had operated steadily for about 100 years by that point. In Iran, the center of the Empire, commodities were still used for trade, along with uncoined silver bullion. If Cyrus were to let go of the Lydian coinage system, it would hurt Lydia's economic supremacy and, thus, the rest of Cyrus' empire. Cyrus kept Lydia's coinage, using the same design that was used

This is a third-century example of India's early square coins.

under Lydian kings: a lion-bull.

It was not until Darius the Great that the Achaemenids minted coins of their own style. Darius, as part of a larger administrative reform, revised the coinage system sometime between 522 and 490 BC. He put his own image wearing a ceremonial dress on the coin and simplified the way coins were struck. Next, he issued a gold coin with an image of himself as an archer, called a daric in Greek. The daric became the most popular coin in the ancient world for at least 150 years.

Precious Metal in Coinage

21 Until the last century, coinage was made of precious metals, mostly gold and silver. Precious metals had many advocates. Aristotle argued that coinage must have an intrinsic value—it must have an exchange value independent of its market value. The Enlightenment thinker John Locke thought along similar lines, though admitted that markets do determine the values of precious metals. The novelist Ayn Rand, though not an economist, argued that precious metal is superior to paper money, which "kills all objective standards and delivers men into the arbitrary power of an arbitrary setter of values." Plato, on the other hand, opposed using precious metal, arguing its lure would incentivize uncivic behavior.

Aristotle's precious metal camp won for most of history. The first coins of Lydia were made of electrum, a mix of gold and silver. Until 1940, the pound sterling had been struck of sterling silver [see: 74]. In 1792, the first dollar of the United States was struck from 24.75 grains of pure gold. However, as fiat and commodity-backed money became the standard type of currency in the 20th century, countries found the extra cost of using precious metals in coinage unnecessary, and they took it out.

With the exception of gold coins created in the Han and Qin dynasties, light bronze coins were dominant in East Asia. Western influences during the 1800s eventually motivated Asia to adopt gold and silver. Why did Asia not use precious metal? Some note that the continent is endowed with fewer gold and silver deposits than Europe is. Others note that European countries had to pay their soldiers more than the Chinese did, necessitating coinage of more precious metal. This allowed for more value in money to be exchanged while weighing less in transport.

House of Egibi: The First Billionaires

22 late 6th c. BC In the 1870s and '80s, archaeologists uncovered some 1,700 business-related tablets from the sixth and early fifth centuries BC. These tablets recorded the existence of one of the first banking houses in history: the House of Egibi. Over more than 100 years, five generations of the Egibi family operated commerce and banking in Mesopotamia.

The Egibi's main enterprise was buying commodities such as barley, dates, onions, and wool wholesale, transporting them and reselling them. This business was likely very profitable because many Mesopotamians at the time were engaged in infrastructure projects rather than farming. The family put their money to use by lending it to partners using an early type of legal partnership called *harranu*. One partner would put up the money, and the other would do the work. The partners then shared the profit.

Soon, the family started buying property. They seem to have preferred land outside of Babylon's city walls, but not exclusively. For example, the head of the House in the second generation, Nabu-Ahhe-Iddin, bought about 80 acres of land along the New Canal for about 11,166 kilograms of silver. Babylon gave important offices to the wealthy, and he was later made one Egibi a royal judge.

Confucianism and Money

23 late 6th c. BC Confucius said: "I can live with coarse rice to eat, water to drink, and my own arm as a pillow and be happy. Wealth and honors that one possesses in the midst of injustice is fleeting like floating clouds." Confucian ideals have dominated Asia for millennia—and his ideas about money are no exception. Confucius was not necessarily opposed to mercantile interests, such as sales and trading, as many other philosophers and religious figures were [see: 10]. However, he was opposed to what those activities imply.

Confucius encouraged hard work and frugality, teaching that the fewer desires one has, the better. Extravagance can lead to insubordination, one of the worst human traits, according to Confucian doctrine. He believed that people should be rewarded based on their merit. Thus, Confucius supported acquiring wealth through hard work, as wealth can serve as a symbol of merit.

Since World War II, countries with cultures traditionally based on Confucianism—namely, China, Japan, and Korea—have experienced some of the fastest economic growth in the world. Confucius believed the government should interfere little in the economy, and focus on maintaining public infrastructure while keeping taxes low—ideas conducive to modern growth.

Early Roman Corporations

24 493 BC Publicans were contractors, or "government leaseholders," for the Roman government. First recorded in 493 BC, publicans were hired for a variety of activities, including construction projects, law-enforcement, leasing of various rights or properties, and tax collection. Publicans' wide-ranging and complex business operations required that they organize themselves into what was the closest thing to a corporation available in Roman law at the time. Publicans modified the structure of the simple Roman *societas* corporation to expand its functions for their needs. By at least the third century BC, publicans were commonly referred to as being organized into these improved societies.

These *societates publicanorum,* as they were called, were similar to corporations in a few ways. First, they were allowed to persist even after one of their members, a *socius,* died. However, if the *manceps,* the person who bid for government leases at auctions died, the *societas* was dissolved. In AD 5, this was changed, and societies of publicans were permitted to change the *manceps* yearly. Next, single members could engage in legal disputes without taking the whole society down. This meant societies could be permanent. Finally, and possibly most importantly, societies of publicans sold shares that could be traded.

Forms of Companies in Rome

25 Rome's economic development was hampered by its inflexible law. Roman law disallowed a truly modern corporate organization but did allow for some approximations of it. The simplest was the *societas,* an association for any purpose. *Societates* could operate out of one building or across seas. They could be banks [see: 45], farms, construction firms, shops, schools, and more. *Societates* were partnerships of only a few men—often two—and thus didn't come near the complexity of modern companies. The *societates publicanorum* were more advanced forms of societies that carried out jobs for the government. These were more similar to modern corporations, as they often managed larger amounts of capital and had more members than the regular *societas.* One society of publicans had 19 members.

The *peculium* was a type of estate that belonged to a slave. This allowed the slave to own things and have some degree of financial independence, while still being subject to his owner's authority. This benefitted the slave owner, as it allowed him indirect control over the slave's activities while being insulated from any liability arising from the slave's decisions. In some cases, multiple people owned a slave through the *peculium* contract agreement. The *peculium* was not used for any large-scale ventures.

A common type of public organization was the *collegium.* These were sometimes religious organizations, sometimes political, and sometimes, closer in character to the medieval guild, places for tradesmen to meet. Some scholars characterize *collegiums* as social clubs of sorts for people working in the same industry. While the *collegium* was not private, its organizational nature showed some development in Roman law. The term is the basis for the modern "college."

Greece Uses Coins to Pay Salaries

26 late 6th c. BC Coinage became widespread in Greece by the year 500 BC. Greek city-states needed coins to pay for public projects and services, most importantly the salaries of soldiers and government officials. It was this role—not creating an easy means to make private market transactions—that motivated the introduction of coinage in Greece. It was in Athens in particular that working for pay in coins became the most prevalent. Greek city-states began paying salaries to jurors, magistrates, assemblies, and military men in the fifth and fourth centuries BC. Because there was not an expectation that coins would be used for small transactions, Greek city states minted more higher denomination coins than lower denomination.

Greek states' governments also misused coinage to make revenue. Some states minted coins to a lighter weight standard, which could then be exchanged for heavier foreign coins with greater intrinsic value. Coins were also introduced for the not-so-practical purpose of demonstrating civic pride. Greek states wanted to show power, and this desire for recognition may explain the quick spread of coinage around Greece.

China Introduces Round Coins

27 early 5th c. BC Round coins were introduced in China over a few centuries. The first series of round coins, called *huan qian*, were minted during the Warring States Period. These coins were modeled after jade rings or spinning wheels. Early *huan qian* coins were large, heavy, and unmarked. Later ones were lighter and marked both with their value and where they were minted. The *huan qian* had a circular hole in their centers. The hole allowed the coins to be stored on strings. They were replaced by round coins with square holes in the center, first introduced in the third century BC under the Qin Dynasty.

The coins' design had an important meaning. The circle symbolized Heaven and the square represented Earth. This design was based on the notion of the "mandate of Heaven," where a Chinese ruler is established by the will of Heaven. If he upsets that will, he is no longer fit to rule, so Chinese emperors made sure that what they were doing was aligned with Heaven. Since money gets its value from trust, establishing a coinage system backed by Heaven helped the coins' adoption.

Greece Taxes the Rich

28 later 5th c. BC Athens did not use a progressive wealth tax, but only the richest paid any tax. It is estimated that, around the fifth and fourth centuries BC, the richest 4–7% of Athenians owned 23–47% of the total wealth in the city-state. They paid a flat percentage of their income based on the types of assets they owned. The wealth tax likely yielded as much as 200–300 talents per year in the fourth century BC.

There were a few other categories of taxes in the fifth and fourth centuries BC. Import and export taxes raised 100–300 talents per year. A tax on silver of between one-tenth and one-twenty-fourth of production yielded more than 100 talents per year. Taxes on foreigners, 12 drachmae for men and six for women, totaled 10–20 talents annually. Municipal taxes and various other ad hoc taxes were levied on goods and religious institutions. However, these revenue estimates should be taken with a grain of salt, as taxes weren't the only way for the government to raise money. Often, the government would directly solicit wealthy Athenians to pay for public goods.

Qin Dynasty banliang coin

Persia Develops Permanent Tax

29 late 5th to early 4th c. BC One of the earliest examples of a fixed, equitable tax is that established under Darius the Great of the Achaemenid Empire. From when the Empire was founded in 550 BC by Cyrus the Great to the rule of Darius the Great, no equitable tax system existed. Conquered provinces had to pay a fixed sum, regardless of their ability to pay. The system was not standardized across the empire. Herodotus notes, "In the reigns of Cyrus and Cambyses after him there was no fixed tribute [for some people], but payment was made in gifts."

Darius implemented a system whereby the provinces, called satrapies, had to pay taxes based on a measurement of the richness of the soil, which indicated how much crop it could yield. Between 10% to 50% of crop yields could be taken as tax, which was to be paid on a yearly schedule. According to Herodotus, 20 satrapies paid 14,560 Euboean talents yearly, which likely equated to about 380,000 kilograms of silver. These taxes paid for government works, with the surplus going to the king's reserve fund to finance important and unforeseen expenditures, such as the war with Alexander the Great.

Trapeza Banks in Greece

30 4th c. BC By the fourth century, Greece—and Athens in particular—was highly commercial, with merchants making many transactions using foreign coinage minted by many city-states. *Trapeza* bankers emerged to facilitate commerce on an expanding scale by managing all of this coinage. *Trapeza*, literally meaning "table bankers," often operated at tables in public places. Though they started as modest currency converters, they eventually started providing loans, holding deposits, and acting as intermediaries for exchanges. These more advanced bankers soon clearly separated from the simple money changers. The *trapeza* bankers were possibly the first middle-class. They were wealthy but had no noble status. Indeed, a number of them were slaves and women.

Trapeza bankers handled many of the tasks that modern bankers do, but without the same legal status. They were unincorporated, sole- or joint-proprietorship organizations unregulated by the government. This is not to say that *trapeza* banks were small. The smallest recorded loan was 100 drachmae, or about 150 days-worth of pay for the typical Athenian. This was only a part of a larger sum of already loaned money, totaling 4,200 drachmae. The word "trapeza" is still the word for bank in Greek.

Greeks Use Bank Money

31 **4th c. BC** Athenians didn't have paper money. "Bank money"—money that is not cash but instead is based on an account balance at a bank—made up for it. Athenian law de jure required that goods be paid for entirely up front. Even so, Athenians made ample use of credit.

Often, people could pay for expensive things like swords or couches in installments, a form of borrowing. Bank payment orders were also common. A payer would tell his banker to give a certain amount of money to a payee. The banker would identify the payee by his appearance, making these transactions paperless. Interestingly, *trapeza* bankers were heavily involved in the perfume business, often lending over five talents to perfume outlets, equivalent to 285 pounds of silver. Banks also financed a wide array of other commercial activities, including mines and ore processing plants, land, and clothes-making factories. They even financed military exploits and political campaigns.

Bank money made international transactions easier. When a traveler went as far as the Black Sea, he carried a bank guarantee of payment and left hard currency back in Athens with his banker. These are all similar types of activities that banks do today to make it easier for customers to buy stuff.

Women and Slaves Bank in Greece

32 **4th c. BC** In Athenian culture, free citizens did not want to work for long periods under a single employer. Work was seen as a disagreeable necessity with no moral value: freemen should work little and carve out ample leisure time. The Greeks were the opposite of Puritans. The full-time nature of banking, therefore, made it an unappealing job for those who were able to work less. Thus, banks were often left to be run by people without the luxury of a lackluster work-ethic.

Slaves and women, two groups who were not free enough to leave themselves ample leisure time, thus went into banking more often than these two groups were able to do in the future. When a banker died, he would often leave the business to one of his male slaves or his widow instead of his son. Bankers had close connections with many of Athens' richest and most powerful citizens. Thus, though women and slaves could not start banks, they were able to gain wealth and influence in a way that was otherwise impossible for them. This made finance one of the first industries to promise upward mobility, even before the term came to exist.

Greek Monetary Standards

33 Today, you don't hear of a monetary standard to support a nation's currency. The gold standard was the last modern monetary standard and was superseded by fiat money in the 20th century. All developed economies now use fiat money, where a currency's worth is determined by government policy and its exchange rate against other currencies. The exchange rate, in turn, is largely determined by the faith that people have in the government backing the fiat currency.

In an economy based on precious-metal coins, however, weight standards matter. One of the most widely used coinage standards, in both Ancient Greece and Alexander the Great's empire, was the Attic standard, based on the Athenian drachma. It used a stater weighing 17.2 grams, with the base unit as the drachma of 4.3 grams. This standard gained prominence due to Athens' economic influence, particularly during the fifth and fourth centuries BC, when Athenian silver tetradrachms became widely accepted across the Mediterranean.

The Aeginetan standard predated the Attic standard and was used by Aegina and many other Greek city-states. The Aeginetan stater weighed slightly above 12 grams, with the drachma being around 6.2 grams. This heavier standard was particularly influential in central and northern Greece and was widely used in maritime trade.

The Babylonian standard, also known as the Persian standard, was another widely used weight system, particularly under the Achaemenid Empire. This standard was based on a shekel weighing 8.4 grams of silver. The 8.4 gram gold daric and the 5.6 gram silver siglos were two of the most common coins.

These standards had a tendency to become lighter over time. This was either to save money by minting coins with less gold and silver in them, or to emulate the worn-down, older coins already in circulation.

The Hidden History of Greek Bank Failures

34 4th c. BC Bank failures are as old as banks themselves. As ancient Greek banking was unregulated and kept secret, bank failures were riskier than they are today and less is known about them. While bank failures certainly occurred in Ancient Greece, there is but a smattering of good evidence as to why, when, and how these failures happened. One historian of Ancient Greek economy wrote, "In Athenian finance nothing is absolutely clear; little is dated; less is quantified for public knowledge."

Records indicate that a sacred building in the Acropolis was once burned to hide losses that were likely caused by a bank failure. There is also a record of real estate speculation that led to the failure of a key banker's business. Another passing reference mentioned a banker making a maritime loan and becoming insolvent before the loan could be repaid.

Sometimes a failure was caused by a single high-profile borrower defaulting, as the Athenian banking system allowed much systemic risk. Sometimes—particularly when a few bankers were working together—a single default could hurt multiple banks. Ultimately, some Athenian banks were passed down through generations, but most did not last long.

Rome's Early Central Bankers

35 352 BC Today, countries have central banks that are in operation year-round to keep the economy running smoothly and to help during emergencies. The Romans had no such full-time organization. On two occasions, however, they entrusted a small group of men with solving economic problems. These public bankers were called *mensarii*. In 352 BC, the government set up the *quinqueviri mensarii* (five bank commissioners), and in 216 BC, it appointed the *triumviri mensarii* (three commissioners) during the Second Punic War.

According to the historian Livy, the Five Commissioners were set up to help pay off private debt, which was becoming an increasingly large problem. The Roman treasury put up the money to pay the private debts, which ultimately helped relieve citizens of their large, accumulating interest burdens. This appears to have been a sort of ancient bailout and an attempt at expansionary fiscal policy.

The job of the Three Commissioners a century and a half later was less clear. The group operated for many years, during which it subsidized slave-owners, trained oarsmen, and attempted to free captive prisoners. These actions often aligned with the Five Commissioners' jobs, as they operated as public bankers, making loans using money from the Treasury.

Aristotle's Economic Theories

36 mid-4th c. BC Aristotle may not be known as an economic philosopher, but his theories dominated European thinking from classical times up to the present. Aristotle differed from his teacher, Plato, on the true value of money. Plato argued that money ought to be an arbitrary symbol with no intrinsic value. Aristotle supported what is now called metalism, which became the dominant practice: money should be an object with an intrinsic value, made of gold or silver.

Aristotle postulated four distinct ways in which money can be used. The first is to replace the inefficient system of barter, which was too cumbersome to be of much use. The second is natural money-making, through the selling of goods. The third way is unnatural money-making in which one uses money merely to make more money, such as by buying goods and reselling them at a higher price (arbitrage). The fourth method is usury—lending at any interest rate—which Aristotle also saw as valueless and unnatural.

Aristotle defined actions based on their ends. Aristotle considered two identical activities to be different if their intended ends were different. Selling goods to make money to fulfill one's needs—the first two natural ways to use money—is acceptable because it satisfies someone's wants. One ends the exchange when one's wants are satisfied, creating a natural conclusion. In unnatural exchanges, however, a trader's goal is simply to make more money. There is no logical end to this endeavor, making the activity irrational and immoral.

Furthermore, Aristotle argued that real wealth is based on the *use values* of goods, which the first and second exchange methods seek to maximize; people try to satisfy their wants by using money to buy the most useful goods. The third and fourth types of exchange, however, just move goods around without creating value.

Made of bronze, the aes signatum square predated round coinage in Rome.

First Coinage in Rome

37 335 BC The Romans were rather late in adopting round, metal coinage. The precursor to coins in Rome, *aes signatum*, were heavy currency bars. These bars, often embossed with a horse, were still in use into the first quarter of the third century. Gold coins were first struck at the end of the fourth century BC, possibly about 335. Silver and bronze coins started in the 260s BC, putting the Romans on a trimetallic system. Judging by the four different styles of coin that have been found, it appears that there were four separate coin mints, possibly one in each of the four Roman provinces at the time.

Rome's disorganized monetary system and limited supply of precious metal left it without the economic power to raise an adequate army to fight the Second Punic War. Rome expanded its coin production rapidly to fund the war, debasing the coinage in the process. After 10 years of fighting, Rome managed to recapture the parts of Greece and Italy it had lost. Rome regained control over a large supply of silver, which allowed it to mint one of its most famous coins, the silver denarius, in about 211 BC.

A Guide to the Roman Coinage System

38 If you were suddenly transported back to Ancient Rome and provided with a single aureus as a stipend to assist with your stay, how much change would you expect back after buying a bottle of wine for one denarius? Here is a traveler's guide to the Roman coinage system. Over the 800-year-long period, from the time that coinage was first introduced in Rome in the fourth century BC to the fall of the Empire in the fifth century AD, the system changed substantially. Under the original system of the fourth or third centuries BC, the *as* was the base coin and weight unit, weighing the same as the Oscan pound under the libral standard: 273 grams. This was equal to 12 *unicae*. The *as* coin was minted of copper or bronze and subdivided into smaller coins as follows:

Semis = 6 unicae = 136.5 g   Triens = 4 unicae = 91 g
Quadrans = 3 unicae = 68.25 g   Sextans = 2 unicae = 45.5 g
Unica = 22.75 g

These coins, minted of bronze and later copper, were not the entire system, just the basic standard. Gold and silver coins were evaluated in relation to them, based on the perceived values of the precious metals.

Under the Augustus reform [see: 53], which established the system used for most of the Empire period, the copper *as* continued to be used as the base unit, but it weighed about 12 grams. The dupondius weighed about 13–14 grams and was worth two asses; the sestertius, worth 4 asses, weighed about 27 grams, and both were made of orichalcum (brass). The denarius weighed about 4 grams and was worth 10 asses, as it was made of silver. And the aureus, made of 8 grams of gold, was worth 25 denarii. Thus, after purchasing that bottle of wine, you would be given 24 denarii in change.

Giro System in Ancient Egypt

39 4th c. BC Money deposit and transfer systems were first used in Mesopotamia as long as 1,000 or 1,500 years before the current era. The Mesopotamian system was rudimentary compared to the giro banking system that emerged in Ptolemaic Egypt around the fourth century BC.

A gyro system is a type of payment transfer system that is almost the reverse of a cashier's check. When a transaction is made with a check, the bank attempts to transfer the money to the payee without knowing the status of the payer's account. With the giro system, a transfer is made of a known, verifiable deposit in the payer's account.

The gyro system allowed Egyptians to transfer money from one bank account to another without moving any physical money. Money at the time came in the form of grain, which was moved among a network of government granaries. Bank-to-bank transactions were much easier than moving large amounts of grain around. The banking system was managed by what was essentially a central bank, located in Alexandria. The giro system only transferred payments and did not yet perform any of the more advanced tasks of banks.

Alexander the Great Changes Money and War

40 330s BC Conquest is an expensive endeavor. Alexander the Great's takeover of the Persian Empire required a very large sum of money. It cost 20 talents per day, or about a half ton of silver, to pay for Alexander's entire army while it was fully engaged in Persia. Macedonian tradition was favorable for a conqueror: the state's wealth of iron, copper, silver, and gold was all personal property of the king. The payment of troops was also his responsibility. Before Alexander managed to subdue the Persians, this battle was only a suck on Macedonian wealth.

As Alexander made progress in Persia, however, the wealth drain ended. The army profited 2,600 talents from the capture of Damascus. The treasury at Susa yielded 50,000 talents, and 7,000 were taken from the capture of Darius. Alexander took over several coin mints, which then started minting coins for him. Many non-combatants, such as scientists and explorers, followed Alexander on his campaign, and the money supply was massively expanded to pay them, along with generous benefits for his victorious soldiers. All great conquerors require money to fund their exploits, and Alexander the Great effectively exploited the new money acquired in his newly expanded domain.

Salt Money in Ethiopia

41 late 1st mil. BC While much of the world came to use metal coins by the first year of the Common Era, Ethiopia did not. Instead, alongside barter, salt was used as full legal tender. Salt was important in the Ethiopia economy from before the Aksumite period (150 BC to AD 960) up to the 20th century. Salt was formed into bars called *amole*, about 20 cm long and five cm wide in the center, weighing about half a kilogram. An estimated three-quarters of a million *amole* were added to circulation each year in the 1830s. Such a large expansion of supply was necessary, as the *amole* were highly fragile and broke easily.

By this time, average citizens in America, Asia, and Europe were using paper money, gold and silver coinage, and had access to robust banking services; those working in finance had even more advanced tools available. Why did Ethiopia not get with the program? The salt bars effectively met the needs of Ethiopians. Like gold and silver, salt was rare, standardized, and portable. Unlike gold and silver, salt is useful for day-to-day needs.

Financial Tools in Mauryan India

42 4th c. BC As there was no large economy in ancient India that could take full advantage of a banking system, banking was likely not widely used. There were, however, many rich merchants who needed financial services (and of course the king required a loan at times). A professional class of bankers, called *sethi*, emerged to provide some banking services during the Mauryan period. This group was composed mostly of Vaishya-caste Hindus.

Bills of exchange emerged in India during that period, too. The bills, called *adesha*, were simply orders for a third party to pay money to a receiver on behalf of the sender. *Adesha* bills seem to have been used on a somewhat sizable scale. Regulation on banks was clearly laid out, according to the *Arthashastra*, a contemporary political document, implying that banking garnished much attention at that time. The maximum interest rate was 15% per annum, except in especially risky industries like seafaring, where 20% per annum was allowed. Charging interest above the legal maximum was punishable by a fine. Unlike China, whose indigenous banking system evolved over time, India made no further innovations in finance until the introduction of Western banking under the British [see: 183].

Trade Guilds in Mauryan India

43 4th c. BC The history of money not only includes tangible forms of money, like coins and credit instruments, but also the institutions that guide the uses of money within the economy at large. During the Mauryan Empire in India, and possibly as far back as the sixth century BC, trade guilds were important in the economy. These guilds were very wealthy, and subscribing merchants were accorded special privileges like not being liable to refund customers for damaged goods. In some cases, trade guilds organized into rudimentary joint-stock companies of sorts and may have later even issued loans. The guilds also had the power to determine the price of goods as a type of monopoly.

Indian law was quite robust in how it addressed guilds. The process of making lawsuits between guilds, for example, was regulated. Even laws from as early as the sixth century BC appear to have been rather nuanced. For example, consumers were protected from unscrupulous behavior by guilds, and the production of poor merchandise was prohibited with a fine. While guilds protected their merchants, they were sometimes taken advantage of by kings.

How Banks (Literally) Make Money

44 Roosevelt opened his first Fireside Chat in 1933 at the height of the Great Depression by explaining a simple fact of banking: "When you deposit money in a bank, the bank does not put the money into a safe deposit vault. It invests your money in many different forms of credit." Many different financial technologies and some simple illusions work together to help banks make bank (figuratively and literally). Much of the development of these methods took place in England and Amsterdam from the 16th through 18th centuries.

Money creation is made possible through fractional reserve banking [see: 145]. The economist John Kenneth Galbraith said, "The process by which banks create money is so simple that the mind is repelled." Money creation occurs when both bank deposits and loans are taken as legitimate money. When a bank creates a loan, it takes a portion of the money from a depositor's account—say $10,000—and gives it to the borrower. Meanwhile, the original sum still remains in the depositor's account—at least on paper. When the borrower uses the $10,000 to buy something, the seller deposits this money in another bank, generating $10,000 out of thin air. A portion of this new deposit will be loaned out again, adding even more to the total supply of money in the system. Under this fractional reserve system, banks have a reserve requirement ratio, putting a limit on how much total money can be created by this process.

Banks act as intermediaries between depositors and lenders. People who have money they are not using expect a return on their deposits. People who need money to borrow expect to pay interest. Banks match people who need money with those who have money, pocketing the difference between interest paid to depositors and interest charged to borrowers, effectively creating money for themselves in the process, too.

Rome's Bankers

45 3rd c. BC The banking profession in Ancient Rome started with a group known as *argentarii* (Latin for "bankers"), who first appeared in the fourth and third centuries BC. *Argentarii* started out as moneychangers and eventually started taking deposits and making loans at interest. There were higher- and lower-ranking *argentarii*, separating simple moneychangers from more advanced bankers. These bankers operated out of shops that were often in a town's forum. They were private entities but regulated by the government and kept clear records in three books: a main record book, a book for deposits, and a registration journal.

While sometimes debts were recorded in writing, often only verbal agreements were made, which was characteristic of early Roman contract law. Wealthy Romans used *argentarii* to solicit money from debtors and negotiate agreements, and, often, they would transfer money on customers' behalf. They may have, in some cases, participated in fractional reserve banking. There are a few brief mentions of *argentarii* in Cicero's orations and in Plautus' comedies, indicating their prevalence in society.

Fractional Reserve Banking in Rome

46 3rd c. BC There may have been fractional reserve banking [see: 145] of a modern type in Ancient Rome. As Roman bankers made payments without the physical transaction of money, we know that credit existed, likely extended by banks. But, as at the time interest made on bank deposits had to be credited to the client's account, it appears that loaning out a client's money would not likely have been profitable for the bank. There were, however, two kinds of deposits. A *depositum* was money deposited solely for safe-keeping without interest. A *mutuum* was considered by Roman law to be a loan, but was similar to a bank deposit. Bankers loaned out *mutuum* deposits to earn interest. This made a profit for the bank, a key purpose of fractional reserve banking.

A sort of overdraft facility also existed. Roman banks' reserve ratios may have been about 30%, as they often were in medieval banks. A number of records exist attesting to the use of loan-making, where the wealthy were both lenders and borrowers. For example, Scipio Aemilanus, a general who fought in the Third Punic War, once loaned 1.2 million sesterces to a bank. There is also a documented purchase of property using credit. Such evidence suggests that, even in Roman times, complex fractional reserve banking was employed to some extent.

Stock Market in Ancient Rome

47 ca. 2nd c. BC The question of whether a stock market existed in ancient Rome is a controversial one. It depends on how one interprets ancient texts and how one defines a company and a stock market.

The first type of legal entity that could sell shares—and the ability to sell shares creates the need for a stock market, a location at which to sell them—was the *societas*, which were first created in the fifth century BC [see: 24]. Cicero once made mention of what could be interpreted as stocks. Egyptologist James Henry Breasted claimed a formal stock market existed in the Roman basilica or forum, where companies were formed and a modern stock market developed. By the later third century and early second century BC, changes in Roman law likely allowed the forming of more proper, yet still rudimentary, corporations. By the following century, those laws were further modernized to create a more efficient and impersonal structure of corporation.

The Romans did not call these entities corporations, though. The fundamental concept of a corporation—that it is a legal person, given rights similar to those of people, such as being able to own assets and assume liability—did not fully develop until the 19th century.

Han Establishes Salt Monopoly

48 **120 BC** The salt trade in China was liberalized in 2014, after having been controlled by the government for much of the preceding 2,000 years. The origin of the salt monopoly is unclear. The Shang Dynasty collected salt as tribute from other countries, and the Zhou collected salt from its own provinces.

The first official salt monopoly was enacted under the Han Dynasty in 120 BC. The Han was founded following laissez-faire economic policy, allowing private salt ownership. But once the salt industry started expanding, it soon came under the control of a few wealthy merchants. When the government became short on cash, it decided to tax revenue from salt and introduced a monopoly. This was not a government-granted monopoly—it was operated by the government. An arm of the Chinese government, controlled by government bureaucrats, produced, transported, and sold salt. The price of salt became a contentious political issue: Should the government raise salt prices to raise revenue, or keep prices low to benefit consumers?

The government salt monopoly was lucrative. While most monopolies drive up prices and decrease quantity demanded, salt is a necessity. This meant consumers won't stop buying salt even if prices rise, creating a steady source of revenue for China's governments.

Promissory Notes in China

49 **118 BC** The Han Dynasty was running low on cash in the form of precious metals and needed a means to meet public expenditures. It did what all self-respecting governments do in times of economic need: it printed money. Unlike future governments, however, the money was printed on animal skins. In 118 BC, *pibi* was created as the world's first fiat currency. *Pibi* notes, literally meaning "skin money," were made from skins of the white deer inhabiting the royal hunting ground. The skins were intricately decorated with multicolored paint.

Pibi were introduced as part of a larger monetary reform made under emperor Wu of the Han Dynasty. Each piece of skin was one Chinese foot square (about one imperial square foot) and was worth 400,000 cash. A numismatist writing in the 1840s reckoned a *pibi* to be worth about 300 francs at his time. For reference, in 1844, the average daily earnings for coal miners was just over two francs. The *pibi* were ultimately not widely used. They never left the royal palace and were withdrawn after 115 BC.

Han Dynasty Financial Reforms

50 **115 BC** During the second century BC, the Han Dynasty's money supply was expanding due to prosperity in both the real economy and in the financial sector. When the Han Dynasty was founded, the responsibility of minting coins was put in the hands of individuals. The result was that wealthy businessmen and people with local political influence started minting debased coins to make a profit. This created inflation and allowed the wealthy an unfair gain.

Emperor Wu, who took power in 141 BC, set out to fix this. He centralized coin minting in 115 BC. Wu set up a specialized government department for casting. Wu introduced *wu zhu* coins, making them the only form of legal tender. This was part of a set of six economic policy changes that Emperor Wu made, including a new tax on merchants. He also levied a 6% tax on the profits from making loans and set the maximum interest rate on loans at 20%. This high interest rate implies that some lenders were charging even higher rates before the rate cap. This is an early example of financial expansion compelling the government to crimp down on unfair opportunities and attempt to stabilize the economy.

Ever-level Granaries in China

51 54 BC When a harvest is good, grain is cheap and plentiful. When a harvest is bad, grain is expensive, and people starve. The ever-level granary is a government-run institution that buys grain during times of plenty and distributes it cheaply during poor harvests.

The first official ever-level granary was founded in China in 54 BC, but the concept had existed for much longer. In the late fourth or early third centuries BC, Li Kui in the state of Wei created the first program to stabilize the price of grain. He used the same model of buying and storing grain in times of surplus and selling grain cheaply during poor harvests. In addition to managing the ever-level granary of 54 BC, the government transported commodities between regions to level public access to grain stores. The ever-level granary could be seen as a sort of rudimentary form of central bank controlling the money supply to keep the economy stable.

Caesar Puts His Face on Coins

52 44 BC To show his new power in Rome, Julius Caesar put his bust on coins minted during and after his rule, from 46 to 42 BC. Slogans such as "parens patriae" (father of the country) or plainly "dictator" were printed alongside the Roman leader's bust. Caesar's face adorned the gold aureus, along with silver denarii of a few different styles. These coins were the first in Roman history to display a living person on it. Previously, Roman mints only produced coins displaying images of gods, wildlife, and nature. We do not know if it was Caesar who wanted his face on coins or if it was demanded by his impressed followers. After Caesar died, Brutus, who was an honorable man and one of Caesar's assassins, minted a series of coins portraying his own bust. He also made another series of coins telling of how Caesar was murdered.

Coin produced by a military mint traveling with Caesar in North Africa in 48–47 BC.

One of coin money's important though lesser-known roles is its propagandistic value. From Caesar on, Roman coins became tools for the emperor to show his authority and to communicate his hopes, ambitions, and persona. Still today, Washington's face on the dollar bill is there for the same reason that Caesar's face was on Rome's coinage.

Augustus Reforms Rome's Coinage

53 28 BC After Caesar was killed, Augustus took over Rome, helping turn the Republic into an empire. During this conversion, Augustus reformed Rome's coinage system. It was not an immediate change. The process of reform lasted from the '30s through the '10s BC. The legality of this move was questionable. Augustus wanted to make the new Roman Empire continue to look Republican while taking much practical power. Though Augustus was not technically consul, he was given the "responsibilities of consul." Not wanting to appear too autocratic, he let the Senate mint bronze coinage but took the right to mint gold and silver coinage, which the military often used.

Augustus' reforms appear to have paid the most attention to low-value coinage. Augustus started minting the *as* coin out of copper instead of bronze to facilitate easier trade with the copper-using provinces. He also adjusted the weights of the sestertius, dupondius, and quadrans. The new system remained in use for about two-and-a-half centuries, at which point bronze coinage lost its value as debased silver coinage caused inflation. Copper minting was eventually abandoned. New rulers often must immediately turn their attention to the financial system, either to promote efficiency or to buttress their power.

Augustus Creates First Pension Plan

54 13 BC Rome had a problem with keeping ex-soldiers loyal after completing their mandatory service to the state. Many soldiers had difficulty finding work after returning to civilian life and felt contempt for those who prospered while they were away. Under the Roman Republic, land and titles were often given to returning soldiers—but on an ad hoc basis that proved problematic. Augustus, the first emperor of what was now the Roman Empire, created a more standardized system.

Legionnaires—retired citizen soldiers—received a lump sum of 3,000 denarii, equal to about 30 ounces of silver. This was 13 times the annual salary for active soldiers. One denarius was about one day's wage for a laborer in the first century AD. The pension system experienced solvency challenges, as it was initially funded by general state revenues and Augustus' generous personal contributions. In AD 5, Augustus established a special fund to pay for the pension, financed by a new 5% inheritance tax and a 1% tax on transactions conducted through auctions. Later emperors occasionally substituted this pension system with land grants. Rome was able to effectively avoid soldier uprisings.

Rome's Contributions to Modern Money

55 In 390 BC, the Gauls entered and attacked Rome. After ransacking much of the city, they marched to take the Capitol Hill. However, it couldn't have been much of a bona fide march as they managed to quietly sneak past the guards and their dogs, attempting to make a surprise attack. They failed, however, to sneak past the geese around the Temple of Jupiter, where much money was held. As the alarmed geese started honking, it was the Gauls who were surprised. The geese warned the Romans, who put up a successful defense. Afterward, the Romans built a shrine to Moneta, the god of warning and advice. Because of Moneta's connotation with the temple where money was stored, her name is the source of the English words "money" and "mint." Additionally, Modern Copper was used for many Roman coins and got its name from Cyprus, where Romans found large copper deposits. These are just some ways in which Rome continues to influence money today.

The English pound, shilling, pence (LSD) system has its origins in Roman coinage, where the libras, solidus, and denarius were used. Financial innovation was important due to the sheer size and complexity of the Roman economy. The coins of Rome started out as rather poor specimens. But as the need to pay soldiers mounted, the production of coinage had to be improved. Rome was an early example of centralizing coin-minting, and subsequent governments have always managed coin production, while often letting private banks take care of paper money.

In the Middle Ages, Jewish merchants held onto Roman ideas about financial transactions. As medieval gentile culture rejected mercantile principles of the Classical era, Jewish merchants prospered by exploiting this financial advantage.

Taxes in the Roman Empire

56 first centuries AD During the Roman Empire, municipalities collected taxes with little oversight from the central government. There were two broad categories of tax: *vectigalia*, or general revenue, and tribute. The main *vectigalia* taxes were 2.5% on customs duties, 5% on freeing slaves, 4% on selling slaves, and a 5% inheritance tax. There was also a land tax, cattle tax, and tax on specific professions. Notably, there was no income tax.

The people of conquered territories and other parts of Italy were required to pay tribute. In at least two provinces, the tax amounted to 1% on personal assets. Taxes on government monopolies were also quite large, with the sale of salt as a notable example. As many mines, quarries, and fisheries were property of the state, people who used them had to pay royalties on them. Additionally, numerous one-off taxes were added for various government purposes.

The most notable flaw in the Roman tax system was the divergence between the amount of money collected from citizens and the amount actually received by the treasury. The Roman government collected an exorbitant amount of money from its citizens, but much of it was siphoned off by people overseeing the collection process.

This is a print of Rome's Capitol Hill, created in the mid-to-late 17th century. The remains of the Temple of Jupiter stand at the left of the print.

Wang Mang Implements "Socialism"

57 9 During the 14-year gap in the Han Dynasty's rule, Wang Mang's Xin Dynasty instituted many economic reforms that are seen as early attempts at what today is termed socialism. Most notably, he took all the land that had become increasingly concentrated in the hands of the wealthy during the Han Dynasty and redistributed it to the common people. He also made three separate and significant changes to the denominations of coinage, causing much confusion and increased counterfeiting. One of these changes was the removal of knife money [see: 12], as the Chinese character for knife is also part of the character for the last name of Han Dynasty royalty, Liu.

Wang eventually nationalized all gold and banned precious metal coinage, allowing only vassal kings to hold gold. The remaining gold was to be brought to Wang's palace and exchanged for bronze coins, sometimes of a higher face-value. After the gold seizures, Wang retained the gold, not even using it in financial emergencies. When he was beheaded by a rebel invasion in AD 23, a few hundred tons of gold were found lying about the capital.

Jesus Cleanses Temple

58 ca. 30 During the Passover likely of AD 30, as many as 400,000 came to Jerusalem on pilgrimage as required by Jewish law of the time. Jesus and his followers decided to make the pilgrimage, too. While in Jerusalem, Jesus went down to the holy Temple and started overturning the moneychangers' tables, where people exchanged Greek and Roman money for the local currency accepted at the Temple. Jesus poured out the coinage on the ground and drove the people who were selling things out of the courtyard and would not let anyone go through. He even kicked out the cows and sheep. The Gospels record him as announcing: "It is written: 'My house shall be a house of prayer'; but you have made it a den of robbers!"

While the historical accuracy of this Bible-given account is questionable, its significance in the development of the culture around money is key. Through this disruption, Jesus informed people of how he thought money should be treated—with scorn. This message has reverberated through the Christian religion—and by extension through the Western world—since.

El Greco's "Christ Driving the Money Changers from the Temple" imagines the scene when Christ made chaos in the Old Temple, showing his scorn for money.

Financial Crisis of AD 33

59 33 A law created in Rome in 49 BC mandated that a certain percentage of one's capital be invested in the area of Italy to limit an outflow of currency. This law, passed as a war measure, eventually fell out of the memories of investors and regulators. In AD 33, the law was revived—possibly by landowners in Italy trying to prop up the prices of their property. All Roman citizens were given 18 months to move two-thirds of their wealth to Italy. The money supply was already unusually low at the time. The sudden demand for cash and insufficient time to liquidate assets and purchase Italian property caused what was similar to a modern credit crunch. Real estate prices crashed and banks called in their loans, further reducing the supply of money.

Emperor Tiberius lent 100 million sesterces (about $37 million today, based on the value of wheat) to distressed landowners through a group of senators, without interest for up to three years. Reducing taxes—an expansionary policy to raise the money supply today—was not a solution at the time, as few people in and around the city of Rome paid taxes. Running budget deficits by increasing public spending, on the other hand, worked. Tiberius' strategy helped stabilize the economy, and his methods mirrored modern ones.

Chinese Coins Reach Japan

60 ca. 1st c. After its invention in Lydia, coinage in the West proliferated around the Mediterranean. The East saw a similar diffusion of coinage after it was first used in China. The first coins to reach Japan in the first century AD were the copper *banliang* and *wuzhu* of the Han Dynasty. Japan did not, however, have a political or economic system sufficiently developed to make use of coins, as rice and cloth continued to serve as the main medium of exchange at that time. These coins eventually influenced Japan's understanding of money. When Japan first minted coins in AD 708, they were modeled on their Chinese counterparts [see: 71].

Korea and Vietnam also copied Chinese coinage. Chinese knife money circulated in Korea while it was in use in the first millennium. However, it was the coinage of the Tang and Song Dynasties that Korea and Vietnam copied. The first Vietnamese coinage was minted in the late 10th century AD, with inscriptions naming Vietnam a sovereign state. The first Korean coins of about the same period initially bore the same inscriptions as their Chinese counterparts, but later versions represented Korea's national identity.

Annuities in Rome

61 ca. 3rd c. One's age of death is unpredictable. If a retiree has a certain sum of money that he intends to live on for the rest of his long life, he would want to use a small amount of it annually. However, he would want to use a large amount of this wealth yearly if he expected to live only a few years more. How can he budget accordingly? Another death-related problem was that wealthy Romans often left end-of-life income for their heirs in their will, and tax collectors needed to know how much was left. These two problems led to the invention of annuities.

Annuity contracts, known as *annua* in Rome, were often sold by those who insured Mediterranean shipping ventures for a lump sum payment up front. One of the most widely used actuarial tables for calculating yearly payout of *annua* was made by the judge Ulpianus in the third century AD. The table is a little impractical, as it predicts that everyone will live to 50 or 60, an age to which many Romans did make it. Those aged 1–20 years old had a predicted 30 years left. Those aged 40 had about 20 years left. Those aged 60 had only 5 years left. This table was used by the Tuscan government until the 19th century.

Diocletian Limits Prices

62 301 Diocletian ascended to the emperorship of Rome in 286, at a time of high inflation: a rate of about 4% annually over the previous 40 years. In 293, Diocletian separated the empire into four sections. This increased governing costs and the need to pay officials, contributing to the start of 23% yearly inflation from 293 to 301. Additionally, in 295, Diocletian enacted a large currency reform to remove the ample quantity of debased currency from circulation and replace it with new coins. Some of these new coins were good quality, but some were still debased, causing inflation to increase further.

In 301, he tried to combat inflation by issuing the Edict of Prices, setting maximum prices for goods. Macroeconomic theory states that if a maximum price is set, there will be more demand than supply, creating shortage. A breakdown of the market system was exactly what happened. Often the maximum prices were ignored, disgruntled buyers tried to take the goods by force, and sellers hoarded goods while waiting for the Edict to be abolished, which raised prices further. Diocletian abdicated as emperor four years after the Edict was enacted, and the Edict went out with him.

China's Equal Field System

63 485 In 485, Emperor Xiao-Wen of the Northern Wei Dynasty introduced a new land-distribution and taxation system called the Equal-Field System. This system remained in use until the middle of the Tang Dynasty period, four centuries later. Under the Equal-Field System, land was assigned to peasant families by the government, based on population. This required an accurate census, a notoriously difficult task for pre-modern governments. The goal of the system was to stop the consolidation of China's land in the hands of the wealthy, which would make it inaccessible to the government.

In the Northern Wei period, a man was given about 80 Chinese mu (13.2 acres) and his wife half that amount. Officials were given 6–15 qing (600–1500 mu). By the Tang Dynasty, the system became more complex. A man was given 100 mu total, 80 of which could be revoked when he died or became too old to work it. The other 20 were his permanently. Officials were given about 10 times more land than in the Northern Wei period, a portion of which they also would have to eventually give up.

III

Money in the Middle Ages:
5th c. – 13th c.

Europe experienced limited financial innovation during the Middle Ages. The sharp pivot from Rome's centralized government to the fragmented system that followed meant political instability, which limited production and trade, slowing economic growth. The first few centuries of this period saw finance evolve in a decentralized fashion. Without standardized Roman coinage, new monetary standards popped up. England, for example, stopped using coinage altogether after the Roman Empire withdrew. Even so, a number of significant financial developments came out of this period. Charlemagne centralized Europe's coinage to an extent, and his administration invented the pound, shilling, and pence system. Without Rome's coinage, the Medieval system was largely cashless and complex banking systems developed to finance the limited trade there was. The Crusades, a set of complex and expensive enterprises, required the development of loan-making. This spurred the creation of one of the first international banks, run by a sect of Christian warrior monks.

Asia had a distinctly different experience. Chinese culture and economy flourished under the Tang dynasty. Paper money was invented in China during this era, making long-distance trade easier. The Mongols abruptly ended China's golden age when they invaded in the 13th century but also introduced their own commodity-backed paper money. Marco Polo brought this concept back to Europe (though Europeans did not implement paper money for a few centuries). In addition to facilitating long distance trade, paper money allowed for monetary expansion, making economic growth quicker. Governments could print additional paper notes, expanding the supply of money to facilitate increased volumes of trade. Paper money, however, was also printed in excess. The Mongols printed too much money during this period, creating inflation. This made China wary of paper money until Europeans reintroduced it in the 19th century.

The Muslim world also contributed a number of important developments. The spread of Islam codified many indigenous Arabian financial systems that had already been in use for centuries. These systems spread with Islam and still dominate the Middle East today.

New Monetary Systems After the Fall of Rome

64 5th and 6th c. After the fall of Rome, the political fragmentation of Europe left various European states with two contradicting applications for coinage. On one hand, there was little need for standardized coins, as smaller kingdoms had little trading to do. On the other hand, the many new countries sought international legitimacy through the minting of sovereign coins.

For example, the Ostrogoths struck coins of gold, which had been the personal prerogative of the Roman emperor. They often used Roman mints, and the coins bore the Eastern emperor's name (with Theodoric's mark on some coins). Bronze coins, which circulated more widely, displayed a mix of Roman and Germanic iconography. Similarly, the Frankish king Theodebert issued coins with his name on them to legitimize the authority that he won for himself.

In the late sixth century, imperial-style coinage was widely replaced by "national" coinage. For example, when Lombardy reached a peace agreement with Byzantium in the 680s or '90s, the Lombard king replaced the Byzantine emperor's bust on the coins with his own. The fall of Rome left a void of power, and new kings intended to use coinage to prove themselves the one to fill the void. Charlemagne streamlined this jumble in the eighth century [see: 72].

Islamic Legal Partnerships

65 7th c. When Muhammed started converting the Arabs to Islam, he adopted many pre-existing Arabian practices into his religion if they did not interfere with Quranic teachings. The tmudarabah and *musharakah* contracts, two of the

This coin was minted by the Ostrogothic king Theodoric the Great, although it bears the name of the Byzantine Emperor.

most well-established legal agreements in Arabia that he adopted, are organizational structures similar to a modern corporation. These two instruments existed before the seventh century, when they were incorporated into Islam. The *musharakah* contract has been described as "the most authentic form of Islamic financing." They are still used today for modern companies, albeit on a small scale.

The *musharakah* contract is a "profit-and-loss sharing" partnership, a technical term in Sharia-compliant finance. It is the riskiest agreement among Islamic financing methods. Two or more partners put up money to fund a project and manage the project jointly. Profits are shared according to a predetermined ratio, and losses are born in proportion to the amount of capital contributed by the parties.

With *mudarabah* contracts, one party provides funding and the other operates the project. While the profits are shared among both parties, the losses are absorbed entirely by the financer. *Mudarabah* contracts are used by banks to take deposits and make loans.

Islamic Finance

66 The evolution of banking over the last two or three centuries is primarily a history of Western banking practices being adopted around the world. This adoption pattern arose either because indigenous banking didn't exist within other countries or the existing banking systems simply weren't up to the task of operating on a modern scale. However, Western banking never fully permeated the Middle East. Islamic banks, which evolved independently, now manage over $4.5 trillion.

Three principles focused on ensuring that money is put toward productive purposes in society govern the Islamic banking system. First, the principle of equity protects the weaker party in a contract. It prohibits predetermined payments (interest) and excessively risky contracts. People must provide ample information before entering a contract. Second, the principle of participation states that "reward comes with risk taking." Investors are allowed to make a profit only if it involves some risk. This principle effectively prohibits interest, which racks up only due to the passage of time. Additionally, investment must benefit the real economy. Thus, return on investment is legitimate only if it is determined to have benefitted the real economy after it is realized. Third, the principle of ownership states that you cannot sell something you do not own. This disallows short-selling and requires respecting property rights and contractual laws.

Islamic banking uses a web of *mudarabah* and *musharakah* contracts [see: 65]. It also uses *murabaha* contracts, where goods are paid for after they are delivered, and *wakala* contracts, where the bank acts as an agent, charging a fee to a customer. On the assets side of the balance sheet, Islamic banks own cash and other securities, conduct *murabaha* loans with other banks, and charge fee-based *wakala* services. On the liability side, banks hold deposits as *wakala*, investment accounts as *mudarabah*, and hold various reserves and shareholder equity.

First Kaiyuan Tongbao Coin

67 621 The *kaiyuan tongbao* coin was the most significant coin of the Tang Dynasty in China. It was first minted in the fourth year of the *Wude* era of Emperor Gaozu (AD 621). It informed the style of Chinese coinage for the next 1,300 years. The order that the characters were printed on the coin—top, bottom, right, left—also became standard in Asian coinage until Western coins were introduced. Unlike earlier coinage, which showed the weight on the coin (such as the *banliang* of the Qin Dynasty or the *wuzhu*), the *kaiyuan tongbao*—literally, the "circulating treasure of a new start"—was minted at 1/10 tael but was only labeled for its symbolic value.

The introduction of a coin that was not marked with its intrinsic value did not result in debasement. In fact, the *kaiyuan tongbao* maintained an intrinsic value closer to its face value than coins that had a value printed on them did. The introduction of the *kaiyuan* coin coincided with the debut of a new decimalized weight standard, suggesting that the coins themselves may have been cast as a standard of weight.

Kaiyuan tongbao coin minted under Emporer Xuanzong of Tang.

Coins Re-Enter England

68 630s After the Roman Empire left Britain in AD 410, the remaining barbarian tribes stopped producing and using coinage. One historian claims they stopped using coinage completely within only a generation. Subsequently, coins were not used in Britain for the next two centuries. Christians were the first to restart the minting of coinage, with some of their earliest works dating to AD 604. The inspiration for this long-lost medium came from the southeast of England—the Merovignians in France. Britons started regularly minting coinage around AD 630, but coins did not penetrate the entire island until the eighth century.

Little information about this early coinage is known. The first of these coins were made of gold and were eventually replaced by a gold-silver alloy. Coin hoards have been found that reveal a coinage-based economy was emerging at this time, but the relative importance of this economy remains unknown. Traditional forms of trade, such as gift exchange, tributes, and other types of exchange, maintained a strong force in medieval British and Continental European life.

Early Chinese Banks

69 ca. 7th cent. Commerce boomed during the Tang Dynasty, and merchants were busy making trades. The inefficiency of China's copper coins, however, weighed merchants down. The first bank-like organizations in China were called *guifang*, meaning "counting house." The *guifang* emerged during the seventh century, and their primary purpose was to keep money safe from theft. Initially, these counting houses simply held gold and silver in reserve. The houses didn't pay interest—they charged storage fees.

Soon, *guifang* started making loans under government guarantees. Customers were required to obtain certificates from the government to deposit or withdraw their money, making the *guifang* more reliable. *Guifang* also created certificates of deposit, which were a sort of check that acted more like promissory notes that could be used by a customer whose money the bank held. Government regulation was ultimately limited, however, and the *guifang* could easily break contracts. Additionally, they often charged interest rates as high as 40%. The *guifang* were some of the earliest banks in the world, developed at a time when banking was essentially non-existent in Europe.

Islamic Coins Standardized

70 693 The *dinar* and *dirham* are Islamic coins with more than just monetary value. They also have religious significance. Byzantine and Persian coins were their predecessors. The Byzantine *dinar*, weighing about five grams, was used in Muslim countries until 693, when an Islamic *dinar* of about the same weight replaced it under the caliphate of Abd al-Malik ibn Marwan.

The *dirham* originated from a Persian currency, and a Muslim equivalent was produced as early as AD 660. However, it did not become widespread until the caliphate of Abd al-Malik ibn Marwan, who imbued the dirhams with religious significance. Religious tithe amounts were denominated in *dirham*, so variation in the value of *dirhams* before they were standardized in 693 led to confusion over the amount to be paid. Additionally, a number of Islamic injunctions were based on the currencies. One scholar reported that a messenger of Allah forbade the destruction of these coins and prohibited the use of leather for money, making the legality of paper money under Islam questionable.

Japan Mints Coins

71 708 Japan was a late comer to the use of coinage for currency. By the latter half of the seventh century, the Japanese state remodeled itself based on China's Tang Dynasty. Japan's government centralized, bureaucratized, and adopted Chinese culture. These changes also included instituting its own coinage based on the Chinese model, rather than using old Chinese coins [see: 60].

The first coins minted in Japan were called *mumon ginsen*, meaning "coins without inscription." The coins were made of silver alloy, round with a square hole in the center, of about three centimeters in diameter and two millimeters thick, and weighed 8–10 grams. The purpose of these coins is debated. As of 2021, only 160 have been found.

A decree from the Chronicles of Japan dating to AD 683 banned the minting of silver coins, and copper coins called *fuhonsen* showed up around that period, though it is not certain that they were used as commercial money. Finally, in 708 the first formal coinage, *Wado kaichin* coins, were minted of silver and later copper. These were Japan's first proper coins, having the full functions of coinage.

Pepin Mints Pennies (and Only Pennies)

72 750s The fall of the Roman Empire left Europe with a void of centralized coinage production. What filled this void in the eighth century became itself an unofficial coinage standard for Europe and influenced the production of coinage for the 13 centuries since. Starting under Pepin the Short, who became the first king of the Carolingian Dynasty in 751, and culminating under Charlemagne, the penny became the dominant coin in Europe.

The penny was a broad, thin, silver coin. Since the coin was made of silver, the metal largely replaced gold for circulating currency in Europe. The size was also significant, as it allowed coins to carry overt indications of royal authority. Under Pepin, pennies bore the letters RP and RF (Rex Pipinus and Rex Francorum). Under Charlemagne, coins bore the words "CARLVS REX FR" along with the name of the mint and the royal monogram.

The minting of pennies was a bit of a franchise. Moneyers across Europe—about a hundred are known—minted the coins to a standard. The penny

This denarius is from 812–14 featuring the bust of Charlemagne.

made it to England under Offa of Merci and continued on the Continent under Charlemagne's ninth century descendants.

Carolingian Monetary System

73 790s "Sing a song of sixpence, a pocketful of rye. Four and twenty black birds baked in a pie." Many know the 18th century English nursery rhyme, but few know the origin of the famed sixpence coin. The pound, shilling, and pence system (£SD or LSD) was first invented in the 790s by Charlemagne. The system was loosely based on that of Ancient Rome. One pound (L for libra, in Latin) breaks into 20 shillings (S, named after the Roman solidus coin) and 240 pence (D, from the denarius). The Romans used the same terms but with different ratios and values.

The weight of the original pound base unit is debated. It was likely based on the Roman pound and thus weighed within the range of 300 to 500 grams. The British pound was broken into 12 ounces, following a Roman convention using a unit basis of 12 that allowed for a whole to be easily divided into two, three, four, or six equal portions. In Charlemagne's time, only pennies were minted—the £ and S were only used as units of account. In 1704, Russia became the first country to decimalize—switch the coinage system to using base-10 . England became one of the last to do so [see: 352].

Introduction of Pound Sterling

74 ca. 800 At the beginning of the eighth century, many small silver coins made by different moneyers started circulating across England. These coins were called pennies after King Penda of Mercia, who reigned in the second quarter of the seventh century. In the 760s, King Offa of Mercia started minting coins more consistently. These coins spread across England within a century.

Sometime around AD 800, people started calling 240 pennies a pound, as per the Carolingian monetary system [see: 73]. A pound of money was supposed to be equal in value to a pound of silver. The weight of silver as money was recorded in pounds, shillings, and pence rather than pounds and ounces. The actual weight, however, of the monetary pound varied. A statute of 1266, possibly recording an older tradition, set the pennyweight at "thirty-two wheat corns in the midst of the ear." The 32 wheat corns likely indicated 24 grains of weight, meaning a pound of currency weighs a little less than a pound weight. Most early coins still in existence weigh 18–24 grains. This is the start of England's currency system.

Flying Cash

75 806 Flying cash, the first quasi-paper-money, was really a form of loan. During the reign of Emperor Xianzong of the Tang Dynasty, the amount of precious-metal money in circulation was dwindling. Additionally, China's use of low-value bronze coinage rather than high-value gold or silver made carrying large sums of coin money a great burden for merchants. In the early ninth century, they started using banknote-like flying cash instead. According to the AD 1060 *New Book of Tang*, when merchants would arrive in the country's capital, they would entrust their metal coin money to the government in exchange for flying cash notes to redeem later.

The Tang Dynasty's government was opposed to the use of paper money, but finally capitulated around 806-12. Flying cash was not meant to be used as legal tender (it was, after all, a bill for deposit), but its occasional use as money made it the first paper money-like exchange medium in history. The notes looked similar to modern banknotes, with the amount of money printed in large numbers. Instead of a signature of authenticity, flying cash notes bore a red stamp, in Asian style. Flying cash paved the way for the first true paper money in the 10th century [see: 80].

Waqf Philanthropy

76 9th c. According to Islamic tradition, Abu Talha, companion to Muhammed the Prophet, donated his date palm grove with over 600 date trees in it after hearing this verse from the Quran: "None of you [believers] will attain true piety unless you give out of what you cherish: whatever you give, God knows about it very well." By the ninth or 10th century, one of the earliest types of philanthropic funds, the *waqf*, was formally codified in Muslim law. *Waqf* operates in perpetuity like an endowment and is more broad than the *awqaf*, which is only for mosques and colleges. There is also the *sadaka* (a cognate of the Jewish *tzedakah*), which was just a donation.

The introduction of the *waqf* and *awaqf* had a notable effect on Islamic culture. The fields of science, art, philosophy, and other activities that produced little profits came to be highly dependent on them, contributing to the flourishing of the Islamic Golden Age. By 1800, an estimated one-half of real estate in the Ottoman Empire was classified as *waqf*, and those 20,000 waqfs produced yearly revenue equal to one-third of the government's revenue.

Why China's Economic Development Was Slower than Europe's

77 Why is it that China and Europe—two areas that historically have had similarly sized populations and similarly robust cultures—diverged so greatly in wealth and living standards between the 17th and 20th centuries? This question has perplexed scholars for at least a century. Max Weber argued that the West benefitted from being more scientific and having a more ascetic value system than the East. Yet, cultural differences cannot explain everything. Perhaps there is something to be said for how economics reacted to and drove politics.

War and national competition is a key driver of the development of financial systems. The question of how to pay for wars and how to pay off the debt that accrued during wars resulted in some of the most important strides in financial development. For example, war was the motivator for the Bank of England, the Bank of the United States, and John Law's bank. Wars often motivated currency debasement, starting a move to paper currency and the invention of new financial instruments.

While the whole of China has, for most of its history, been managed by one big dynastic state or another, Europe has been made up of many small competing countries since the fall of Rome. This means more wars and competition in Europe, and thus, greater financial innovation. Additionally, small states inherently have less power. They have a smaller tax-base, fewer alternative sources of revenue, and less control over citizens. Financial development allows small states to make their limited resources more productive and become more financially efficient.

Financial innovation in Europe picked up in the 16th century, as the modern notion of the state matured and wars became larger and more expensive. Conversely, China had fewer internal conflicts and little incentive to develop its financial systems.

Islamic Sakk

78 9th c. Today, the Islamic *sakk* (plural: *sukuk*) is a financial instrument that functions similarly to a conventional bond that follows Islamic financial principals [see: 66]. While interest-bearing bonds are prohibited in Islamic finance due to riba (usury laws), *sukuk* allow effective lending by representing an ownership stake in an underlying tangible asset, project, or business venture rather than a simple debt obligation. *Sukuk* provide returns based on the profits generated by the ownership share of the underlying asset, rather than fixed interest payments.

Sukuk originated in the medieval Islamic world. At the time, however, they had a slightly different purpose. Early *sukuk* acted like checks or promissory notes to help facilitate financial transactions and long-distance trade. Some scholars suggest that the Arabic term "Sakk" was introduced into European financial systems through trade with the Islamic world and evolved into the term "check".

Today, Malaysia and the Gulf Cooperation Council (GCC) countries issue *sukuk* for facilitating government and corporate financing. Many non-Muslim countries, such as the UK, Hong Kong, and Luxembourg, also issue *sukuk* to attract investment from the Islamic finance sector. There are nearly a trillion dollars of outstanding *sukuk* as of 2024, showing that alternatives to Western financial systems have strong support.

Athelstan Unifies England's Coinage

79 928 King Athelstan, the first king to rule the entirety of what is today called England, had a coin-minting problem. He needed more mints, but having more mints meant having more coordination difficulties, giving the king less control over each one. To maintain his power, Athelstan tightened laws for moneyers. In 928, he enacted the Statute of Grateley.

The new law stated that if a moneyer was found guilty of illegally minting coinage, his hand would be cut off. England thus became the first country in Europe to establish a single national currency, which was important for promoting economic development. Athelstan also specified how many mints are permitted in each region: eight in London, seven in Canterbury, and, excluding other explicitly-mentioned cities, one per borough. The best way to control the styles of coinage was to control the distribution of dies, and Athelstan controlled the dies. He also established the norm of printing the name of the mint and moneyer on the coins (presumably so he'd know whose hand to cut off, if necessary).

Athelstan was not entirely successful, however. Moneyers and mints continued to organize themselves on a regional basis, with the designs of their coins manifesting earlier, pre-unification designs. Kingdoms battling over territory on the English island also hampered unification until the Norman Conquest in 1066.

True Paper Money in China

80 995 Due to the cumbersome nature of the iron and copper coins, merchants in Sichuan Province during the Song Dynasty started issuing *jiaozi* (not the food item) as the world's first paper money in 990 or 995. From a legal perspective, only some types of *jiaozi* notes were true legal tender in the modern sense. Initially, the notes were no more than written slips verifying that a recognized merchant retained the money someone had left with him. It was the *guanjiao* variant of *jiaozi* that could be taken at face-value anywhere, and became the first paper legal tender.

The first issue of *jiaozi* was worth approximately 1.3 million *guan* in Sichuan iron coins, with 360 *guan* (28%) coin reserves. This indicated an expansion of the money supply, an important characteristic of paper money. When *jiaozi* notes were first introduced, many merchants printed them. Some of these merchants were less than trustworthy. To rectify this, 16 wealthy merchants took over printing all *jiaozi*. These 16 merchants were replaced by the government a couple of decades later. Soon, *jiaozi* were used all around China. Some *jiaozi* notes have illustrations of coins on them, showing an understood connection between paper money and coin money.

This jiaozi note is from 1024–1108. The coins on the top of the note indicate a connection between paper money and coin money.

China's Commercial Revolution Starts

81 10th c. Starting during the Tang Dynasty and culminating under the Song Dynasty, China underwent what could be called a commercial revolution due to the innovation and expansion of financial technology in the country. This innovation came during a time of flourishing culture, as the population grew from 50 million in AD 800 to 100 million in AD 1100.

This development started in the aftermath of the An Lushan Rebellion of 755, during which the Tang Dynasty underwent an eight-year-long political convulsion. The rebellion was significant in China's economic history because it required a change in tax collection. After the rebellion, the central government lost control over much of northern China to warlords and could only expect taxes from eight southeastern provinces. Additionally, many fled the warring north, moving south to loyal provinces. The level of migration made collecting taxes difficult. Emperor Dezong, who took power in 778, instituted a system of paying taxes with newfangled paper cash rather than in-kind currency.

The greater and denser population of the south allowed for agricultural innovation as well as larger and more specialized commercial markets. The Tang Dynasty fell in 907 and gave way to the Song Dynasty in 960, the year when the first commercial tax law was penned down. The economy remained strong under the Song Dynasty, and commerce boomed between 960-1127, as 3,422 market towns opened in China.

This commercial expansion resulted in China producing some of today's most important financial advances over this period, such as early bank-like institutions, "flying cash" paper money, and true paper money [see: 69; 75].

Government Monopolizes Banknotes

82 early 11th c. The first government-issued paper money was that of China's Song Dynasty. After delegating the task of printing money to a collection of printing shops, the government took the job over and created a government monopoly on note issue in the early 11th century. This coincided with the government's broader efforts to exert greater control over the economy. The Song Dynasty thus consolidated economic management under a dedicated government department.

The newly issued *jiaozi* notes were initially valid for three years and were backed by the government. About a century later, Song issued *huizi* banknotes, further solidifying government control over the monetary system. In most cases in the 17th, 18th, and 19th centuries in Europe and America, banknotes were issued by private banks. This change foreshadows how, by the 20th century, banknotes would increasingly come under the control of the government, albeit due to different circumstances.

Domesday Book Makes Judgment

83 1086 Effective account-keeping is imperative for any type of large-scale financial systems, whether it is the government keeping a census for tax purposes or a company keeping a balance sheet. After William the Conqueror became the king of England in 1066, he realized that, in order to better manage his kingdom (and to better legitimize his somewhat stolen rule), he needed an inventory of everything in his domain. By 1086, his government produced the *Domesday Book*. The *Domesday Book* was one of the most comprehensive national surveys in history, named after the sense that its records were as final as those of the last Day of Judgment.

To create the *Domesday Book*, William required each tenant-in-chief and sheriff to send a list of feudal manors and the people within them. Then, investigators scoured the country to cross-check the list and create an exhaustive inventory of manors and their resources. This census included much detailed information, such as the number of mills and fisheries on a given property, and culminated in the 38-volume-long series. Unlike modern accounts, the *Domesday Book* recorded information in narrative format. In addition to its immediate significance for William's kingdom, the Book was also a model for later account-keeping, like that of the Exchequer.

Why England Invented Modern Finance

84 Most of the economic development recorded in this book is a product of England. Why was England so prolific and able to rocket itself to the forefront of innovation, particularly in the 19th century? Luck surely played a role, but looking at what is measurable, two key factors stand out: intellectual innovations and coal.

The Scientific Revolution lasted from the mid-16th century to the late 17th century, which then bled into the Enlightenment from the late 17th century to the early 19th century in England. The Scientific Revolution started on the Continent; but, following the freedoms promised by England's Reformation, it moved to the British Isles. The Scientific Revolution set the stage for the Enlightenment, where scientific methods were applied to the study of humans.

Ideological products of the Enlightenment were often economically beneficial. Classical Liberalism, for example, stressed the importance of free markets. The works of Adam Smith, the Scottish scholar and inventor of modern economics, were first adopted by a British audience [see: 187]. By more or less inventing the study of modern economics, England had a large advantage.

Coal also played an important role in Britain's success. In the 19th century, coal drove industry as oil and electricity do today. England had the most coal reserves, digging up 72 million metric tons of coal annually from 1853-62. France never managed to achieve that number, even at its peak production of 40 million tons in 2013. Further, technology to mass produce steel and steam engines were invented in the 18th and 19th centuries, facilitating the scaled production. The technological groundwork laid by the Scientific Revolution quickly made England the world's first industrial state. Scale necessitated better financial services, which Enlightenment thinking helped develop. These ideological and geographic factors put England in the center of financial innovation and made it the richest country in the world.

Japanese Za Guilds

85 1092 The Japanese *za* was an organization very similar to the Medieval European guild. The *za* limited competition in certain trades to increase its members' profits. Though Japan had less developed, guild-like organizations in prior centuries, the earliest-recorded *za* was founded in 1092. This *za* was formed by a group of woodcutters who wanted exclusive privileges to deliver firewood to Kyoto.

Within a few years, more *za* guilds were founded to provide lamp oil, charcoal, and needles. The number of *za* grew in the 12th through 14th centuries. Most were located in Kyoto, but some operated in other regional cities. *Za* guilds were usually sponsored by temples, shrines, and court nobles.

The existence of *za* guilds came to an end after the close of the Onin War, which lasted from 1467 to 1477, and started the Sengoku or "Warring states period" when warlords controlled Japan. They let the *za* guilds continue in order to raise money for their battles. However, as the warlords gained security by the mid-16th century, they realized that removing trade restrictions would result in greater economic activity and higher tax revenue, and they outlawed *za* guilds.

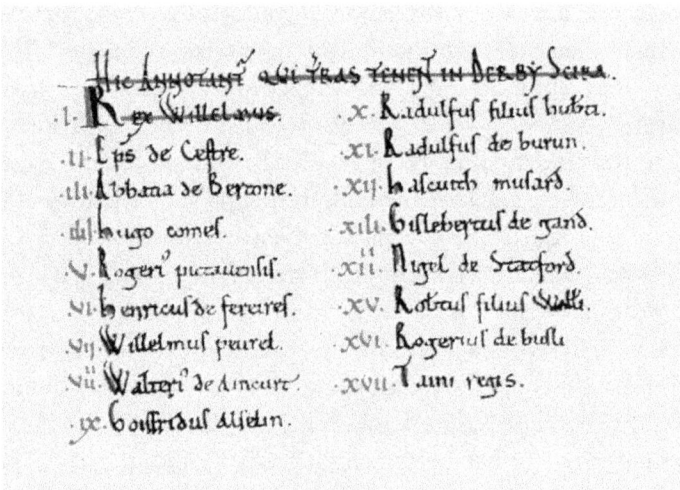

List of names of Derbyshire tenants-in-chiefs from the Domesday Book.

Medieval Guilds

86 11th c. Guilds were associations of craftsmen and merchants that emerged in Europe during the Middle Ages. Guilds began to form around the 11th century, with merchant guilds (for long-distance and wholesale traders) appearing in Italian cities during the 12th century and craft guilds (based on specific trades) becoming widespread by the 13th. After the Black Death in the mid-14th century, the number of guilds quickly grew further.

Guilds served multiple functions. They regulated trade practices, maintained quality standards, controlled prices, and provided mutual aid to members. Guilds also wielded significant political power. They often monopolized trade within a town, protecting their members but also creating inefficiencies characteristic of pre-modern mercantilism [see: 118]. The structure of guilds typically included a hierarchy of apprentices, journeymen, and masters. Apprentices trained under masters to learn a trade, eventually becoming journeymen who worked for wages. After producing a "masterpiece" and meeting other requirements, a journeyman could become a master and open his own workshop.

Guilds began to decline in the early modern period, particularly from the 16th century on. The modern market economy undermined guilds. In some regions, guilds persisted into the 19th century, but their economic functions had largely diminished by then.

Crusaders Take Loans

87 1096 Crusades were expensive. The distance from Paris to Jerusalem is more than 2,600 miles. Before the era of mechanized means of transportation, and in a time when only the wealthy had horses, traversing this distance was difficult and costly. Additionally, individual crusaders were responsible for paying for the trip, meaning that the poor often could hardly afford the endeavor. Indeed, even the wealthy struggled to pay for the journey.

Many crusaders turned to loans. There were some fantastic loans, such as when Duke Godfrey of Lower Lorraine sold his castle with the right to reclaim it when he returned. There were also more modest loans, such as when one king would loan a sum of money to another without interest. A common type of loan arrangement had the lender take a parcel of land from the borrower, who would eventually pay back the principal with interest, to reclaim the land. There were various adaptations of this model. Some types of loans were condemned by the Church as usury, but other models escaped such condemnation. Loans were so common as a means to pay for the Crusades that the Popes got involved, sometimes in protecting loan-making, sometimes outlawing it.

Knights Templar and Hospitallers Bank for Crusaders

88 1113 The Crusades, a massive movement of troops across Europe and into the Holy Land, required extra special methods of managing money while on the expedition. Two orders of Catholic monks—the Knights of the Temple (Templars) and the Brethren of the Hospital (Hospitallers)— used their multinational networks as banking systems to finance the Crusades. Both of these orders were headquartered in Jerusalem, founded soon after Christians established a hold in the city in 1099, 1113, and 1118.

The financial systems stretched from England to Israel, facilitating most of the operations of modern banks. Deposits made in Europe could be withdrawn in the Holy Land and vice versa. The Templars and Hospitallers made loans, collected taxes, and even minted legal coins. The establishment of these two banking systems was made possible by the orders' ownership of many ships, castles, and store-houses. The monks managed private armies and received large donations of land and capital from wealthy European nobles.

The Templars and Hospitallers continued business and religious operations for centuries after they were founded. In 1312, the Templars were disbanded by the Pope and their property dispersed. The Hospitallers did not disappear until the 19th century, by which point their banking activities had long ceased.

English Use Tallies

89 12th c. In Ancient and Medieval Europe, a system of notched wood sticks called tallies were used to keep financial records, due to the high cost of paper and low literacy rates. Though tallies were common in Europe going back to Ancient Greek times, it was Medieval England that made the best use of them.

In 12th century England, tallies were mostly used as tax receipts by the Exchequer, historically the Crown's tax collection and treasury department. Tallies also were used as credit devices for making loans, thus assisting money creation when the amount of money the economy needed was larger than the supply of coins [see: 44]. These debt tallies could be sold or exchanged, in which case the new owner would become the debt collector. Once the debt was paid, the tally was broken in identical halves, with each half acting as a receipt for the two parties.

England formally stopped using tallies in 1826. In the 1850s, Charles Dickens shrewdly recalled, "In the reign of King George IV an enquiry was made by some revolutionary spirit whether pens, ink and paper, slates and pencils, being in existence, this obstinate adherence to an obsolete custom ought to be continued."

Tally sticks

Taxes to Support the Crusades

90 1146 In addition to taking loans to fund the Crusades, kings and lords levied taxes to raise money for their expeditions and maintain their holdings while in the Holy Land. One of the earliest official taxes was levied in 1146 to finance the Second Crusade. (Though even before that, kings and princes requested aid from their subjects.) In 1166, Pope Alexander III requested a general tax in France and England.

The most extreme tax was levied in 1183 by the Christian-controlled King-dom of Jerusalem to pay for its defenses. Everyone, including peasants, women, and non-Christians, were subject to the tax, which was one bezant per hundred of assets (some 70 grains of gold—a considerable sum). Alternatively, people could donate as much as they could afford. Clergy and nobility were taxed on their revenue. This was considered the first national tax, the first tax based on a valuation of one's property, and the first income tax in history.

While the Medieval feudal system is characterized by decentralized government, taxation requires centralization. These Crusades taxes are credited with contributing to the downfall of the Medieval system and the rise of government centralization during the Renaissance era.

Commenda contract

91 1156 The *commenda* contract was an early form of incorporation, though they were often closer to loans than to companies. There were two types of *commenda*: unilateral and bilateral. For a unilateral *commenda*, one or more investors known as a *commendator* would lend money to a crew, bearing all liability of loss. The crew would use the money to fund an overseas expedition. Upon their return, they repaid the original sum of money plus a share of the profit, with the investor typically getting three-fourths and the sailors one-fourth. The bilateral commenda more closely resembles the modern joint-stock corporation. Both the traveling party and the *commendator* invest in the project (usually the *commendator* invests two-thirds and the traveling party, one-third), and the total profit is split in half.

The *commenda* contract was a slow development. The first reference to a Venetian form comes from AD 976, and the first municipal statute permitting them was from Pisan in 1156. The benefits of the *commenda* were the same as those of modern corpo-rations: it helped raise capital and assemble expertise. Poor sailors would benefit from having their expeditions funded by investors, and investors had the opportunity to make a profit on someone else's work.

Usurers Excommunicated

92 1179 The Third Lateran Council, convened in AD 1179 by Pope Alexander III, was one of four Lateran Councils held by the Catholic Church to address various ecclesiastical, political, and moral issues. Among its many rulings, this council played a significant role in the history of finance by reinforcing and formalizing the Church's stance against usury. At the time, usury—defined as charging any amount of interest on loans—was increasingly viewed as immoral and exploitative, particularly when it targeted the poor.

Canon 25 of the council explicitly condemned usurers, declaring that "caught-in-the-act usurers" (*usurarii manifesti*) were to be denied communion and a Christian burial. That is, excommunication. Additionally, any priest who performed burial rites for a known usurer would face temporary suspension from his duties until his bishop could determine an appropriate punishment.

This ruling continued the Church's broader effort to stop usury, which was banned by the Bible [see: 11]. The council also reinforced the Church's power in the financial sector, which limited the development of banking through the Middle Ages. It wasn't until the Renaissance that usury restrictions were softened [see: 116].

Cash Use and the Manorial System's Fall

93 12th c. Traditionally, the manorial system—the economic component of the feudal system in which peasants work for their lord on his manor—used in-kind payments for making transactions. By the 12th century, money payments came to be more widely used in place of indentured labor services. As the population grew, labor started showing diminishing returns, decreasing the real value of a peasant's labor. Payment in money allowed lords to improve their profits. The development of a more robust commodity market further incentivized the use of cash money.

In the 13th century, the situation changed. Inflation hit much of Europe, making money payments less ideal. Inflation subsided in the 14th century, and the Black Death created a severe labor shortage, giving tenants more bargaining power and greater rights. Lords reduced labor obligations and gave tenants life leases that were paid off in both labor and money. These life leases became standard in the 15th and 16th centuries, when the agreements came to be seen as equal to copyholds—a type of land ownership—and paid in fixed payments. Thus, not only was cash adopted, but the manorial system also allowed peasants to choose employment, putting an end to the economic system that characterized the Middle Ages.

Merchant Banks

94 12th c. The term merchant banking has been defined as having "No precise meaning and is sometimes applied to merchants who are not bankers, to bankers who are not merchants, and even to Houses which are neither merchants nor bankers." These sorts of bankers evolved in 12th and 13th century Italy, the center of banking and merchant activities across Western Europe at the time. Small merchant houses started financing foreign trade, often voyages, which were highly risky. Later, merchants would act as sorts of banks, taking deposits and making loans. Development of medieval credit devices like bills of exchange freed merchants from the burden of carrying precious metal.

Merchant banking was highly interconnected with regular banking during this period. Soon, the center of trade and finance moved to Amsterdam and then to London, and merchant banking moved with it. In the 18th and 19th century, merchant banking became more similar to traditional banking, though still focused on financing trading. Today, it is synonymous with investment banking.

Ghost Money Spreads

95 13th c. One of the purposes of money is to act as a unit of account. While today most units of account also have an associated physical form with the same name, this wasn't possible in the Middle Ages and early modern period, giving rise to so-called ghost money, or money of account.

Why could the physical and accounting currency not be the same? There were two reasons. First, starting in Charlemagne's time, only pennies were minted. It was difficult to express large sums in pennies, so larger units came to be used on paper, with no corresponding larger coins minted. Thus, the ghost pound referred to 240 pennies. Second, though larger-denomination coins were eventually minted, medieval mints did not effectively keep an equivalent exchange rate between the larger and smaller units, often because coins were simply not precisely minted. In 1252, a certain Genoese gold coin was equal to 120 pennies, but by the 16th century, that coin equaled about 720 pennies. Accounting for changing exchange rates between coins of the same currency was complicated, incentivizing the use of a different ghost currency with fixed rates between units.

Ghost currencies had different names than their physical counterparts to reduce confusion. As a result, Continental Europe used the pound at least into the 16th century.

Fibonacci Introduces Better Numbers

96 1202 Europeans did not know about the number zero or place-value notation with base-10 until Leonardo Pisano, a citizen of Pisa, brought that knowledge back from his travels. Leonardo, known commonly as Fibonacci, traveled throughout the Mediterranean and Near East on business. It was there he learned of Greek mathematics and theories, and most importantly, studied Arabian mathematics.

Fibonacci first published his book *Liber Abaci* in 1202, in which he introduced Arabic numerals to the West and first brought the number zero to Europe. The Arabic numeral system allowed for more efficient computation of math, making financial reporting easier.

This new system of arithmetic was not quickly accepted, however. In many parts of Europe, the Catholic Church and other powerful groups did not support the system. Arabic numerals were even banned in Florence in 1299, allegedly because they were harder to read. Other cities followed suit. The bans did not hurt everyone, though. Jewish merchants and bankers were quick to adopt Arabic numerals, giving them a notable advantage. By the 16th century, Arabic numerals had become entirely accepted, and Roman numerals began to fade into the past.

How Our Number System Works

97 The numerical digits and the system we use today (1, 2, 3, 4 . . . 42, 43 . . .) are not a European invention, but an Indian invention. The importance of the introduction of this system to Europe by Fibonacci cannot be understated. Called Arabic numerals today, these Indian characters use the place-value notation system, where a digit's value depends on both its absolute value and on where it is located in a recorded number. The digit 8, when located in the hundreds place, for example, is worth its value multiplied by 100—that is, 8 in the hundreds place denotes the value 800. If 8 is moved one space right to the ten's place, the number's value is now 80. Right one more space to the one's place, the value is eight. This is the system we all use today.

Before Arabic numerals were adopted in Europe, Roman numerals dominated math and business dealings conducted in the West, often making even simple arithmetic difficult. Try adding XCIV (94) to XXXVI (36) using Roman numerals. There is no easy way to do it. The place-value notation system, however, allows for vertical addition that even first-graders can easily grasp for any size value:

$$
\begin{array}{r}
94 \\
+ 36 \\
\hline
= 130
\end{array}
$$

Now imagine trying to use Roman numerals to calculate the profit on an initial investment of $100,000 after 15 years of 3.8% compounding interest!

In addition to using place-value notation, the Arabic numeral system also uses decimals and the number 0, making algebra possible, which is frequently required for financial analysis. Arabic numerals were looked down upon in Europe after Fibonacci introduced them, only becoming prominent after they were used in the book *Summa de Arithmetica*. Written by Luca Pacioli, this book of algebra and geometry was the first book describing double-entry bookkeeping [see: 123].

Axe Money in Mesoamerica

98 early 2nd mil. AD Sometime in the early second millennium AD—in the 1200s in many areas, but as early as the 800s in others—people in Mesoamerica started using axe-shaped money. Primarily made of copper-arsenic alloys, this money was thin, axe-shaped pieces of metal that were widely used for trade, tribute, and the storage of wealth. Some axe money had standardized weights, similarly to cacao beans, which were also widely used for trade in Mexico. Axe money has also been found in elite burial grounds, suggesting it also had religious significance.

The tool money originated in the Andes, particularly in Ecuador and Peru. From there it spread to Mesoamerica through maritime trade networks. The introduction of metallurgy from South America to Mesoamerica led to the development of distinctive regional forms of axe money. West Mexico, particularly Oaxaca and Guerrero, became prominent centers for the production and use of the tool money.

Archaeologists have also found *naipes* (I-shaped metal sheets) and metal feathers, suggesting that axe money may have been just one of many metal devices that Pre-Columbian Mesoamericans used for trade. China similarly used tool money some 2,000years prior.

The Magna Carta as a Financial Document

99 1215 The Magna Carta, one of the first democratic documents in history, was in a large part motivated by a tax dispute. It was one of the first documents in history to regulate a king's ability to tax. After taking the throne in 1199, King John of England was strapped with high expenses. Prices were rising with inflation, while the loss of revenue-producing lands in France hurt the treasury, and continued conflict between the two countries cost money. Instead of creating new taxes, King John found and re-upped some old yet still-on-the-books taxes, creating resentment.

A number of barons, already upset, capitalized on this opportunity and threatened to rebel, forcing King John to agree to their demands and sign the Magna Carta to regulate the king's discretionary power. In the history of taxation, clause 12 and 14, banning taxes without "general consent," and outlining how to get said consent, are key in developing more fair taxation. Initially, general consent only meant the agreement of lords who answered directly to the king. But, by 1297, it came to refer to the whole kingdom. Provisions other than those relating to money were included in the Magna Carta, but it was taxation that was the ultimate motivation.

Money Leads to the Rise of Democracy

100 13th c. onward Why was democracy invented? Some say it was born of some flowery notions that all men are created equal. Historians will say it arose during a time of abuse of power by kings. Here is the economic perspective, which boils down to the fact that, throughout history, governments needed money, often acquired it through taxes. People did not want to part with their earnings unless they had a say in what the money was being spent on. It is one thing for a king to demand taxes; it is another thing for him to actually receive them. And kings had to be efficient at raising taxes, as they were perpetually short of money.

Securing revenue was a key reason that King John complied with his barons and signed the Magna Carta in 1215. In 1241, Henry III called together several wealthy merchants to raise tallage, which is a type of tax typically levied by lords upon their tenants. He promised benefits to any contributors. The development of Parliament, which first met in 1254, similarly may have been a means of getting money from the wealthy groups that held it. The constant need for tax revenues motivated the Crown to create a body to consistently approve of its provision. The medievalist Carl Stephenson wrote, "Without the recurring need for general taxation, there would, I believe, have been no House of Commons." Parliament later became an agent for democratic change.

The English Civil War, which ultimately strengthened Parliament, was in part set off by tax disagreements. This put King Charles I in an odd position where he needed a Parliament to get tax money, but he did not want to summon it, lest he be forced to address their grievances.

The American Revolution was motivated by an excessive tax burden, while the French Revolution was sparked by the need to reform France's tax system. In all these cases, the need to raise taxes moved the world closer to democracy.

Mongols Use Paper Money

101 1236 At its peak, the Mongol Empire spanned nine million square miles, covering much of Asia, the Middle East, and parts of Europe. The Mongols issued paper money in an attempt to unify the currency in their realm. The first notes issued in 1236 AD were backed by 100,000 ounces of silver. Under Kublai Khan, the currency supply expanded substantially. Additionally, the Khan made paper money legal tender in China.

However, as the amount of paper money in circulation expanded, it soon grew larger than the quantity of precious metal, and inflation set in. Mongolia stopped using paper money in 1356. China also experienced inflation because of paper money. It did not, however, get away from paper until the 15th century.

The effects of this event on the non-Mongol world were more significant than on the Mongol world. Marco Polo, who brought the idea of paper money to Europe, specifically referenced the Mongols and the Chinese as its inventors. Paper money did not catch on in Europe for a few centuries, by which point Asia had almost entirely stopped using it.

Yuan Dynasty Makes Paper Sole Legal Tender

102 1260 In 1260, the Mongol-run Yuan Dynasty in China created a new currency, the *zhongtongchao* ("zhongtong" is the name of the Khan era, and "chao" means money). The Mongol Empire expanded to cover the entirety of China and Korea. This far-eastern portion of the empire was called the Yuan Dynasty in 1271. This paper currency was initially backed by silk and later by silver. The Yuan used only the *zhongtongchao* and was the first dynasty to rely on paper money exclusively. Additionally, the *zhongtongchao* was one of the first commodity-backed monies in history. Silver was the metal of choice for tribute to the Mongol Empire and was exacted from all the Empire's territories.

After a decade of stable monetary policy, the government ran low on silver and amassed high expenditures from its southward expansion. When the Yuan Dynasty started printing more paper notes, the currency became inflated. The government responded by issuing a new currency. Four new currencies were issued in total. When the Yuan fell and the Ming Dynasty replaced it, the government intended to do away with paper money but did not have enough copper to do so until the 15th century. From that point on, China did not care to use paper money again until Western banks showed up.

Venice Consolidates Debt

103 1262 During the reign of Doge Ranieri Zeno, things were difficult in Venice. The city was fighting a war with Genoa while trying to defend its trading routes and maritime empire. The city was also trying to expand its trading farther east. Fighting on multiple fronts while trying to expand a fleet of ships and aid merchants is expensive, and Venice borrowed extensively from its wealthy citizens. The Doge also mandated many forced loans called *prestiti*.

To manage these debt obligations, the Republic of Venice centralized its debt by pooling these loans into a single, state-controlled fund. In return, creditors received interest payments (often around 5%) that were backed by state revenues, particularly from customs duties and trade taxes. These debt obligations were then made transferable, allowing lenders to sell their claims to the government.

This effectively created an early secondary market for public debt. This system not only helped Venice finance its wars and infrastructure investments, but it also helped establish long-term investor confidence in Venice, making future borrowing easier. The Venetian debt model became a precursor to later European public finance innovations.

Marco Polo Brings Paper Money to Europe

104 1270s Marco Polo introduced the concept of paper money to Europe. Polo, a Venetian merchant, traveled along the Silk Road. He reportedly reached China, which at the time was ruled by Mongols, and met with the great Kublai Khan. Historians debate the extent of his travels. Regardless, he ventured far enough to witness the widespread use of paper currency in the Yuan Dynasty. In his autobiography, *The Travels*, Polo described how the Chinese government issued paper money backed by the state. Polo detailed the highly organized monetary system in China, noting that merchants and officials readily accepted these banknotes.

Marco Polo's discovery of paper money did not, however, immediately make waves in Europe. European economies at the time only used precious metal coinage and a limited number of debt instruments. It wasn't until the 17th century that Europe broke with this trend when a public bank in Sweden issued the continent's first paper money. By that point, paper money had created rampant inflation in China and went out of use, to be reintroduced by Europeans two centuries later.

Watermark Invented

105 1282 Today, watermarks are one of the many standard features of banknotes designed to make them harder to counterfeit [see: 488]. The first known watermark dates to 1282 in Italy. Early watermarks were used to mark the origin or craftsman of paper and were hidden in the pages of old books. Different watermarks denoted which papermaker made which book. One early example of insignia was an eagle inside a circle, with a crown on top of the circle. Watermarks were later used to denote the grade, quality, or size of paper.

The first watermark to appear on a banknote was from 1697 on an English banknote. The watermark was added by a Berkshire man named Rice Watkins. Since then, watermarks have been standard on banknotes as a security measure.

Lombard Banking

106 late 13th c. The Lombard bankers showed up in Italy near the end of the 13th century. Lombards were a group of people in northern Italy, and the Lombard bankers were often, but not always, ethnically from Lombardy. The Lombard bankers participated in more rudimentary money-lending than proper banks like the Medici [see: 114]. They owned pawnbroking shops, though with somewhat shaky legal status. They also lived in constant fear of societal expulsion, in a position much like that of the Jews.

The Lombards' problem was that their business was borderline usurious. Technically, their pawnbroking operations were the discounted sale and repurchase of goods, though that could be interpreted as charging interest. The technical definition of their activities must have been good enough for the Count of Flanders, who gave the Lombards licenses to operate. These licenses were issued for a few centuries. The number of bankers receiving them appears to have been quite small, and none of them were from major houses. The licenses were also terribly expensive. One partnership paid over £133 in the local unit of account in fees to the city in 1308. It must have been worth it to dodge usury laws.

Sterling Silver Introduced

107 1298 Sterling silver acted as the standard to which British coins were minted for at least a thousand years until it went out of use in 1920. Sterling is a 92.5% silver alloy, with its origins in the standard set under William the Conqueror after he invaded England in 1066. Some evidence indicates that it may have been used even earlier.

Coins bearing the title of sterling first appeared in the early 12th century, possibly named after the Old English *steorra*, meaning "star," a shape that appeared on some coins. Alternatively, the name may come from the birds, *staer* or starling, that appeared on coins of Edward the Confessor. King Edward I made the 92.5% standard official in 1298. From then, English coinage became well-respected for its consistent quality, though many debasements and recoinages would follow.

IV

The Birth of Banking:
14th c. – 1601

Modern banking, which has made money ever more accessible and efficient, has its roots in the Middle Ages. The first major banking houses were the Bardi and Peruzzi in Florence, Italy. The famous Medici house came about a century later. This period was the heyday for financial innovation in Italy, the center of medieval banking and where the Renaissance soon originated. Banking at the time was remarkably complicated and well organized. It benefitted from innovations in math and accounting, such as the introduction of double-entry bookkeeping.

This period also saw the beginning of the Age of Exploration. Spain conquered the Aztec empire, bringing so much gold home that Europe's economy was hurt by inflation. In time, more advanced corporate organization were needed to finance colonial expansion, as we will see in the next chapter.

Another notable change was the world's center of influence shifting from being in both China and Europe to being solely in Europe. China contributed several valuable inventions to financial history, such as paper money. However, China failed to put those inventions to use nearly as well as did Europe. Additionally, the Mongol invasion of China in the 13th century brought the golden age of the Tang and Song to an end. Within a few centuries, Europe's Renaissance hit, and its development outpaced that of Asia. Because of this macro realignment, Asia didn't make many more notable contributions to the history of money after this point.

By the beginning of the 16th century, banking still had a ways to go to develop into a system comparable to what banks are today. The Bardi, Peruzzi, and Medici, though highly efficient, still lacked many modern elements. But the fundamentals of modern banking were now set. Money's definition strayed further from the idea that it is little more than coinage. Europe was now on track to create the modern financial system.

Rise of the Bardi and Peruzzi Banks

108 early 14th c. Two families, the Bardi and the Peruzzi, were giants in Italian banking in the early 14th century. Combined, their fortune was larger than even the Medici family of the next century [see: 114]. The nobility of the Peruzzi was recorded from as early as the 11th century, and the Bardi nobility was first noted in 1164. Though known in this book as bankers, these families both got their start in the wool trade.

By 1336, the Peruzzi family had established 15 branches across the Mediterranean, including as far away as modern-day Israel and England. In its prime, the company employed about 90 clerks and commanded 103,000 gold florins in capital. This would be over $40 million based on a gold price of about $3,200 per ounce. While only about 60% of the Peruzzi bank was owned by the Peruzzi family, it was not a joint-stock company. Instead, it was a type of partnership that continues even after one partner dies. In 1300, there were 17 partners. The Bardi family bank was about 50% larger. Its business particularly excelled in England, where it operated since the 1270s. Though these banks were giants by medieval standards, they came toppling down within a few decades.

Failed Token Money in India

109 1329 Muhammad Bin Tughlaq, Sultan of Delhi, introduced a type of token money used to facilitate economic expansion and make up for a lack of precious metal in the government's vaults. This lack of metal was in part due to the Sultan's lavish lifestyle, the fact that he attempted to expand the kingdom while it was experiencing a general lack of prosperity, and his plan to move the country's capital from Delhi to Devagiri, a more strategic location about 700 miles away.

In 1329-30, a copper coin was introduced and it was required that it be used just like a silver or gold coin. Though these coins were made of base metal and had insignificant intrinsic value, their face-value was legally set equal to that of silver coins. The coins were known for being artistic in their design, but their use did not last long. Delhi didn't trust the coins' value, and easy copying made for rampant forgery. Copper coins started falling in value against gold coins until Muhammed Bin Tughlaq repealed the edict, requiring that all copper coins be brought to the treasury and exchanged with gold.

King Edward III Defaults

110 1340 In 1340–41, King Edward III defaulted on the debt lent to him by the Bardi and Peruzzi families. The previous few years were financially challenging for the Crown. The ongoing war with France had left the country £300,000 in debt, with £230,000 owed to the Bardi and Peruzzi families (worth some £240 million today). Edward had to raise money quickly.

The magnates and Commons agreed upon a one-ninth tax on all produce. The national shortage of coinage required this tax to be paid in-kind. The collected goods would be sold to the public. The public, however, was unable to buy them back due to the shortage of currency. The Crown, which needed to collect £100,000 to pay the debt, could only round up £65,000.

Further, this financial struggle occurred amidst general political turmoil. The King's authority was weakening, government officials were acting immorally and unlawfully, and those in charge of collecting tax revenue collected more than they deposited at the treasury. Ultimately, the country was unable to raise enough money to pay its debt. England defaulted on its loans with the Bardi and Peruzzi families, which, combined with other factors, resulted in the largest bank failures up to that point [see: 112].

How Debt Helped Medieval Business

111 In the Middle Ages, the supply of coinage provided by the Roman Empire dried up. While Charlemagne minted a series of pennies that could be used for small transactions, in the day-to-day life of most people, the cash economy of the Classical period evolved into one based on non-cash transactions. Goods were largely traded in kind, making economic exchange extremely inefficient. As a result, a remarkably complex system of credit instruments sprung up mostly by the High Middle Ages.

Bills of exchange were used for satisfying foreign transactions. During the politically fragmented Middle Ages, which lacked both international and intranational policing, it was unwise to move large quantities of precious metal across borders. Bills of exchange allowed international payments to be made with an extension of credit over two months and with foreign currency exchange built in. The exchange rate could also be manipulated, allowing for the charging of interest in a manner hidden from Church prohibition.

A larger suite of tools was available for completing domestic transactions. For example, notched wooden sticks called tallies were used to record sums of money. Sometimes people used them simply to keep tax-receipts. At other times, they denoted credit that was owed [see: 89]. Often, credit relationships operated outside of formal credit instruments and money, and exchanges were often enabled by book transfers.

Debt owed to a person was seen as an asset to that person, as it is today. For example, the moveable assets of a certain London merchant were evaluated at over £4,842 in 1424. Of that total, only £1,815 was cash and goods, while £3,027 was debt owed to him. These are just some of the ways that finance advanced in the Middle Ages to account for the lack of coinage.

Bardi and Peruzzi Collapse

112 1343 For all their grandeur in the banking sphere, the Bardi and Peruzzi families had rather short runs. The Peruzzi bank failed in 1343, and the Bardi in 1346, after Edward III of England defaulted on his debt owed to them [see: 110]. Edward borrowed—and failed to repay—600,000 gold florins from the Peruzzi family, and 900,000 from the Bardi.

The default, however, could not have been the only reason for the banks' demise, as they did not collapse until a few years after Edward defaulted. Also, Florence's third-largest bank followed the Bardi and Peruzzi into bankruptcy, even though it had not made loans to England. It was the banks' involvement in politics that were a key cause of their failures.

In 1340, Walter VI, Count of Brienne, was installed as ruler of Florence, supported by both the Bardi and the Peruzzi families. Three years later, public opinion of him changed and he was overthrown. The lower classes in Florence then overthrew the governing regime established by the merchants, thus putting the Peruzzi bank out of business. The Bardi bank went bankrupt when an important institution in the government restructured its debt, much of which was held by the Bardi bank.

Economic Effects of the Black Plague

113 1346 In the winter of 1346-1347, the Black Death emerged in Southeastern Europe and quickly spread across the continent. This wave of disease, thought today to have been the Bubonic Plague, killed one-third of Europeans between 1347 and 1353. This was the largest population decline in European history. The plague subsided after 1353, but returned in the 15th, 16th, and even 17th centuries.

There are estimates assessing the Plague's effects on wages, GDP, and prices. The Plague raised wages in the long run as business adjusted to the scarcity of labor. In the short run, however, wages dropped 20% in England, due to the breakdown of the economy (though, oddly, wages increased in Florence). GDP per-capita in England decreased 6% in the first year. The resulting inflationary effects were dramatic. The supply shock (fewer goods) combined with increased wages resulted in a 27% jump in the consumer price index between 1348 and 1350 in England. The following economic recovery was mixed. Farmers got back to farming as usual, though the disintegration of traditional trade networks mitigated the economic rebound. The Black Death often marks the end of the Middle Ages, as it took down the Middle Ages' dominant manorial system [see: 93].

Medici Bank Founded

114 1393 The Medici was one of the richest and most powerful families in history. They were neither the first family to establish a bank in Italy nor the most innovative, but structural aspects of their bank allowed it to expand to be the largest bank in Europe at the time. The family established itself as elites. From their ranks, two became popes, two were queens of France, and three were dukes in Italy. This was remarkable upward-mobility, given that the family started as criminal gangsters.

The Medici bank was founded in 1393 by Giovanni di Bicci de' Medici, who exchanged currencies in Florence. Giovanni quickly expanded his operations, opening multiple offices around Italy. In 1429, Giovanni's son, Cosimo, took over the business and continued to expand it, opening a branch as far away as London. The Medici bank partnered with other banks that managed their dealing in locations without a branch.

The Medici bank failed for the same reason many modern banks fail. It traded heavily on equity and issued bonds to assist in expansion. Even when company profit fell, the bank worried that cutting interest rates on its bonds would hurt its prestige. It was right. Eventually, it was forced to cut rates, the bank's losses became public, and it collapsed in 1494.

The Birth of Venus was painted in the 1480s by Sandro Botticelli, one of the many artists that the Medici patronized.

How the Medici Bank Worked

115 In the High Middle Ages, most banks were monolithic structures. If a high-profile client defaulted, the entire bank could be brought down. The Medici, on the other hand, was essentially designed as a loose confederacy of branches—almost like a franchise. The central office in Florence contracted with each Medici branch separately, and each branch had its own balance sheet, capital, and liabilities. To maintain control of the branches, the central office owned at least 50% of each branch subsidiary company. At the central office, there was a general manager for all Medici Banks. There was also a manager for branches in Italy and another for branches outside of Italy, and each individual branch had its own internal structure.

The Medici Bank provided comprehensive interbank and foreign currency exchange services. Each branch had a nostro and a vostro account. A nostro account was an account with another bank in that bank's local currency. A vostro account was a bank account on behalf of a foreign bank—that is, for the central Medici office. In addition to standard savings and loan accounts, this Medici bank participated in speculative investments. It used bills of exchange widely, a type of contract specifying one party's obligation to pay another at a set date.

The Medici Bank had a modest seven or eight branches, along with 40 or 50 factors (excluding branch managers, who were not full employees), and possibly a dozen clerks in Florence. Yet it was the largest bank in existence at that time. It was so large for its time that it often struggled with finding outlets for all the cash that came in. In fact, the need to spend its cash incentivized the risky investments that ultimately brought the bank down.

Usury Not So Bad After All

116 15th c. Usury, which in the past meant charging any amount of interest, was strictly forbidden in Classical times and the Middle Ages by Biblical decree and later Christian law [see: 11; 92]. By the beginning of the Renaissance, however, religious hatred of usurers started to soften.

Usury became less sinful for two reasons. First, as the late-Middle Ages and early Renaissance became more money-oriented, the values of the time shifted to allow money to be considered morally-okay. Lending is key for financial development. By restricting lending, usury restrictions limit business' ability to operate efficiently. Second, the invention of Purgatory, the in-between place where someone goes after he dies but before he can be sent on to heaven, lightened the damnation given to usurers. Purgatory seems to have appeared in Catholic doctrine around the 12th century, and usurers, in going to Purgatory, could escape eternal damnation in Hell, which opened the door for more liberalization around money-lending. This allowed the economy of modern banking to get moving.

Barcelona's City Bank

117 1401 Sometimes described as the first central bank, the Taula de Canvi was founded in 1401 in Barcelona. Barcelona's city government was facing two problems: high public debt and private bank failures. The city realized it needed a stable and reliable bank that could take deposits. The bank would help the city finance its debt cheaply.

While the Taula de Canvi was meant to loan only to the city, it allowed private customers to have overdrafts, which essentially meant giving them private loans. The city guaranteed the bank, giving it a monopoly and many other privileges that attracted depositors and hurt private bankers. In 1433, the Taula de Canvi had 1,460 depositors and helped cut the city's debt in half. The bank was eventually incorporated into the Bank of Spain in 1853.

The Taula de Canvi differed from a modern central bank in that it did not act as a lender of last resort, and it deliberately made policies to hurt private banks. Additionally, it did not regulate the money supply or have a monopoly on banknote-issue. These key differences disqualify it from being considered the first central bank—a title that goes to the Bank of Amsterdam [see: 143].

Rise of Mercantilism

118 15th c. During the Middle Ages, the nation-state as we know it today did not exist in Europe. Instead, there was a complex mosaic of kingdoms bound together under the Christian religion. With the innovation of the nation-state—the modern country—as a governing institution in the Renaissance, international trade became safer and expanded widely. This required new economic paradigms to manage commerce and trade.

Mercantilism was a theory about the source of a nation's wealth. Wealth was determined by the amount of precious metal a country owned. Nations tried to maximize exports to bring more gold and silver payments into the country and minimize imports to prevent it from leaving. Nations imposed tariffs and quotas on imports, granted domestic monopolies, and made new companies exempt from taxes or guild rules. The mercantile classes liked these protectionist policies, as they kept competing foreign businesses away.

Mercantilism motivated economic competition between European countries. Politically, countries built up their armies and replaced volunteers with professionals. Economically, Spain sailed her armadas to the Americas and brought back large amounts of gold and silver, which appeared as a grand show of power. Spain's obsession with gold, however, uncovered the flaws of Mercantilism and sparked the Price Revolution [see: 133].

Adam Smith refuted Mercantilism, recognizing that a country's wealth was determined by how much it produced and traded with other nations. Smith claimed that a means of exchange and wealth itself—two different aspects of what is called "money"—were in fact different things. Conflating the two, he claimed, allowed the mercantile class to take advantage of the government so it would make laws benefiting them. Smith illustrated that free trade (and laissez-faire policy in general) made countries more prosperous than protectionism. Free trade benefits both parties involved, limits market distortions from government intervention, allows businesses to operate more efficiently, and minimizes the monopolistic practices common under mercantilism that hurt the general public.

Chinese Merchant Guilds

119 15th c. China's *huiguan*—provincial guild halls—were guild-like associations where membership was based on common geographic origin. The first such associations emerged in the 15th century in Beijing, providing hospitality to gentry who were traveling to the capital on official business or to take government examinations. Those traveling to Beijing found *huiguan* useful, and the guild halls spread around China. Merchants started contributing to the halls in the 18th century, though weren't fully allowed into Beijing's *huiguan* until the beginning of the 19th century.

Unlike in Beijing, merchants could be members of the *huiguan* in the commercial southwest from the 16th century on. These organizations provided aid and protections for their members, many of whom were not all that wealthy. Since *huiguan* guilds were organized by region, not by trade, they could be seen as contributing to localism and inhibiting economic integration. However, the networking opportunities *huiguan* organizations offered benefitted merchants, who could connect with other businessmen and politicians in their region. The guilds boosted economic growth in the Qing Dynasty.

The Unusual Incan Economy

120 15th c. The Inca is one of history's greatest empires. However, while the Roman and British Empires were built on an effective financial system, the Incan Empire did not use money at all.

The basic social unit was the *ayllu*, similar to a clan. In the Incan Empire, there was a great homogeneity of dress, food, religion, and language, making collective ownership of land an easier idea for the Inca to get behind. While the capitalist is motivated by profit, the Inca was motivated by mutually beneficial work for his neighbor. This took all sorts of forms, such as a community building a house for a newlywed couple. These communitarian inclinations ensured that the Incas achieved a high standard of living.

A downside of a non-monied economy was the difficulty of collecting taxes. The

Incas used a system whereby laborers, after completing the labor necessary for themselves, spent the rest of the year working for the government. There were up to 40 different types of labor tasks that the government could require. In this way, the Incan Empire managed to maintain a large infrastructure. While this sounds socialistic, it has been argued that the Incan Empire was in fact more of an authoritarian command economy.

Great Bullion Famine

121 mid 15th c. Mercantilism was generally stable, except when countries ran out of precious metal. There was a constant drain on Europe's precious metal resources, as Europe imported high-priced luxuries such as spices, silks, dyes, and pearls from the East without making sufficient exports to bring the precious metal back home. That is, in the early modern period, Europe got itself in a massive balance of payments deficit that consumed much of its gold and silver reserves. Two shortages of gold and silver in Europe, one at the beginning and one in the middle of the 15th century, were the worst shortages since the seventh century. The shortages were termed the Great Bullion Famine.

The reduced supply of precious metals meant a reduced supply of money in Western Europe. Miners were digging up insufficient amounts of gold and silver to replace the lost reserves, and lower production of coins was reported. Coins were taken out of circulation and hoarded. Bullion prices rose, and speculators attacked the now undervalued national currencies. European trade was stifled. It took the continent about a century to fully recover from the Great Bullion Famine, only to be struck by more problems when too much gold was imported into Europe [see: 133].

Quipu Accounting Strings

122 15th c. The Incan Empire recorded financial transactions in a way that may sound unusual but, in fact, was quite universal for pre-writing civilizations. The Incas widely used strings, called *quipu*. The *quipu*, which may have emerged during the first millennium AD (although records of them don't exist before the 15th century), are sets of cotton or wool strings that are all tied onto a rope on one end. Both the rope and the strings were often more than a yard long and dyed in many colors. Incas recorded numerical values by trying knots onto the strings.

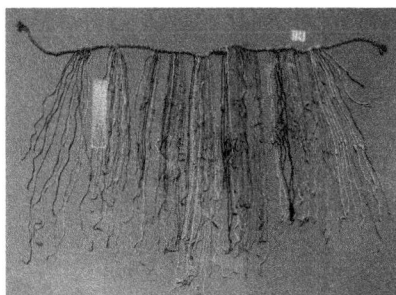

Fragment of a quipu accounting string, likely from the late 15th or early 16th century

It is unclear exactly what format the Incas used to record onto the *quipu*. Illustrations made by Spanish conquistadors show Incas using abacus-like devices alongside the strings. The device was a box with 20 compartments, each with black and white beads in them, which were likely used to indicate zeros and ones. An Inca may have used the *quipu* to record data stored in the box. The Incan government and economy was highly advanced, and with these *quipu* strings, Incas recorded debit and credit transactions and may have even used double-entry accounting.

Double-Entry Accounting

123 1494 Double-entry bookkeeping is an accounting method where every transaction is recorded as both corresponding credits and debits in the same account. For example, a bank considers a loan to be an asset and would write the loan amount as a number on the debit side of the ledger. However, it would consider the decreased reserves as a liability and record the same amount of money on the credit side of the ledger. In general, credits are written on the right side of the page and debits on the left. Since every change is recorded on both sides, the accounts are always "balanced."

Improvements in Accounting

124 Businesses and governments have always kept accounts. Today, double-entry accounting is standard; but throughout history, people have used other accounting systems. The earliest society that had enough economic activity to require bookkeeping was Mesopotamia. The region has provided historians with hundreds of thousands of clay tablets to attest to this need. In the very early days of Mesopotamian history, pictographic scripts were used, and Cuneiform was developed later [see: 2]. Mesopotamian accounting records were fairly detailed and mostly written out in prose.

The three-column accounting method, invented under China's Zhou Dynasty, was the most robust accounting method for its time. It was improved upon with the four-column method during the Tang Dynasty, in which starting balance, increase, decrease, and ending balance were all recorded. The Romans also realized the importance of accounting, and many of the wealthy wrote up their accounts every month. Roman advances in accounting allowed them to conduct high-level financial transactions, and imperial accounts were kept from Augustus' time onward. It appears that the Roman emperor had massive amounts of economic information available to him.

A 1396 ledger from Europe described credits and debits in full sentences, with credits written on one side of the page and debits on the other. Each transaction was recorded only once. Double-entry was invented in 1494, and early examples write on one side how much will be given and paid, and on the other how much will be received and paid. In the late 15th and early 16th centuries, prose was slowly replaced with numerical columns.

The earliest known example of double-entry accounting was from Florence in 1211. The method continued to be developed as increasingly complicated financial exchanges required more advanced accounting methods. Modern double-entry book-keeping was first outlined in the famous *Summa de Arithmetica* (*Everything about Mathematics*, published 1494) by Luca Pacioli, who is today known as the father of accounting. As England began to become more industrialized, it became the first country where businesses started using double-entry bookkeeping on a large scale. This method is still used today, even by the largest companies.

Date	Account Titles	Debit ($)	Credit ($)
2025-06-06	Office Supplies	500	
	Cash		500
To record office supplies purchased with cash			

This double-entry account shows that the company purchased $500 of office supplies and paid with cash. The $500 debit to Office Supplies reflects an increase in assets, while the $500 credit to Cash reflects an equal decrease in assets. Thus both sides are balanced.

Great Depression of the Renaissance

125 late 15th c. Though the Renaissance was a time of cultural revolution, it was not necessarily a time of economic expansion—at least at its start in the 15th century. The evidence, though vague, points to an economic downturn occurring after an initial period of growth in the centuries marking the end of the Middle Ages.

An example attesting to this downturn is that, between 1424 and 1453, the percentage of people in Basel (modern-day Switzerland) who did not possess the minimum taxable capital increased by about 10 percentage-points. In another example, construction records of the expansion of town walls in Italy show that there was a boom in the 13th and 14th centuries. However, this was followed by a notable decline in construction in the 15th century and first half of the 16th. Further, England's population declined during the latter-half of the 1300s, and Italy followed this trend in the 1400s.

More poor people, less construction, and a declining population all point to circumstantial evidence of economic troubles during the Renaissance. Historians postulate that a key reason for the contraction was that population growth outpaced improvement in productive technology. Thus, there wasn't enough food to feed everyone. This was solved with the Industrial Revolution a few centuries later.

American-Indian Wampum

126 16th c. Native Americans used *wampum* beads as money. The full name, *wampumpeag*, means a string of white beads. "Wampum" means white, and "peag" means a string of beads in the New England Algonquian language. *Wampum* strings were most widely used east of the Mississippi River, though they traveled west and were treated as a rarity by American Indians near the Rocky Mountains.

We do not know when Native Americans first used *wampum*. American Indians may have been using them for centuries before Europeans arrived. The earliest remaining records of *wampum*, however, are from Europeans. Making *wampum* was a meticulous job. The beads' sizes ranged from less than an inch long to two inches long, and often had a texture like glass. Sometimes strings of beads would be attached together to make wide fabric-like products.

When Europeans arrived, they started using *wampum* to trade with the American Indians because European currency was lacking on the American continent. To increase trade, European settlers started mass-producing *wampum*, creating inflation and damaging the indigenous system. New Netherlands banned low-quality *wampum* in 1641, and Connecticut followed suit. In 1648, Massachusetts made *wampum* de jure legal tender, but this status was repealed in 1661. *Wampum* continued to be used as money well into the 1700s.

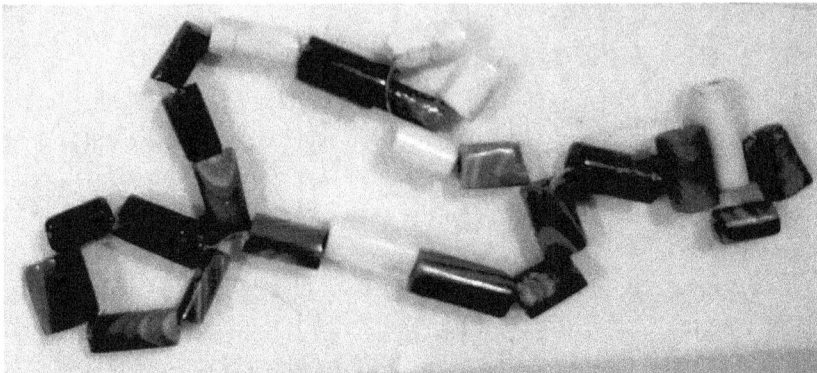

A wampum bead string, ca. later 18th c.

King Henry VIII Dissolves Monasteries

127 1536 Between 1536 and 1541, King Henry VIII of England disbanded Catholic monasteries and other Catholic institutions. As part of his separation from the Catholic Church, Henry tried to reduce the Church's power in England. He was also short on money and wanted to take advantage of the wealth held in domestic monasteries to alleviate the burden on his treasury created by the growing population and wars with France and Scotland. At the time, there were about 900 Catholic religious houses in England and Wales, many having been there since the time of the Roman occupation.

The main source of income for these organizations was their landholdings, which were mainly used for agriculture. Monasteries owned about one-third of all land in

England and Wales, which brought them between £100,000–200,000 per year, equivalent to three-quarters of the Crown's annual income. The dissolution of the monasteries was done through several acts of Parliament. Originally, the land was meant to be managed by a dedicated government ministry. However, Henry decided to quickly sell off much of it to raise money, and the Crown was unable to fully realize potential profits.

Religion and Economic Growth

128 The economist and historian Niall Ferguson wrote of Europe's recent trend toward secularism: "To put it bluntly, we are witnessing the decline and fall of the Protestant work ethic in Europe. This represents the stunning triumph of secularization in Western Europe—the simultaneous decline of both Protestantism and its unique work ethic." Is Europe really on the decline because of secularization? Maybe. It has been well documented that Protestant countries economically outperform Catholic countries.

This theory was first posited in the early 1900s by Max Weber. Weber argued that Protestants have a stronger work ethic, are more individualistic, focus on education, are more modest, and are more inclined to find their career calling. This results in Protestants being more entrepreneurial, which leads to greater economic growth. These supposed character traits have a theological basis in Protestant religion. Protestants gain salvation by having an individual relationship with God rather than by going to church or performing rites. Protestantism encourages every person to read and interpret the Bible for himself. A later scholar added to Max Weber that, since salvation is uncertain, one must work hard to achieve it. Further, entrepreneurship was one of the few ways for members of the prosecuted new religion to thrive.

Jews have also been economically successful for similar reasons to Protestants. Judaism strongly values education and critical thinking. Historically, Jews have been discriminated against and denied opportunities and access to wealth. Turning to entrepreneurship, law, and medicine requires little working capital but intelligence and commitment. On a similar note, one study suggests that worship of traditional sages in China negatively affected economic growth in the country. The more sage temples there were in a prefecture zone (indicating greater reliance on traditional Chinese religion), the slower that zone adopted Western business practices and, thus, the zone experienced less economic growth.

Great Debasement in England

129 1544 King Henry VIII's England was forced to bear large expenses from wars with France and Scotland. His lavish lifestyle and other big-ticket items (starting a new Church is not cheap!) started to add up, too. English coinage of the Middle Ages was some of the most reputable, known for its high precious metal content of 92.5% for silver coins and 99.5% for gold. But Henry realized that he could make a large profit from debasing the coinage.

Initially, the project was kept secret. The debasement occurred in multiple steps over eight years. In 1544, the gold content of coins was reduced to 95.8% and the silver to 74%. This failed to solve the treasury's problems, and Edward VI, who took power in 1547 after Henry died, recalled all coinage previously issued and recoined it at a lower amount of precious metal. In April 1551, the fineness of silver coins was reduced to 25%. By October of that year, the fineness of silver coinage was restored.

Over eight years, the Crown profited £1.01 million. The effects of the Great Debasement were massive and took years to be reversed. Trade with the rest of Europe was disrupted, and price levels rose dramatically—as much as 50%.

Silver Discovered in Americas

130 1545 In 1545, an Andean prospector named Diego Huallpa discovered the Cerro Rico de Potosí, a 16,000-foot-high volcanic neck that has yielded 60,000 tons of silver since its discovery. These deposits formed about 13.5 million years ago. Within a few decades, the Spanish, the new owners of the region, had thousands of indigenous furnaces set up to smelt silver around the clock. In 1572, more advanced smelting machines were put into use that could separate the silver from zinc, lead, and tin—something indigenous furnaces could not do. Many Native Americans were employed or enslaved to operate the mines, which was a highly dangerous operation.

Production peaked in 1592 when the city of Potosí had a population of 100,000. Europe was enthralled with the massive quantities of silver; large amounts of Potosí silver made it as far away as China. The city started to decline in the 17th century, along with the Spanish Empire. It had a slight resurgence in the 18th century, but in 1800, drought and human rights concerns finally closed the mine. South American rebels tried to overthrow the Spanish government and succeeded in 1825.

First Machine-Made Coins

131 1550 As gold and silver flowed from the Americas to Europe, mints busy trying to coin it all started churning out increasingly poor coinage that was easily clipped and counterfeited. By Gresham's Law, these bad coins circulated more, undermining the entire coinage supply [see: 230]. Before 1550, German engineers were working on ways to mechanize mints. They made experimental designs for machinery that could roll metal out, cut out coin blanks, and press designs onto them.

However, using these machines proved troublesome, as the components were prone to break.

In 1550, a man appeared who could seemingly make all the pieces work together. Only Charles de Marillac, the French ambassador to the city of Augsburg in Germany, knew of this man. Marillac wanted France and France alone to capitalize on the invention of machine-made currency to gain an advantage over the Holy Roman Empire. Marillac kept his dealings with the inventor secret and snuck the technology back to France, where it was quickly put in use for French coinage. Eventually, the secret got out, and milled coinage was implemented across Europe in the 16th and 17th centuries.

Illustration of Potosi mine

Russia Company Chartered

132 1553 The development of modern companies is significant in the history of money, as companies are key to economic development. The Muscovy Company was an early form of joint-stock company. Founded two years after Richard Chancellor discovered Russia while looking for the Northeast Passage to China in 1553, the company facilitated trade between Russia and England and helped develop friendly relations between the two countries.

The company was founded as a partnership among 250 men. It had £6,000 of start-up capital, a small sum which quickly grew. About three-quarters of the charterers were London merchants who maintained a strong hold on the company's operations.

The Muscovy Company was a predecessor to the first true joint-stock company, the Dutch East India Company [see: 139]. The Muscovy Company's stock was not freely transferable, and it operated more like a regulated trading company with a fixed group of chartered members rather than as a corporation with publicly traded shares. The company was less financially flexible, and money couldn't be taken out as easily. As such, it represents a node in the development of modern corporate structure.

Price Revolution in Europe

133 16th c. When money is added to circulation faster than the growth in real transactions, inflation ensues. While printing too much fiat money can easily result in inflation, basing the value of money on precious metals usually helps keep inflation in check. This is because additional mining decreases the value of precious metals, which, in turn, lowers the value of mining and raises the value of alternate uses for precious metal in ways other than trade. This creates deflation, balancing things out.

Through the 16th century, however, the influx of gold and silver from the Spanish Americas was so great that inflation was inevitable. Spanish colonies in the Americas shipped tens of thousands of tons of precious metals to Spain. The new money diffused across Europe.

As a result, prices in Europe rose by a multiple of three or four over the 16th century—massive for the time. Between 1525 and 1600, the largest amount of precious metal was mined, and consequently, the highest inflation of the period occurred. The damage done to the economy and the current account deficit that resulted when Spain spent its new money left Spanish industry undeveloped and uncompetitive, contributing to the fall of the empire.

Spain Defaults on Loans

134 1556 In the early Renaissance, European governments periodically spent heavily on military activity. For instance, in the 16th century, military spending typically constituted 60% of the Spanish Crown's total expenses at a time when Spain's income was volatile. Sales tax and a tax on silver imports from the Americas were the main sources of income, and the profit from the latter fluctuated significantly. With changing war expenses and volatile income, Spain needed the ability to borrow heavily at times. Often unable to pay back its loans, Spain became the first country to be considered a sovereign credit risk—a label it still holds today.

The king borrowed heavily by issuing bonds and by taking loans from Genoese bankers. In the average year between 1566 and 1600, King Phillip II had 6.6 million ducats in revenue and 34.9 million in debt. The Crown defaulted twice in 1556, and then declared a third bankruptcy in 1575, and a fourth in 1596. After each of the defaults, the Genoese bankers negotiated with the Crown and were paid back a percentage of the amount they were owed. These defaults—unlike modern defaults—did not significantly weaken the Crown's borrowing ability, and the Genoese continued lending and ultimately benefited.

West Africa Bracelet Coinage

135 **16th c.** Coinage does not have to be round to operate as a means of exchange. In western Africa, particularly in Nigeria and in the Congo, bracelet-shaped coins were used. These bracelets, called manilla bracelets, were first produced in the 16th century. They were still used as late as the 1940s and may even continue to be used today in some remote villages. Used mostly as a means of payment for slaves during the Atlantic Slave Trade, manilla bracelets often had little hoof-like flanges at the end.

The bracelets were typically made of copper, brass, and, later, iron. One manilla bracelet dating to the mid-18th century was found embedded in a coral reef in the Caribbean, likely having fallen off of a wrecked slave ship. The bracelet was given a composition analysis test, which showed that it was made of 64% copper, 26% lead, 7% tin, and a few other trace elements including 0.98% silver.

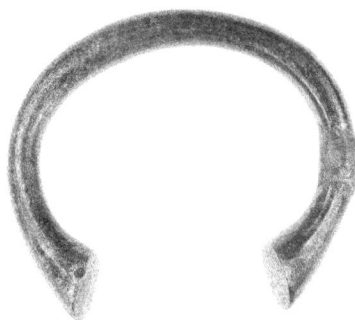

Manilla money bracelet

Yamada Hagaki: Japan's First Paper Currency

137 **1600** The *yamada hagaki* was Japan's first paper currency, introduced around 1600. There are two major Shinto shrines in the city of Ise. Many pilgrims came to these shrines, fostering commercial development and trade there early on. The influx of commerce led to a shortage of small-denomination coins, prompting local Shinto priests, who also engaged in mercantile activities, to create paper money.

The *yamada hagaki* were a form of promissory note or deposit receipt. The notes were backed by silver and could be used in everyday transactions. The largest denomination was typically one *momme*, equivalent to approximately 3.75 grams of silver—not a very large sum. The notes were printed with woodblocks and gained widespread acceptance over time.

In 1631, the Tokugawa shogunate recognized the utility of these notes and brought their issuance under official oversight. Control was vested in the Sanpo Kaigosho, a regulatory body that authorized select groups to issue and redeem the notes for silver. This formalization aimed to standardize the currency and integrate it within the broader monetary system of the Edo period. People continued to use *yamada hagaki* for over three centuries.

What is Inflation?

136 Inflation, the most well-known term in economics, is also the most hated. US president Ronald Reagan said, "Inflation is as violent as a mugger, as frightening as an armed robber, and as deadly as a hit man." Milton Friedman described inflation with less strong terms, as "Too many dollars chasing too few goods."

Inflation occurs when the supply of money grows faster than the production of things to buy. Specifically, when the money supply grows, there is more money to spend and demand for goods increases. If the supply of goods does not change, however, then prices simply must go up. Inflation sometimes coincides with economic growth. When the economy grows and there is more money available, inflation is often the result. The US Fed and most other central banks have a target inflation rate of 2%. Maintaining a target rate is one of central banks' key jobs [see: 165].

Though inflation has certainly been around for a very long time, the amount of steady inflation we experience today largely has only existed for the past couple of centuries. Except for during periods of bad economic policy, prices generally didn't change as quickly when precious metal was used for coinage. Even the Price Revolution, a period of then-considered large, long-term inflation, was relatively minor by modern standards. The Great Inflation of the 1970s was a more recent inflationary spell [see: 337], and since then, inflation at a pace much quicker than ever experienced in the pre-modern world has become standard.

Supply shocks—when supply suddenly drops but demand stays the same— also cause inflation, often after wars. Since most currencies are fiat currency today, inflation burdens poorer countries with governments unable to create trustworthy monetary policies. Sometimes this turns into hyperinflation, such as when goods in Zimbabwe got 500 billion percent more expensive in 2008 [see: 453].

Poor Relief Act

138 1601 The social welfare programs we have today, such as Social Security, have their origins in two major changes in England, which uprooted the traditional system whereby the Church and the wealthy were responsible for assisting those in need of aid. The two changes were the dissolution of monasteries under Henry VIII [see: 127] and the end of the manorial system. Both left the poor without charity help or a home. The first program to help the poor was initiated under Henry VIII in the 1530s. These laws were expanded upon in the famous Poor Laws, officially the Poor Relief Act of 1601, under Queen Elizabeth.

The administrative unit for the Act's charity program was the parish. Each parish was tasked with supporting those who were poor or unable to work with food, shelter, clothing, and cash. They helped find employment for the poor who could work and punished the poor who were able but refused to work. The program also permitted the poor to use common land. In some cases, the parish would raise funds for the program by taxing its citizens, but these taxes were generally ineffective at raising large sums.

V

The Company and the Market:
1602 – 1835

A corporation is a group of people who act as a single entity. It dilutes risk by protecting owners and employees from losses, and operates more efficiently than a sole-proprietorship can by pooling people's investments and combining many people's skill sets. The company is a key part of the foundation of modern capitalism. The founding of the Dutch East India Company (VOC), the very first modern-style joint-stock company, is the first event in this chapter. The VOC was created to buy spices from India, which was an arduous task at the time. Ships had to sail from Europe, around the Cape of Good Hope under Africa, and up through the Indian Ocean. This was a very expensive trip that required the pooling of risk, advanced logistical coordination, and complex organization to finance it all effectively. These needs were met by the joint-stock company.

The existence of a company necessitated issuing ownership shares to raise money. In turn, this required developing a market for issuing, buying, and selling such shares. The first stock market emerged in Amsterdam, allowing investors to quickly and efficiently exchange VOC shares on a large scale. Companies—and now investors—still needed access to more capital. In order to help finance the burgeoning stock market, Amsterdam developed a stronger banking system.

The beginnings of the modern banking system, which were described in the previous chapter, quickly expanded into something more recognizable today. Many European countries adopted central banks, while more and more citizens started using private banks. New forms of money also developed during this period. By the end of the 17th century, the amount of paper money in circulation exceeded the amount of coin money for the first time. Financiers invented tools to store and use investor money more efficiently, such as options and futures, as well as annuities and life insurance.

These new tools meant that the amount of effective money in the economy expanded beyond the actual amount of coinage available. This encouraged industrial expansion and made it possible to build and buy large machines with loans. Individuals now had more and better ways to save their money. Credit also became more available, allowing people to buy more goods they wanted.

Adam Smith published his *Wealth of Nations* in 1776, creating the field of modern economics. This period saw the transformation of finance from its Classical and Medieval version to more closely resemble the system that operates today.

VOC Chartered

139 1602 Several early forms of companies have been featured in this book. They were predecessors to the first true joint-stock company, the Vereenigde Nederlandsche Geoctroyeerde Oostindische Compagnie, or the United Dutch East India Company (VOC). Before the VOC was created, every voyage to the East Indies to trade for spices required its own contract. This contract would fund—and bear the risk of—only that single voyage. Most investors could not cover multiple contracts to spread the risk of such arduous and perilous journeys. To expand trade and compete with Spain and Portugal, the Netherlands needed a single, coordinated business entity to efficiently pool investor funds.

The VOC was chartered with 6.54 million guilders (about 100 million euros today). Its management was split between six Dutch cities that would send delegates, collectively called the Seventeen Lords. The government gave the company a 21-year charter, and the company agreed to liquidate after 10 years, at which point investors could then reinvest. The first subscribers paid in four installments, were given receipts that could be resold, and their names were put on a stock ledger. There were 1,143 subscribers in Amsterdam alone, from all social classes. Thus, the modern corporation was born.

First Stock Market

140 1600s The founding of the Dutch East India Company in 1602 necessitated a secondary market in which shares of the company could be bought and sold by a large and diverse set of investors. This secondary market became the world's first modern stock exchange.

The VOC rule book laid out clear procedures for trading its ownership shares. To trade, the buyer and seller must go to the East India House and ask the bookkeeper to transfer the shares to the buyer's account from the seller's account in the VOC's main account book. The clear rules made trading safer and incentivized broader investment.

The secondary market became more important after the VOC became permanent when Amsterdam's States General extended its original 10-year charter. Previously, medieval shipping companies were founded for the duration of a single voyage. Once completed, the company dissolved and investors (sometimes) got their money back. After the VOC was created, investors could sell their shares on the secondary market if they wanted to cash out, lowering investors' risk and encouraging investment. The new stock market facilitated the efficient organization of financing global markets and helped Amsterdam rise to economic preeminence.

Short Selling Invented

141 1608 You may think that it is only in recent times that investor speculation disconnects stock values from their company's actual performance. However, the stock market has been a tool for gambling for as long as it has existed. Speculation on stocks was invented no more than six years after the first joint-stock company, the VOC, sold its stocks. The quick turnover in the secondary market for the VOC's shares offered opportunities for profit seekers to exploit.

Isaac Le Maire launched the first short-selling attack in history. He was a sizable shareholder and director of the VOC, until he was removed from the directorship for embezzling funds in 1605. In 1608, Le Maire formed a syndicate that borrowed VOC shares and sold them. He tried to exploit a trading mechanism unique to the VOC to drive its stock prices down. The attack worked in the short term, allowing the syndicate to rebuy shares at a profit, but it did not hurt the VOC in the long term. Short selling was banned in the Netherlands in 1610.

How the VOC Worked

142 The Dutch East India company was founded in 1602 and shut down in 1799, nearly 200 years later. In addition to using the revolutionary system of issuing freely tradable stocks making it the first joint-stock company, the VOC also issued bonds to raise long-term capital and paid dividends. Early on, annual returns on dividends was an estimated 5–10%.

The Dutch Republic gave the VOC a monopoly on trade in Asia—everywhere east of the Cape of Good Hope. The VOC established trading posts in South Africa, India, and Indonesia. The VOC operated two different trade networks. In addition to moving goods from Asia to Europe, the Dutch transported goods around Asia, often taking payment from Eastern companies or rulers to do so. The VOC had sweeping power in Asia. It was, in a way, its own country. It waged wars using its own army and navy, it signed treaties, it governed its colonies, minting its own currency, and operating its own courts. The VOC's private army was key to protecting its trade routes from Asian leaders who sought to challenge it. The army did, however, often go astray. The VOC was known to be war-like. It both intervened in efforts at liberation in its colonies and picked fights with other European countries to try to take over their trade routes.

The VOC was in many ways similar to the British East India (EIC) company, which was founded two years prior. However, the British EIC was initially chartered with stronger capital limitations, and it was thus initially not an official joint-stock company. Eventually, however, the British adopted the joint-stock format of the VOC and improved upon it. It imposed lesser limitations on the size of British EIC stock. The British EIC closed in 1874, by which point it had operated as the government of India.

Bank of Amsterdam Founded

143 1609 The Bank of Amsterdam (Wisslebank in Dutch) is, by most definitions, the world's first central bank. However, it differed markedly from central banks today. It did not act as a lender of last resort or try to promote GDP growth. The bank managed monetary policy in a more rudimentary way.

The Dutch Republic of the 17th century had a complex currency problem. The country used the florin as a unit of account, but the florin wasn't minted to a single standard. There were 40 mints in the country, 14 of which were official—either provincial or municipal—and the rest local. Additionally, at the time, small countries like the Netherlands used many foreign coins, which were often debased. These factors combined to create higher inflation and complicate financial transactions.

The Dutch Republic founded the Bank of Amsterdam to address this issue by standardizing minting policy and requiring up-to-par coinage for deposits, forcing higher-quality coinage across the country. Additionally, the Bank created a system of intra-bank deposit transfers, meaning that coins were increasingly seldom withdrawn from the bank. The Bank of Amsterdam used these rudimentary means to essentially promote stabilization, much like modern central banks.

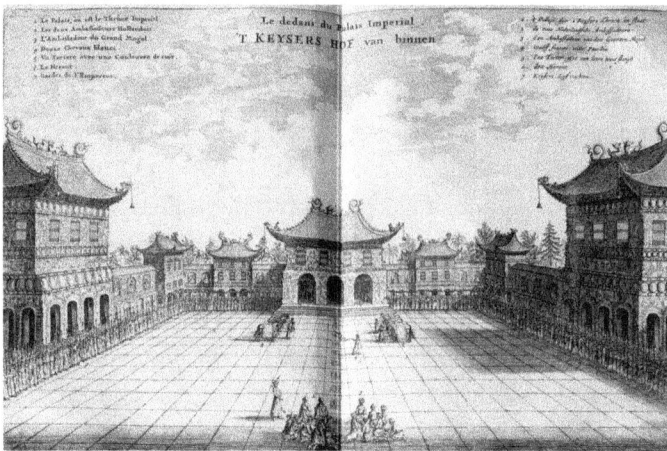

This illustration from a seventeenth-century Dutch travel account depicts envoys of the VOC paying tribute to the Chinese emperor in the Forbidden

Dutch Cities Copy Bank of Amsterdam

144 1616 The Bank of Amsterdam worked so well that other Dutch cities looked to establish their own banks on a similar model. Many parts of the Netherlands outside of Amsterdam also needed more stable coinage. These new, regional banks initially were mere copies of the original. The first was founded in Middelburg in 1616, with two more founded over the next 20 years.

The Bank of Amsterdam invented non-tangible "bank money," which was used for facilitating interbank transactions. Bank money differed from current money—coined money that circulates in a country. Regional banks let customers have separate accounts in current money and bank money, which was very convenient for merchants who needed the different forms of money for different types of transactions. Bank money in regional banks was valued at the market premium in Amsterdam, standardizing its value nationally. However, as the money supply improved in the 1690s, coined money became more stable, and the need for bank money disappeared. Thus, the need for exchange banks to manage bank money also disappeared. By the end of the 18th and the first decade of the 19th century, the regional exchange banks in the Netherlands closed their doors.

How Fractional Reserve Banking Works

145 When you deposit your money at a bank, the bank does not just leave it in the vaults and wait for you to come get it. The bank only retains a percentage of the total customer deposits, meaning the bank loans out or invests much of the money deposited with it. The difference between interest rates charged to borrowers and the interest rate paid to depositors allows banks to make a tidy profit. Some banks also profit on their investments. This is how a fractional-reserve banking system works, and this system is used by all modern banks.

The percentage of deposits that the bank keeps is called the "reserve ratio." Changing the ratio influences the total amount of loan making and is a way that a central bank can increase or decrease the total amount of money within the economy. The higher the reserve ratio, the fewer loans a bank can make. Making loans is akin to printing money because the bank is giving out money for someone to use that someone else also owns but is otherwise idle as a deposit in the bank at the same time. The money is effectively being used twice. On a large scale, this expands the supply of money in the economy. For transactional accounts, a reserve ratio of about 10% is typical across central banks.

Some early banks used full-reserve banking. The early Bank of Amsterdam used a reserve ratio of around 100% in its early years. When the required reserve ratio is too low, bank reserves may be insufficient to meet depositor withdrawal demand. This can result in a bank run, where fear of a bank's illiquidity can cause people to rush to get their money out of the bank before other depositors do so. If the reserve ratio is too high, banks can't make a profit (and have to spend a lot of money guarding all the cash in their vaults).

Baysa Cotton Money in the Sahara

146 17th c. Metal coinage has its obvious benefits as a means of exchange. However, it is not the only means of exchange. In the Sahara in Africa, cotton money called *baysa* emerged around the 17th century, possibly getting its name from the French or Portuguese word for "piece" or "coin." *Baysa* were reams of cotton, often 30 *dhira* (15 meters) in length and three wide—a measure that remained constant for centuries. This cotton money could be used for the standard functions of money by the 19th century, at which point it had become a standard unit of account in Saharan exchange for transactions, taxes, property values, and tributary payments.

One 19th-century account suggested that a *baysa* was worth three young male sheep. Large transactions would be counted in whole *baysas*, while smaller transactions used the *dhira* measurement. Naturally, the type of cloth used varied, and so did the value of the *baysa*. Cloth type also determined how stylish *baysa* were, as the means of exchange sometimes doubled as clothing.

Kipper und Wipperzeit Crisis

147 1619 The Kipper und Wipperzeit Crisis—literally meaning "tipper and see-saw time" in 17th-century German slang—was caused simply by coin debasement rather than complex financial mechanics. Before modern banking and lending developed, countries like the Holy Roman Empire (HRE) found it difficult to raise money. The HRE especially struggled because the "Empire" was just a collection of small, loosely coordinated states that were difficult to tax. With the start of the Thirty Years' War in 1618, the HRE realized that it had to raise money quickly.

HRE states exploited a long-known trick. Minting coins with less precious metal but labeled with the same face value makes a profit for the minter off the difference in cost to produce and sell the coinage. Unscrupulous minters would then take these debased coins outside their state of origin, use them somewhere else, and exchange them for the better coinage in circulation there. The better coinage was brought back, and the cycle was repeated. Entrepreneurs quickly got into the coin-debasing industry. The quantity of precious metal in coins continued to decline as more mints were opened. Legend holds that children would play with these worthless coins in the streets. Hyperinflation set in until the debasing stopped in the HRE about 1623.

Options and Futures Trading in Amsterdam

148 early 17th c. As the center of European commerce moved from Antwerp to Amsterdam, many new innovations followed. One of Amsterdam's key developments was options and futures trading. A contemporary source describes a rather rudimentary method of investing in options: not formally buying them, but rather simply not fulfilling your contracts until you want to, turning the contracts effectively into options. Over time, the legality of options became thoroughly fleshed out.

By the mid-17th century, investors could buy put and call options of Dutch East India Company stock, which often expired on regular schedules. However, the business degraded such that by the 18th century, "Options were the province of the out-

and-out gamblers," one historian wrote.

Futures trading also developed. Unlike options, investors initially used futures contracts to buy commodities such as grain and herring. Later, investors could also buy futures on stocks. These tools allow traders to allocate their money in investments across time more efficiently. It was not long, however, before these developments caused problems. For example, the Tulip Mania was the first speculative bubble of many to be fueled by such new investment technologies as options and futures.

Tulip Mania

149 1634 In around 1634, people who did not specialize in horticulture began entering the tulip market in the Netherlands, speculating on tulip prices as investment commodities. A bubble soon formed as investors used futures contracts to trade tulips. Traders over-extend their assets by exploiting lax rules on margin trading. In most tulip transactions during the bubble, the buyer did not have enough cash to pay for the tulip bulb at the settlement date, and the seller did not have the tulip bulb yet.

The bet was on the change in price when the bulb could be resold. The Mania had little impact on the quantity of tulips being traded or on the price of tulip production. However, at the height of the bubble, individual tulip bulbs traded for $50,000-150,000 in today's money.

The tulip market bubble burst in the autumn of 1636. Soon, everyone was selling their tulips, and prices fell by 90% within six weeks. The strike prices, or the price agreed to be paid in the futures contract, didn't fall until February of the following year, financially ruining many traders. In 1537, the Dutch government nullified purchase obligations created by futures contracts signed after November 30, 1636. Tulips were the first commodity to be traded in a speculative bubble.

Goldsmith Bankers Emerge

150 1630s Traditionally, goldsmiths simply made things out of gold. However, during the 1630s and '40s, London goldsmiths expanded their services beyond metalwork. They started offering foreign currency exchange and secure storage for clients' valuables. This shift was partially motivated after King Charles I seized bullion stored in the Tower of London in 1640, undermining public trust in traditional methods for safe-keeping money.

The goldsmiths soon took on more roles commonly performed by banks. They started accepting deposits and issuing receipts that soon evolved into transferable promissory notes. This meant people could use the notes as a payment, making them an early form of cash. Further, Goldsmiths lent out a portion of the money deposited with them. They paid low interest on deposits and charged high interest to borrowers, pocketing the difference. Thus, goldsmiths effectively practiced fractional reserve banking.

By the 1670s, London was home to 44 such goldsmith bankers. Notable among them was Edward Backwell, who began his banking activities in 1654. Backwell served notable clientele, including the East India Company, and prominent individuals such as diarist Samuel Pepys. He also engaged in tax farming and international bullion trade. Goldsmiths were the beginning of modern banking.

First Mint in America

151 1652 When the Puritans landed on Plymouth Rock, they arrived with the coinage they had on them, plus some extra for what they anticipated they would need. What they brought turned out to be insufficient for transactions necessary for establishing a colony. In 1652, the General Court, the administrative body of the Plymouth Colony, passed a law establishing a mint.

John Hull, a 28-year-old British-born colonist, became mint-master. He began minting silver coins displaying willow trees, oaks, and most famously, "pine tree shillings." Primarily, the silver came from melted-down foreign coins, especially Spanish pieces of eight, which widely circulated due to Spain's presence in the Americas.

A legal problem soon cropped up. Minting coinage was the prerogative of the Crown of England. It was decided that for the mint to continue operations, it would need a royal charter, which it never received. The mint closed around 1686. There is no record of how much coinage was minted by John Hull's mint. However, the first mint in America probably produced hundreds or even thousands of pounds of coins and effectively provided enough money for exchange in the colony.

John Hull's silver pine tree shilling.

Chinese Gongsuo Guilds

152 late 17th cent. Qing China's *gongsuo* were guild-like associations primarily based on shared occupation. They differed from *huiguan* guilds, which each drew members from a specific hometown [see: 119]. The guilds played an important role for the businesses of artisans, traders, and merchants, particularly in urban centers. *Gongsuo* helped standardize wages, control the supply of goods, and mediate disputes among members. They also regulated trade, negotiated with government officials, and managed market competition within a particular industry.

Gongsuo had a degree of self-governance, with elected leadership overseeing internal affairs. However, the guilds were not completely independent of state control. While the central Qing government often left guilds alone, local authorities took advantage of them. Guilds helped governments collect taxes, carry out municipal functions, and organize charitable events. Some *gongsuo* guilds also helped enforce market regulations. Others, however, resisted state intervention to maintain their autonomy.

Gongsuo guilds also had important social functions. Like the *huiguan*, many *gongsuo* maintained temples dedicated to patron deities, organized religious ceremonies, and funded constructions like schools and burial grounds. The *gongsuo* declined in the late Qing era and early 20th century due to industrialization and government attempts to modernize trade associations.

First Banknotes in Europe

153 1661 In 1657, Stockholm's Banco was founded by Johan Palmstruch, a twice-failed bank founder, as a sort of central bank partially managed by the Crown of Sweden. In 1661, the Banco issued the first paper money in Europe, called *kreditivsedlar*. Banknotes were introduced as a solution to a banking crisis caused by coinage. After a government decree lowering the quantity of copper in the country's copper-plated coinage, depositors started hastily withdrawing money from their bank accounts in hopes of getting the old coins with higher copper content back. This caused a run on banks, particularly the Banco.

Palmstruch came up with the idea of creating paper notes backed by faith in the bank, rather than having bank money be tied to specific deposits in the bank. The notes could be redeemed for physical money at any time. This allowed the Banco to print out enough money to stop the bank run and allowed the government to debase the coins. The banknotes achieved a level of recognition for a few years. But soon, the Banco started over-issuing notes, weighing on the liability side of its balance sheet, and bringing down the whole bank.

Collapse of Stockholm Banco

154 1664 The very thing that put Stockholm's Banco in this book also caused its demise. The banknotes issued by Stockholm's Banco were essentially loans: the paper note is a guarantee that the bank will exchange a quantity of metal equivalent to the value printed on the paper. By 1663, two years after banknotes were introduced, bank employees realized that the Banco was running dangerously low on capital.

This was caused by excessively large creation of loans, and issue of banknotes, backed by too little copper and silver. By mid-December 1664, there were some 2.7 million copper dalers of paper notes in circulation, about 10-20% of the money supply. The value of the banknotes fell as the Banco couldn't afford to redeem them for precious metal

Operations ceased in 1664, and the Riksdag—the Swedish parliament—took over. Loans were terminated, and all banknotes were to be taken in and exchanged for coin, which took longer than expected due to a shortage of coinage. The bank was entirely liquidated by 1667-8, and Palmstruch was imprisoned. The Riksbank was founded in 1668 to take over operations as the central bank of Sweden.

This Stockholm Banco banknote was minted in 1666 (possibly by the Swedish government itself, as the Banco collapsed in 1664) and is signed by John Palmstruch. It is worth 100 daler silvermynt, equivalent to several months' wages for a skilled worker.

Collateralized Treasury Orders

155 1667 The English and the Dutch engaged in war between 1665 and 1667. As was often the case with early-modern wars, neither side achieved a decisive victory, but both sides ran broke. For this event, it is the English running out of money that is of interest. To help relieve the country's pocketbooks, the collateralized treasury order, also called the fiduciary order, was invented. Fiduciary orders were the predecessors of modern bonds and mortgage-backed securities. They were interest-bearing negotiable securities that were backed by tax revenue.

Initially, it was specific tax revenue backing them; but soon, they started being issued against the credit of the Exchequer itself, thus acting as a sort of paper money. The orders first appeared in early 1667, and goldsmith bankers bought up large amounts of them, becoming the Crown's principal creditors. As the story often goes, these orders were over-issued, and in 1672, King Charles II realized the problem and stopped payments on them, creating what became known as the Stop of the Exchequer [see: 159]. This piece of financial innovation set the stage for the proliferation of other advanced financial instruments in the modern age.

Spanish Dollar Used in China

156 17th c. While today's dominant international currency is the US dollar, a few centuries ago it was the Spanish dollar, colloquially known as the "piece of eight." In fact, this is the reason NYSE prices used to be quoted in eighths. The currency's main use outside of Spain was to buy goods from China, which were in high demand across Europe. Spanish dollars first entered China at the end of the Ming and start of the Qing Dynasty in the late 17th century, and their usage there drastically expanded by the 19th century.

Spanish dollars were convenient for Chinese and European merchants alike because they were abundant, clearly marked, and standardized. In contrast, the Chinese coinage system was in disarray. Pieces of eight began trading at a premium, above the value of the silver they were made of. As the coins were mostly minted in Mexico, Mexico's declaration of independence in 1821 meant Mexican pesos replaced Spanish dollars in international trade. Other countries followed Spain and Mexico, issuing dollar-like coins specifically for trade with Asia [see: 245]. However, these generally failed to become as well received as were the original pieces of eight.

International Currencies Before the Dollar

157 North Korea has one of the largest anti-American propaganda forces but cannot wean itself from the US dollar. The wealthy and poor alike use US dollars over the unstable sovereign won. International currencies, like the US dollar today, have a long history.

Rome's monetary standard was maintained across its European Empire. During the Middle Ages, the Roman *solidus*, maintained by the Byzantine Empire and Germanic tribes in the West, acted in its place. Eventually, in the eighth and ninth centuries, silver pennies dominated the continent [see: 72]. In Asia, knife money was widely used outside of China [see: 12].

Western trade with the East increased in the 18th century. Spanish dollars came to be used for trade with China, Japan, India, Persia, Constantinople, and other places. During the 1880s, one author wrote, "Hardly any other currency circulated among those remote peoples than pieces of eight [nickname for Spanish dollars] and Castilian doubloons." The Far East was described as an "abyss" that ate up currency as quickly as silver could be dug up to mint it [see: 156]. The Spanish dollar's consistent weight and reliable silver content garnered much trust from Eastern merchants.

When the UK became the center of global finance, the pound sterling became the top international currency. Britain benefited from the wide use of its currency, though it eventually became a burden on the country's economic system. Maintaining sterling's international role required Britain to sustain large overseas liabilities and provide liquidity to the global monetary system that mitigated its ability to address growing domestic economic problems. After the US dollar became the world's reserve currency under the Bretton Woods system, a protracted shift away from the pound began. As of 1960, nearly 60% of reserves were in pounds; by 1980, it was under 5%.

Riksbank Founded

158 1668 Sweden's Sveriges Riksbank (Bank of the Estates of the Real) is the fourth-oldest central bank and the oldest currently-existing central bank.

Originally (and aptly) named "The Bank," its name was changed to Riksbank in 1866. The Riksbank was founded in 1668, after the collapse of Stockholm Banco left Sweden without a central bank [see: 153]. Sweden's government put the Riksbank under the control of the Riksdag, Sweden's parliament.

The Bank started out merely taking deposits and making loans. Beginning in 1800, however, the Bank adopted an unusual method of governing. Each of the four Estates—a class system similar to France's Three Estates—sent three delegates to the bank's governing board. Riksbank became an official central bank in the modern sense in 1897. That year, the Riksbank Act gave the Riksbank sole authority to issue banknotes. Private banks were, from then on, required to hold Riksbank banknotes.

Stop of Exchequer

159 1672 Over the 1660s, King Charles II borrowed heavily to pay for government expenditures and a few wars, as the money the government collected in taxes proved insufficient. Much of this borrowing consisted of selling bonds to London's goldsmith bankers. To make these bonds appealing, Charles II paid interest rates of about 8% to 10%, far above the 6% legal maximum imposed on bond returns. The debt increased to as much as £1.5 million.

On January 12, 1672 (January 2, 1671, OS), King Charles II declared that the Exchequer would cease payment on bonds, an event known as the Great Stop of the Exchequer. He intended for these payments to cease for about a year, until the Exchequer had collected money to pay them off in full. The end of the Stop was postponed, first for two years, and then indefinitely.

The effects ranged from bad to very bad for many London goldsmith bankers. In 1677, these bankers held 97.5% of the Crown's debt, and many went into bankruptcy during this period. Though the Crown conceded some small sums here and there, ultimately, the goldsmith bankers only had about half of their original investment returned.

Playing Cards Used as Money

160 1685 In the late 17th century, the New France colony (now part of Canada) faced a severe shortage of currency for the simple reason that it was difficult to import large amounts of cash or coinage from Europe into the Americas. Things worsened when the intendant of the colony, Jacques de Meulles, couldn't pay the troops who fought against the Iroquois in 1684. He came up with an unusual solution. In June 1685, De Meulles issued playing cards as a form of emergency currency. He collected available cards, cut them into quarters, and marked them with his seal and signature to denote various denominations. He declared the card money legal tender and used it to pay soldiers and civil servants, facilitating trade and daily transactions until official currency could be imported.

This practice of using playing cards as currency continued intermittently in New

France until 1719. Indeed, it almost became a staple of exchange in North America, which continually lacked cash. Similarly, in the early 18th century, the French colony of Louisiana experienced financial difficulties following the collapse of the Mississippi Bubble [see: 175]. The colonial government in Louisiana similarly issued playing cards until it could implement a stable monetary system.

Options Trading in England

161 1680s The earliest surviving English stock options contract was a request for the delivery of £1,000 of East India Stock at 200 for a premium of 150 guineas. The contract was dated July 29, 1687, and was set to expire on March 1, 1688. Options trading in England developed as part of the broader financial innovations that moved from Amsterdam to London in the late 17th century. These instruments allowed investors to speculate on stock prices without the need for full ownership, providing both opportunities for profit and lower risk of loss.

The stock market crash caused by the recoinage of 1696 led to a shift in trading from the Royal Exchange to coffeehouses, where options trading continued in an informal but increasingly active market. By the start of the 18th century, the rise of speculative trading prompted government intervention. An act in 1697 sought to regulate financial speculation, including options, while another in 1733, known as Barnard's Act, indirectly influenced options markets by increasing broker liability in financial transactions, forcing greater honesty from options traders. These measures contributed to the gradual formalization of stock and options trading, laying the groundwork for the eventual establishment of the London Stock Exchange.

First Paper Money in the Americas

162 1690 The first banknotes of the American colonies were issued in 1690 in Massachusetts. Soldiers returning from a failed occupation attempt on Quebec were looking to be paid. The colony, however, could not afford to pay them. To pacify the soldiers, the government issued debentures which could be used to pay taxes, though this did not satisfy them.

After John Hull's first mint in the state was shut down by Royal decree four years earlier, in December 1690, the Colony agreed to pay £7,000 with new paper money, technically called "bills of credit." The bills could be converted for precious metal, but never were, making them de facto fiat currency.

Why were they called "bills of credit" and not simply referred to as "paper money"? For legal reasons. England did not want colonies minting their own currency and disallowed colonies from printing "money." However, a debt printed on paper, or an IOU, was accepted, and that is just what these notes were disguised as. Allowing convertibility into precious metal was required for them to be considered debts, even if the notes were never actually converted. The other colonies caught on, and Virginia was the last to do so in 1755.

Brazilian Gold Rush

163 1693 In the days of mercantilism [see: 118], the amount of gold that a country had was incredibly important, not only for its ability to purchase goods but also for its image as an international power. Gold was a key reason for European colonization of the Americas. Portugal's efforts in the New World were rewarded when gold was found in Brazil in the 1690s.

The gold deposits were discovered by wandering slavers, colonizers, traders, and natives in Minas Gerais, a part of south-east Brazil, and exaggerated rumors about the massive size of the deposits spread quickly. Within five years, 50,000 people arrived in the province hungry for gold and were accompanied by hundreds of thousands of slaves. Over the 18th century, miners dug up 800 tons of gold (worth just over $40 billion today) and exported it, according to official records. However, many more tons were likely smuggled illegally or retained in Brazil. The small Portugal capitalized on one of the largest and longest gold rushes in history. Portugal showed Europe the value of the new American colonies.

Bank of England Founded

164 1694 The Bank of England (BoE) opened on August 1, 1694, with 17 clerks and two doormen—a rather modest operation. The BoE was founded at a time when the Crown was constantly in need of money and looking for places to borrow, including from the East India Company and the City of London itself. But the Crown had bad credit.

England was facing other financial problems as well. No entity existed to set and update the interest rate. The goldsmith-bankers [see: 150] were often unreliable, and there was no centrally organized, government financial organization to address the nation's problems.

William Patterson proposed a plan that was the basis for the Tonnage Act, also called the Bank of England Act of 1694. The Act opened subscriptions to establish the BoE. Once £1.2 million was raised, the corporation was converted into a royal charter to last 12 years. The charter required that the Bank elect a governor, deputy-governor, and 24 directors

Mercer's Hall, the original rented location of the Bank of England and the building in which it resided for forty years.

every year. After its founding, attempts were made to legitimize the BoE by, for example, giving it a monopoly on banknote issue [see: 219]. Even with its apparent benefits, the BoE did not escape criticism.

What Do Central Banks Do?

165 The core functions of a central bank include regulating the money supply, setting key interest rates, and controlling inflation to ensure price stability in the nation's economy. The central bank also acts as a lender of last resort to commercial banks, overseeing the entire banking system to maintain public confidence. These actions foster conditions for sustainable employment, stable financial markets, and long-term economic health. To promote a more stable and predictable rate of economic growth, modern central banks implement three types of monetary policy.

The most well-known policy is setting the discount rate, which is the interest that the central bank charges other banks for very short-term loans. Banks usually need such loans to address short-term liquidity issues. The discount rate can be raised if the economy is growing too quickly and exhibiting price inflation. The higher rate disincentivizes loan-making and promotes economic contraction. Conversely, lowering the rate encourages loan-making and growth when the economy is under-performing.

Central banks can also change the reserve requirement ratio (RRR) of commercial banks, which is the share of all deposits that must be immediately available for withdrawal. Raising the RRR decreases the quantity of loans that can be created, which dampens a nation's economic activity. Decreasing the RRR has the opposite impact, growing the economy by allowing banks to make more loans.

The third type of monetary policy is called open-market operations, where the central bank buys or sells government bonds. As the central bank sells bonds, more money is collected from the public and removed from circulation. A smaller money supply slows economic growth. When a central bank buys bonds, it dispenses money into the economy, expanding the money supply and promoting growth. Central banks are usually designed to be independent and free from political influence. This gives them immense power to unilaterally make decisions in an almost authoritarian way. This freedom from day-to-day politics, however, often lets central bankers make the best decisions without popular influence.

Controversy Around the Bank of England

166 1690s England immediately reaped the financial benefits of establishing the Bank of England. However, the bank's creation did not escape criticism. Many people thought the Bank would either unfairly benefit London's wealthy or, on the flip side, hurt business as a whole. Some critics saw issues in technicalities of the BoE's construction. Others simply felt that such a large institution would naturally hurt smaller ones.

John Locke wrote of how the Bank would unfairly benefit the wealthy: "[T]he money in the bank is, and I conclude always will be, managed by London merchants." Locke thought that, while the system of goldsmith bankers was decentralized and therefore inherently fair, the BoE would act as a monopoly and allow consolidation of both money and power. One author wrote that the Bank would start "[engrossing] much of the ready money in London," imposing unfair competition onto the goldsmith bankers. There was also concern that the Bank's dividend payments would be distributed unequally, which the Bank made clear attempts to avoid. The criticisms did not stick, however, and the bank's charter, originally 11 years long, was renewed nine times until it was made permanent.

Bank Money Exceeds Physical Money

167 late 17th c. By the close of the 17th century, England was one of the first countries to see the value of paper money in circulation exceed the value of coinage and specie in circulation. Charles Davenant, an English economist, estimated that in 1698 there was £11.6 million of coinage in circulation and £15 million of paper money and bank money. He also estimated there was £20 million of land securities, such as mortgages. Though mortgages didn't fully count as money at the time, this combined £35 million of non-coin value shows significant growth in the importance of bank money.

This trend is important for two reasons. First, it reveals the notable expansion of the banking sector, which barely existed only a century earlier. Second, the turn toward banks marked a shift in economic power in England that still affects us today. When people are using coinage, the guy who mints the coins—such as the king—exercises significant economic power. The greater public acceptance of paper bank money meant that the king cannot just create money whenever he needs it. He now must find other sources of money to exploit, perhaps seeking consent from Parliament to enact taxes and goodwill from bankers to get loans. Thus, banking became necessary for governments to operate.

Great Recoinage of 1696

168 1696 In the late 17th century, England's coinage system was a mess. The coinage became so heavily clipped that, when in 1695 the Exchequer measured 100 bags of silver coinage that were supposed to weigh 39,000 ounces, they only weighed 19,588 ounces. The hand-struck coins minted before 1692 were unevenly shaped, making them easily targeted by coin clippers. After 1692, milled coins were introduced, which maintained the correct shape and weight. However, since they were heavier than the other coins, these new coins were hoarded, as predicted by Gresham's Law [see: 230].

The preeminent economists (and philosophers) of the time were called on for a solution. John Locke argued that money was silver coinage, and the government had an obligation to provide a stable currency for its citizens. Thus, he advocated for re-minting England's coinage to its original purity. Locke's suggestion was adopted as a recoinage bill, passed in January 1696. On May 4, clipped coinage was demonetized, and it ceased being accepted as payment for taxes in June. The problem still was not solved, however, as the insufficient supply of new coinage resulted in an economic contraction, throwing England in a short financial crash.

Locke's Theorizes About Economics

169 late 17th c. John Locke, known as the father of Classical Liberalism in political theory, also theorized about economics. He contemplated property rights, seeking to answer the question of why people rightfully own what they own. Locke avoided the notion that rights existed "because society says they do." Instead, he proposed that one's property was any physical thing with which he "mixes" his labor. For example, if someone picks up an acorn, or anything else provided by nature, he then owns it. Similar to Marx [see: 224], Locke postulated that added labor deter-mines the underlying value of goods. However, he differed from Marx by claiming that men are simply more inclined to labor over those things that sell at a high market price, which is largely determined by the item's intrinsic value.

Locke was also involved in economic policy development of the time. He argued that the government is unable to control interest rates, as people are inclined to borrow at the cheapest price. Locke argued against a bill in Parliament to lower the interest rate, which he claimed depends solely on money's "natural value." This value is determined by "the whole quantity of the then passing Money of the kingdom, in proportion to the whole Trade of the Kingdom, (i.e.) the general Vent of all the commodities." Locke was a Mercantilist [see: 118], and believed that naturally lower interest rates would attract more wealth.

During a period of economic weakness, millions of pounds of silver flowed out of England, resulting in the mint debasing its coinage. The currency had to be recoined, and the question was if new coins should be minted at their face-value in silver. Locke thought that the role of the government is not to set money's value but to assure the right to use money, which ought to be a stable value.

Rice Futures in Japan

170 early 18th c. The Dojima Exchange was founded in 1697 on the newly inhabited island of Dojima in Osaka, Japan. It was the world's first organized commodity futures market. Rice was not only the staple food in Japan but also the primary medium of exchange and a measure of wealth. Samurai and feudal lords re-ceived stipends in rice, which they often needed to convert into currency to finance their expenditures. Osaka was well located to become the central hub for rice distribu-tion.

Traders gathered on the island to trade. Futures trading had in fact been banned since 1693 as it was thought to artificially raise rice prices. However, in the 1720s, Japan had unusually good harvests. The influx of rice depressed prices, hurting the samurai and feudal lords. Japan's shogunate lifted the ban on futures trading to help raise prices and officially authorized the Dojima Exchange in 1730.

The Exchange helped standardize contracts and centralized clearing, making rice trading more efficient. It ultimately stabilized rice prices and allowed growers and merchants to hedge against losses. These developments were key in the evolution of efficient financial markets.

How the Dojima Rice Exchange Worked

171 The practice of making forward contracts started in Japan in the 17th century. Mostly used for rice, a forward contract stipulated that a farmer agreed to sell his harvest to an investor at a future date for a set price. Early forward contracts originally were made ad hoc with individual farmers and could not be traded between investors. Eventually, the "rice bill" was developed, a futures contract that was traded by investors.

There were two types of rice bills. A backed bill was one backed by harvested rice that was sitting in a warehouse. A trader would bid on the rice, paying one-third of the set price at an auction and the rest 7 to 10 days later, when he would be given a backed bill. The bill could be exchanged for the rice, which the trader was supposed to do within 30 days, though, in practice, some traders held bills for as long as a year. If at the end of the year, rice prices have risen, the trader profits on the difference between the amount he paid to get the bill and the new price of rice. Backed bills allowed traders to speculate in future rice prices without holding rice themselves.

The unbacked prepayment bill was introduced later in the century and was essentially a loan collateralized by future rice harvests. An investor would buy a bill for rice that had not been harvested yet. The bill required no up-front exchange of rice. A year after the investor purchased the bill, the rice seller would pay the investor the principal (the original rice) plus interest in cash or rice. If the seller could not pay in cash, the unbacked bill would be exchanged for a backed bill, which was exchanged for rice.

John Law Opens Bank Generale

172 1716 John Law was a peddler of banks. He tried to sell banking schemes in his home country of Scotland, England, and to the government in Paris soon after arriving in France in 1713. France's economy, already in a slump after the end of the War of Spanish Succession in 1714, faced other trying internal economic issues. John Law proposed a plan to the French government that entailed establishing a bank that would help the economy recover. Law was given a charter to open the Banque Generale in 1716.

Law had two goals. First, to use the bank to help pay down France's debt. Second, he wanted to issue banknotes, creating monetary expansion that would boost France's economy. Though Paris had given Law a charter for a private bank, Law managed to transform it into a government concern. Law started manipulating the sovereign coinage: he reduced coins' silver content and thus made banknotes more valuable. Law's venture expanded into the Americas, where it quickly became one of the largest banks in history. Yet, men who are too ambitious can seemingly never win, and Law's bank collapsed within only a few years.

Dojima Exchange

Isaac Newton and the Mint

173 early 18th c. Though he is best known for inventing calculus and discovering gravity and the light spectrum, Isaac Newton also ran the English mint for a while. He was appointed as Warden of the Mint in 1696 and was promoted to Master of the Mint the next year, all while keeping his position as Lucasian Chair of Mathematics at Cambridge. His first action as Master was to complain about the £400 salary, and he was given a raise.

The next major task of his career at the mint was to oversee the Great Recoinage of 1696, though this effort did not go smoothly. The quantity of old money melted was not clearly recorded, and the new money was not put into circulation fast enough. This forced the Bank of England to suspend its payments. Newton knew what kind of job he had gotten into.

Once the Recoinage was over, Newton focused on ensuring that coinage was minted to the correct standard. He noted discrepancies such as that "Some pieces [were] 2 or 3 grains too heavy, and others as much too light." Seeing that 2 or 3 grains is less than one-tenth the weight of a penny, we can tell he was meticulous to the utmost. He added, "The heavy guineas were called 'Come-again guineas' because they were culled out and brought to the Mint to be recoined."

England Adopts De Facto Gold Standard

174 1717 The first gold standard was adopted in England with little pomp or circumstance. This was a de facto standard, not legally enacted, and created due to an overvaluation of gold to silver.

In the 17th and early 18th century, England's monetary system was based on silver. However, in 1717, Mint Master Isaac Newton overvalued the guinea coin, changing it from being worth 20s to 21s. Previously, the value ratio of silver to gold had been 14.37 to 1. In practice, this ratio was designed so that, if a pound-weight of gold were separated into 44.5 pieces, each piece would be worth about £1, coined in silver. Newton changed this ratio to 15.07 to 1, raising the value of gold against silver.

Gold was thus overvalued, as it was worth more in England than it was on the Continent. In England, 21s of silver could get one guinea of gold, whereas on the Continent, that much silver could buy more gold. Gold was overvalued and silver was undervalued in England compared with on the Continent. As predicted by Gresham's Law, gold remained in circulation while silver was increasingly shipped out of the country. This effectively put England on a de facto gold standard, as very little silver went through the English mint afterward.

Law's Bank Collapses

175 1720 John Law's Bank Generale was a proven success [see: 172]. It had effectively financed a war with Spain in 1718–9 while managing overseas trade in the Americas through Law's Mississippi Company. Law held the wide-spread belief that a larger money-supply would create lower interest rates, something he thought France urgently needed. To raise the money-supply, he increased the share price of the Mississippi Company from 500 livres in January of 1719 to 10,000 that December. This prompted a 23% inflation rate.

People quickly realized that Law issued more value in paper money than he had in gold. The public and the government lost trust in Law's bank and started converting paper money into gold. Share-prices plummeted starting in December 1720 and returned to 500 livres by September 1721. A bank-run followed. Law was fired from the Bank Generale but rehired a few days later to fix the bank's problems. His corrective measures failed, and his notes were demonetized. Law left France in December 1720.

The French government bailed out the Mississippi Company, taking over the company in January 1721. Its liabilities were converted to government bonds. A half-million banknote-holders filed claims, which were compensated. In the end, France's debt ended up where it had started before Law came onto the scene.

The South Sea bubble

176 1720 The South Sea Company was founded in September 1711 under Queen Anne of England. The company was created as a place to store the national debt, and it took up slave-trading as a cash-generating venture.

In 1719, the South Sea Company bought the right to purchase all outstanding government debt, totaling £31.5 million, in exchange for a certain pound-value of its own stock and £7.6 million in cash. However, the agreement did not specify the *quantity* of shares to be exchanged. This meant that, if the price of each share increased, the number of shares the South Sea Company would need to give away would decrease. As a result, the company was motivated to drive up the share price.

There was not much of a way for the Company to expand except for on paper. Each share cost £130 in February 1720. The Company used psychology and government connections to raise its share prices. One method it used was raising dividend payments, incentivizing more share purchases. The share price hit £600 in May and £1,000 by mid-June. The bubble burst when investors began to doubt the company's actual profits and started selling off their shares en masse, triggering a panic. Then, the stock fell to its pre-bubble levels by the last quarter of 1720, ruining thousands of investors.

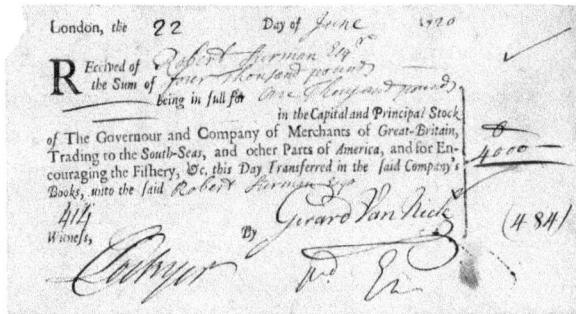

A 1720 certificate for £1,000 of stock of the South Sea Company. The buyer paid £4,000 at a market price 400% above the stock's nominal

First Modern Insurance

177 1744 An important innovation in finance is the ability to predict risk and standardize financial outcomes. Predictability is the basis of many tools central to finance, such as bank loans, bonds, and, in this event, insurance. All of these tools require predictability, as they expect constant financial returns, often scheduled years into the future. No bank is going to give a 30-year mortgage if it can't be reasonably assured that the environment will continue to be stable in 30 years (though, in fact, banks often do make uncertain loans).

The actuarial fund—essentially life insurance—was first conceived in 1741 or 1742, as the Scottish Ministers' Widows' Fund. Its goal was to provide a yearly stipend to the wives and children of ministers who died. The Widows' Fund was not the first actuarial fund, though previous attempts had failed to gain traction. Robert Wallace and Alexander Webster were the founders. Webster collected data on the ministers in the Church of Scotland, while Wallace designed a theoretical basis for financing the program. To determine the quantity of money needed to support the program, Wallace considered the necessary amount of payouts, the likelihood of ministers dying based on their health and age, and how long the wives would live to collect program payments. Parliament approved Wallace and Webster's plans in March 1744, and the world's first life insurance was born.

Modern Annuities in England and Amsterdam

178 18th c. Annuities have been around since Roman times [see: 61] and, from then on, slowly evolved into their modern form. As one author put it, by the 18th century, annuities were no longer based upon "guesswork, high expectation, and the sort of literary exploitation which today is known as 'high-pressure salesmanship.'" By the 18th century, annuities became more technical and analytical.

New interest tables published in 1726 contained information for annuities. Around the same period, the London Bills of Mortality—recording every week's deaths—started publishing people's ages at death. In 1756, the Equitable Life Insurance Society of London was founded. Age, health, and other circumstances were considered when selling annuities and setting premiums. In the US, the first organization for providing funding to widows of ministers was founded in Pennsylvania in 1759.

Interestingly, the demand for annuities slowed in the 19th century, while demand for life insurance picked up. This was because, in general, people who worried about dying unexpectedly tended to buy life insurance, while those who have no relatives to support them while they are living bought annuities. With the decline of multigenerational households that provided support to elders in the 20th century, the annuities market was revitalized.

Amsterdam Banking Crisis

179 1763 Dutch bankers in the mid-18th century made heavy use of an instrument called a bill of exchange. Bills of exchange were originally orders to pay, like modern cashier's checks. However, they turned into a type of loan that could be resold, whereby the original seller and every successive seller were jointly liable for the bill. These were short-term loans that were often rolled over to act as long-term loans. Bills made Dutch financial institutions highly interconnected.

After the Seven Years' War ended in 1763, the banker Leendert Pieter de Neufville agreed to buy a large amount of Russia's grain that was left in Poland. When war prices ended, grain prices fell 75% between May and August, a fall much steeper than expected. Banks in Amsterdam lost so much money they could not effectively make and take loans. The resulting credit crunch was exacerbated by bills of exchange, and dozens of banks across Amsterdam and Germany fell.

The Bank of Amsterdam responded by extending liquidity through repurchasing coins and silver bullion. Along with some other measures, this resulted in a 40% increase in the supply of Bank of Amsterdam money in six months and allowed some failed banks to eventually reopen.

Moral Hazard

180 Moral hazard occurs when one party in an agreement will not suffer consequences of risky behavior and thus doesn't have an incentive to avoid risk. The other party in the agreement will bear the burden of those consequences. Moral hazard can allow morally-reprehensible behavior because one party can do bad things without liability. For example, when someone buys and insures a car, the insurer is expecting the car owner to take care of it. However, the owner will not bear a large financial liability if the car is damaged in an accident. The car owner is thus not incentivized to drive as carefully as he would if he did not have insurance. Moral hazard also arises in investment and financial transactions

The concept behind moral hazard dates to the beginning of modern insurance in the mid-17th century. At the time, many believed that events such as fires, sinking ships, and other catastrophes were the will of God and cannot be controlled by humans. As people came to believe humans can exercise some control over the risks surrounding such events, the concept of insurance evolved. In 1865, the first definition of moral hazard appeared in *The Practice of Fire Underwriting*, expressing "the danger proceeding from motives to destroy property by fire or permit its destruction."

Moral hazard also contributed to the 2008 financial crisis [see: 440]. Loan originators repackaged risky mortgage loans into bundles with safer loans and sold these bundles to investment banks, with little incentive to ensure they were safe. The buyers failed to perform their due diligence and purchased these bundles at prices far too high for the true underlying risk. When the risky loans failed and created significant financial losses for the investment banks, many banks called on the government to bail them out and thus suffered limited consequences of their poor judgment.

Currency Act

181 1764 The Currency Act, passed April 19, 1764, was imposed on the American Colonies by the British. The Currency Act of 1751 already made the minting of legal tender paper money in New England illegal, and the 1764 act made it illegal to the south of New England. That 1764 act also required colonies to retire all circulating paper money, making coinage and British-printed paper money the sole form of legal tender.

Paper money from the Colonists didn't have a good reputation. Frequent local wars and a general lack of funds forced colonies to turn to the printing press to pay their debts. Virginia was one of the worst, minting £440,000 between 1755–62. To protect British assets within the Colonies, the British Board of Trade preferred coined gold and silver—hard money. Merchants also needed stable money, and stopping excessive printing would curb inflation.

The Currency Act forced the colonists to use coins, which limited monetary expansion and slowed economic growth. The 1764 Act was one of the British-imposed limitations that motivated the American colonists to declare independence, which let colonists liberalize trade and monetary policy.

First Paper Money in Russia

182 1769 In Tom Lehrer's song "Who's Next?" he comedically sings about nuclear proliferation. He starts, "First we [the US] got the bomb and that was good, 'cause we like peace and motherhood." From there, the number of countries with nuclear weapons expanded, just like the number of countries with paper currency expanded through the 19th century. Here, Russia gets the bomb. Or, at least paper money.

Under Queen Catherine II, the Russian Empire began printing the assignation ruble in 1769. Two assignation banks were established with a capitalization of 500,000 copper rubles each. One million assignations total were issued, redeemable for the copper. The purpose of paper notes was to make long-distance transactions easier.

The classic story of banknote over-issue followed. Redemption for copper was eventually discontinued in 1777. The maximum permitted issue jumped to 20 million in 1784, then to 836 million by 1817 after the Napoleonic Wars, creating damaging inflation. In 1841, a new type of paper note, "credit notes," was issued. The bank exchanged assignations for credit notes, and assignations were taken out of circulation. Credit notes then faced the same fate until Russia moved to the gold standard in 1897.

British Banking in India

183 1770 China had the Shanxi banks [see: 210], which was a robust indigenous banking system. However, India could not claim to have invented any comparably-effective banking system, even with its various early financial tools [see: 43]. Things changed when the British established colonial rule there. The East India Company managed India from the mid-18th to the mid-19th centuries, during which period many European-style banks popped up. The Bank of Hindustan, established in 1770, was one of the first banks to issue banknotes in India.

Many of the banks established early on in England's colonial rule were headquartered in Calcutta. By the time the United Kingdom left India, many Indian banks were headquartered directly in London. In a way, English banking power had outlasted English political power in India. Many colonial banks outlived the bone fide colonial period, including India's largest and oldest bank today: the State Bank of India.

1772 British Credit Crisis

184 1772 The crisis of 1772 started when Alexander Fordyce, a London speculator, lost £300,000 on a short position on East India Company stock. He financed this position with a loan from his own heavily leveraged bank, which was indebted to the Scottish Ayr Bank. Ayr Bank accounted for 40% of all Scottish bank assets in 1772.

When East India Company's stock failed to decline as expected, Mr. Fordyce became bankrupt and fled to the Continent as his bank collapsed. Ayr Bank, having lost a key debtor, suspended its payments. Panic and bank runs started in London, and quickly moved to Edinburgh, where they became even worse.

At the same time, a group of banking houses in Amsterdam were conspiring to raise the price of British East India Company stock, which was trending downward since the Company was having trouble with the Sultan of India. Those banking houses were suddenly 700,000–800,000 guilders in debt. Trade between England and Amsterdam declined as the crisis spread farther across Europe.

By 1773, the Bank of England stepped in, allowing gold and silver to be drawn against notes and government bonds. It also increased bill discounts and extended loans and bailouts to many banks and even to the East India Company itself, soothing the crisis.

First Mutual Fund

185 1774 A common way for small investors to diversify their portfolio is to invest in mutual funds. In 1774, the first mutual fund was launched in Amsterdam by a banker named Abraham van Ketwick. Amsterdam was the first city with a financial system advanced enough to be able to facilitate this type of fund. Ketwick's fund invested in foreign government bonds, banks, and plantation loans in the West Indies, paying out a 4% dividend yield. The fund was to operate for 25 years and then be dissolved. Initially, 2,000 shares were sold to the public, and once they were all purchased, shares could only be bought from pre-existing shareholders, making the fund's shares freely tradable.

The first modern mutual fund was established in 1924 and sold by the Massachusetts Investor Trust. This fund was different in that it allowed continuous issue and redemption of shares at a price that tracked the market value of the underlying assets. Other than that difference, these two funds, separated by 150 years, were very similar.

American Colonies' Bad Economic Policy

186 1775 In April 1775, the Thirteen Colonies in America did not have enough money to fight a war against the British. In total, there was about $22 million in paper money and $12 million in specie in the colonies. The prospects of raising more money were poor. Taxation would be too slow and would draw from an insufficient cash tax base. The Continental Congress could not get a loan from a foreign bank because it had no tax revenue to use as collateral.

In June 1775, Congress implemented the last alternative: printing money. Several states also issued more money, and inflation followed. By 1777, the specie value of a Continental dollar fell to 30% of its 1775 value. At the end of 1777, Congress imposed a currency requisition on the states, which produced sufficient income for a time. But by 1780, states were falling behind on payments, forcing Congress to turn the Continental Army against them.

In 1781, Congress started pursuing a national tax with the right to use force against the states. However, in October of that same year, the British surrendered. The problem was not yet over, though: now Congress turned to creating a functional taxation system to effectively run the new country.

The Rise of Adam Smith

187 late 18th c. Adam Smith was born—or at least baptized—in Scotland on June 5, 1723, in the middle of the Enlightenment. John Locke's *Two Treatises of Government* were published only a few decades earlier, while other great thinkers, including Voltaire and Rousseau, were just getting their start. Smith's father, also named Adam, died when his second wife, Margaret Douglas, was pregnant with their son Adam (the one you are reading about now). A sickly boy, Smith excelled at academics, something his mother entertained. He was sent to Burgh School of Kinkardy, one of the best secondary schools in Scotland. An autographed copy of the Latin textbook he started studying in 1733 still exists today.

Smith then went to the University of Glasgow at age 14. After graduating, he received a scholarship to go to Balliol College at Oxford, but soon left to become a professor back at Glasgow. He also took a job as a tutor, allowing him to travel around Europe. The spare time and extra money he had from tutoring allowed him to develop his ideas on economics, which after developing them for 12 years, he published as *The Wealth of Nations* in 1776. Some of his ideas came from observing how much more efficient English production was than Scottish production while on his trip to Oxford years prior. Smith's ideas were incredibly popular in his time, and his book went through nine reprints by 1800. Smith died in 1790, known as the father of modern economics.

Though Smith excelled in the academic world, he struggled in the personal world. Women found him charming, but they made him rather nervous. He had some odd tendencies, such as talking to himself and suffering from various imagined illnesses.

Adam Smith Published Theories

188 1776 Adam Smith's *The Wealth of Nations* was published on March 9, 1776. The treatise took him 12 years to write and possibly 12 more years of contemplation before that. The book was published in two volumes and sold for £1 16s. Smith was likely paid £500 for the manuscript, which was a comfortable sum in that time. The first edition of *The Wealth of Nations* sold out in six months, though it is not known how many first edition copies were printed.

Hume said of the sales of Smith's book, "[T]hough not near so rapid, has been more than I could have expected from a work that requires much thought and reflection (qualities that do not abound among modern readers)." Some of Smith's friends doubted his ability to write a book on commerce, given that Smith never participated in business himself.

Smith's book was first quoted in the House of Commons in 1783, showing its relatively quick adoption. The first Parliamentary budget after its publication used its advice to raise tax revenue. By the 1790s, further editions and a few translations rolled off the presses as its fame was solidified.

Number of Banks in England Explodes

189 1780s As real banks started to replace goldsmith banks, and the need for banking increased with the start of the Industrial Revolution in the latter half of the 18th century, the number of banks in England expanded quickly. Only 20–30 banks existed in London between 1750-1760. This increased to 50 in 1770, and to 70 by 1800.

In the countryside, banking-like business was initially under the purview of merchants who did not specialize in banking and did not issue notes. For example, the Gurneys family of Norwich was seen as essentially bankers starting in the 17th century, but did not incorporate as a real bank until later in the 18th century. Only a dozen banks existed outside of London by the middle of the 18th century. By 1775, there were 100–150 banks, and by 1793, there were about 280. By 1810, after some laws relating to licensing were made, there were 783 licensed banks. This expansion of banking services was part of the larger expansion of the British economy in the 19th century and showed how many more people needed access to banking services.

How Debt Caused the French Revolution

190 1789 With a debt-to-GDP ratio of over 120%, economists worry about the economic implications of the US' burgeoning federal debt. For France, a high debt ratio was one of the causes of the French Revolution. Under the Ancien Régime, spending was controlled by the Crown, but taxation was controlled by the Parlement de Paris. New taxes could not be levied except by the agreement of the entire country, as represented by the Estates-General, which had not met since 1614.

The Revolutionary War in America required the French government to borrow funds and subsequently trim expenses to keep the budget balanced. The French Crown soon abandoned a balanced budget. Its expenditures, including interests on loans, grew even larger than its long-term budget constraint—the amount of money a government can borrow given its revenue. This created a looming national financial crisis.

The taxation system in France was highly inequitable, meaning that an attempt to raise taxes would inevitably incite talk of tax reform (and other reform). Even if the largest tax exemption—that for the clergy and nobility—were corrected, the government still would not be able to raise sufficient revenues. Thus, growing debt meant reform would soon be an explosive political issue, setting the stage for the French Revolution.

What Adam Smith Thought

191 Adam Smith made three main contributions to economic thought. The first is the "Invisible Hand" of the market. Smith argued that competition between buyers and sellers brings about the best prices and most efficient levels of production. For this reason, he thought markets should not be regulated. Smith posited that self-interested buyers and sellers competing with each other inadvertently create the best market outcomes through supply and demand. In this way, a buyer or seller is promoting social good by pursuing his own self-interest, as if, as Smith said, "he is [...] led by an invisible hand to promote an end which is no part of his intention."

Smith's second main contribution is the idea of economic growth through specialization of production. Looking at the production of pins, Smith writes, "A pin-maker [...] could scarce, perhaps, with his utmost industry, make one pin in a day." But he found that pin-making was "divided into about eighteen distinct operations," and that, "When ten men only were employed, and [...] performed two or three distinct operations. [...] they could, when they exerted themselves, make among them about twelve pounds of pins in a day." Smithian growth is just that: specialization—often necessitated by geographical expansion—is the driver of economic growth.

Third, Smith disagreed with the prevailing Mercantilist view that using gold to buy imported goods was bad for the nation's economy [see: 118]. He wrote, "In the restraints upon the importation of all foreign commodities which can come into competition with those of our own growth or manufacture [viz., Mercantilist policies], the interest of the home consumer is evidently sacrificed to that of the producer," which hurts consumption, the ultimate goal of production, and thus the economy as a whole. Smith argued that the amount of national production, not gold, determines a country's wealth.

French Assignat Introduced

192 1790 There are four ways for governments to finance wars: raising taxes, selling public property, taking on debt, and printing money. The storming of the Bastille in July 1789 helped the revolutionaries, but it did not alleviate any real economic problems like poor harvest, which shrunk the government's tax base. France lost more money as revolutionaries repealed many unpopular taxes. The new government was soon effectively broke. In 1789, total expenses summed to 500 or 600 million livres, with a 162 million livre deficit.

The government seized property owned by the clergy and monarchy, estimated at about 3.5 billion livres in value. The government's plan was to issue banknotes to first pay its expenses and then pay for the seized property. In September 1790, 1.2 billion livres in assignat banknotes were issued, followed by millions more. Still low on cash, the revolutionaries started printing money. The assignat fell to 82% of its face value by November 1791, and then to 57% in June of the next year. Leaders under the Reign of Terror tried and failed to solve the problem, and high inflation was added to the list of problems that arose during the French Revolution.

US Government Assumes States' Debts

193 1790 After the American Revolutionary War, the Thirteen Colonies had a combined $25 million of debt. While the southern states were able to mostly pay off their debt by raising enough money through taxes, the northern states could not. Secretary of the Treasury Alexander Hamilton proposed a plan in 1790 whereby the federal government would assume all the states' debts.

This plan was incredibly controversial. Hamilton argued that for the new and weak country to legitimize itself, it needed a strong national financial system. Along with the assumption of debts, he proposed other financial policies, including establishing the Bank of the United States. Hamilton's main opponents on the issue, Thomas Jefferson and James Madison, did not agree that so much power ought to be given to the federal government. They worried that Virginia, which had paid off much of its own debt, would be strapped with the debt of other states.

Finally, Hamilton, Jefferson, and Madison famously arranged a deal exchanging votes for Hamilton's plan for moving the US capital south, and Congress passed the Funding Act on August 4, 1790. Effectively managed government finances played a crucial role in the country's establishment, and this laid the building-blocks for American development for the next two and a half centuries.

First Bank of the United States Founded

194 1791 Alexander Hamilton, the first Secretary of the Treasury under President George Washington, sent a proposal to Congress in 1790 for a central bank that would be subsidized by the federal government. Neither Thomas Jefferson nor James Madison liked the idea. Contemporary banks were known for risky speculation and being misused by politicians. Jefferson wanted a more decentralized and agrarian country than Hamilton and worried that a new central bank would hurt existing state banks. Madison believed a federal bank was unconstitutional and would concentrate power among a select few.

Hamilton's bill finally passed in 1791, and the First Bank of the United States (BUS) was established. Hamilton modeled his bank after the Bank of England, the then-premier central bank. The BUS was granted a 20-year charter with a capitalization of $10 million, only $2 million of which the government owned. The BUS collected taxes, made loans to the government, printed banknotes, and acted as a commercial bank through its eight branches. In 1811, the 20-year charter of the bank was up for renewal and rejected. Five years later, the necessity of a federal bank was realized, and the Second Bank of the United States was founded [see: 206].

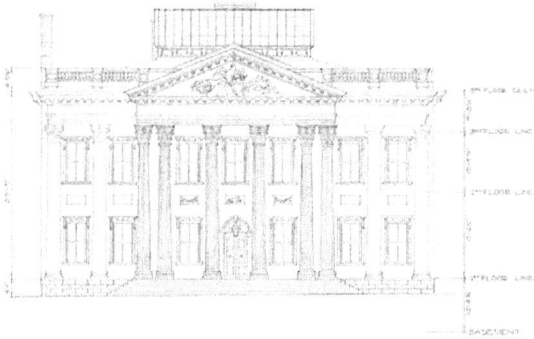

Plans for the building First Bank of the United States.

The Rise of Upward Mobility

195 late 18th c. How did the US take the title of the world's largest economy from the United Kingdom? Why is the US now so much wealthier than Europe, which has double the population (and history)? While the US is more generously endowed with natural and human resources than Europe, cultural factors also play a role—particularly in motivating productive activity. This motivation is often driven by promises of upward mobility and the American Dream. This differs from the culture of England, which George Orwell called "the most class-ridden country under the sun."

Interestingly, by the 20th century, England was in fact not actually more "class-ridden" than the United States. Though differences in constraints by class may not have been real, the cultural effects of the notional existence of these constraints are. These affections determine modern economic development. Similar to England, many European societies, such as Germany and France, shared historically rigid social hierarchies that mitigated class mobility and reinforced aristocracy, bureaucracy, and inherited privilege in society. Though meritocratic elements have increased over time across many European countries, deep-rooted notions of class continue to influence class mobility for their citizens.

In Asia, similar cultural dynamics exist, albeit in different forms. In China, the imperial-era Confucian system emphasized hierarchy along with social harmony, yet the civil service exam offered a rare path for upward mobility. A similar path existed in ancient Korean governments that were modeled on the Chinese system. Even so, Korea and Japan, shaped by Confucian values, traditionally emphasized seniority and social stability over individual ambition. However, rapid industrialization in the 20th century led to new-found economic mobility, particularly in Korea, where education and corporate success now define social standing.

American culture, historically rooted in ideals of freedom and self-determination, fuels productivity and economic development, even if those ideals remain inaccessible to many. The fact that these ideals are too abstract to be tangibly achieved results in a constant upward struggle that contributes to America's rapid economic growth today.

United States Dollar Created

196 1792 The creation of the US dollar sparked debate over the role of the government in issuing money. Some, like Alexander Hamilton, argued that a strong national currency was essential for economic stability and growth. Others, like Thomas Jefferson, feared that centralized control over money would lead to government overreach and favoritism toward financial elites.

The legality of paper money was also contentious. The Constitution did not explicitly authorize the issuance of paper money by the federal government, leading to early debates over whether banknotes should be considered legal tender. While the First Bank of the United States was given the power to issue notes with congressional approval, critics saw this as an unconstitutional delegation of power and a betrayal of the Revolution's fight against centralized British economic control.

Ultimately, the Constitution gave Congress the sole right to mint coinage. In 1792, Congress passed an act establishing the Mint. Unlike today, the government did not issue banknotes for most of the 19th century. However, non-government banks did, with the approval of Congress. The first coins to be minted were made of gold and silver and adhered to the decimal system, as recommended by Thomas Jefferson.

NYSE Founded

197 1792 Today, the New York Stock Exchange (NYSE) is the largest exchange in the world, with a market capitalization of over $30 trillion. Most US stocks are listed on the NYSE. The exchange also grew by acquiring other exchanges. In 2007, it merged with Euronext, an exchange in Europe. The next year, it acquired the American Stock Exchange. In 2012, the NYSE was itself acquired by Intercontinental Exchange.

The NYSE was founded on May 17, 1792, by the Buttonwood Agreement, which was signed by 24 stockbrokers who convened under a buttonwood tree at 68 Wall Street, New York. When the exchange was founded, five securities could be traded: three government bonds and two bank stocks. In 1824, the New York Gas Light Company joined (later renamed Consolidated Edison) and is now the longest-running stock on the exchange.

An artist imagined the signing of the Buttonwood Agreement. Men in top hats crowd around a park bench located under the tree, talking and pouring over a stack of papers. The tree is in the middle of a dirt road with red and orange brick town houses on both sides. A couple of women stand in the otherwise empty background, wearing elaborate dresses, one carrying an umbrella.

Artistic depiction of the signing of the Buttonwood Agreement on May 17, 1792 on Wall Street in New York City

Panic of 1792

198 1792 In December 1791, William Duer and Alexander Macomb tried to corner the market on US debt securities, which were required to buy stocks of the First Bank of the United States (BUS). Between December 1791 and January 1792, the price of BUS securities rose by $15 (nearly $500 today). However, prices began falling in February and March, hitting the trough in April, when the duo ran out of money.

The BUS also made a few bad moves. Since its founding, it significantly expanded its balance sheet, claiming $2.17 million in liabilities and $2.68 million in discounts. In February and early March, realizing the bank had over-extended itself, it began sharply correcting its balance sheet. William Duer and Alexander Macomb's failure, combined with the First Bank's correction, threw the market into turmoil. Securities prices fell 20%.

Officials from the bank and the US government authorized the Treasury to buy at least $100,000 of securities, and at most $500,000, if the Bank of New York ended up with excessive collateral. This helped stabilize the market. Hamilton also took several steps to resume normal function of markets. Interestingly, his actions followed Bagehot's rules, 90 years before Bagehot even wrote them [see: 235].

The Rise of Alexander Hamilton

199 late 18th c. Alexander Hamilton was born in either 1755 or 1757 on the island of St. Nevis in the West Indies, a place where little opportunity was available to a bastard orphan like Hamilton. Even so, Alexander was a precocious kid, became a clerk in a counting-room at 12, and soon was put solely in charge of a small business. Yet, the island economy proved too small for him. In 1772, still a teenager, Hamilton was sent to Boston. There he spent a year at a grammar school before matriculating at King's College (now Columbia University in New York). He studied around the clock, taking particular interest in finance, government, and politics.

Hamilton enrolled in the Continental Army in 1776. Three years later, he met the lovely Elizabeth Schuyler, to whom he was engaged the next year. After winning the Battle at Yorktown in 1781, the Colonies gained their independence. However, the deficits of the Articles of Confederation, the Colonies' governing documents drawn up earlier that year, were quite glaring. Hamilton wrote that the Articles were "neither fit for war nor peace." He resigned from the army and took to studying law, passing the bar in 1782. He was then elected to the Continental Congress, giving him an inside look at the government. He joined the Constitutional Convention in 1787, at which he argued for a strong central government. Once the Constitution was written, Hamilton produced 51 Federalist Papers to try to sell the document to the public.

George Washington, as the first President, appointed Hamilton as Treasury Secretary in 1789. Hamilton got the American economy moving by convincing the government to assume the states' debts from the war, creating a national bank, and devising a plan for bailing out the bank during its first panic. He died in a duel with Aaron Burr in 1804 and was buried at Trinity Church in New York.

First Union: Journeymen Cordwainers' Society

200 1794 The Federal Society of Journeymen Cordwainers, established in Philadelphia in 1794, was the first trade union in the United States. Formed by shoemakers known as cordwainers, the society sought to protect wages and working conditions for those whose jobs were being taken by growing factories. The union sought to prevent wage undercutting by "scab labor"—workers who refuse to go on strike—and to ensure fair compensation for its members.

In 1805, the society organized a strike demanding higher wages for shoes produced for export to the American South. The strike led to the Commonwealth v. Pullis court case. Employers accused the union of criminal conspiracy to raise wages, and the court ruled in favor of the employers, imposing fines that effectively bankrupted the union.

Despite its dissolution, the Federal Society of Journeymen Cordwainers set the stage for future worker-led attempts for better working conditions. Nearly 30 years later, in 1842, the decision in Commonwealth v. Hunt deemed labor unions legal, provided they used lawful means to achieve their goals. Workers' rights continue to be a contentious issue in the capitalist system, showing a pull between financial efficiency (that is, ensuring no rights for workers) and the job of the government to protect people.

US Dollar: International Currency

201 Today, the US dollar is the preeminent global currency, comprising nearly 90% of all foreign exchange transactions. Dollars make up about 60% of all international central bank reserves, and about half of all international exchanges, loans, and debt securities.

This situation arose after World War II, as the US surpassed the UK in political and economic power. The economically-weakened European nations adopted the Bretton Woods system, which cemented the value of the US dollar to gold and named the dollar as the standard currency for international trade across European economies and the US [see: 313].

The reliance on dollars comes with benefits and downsides internationally. On the one hand, using a single global currency makes international transactions easier. Businesses can avoid any losses from exchanging foreign currency. On the other hand, poor and unstable countries often must borrow from international finance organizations, like the International Monetary Fund. These loans are denominated in dollars and are expected to be repaid in dollars. The problem is that these countries typically have unstable national currencies. If the local currency loses value against the dollar, these governments must use ever larger sums of local currency to repay the same sum of dollar-denominated debt, which can be incredibly harmful.

The global power of the dollar also has benefits and downsides for the US, which can pay its international debts in its own currency. However, increasing global trade increases demand for dollars, driving up their value. This makes US exports become relatively more expensive and thus less competitive, boosting the trade deficit. In recent years, US dollars have represented a decreasing share of international currency reserves, raising questions about the rise of a new world reserve currency. China's renminbi is an obvious competitor, but due to China's lack of fiscal transparency, it is only the eighth most-traded currency globally as of today.

Qianzhuang Banks

202 18th cent. In the 18th century, China used a diverse array of coinage. *Qianzhuang* banks emerged to offer a remedy to the resulting confusion. Early *qianzhuang* banks initially specialized in coinage exchange, but became more advanced over time. Unlike the *piaohao* banks [see: 210], *qianzhuang* banks didn't have branches. Additionally, *qianzhuang* were mostly located in the south, near the Yangtze River. They were local businesses that, in addition to money exchange, took deposits, offered cash notes, and made loans. Many *qianzhuang* banks operated 24 hours a day, and customers could knock on the door of a *qianzhuang* at midnight if they needed cash immediately.

Qianzhuang banks mostly offered services to merchants. Between the 1840s and 1895, Shanghai's foreign trade jumped from essentially zero to 381 million taels of silver annually. *Qianzhaung* acted as intermediaries between foreign firms and Chinese merchants, taking money from the former to lend to the latter. They were extremely leveraged. One Shanghai *qianzhuang* with 20,000 taels in capital made 1,040,867 taels in loans in 1907. There were around 10,000 *qianzhuang* in China by the 1890s, and almost all merchants relied on them, making them similar to Western banks.

House of Rothschild

203 1798 The Rothschild banking dynasty was established in the late 18th century by Mayer Amschel Rothschild. Born in 1744 in the Jewish ghetto in Frankfurt, Germany, Mayer Amschel laid the foundation for a financial empire that earned him the title of "founding father of international finance."

Amschel dispatched his five sons across Europe to start Rothschild branches. His sons went to Vienna, London, Paris, Naples, and one remained in Frankfurt. This branch model allowed the Rothschild Bank to efficiently move capital across Europe. Nathan Mayer Rothschild founded the British branch in 1811. The bank helped the British government provide subsidies to its allies during the Napoleonic Wars. Nathan Rothschild also funded the Duke of Wellington's armies in Portugal and Spain, helped build the London Tube, and provided private wealth-management services.

The Rothschilds also played a large role in financing international projects, including the British government's 1875 purchase of Egypt's interest in the Suez Canal, the Spanish-founded Rio Tinto mining company, and De Beers diamond mines. The Rothschilds' influence also extends beyond finance. The family bank owns dozens of subsidiary companies. They have provided aid to European governments, produce fine wines, and rank as nobility in the United Kingdom.

First Income Tax in UK and US

204 1798 War is the most prolific mother of financial instruments. In 1798, under Prime Minister William Pitt, England created the first income tax to help pay for the war against revolutionary France. Nothing came of the 1798 tax; but, in 1799, another 10% tax was imposed. This was definitely a better rate than what the Beatles had to deal with ("There's one for you, 19 for me, 'Cause I'm the taxman!"). The tax was repealed, reinstated with the tides of the wars, and fully removed after Napoleon was defeated in 1816. In 1842, the basis of the UK's modern income tax was instituted, with a rate of 3%.

The US had a similar experience. The expense of the Civil War resulted in the country's first income tax in 1861. The first tax day was set as June 30, 1862. After delaying the details and pushing the effective date of the act back a year, Congress finally landed on a 3% tax on income above $600. This was, however, just one of many measures taken to raise revenue for the war and was quickly abandoned, not to be replaced by a permanent income tax until 1913.

William Pitt as a doctor talking to Napoleon about the remedy for Europe

Banks Help Buy Louisiana Territory

205 1803 Even at the bargain price of $15 million, the Louisiana territory was too expensive for the 14-year-old United States to afford. Baring Brothers, a large British bank, and Hope and Co., a Dutch Bank created to conceal any British-French involvement, forwarded the money to France, making the purchase possible.

The deal worked as follows. Alexander Baring, along with US Treasury Secretary Albert Gallatin, presided over the transaction, sailing back and forth between London and Washington to carry out the deal. The United States would pay a little under one-third of the price up front: $3.75 million. The two banks bought $11.25 million in 6% interest US government bonds with plans to resell them. The bonds were then sent to the banks in Europe. There, the banks advanced the money to France in cash and then turned the property, Louisiana, over to the United States. Essentially, the banks bought the Louisiana Purchase from France, and then the US bought it from the banks. The bank's profit from the transaction is estimated to have been about $3 million.

Thus, the first American expansion, and one of the largest land sales in history, was almost entirely financed by banks.

Second Bank of the United States Founded

206 1816 The banking sector in the United States greatly expanded during the five years after the charter of the First Bank of the United States failed to renew [see: 194]. Many of the new banks were unit banks, which meant that each bank only had one building in one location. This made their business inherently unstable. The War of 1812 put added pressure on the banking system, disrupting its normal functions. The Second Bank of the United States was set up in 1816—essentially a replica of the First Bank—to get the economy back on track.

The Second Bank worked to keep the risky banking system in check in a few ways, primarily by redeeming privately-issued banknotes for specie. This checked private banks' banknote-issuing power, as well as their lending power. The Bank also printed its own banknotes. By 1831, it had 24 branches around the country, most of which were built in Greek revival design, contributing to today's image of the classic bank look.

Like the First Bank, the Second Bank was given a 20-year charter, which expired in 1835, setting the United States' economy on a turbulent path for the remainder of the 19th century [212].

England Adopts Gold Standard

207 1816 England started operating on a de facto gold standard in 1717, but was still operating on a de jure bimetallic standard. That is, while England was legally based on a bimetallic standard, it was actually using a gold standard. The Coinage Act of 1816 established the gold standard legally. It set one pound sterling (one troy pound of silver, or 0.82 lb) to 123.25 grains of gold, and issued a gold coin known as the sovereign, worth 20 shillings.

England also resumed convertibility of notes to specie, which was suspended for the Napoleonic Wars. Thus, the gold standard, one of the most important systems in the history of money, officially began after unofficially beginning 99 years earlier. It would take a few more decades before the rest of Europe and the world followed England's lead and moved to the gold standard [see: 240].

1819 Financial Crisis

208 1819 After the Napoleonic Wars ended in 1815, prices of goods began to fall across Western Europe. Falling prices were due in part to a deficiency of precious metal coinage, as Napoleon's conquest decreased precious metal imports from the American colonies. Additionally, Britain's manufacturing industry had expanded to produce goods that fueled the Napoleonic Wars. The end of the Wars meant cheap goods flooded the market.

As Europe's farming industry suffered from crop failures, booming American agriculture filled the high demand in Europe for farm products. However, cotton turned into a speculative bubble in the American South, which burst in 1818 when agricultural conditions in Europe improved and cotton imports from British East India resumed. The prices of US goods plummeted 50-75%.

The Second Bank of the United States exacerbated the crisis. Cheves, the Bank's president, implemented a conservative fiscal policy, cutting liabilities in half, tripling specie reserves, and reducing the amount of banknotes in circulation. These deflationary policies exacerbated the falling prices of American goods on the world market. As a result, many American debtors were unable to pay back their loans. Bank failures followed, worsening the panic. The federal government passed minor debtor relief laws, but never took substantive action. The economy managed to stabilize itself within a few years.

US State Bank Insurance Programs

209 1829 Before the FDIC was founded, there was no nation-wide insurance for US banks. However, states created insurance programs to fill the gap. The first such program was launched in 1829 in New York state. Businessman Joshua Forman, who apparently was inspired by merchants in Sichuan, China, devised the plan. He established an insurance fund that all banks paid into, and a board of commissioners that could audit these banks. If a bank was having trouble, the fund would pitch in.

Between 1831 and 1858, five more states adopted similar measures. Interestingly, none of the systems imposed a dollar-limit up to which depositors were insured. In addition to helping struggling banks pay their creditors, these insurance programs protected banks in other ways. For example, some programs redeemed banknotes for precious metal if the bank that issued the banknotes could not afford to do so.

Only a few years after the first program was started, a legal change brought on by the Free Banking Era laws altered the way banks could insure notes, and nonconforming banks were disqualified from participating in state insurance programs [see: 213]. By 1866, a few years after the start of the National Banking Era, all state bank insurance programs closed.

Piaohao Banks Emerge

210 1831 Around the 1820s, a unique form of banking emerged in Shanxi province, an interior region of northern China. These financial institutions, known as *piaohao*, functioned in many ways like Western banks, though they were a distinct Chinese innovation. *Piaohao* provided key financial services such as long-distance remittance, secure deposits, and loans with interest. They were developed to assist Shanxi's merchants and allowed them to travel without carrying large amounts of silver or copper. Merchants could instead use *piaohao* drafts that could be cashed in different cities, akin to modern checks.

Unlike previous Chinese moneylenders, *piaohao* operated with a structured system resembling joint-stock companies. Ownership was divided among stakeholders.

How Piaohao Banks Worked

211 Providing services for merchants and wealthy individuals, a few dozen *piaohao* bank chains operated across China from the 1820s to 1910s. They offered merchants bank drafts. Someone buying a good would deposit money in a local bank and be provided with a slip, ripped in half. One half was sent to the seller and the other half to the seller's bank. After the transaction was made, the seller would claim the other half of the draft and the funds would be transferred. Banks also exchanged currency, as 20 different types were used at the time. *Piaohao* banks took deposits at 0.2% or 0.3% interest and loaned at 0.6% or 0.7%.

While the Qing Dynasty legal system of the time did not offer an enforceable corporate system, the *piaohao* banks developed a robust management organization and corporate structure. *Piaohao* banks issued dual-class shares: one class for cash-flow rights and the other for voting rights. They also had two classes of equity: capital shares and expertise shares, which differed from voting and non-voting shares. Capital shares were the underlying capital for the bank. Capital shareholders owned all the bank's capital, which could be passed to their heirs. These shares were not traded but could be redeemed. At the end of the three- or four-year-long fiscal cycle, the performance of the bank would be assessed by capital shareholders.

Capital shareholders had no say in a bank's affairs but bore full liability. Expertise shares were owned by those actually conducting the business. A manager or vice president usually got about one share, the dividends on which could be 12,000 taels in a good fiscal cycle, though 1,500 to 2,000 was more the standard. These dividends provided incentives for the shareholders to manage their banks well.

Employees could receive pensions, a rare practice at the time. Shanxi's banking houses became the backbone of China's financial network, establishing branches in key commercial centers including Beijing, Suzhou, and Guangzhou (Canton). *Piaohao* handled the transfer of government tax revenue and facilitated trade across China. However, with the rise of modern Western-style banks in the early 20th century, *piaohao* gradually declined. It remains a matter of interest how a system so similar to Western banking was developed relatively independently.

VI

Booms and Busts:
1835 – 1910s

The 19th and early 20th century was a volatile period in financial history. One cause of these troubles was the closing of the Second Bank of the United States in 1835, bringing to an end the federal government's second attempt at a central bank. While the US was not yet a major economic force in the world at that time, this event proved important internationally, with a direct and destabilizing effect on the stability of Western finance. After the closing of the Second Bank, the US was left without a central bank or any central regulatory body for monetary policy for nearly 80 years. Additionally, since the federal government was substantially weaker at the time, it couldn't make impactful fiscal policy. Further, legal changes in the US made chartering a bank much easier, leading to a profusion of undercapitalized banks. These factors combined to make US banking highly unstable during the 19th century. The country faced financial crises almost every decade.

The US was not the only place with an unstable banking industry, as Britain became notorious for its own series of financial crises. However, as the financial sector in the Anglo-American world grew faster than effective banking regulations, crises were to be expected. Indeed, the frequency of financial crises grew with the size of the financial sector.

Despite this volatility, banking became ever more part of daily life and average people's relationships with money started to resemble its modern form. By the dawn of the 20th century, most people in industrialized nations had bank accounts, and business relied ever more heavily on the financial sector. Finance also increasingly became a professional vocation, as growth and advances in the sector created more jobs at banks and other financial firms. While the Medici had made a name for itself as bankers back in the 1400s, 19th-century men grew wealthy by investing, leveraging, and managing money to become part of the rising Gilded Age industrialist class. J. P. Morgan was the foremost among these new financiers.

Not only did private citizens and businesses start banking in greater numbers, governments also came to rely more heavily on financial services. By the end of this period, almost every large country (except for the US) had a central bank. This was not merely a European phenomenon, as Asian nations emulated modern European financial systems. The first British bank opened in China during this period, and a Chinese entrepreneur established the first Asian bank modeled on Western practices, too. Finance was truly becoming an international endeavor. Indeed, by the end of this period, Britain had lost some of its prestige as the financial center of the world.

An economy with more banks, however, doesn't simply mean that more people have bank accounts. New financial services became available, and the increased size of the financial sector changed the forms and uses of money. People started using more checks, wire transfers, and other forms of "bank money." Indeed, when paper cash became mainstream in the 19th century, banks rather than governments issued it, making cash a type of bank money.

These financial developments unfolded against a larger backdrop of industrialization and modernization—and helped fuel those trends. Finance played a role in the rise of train travel, the spread of manufacturing, the expansion of cities, growing homeownership, and much more. In turn, an explosion of wealth across developing societies helped to drive the world of finance to ever greater heights.

Jackson Ends Second Bank

212 1835 Andrew Jackson ran on a pro-agrarian, anti-elite campaign. One of his last resolutions while in office was ending the Second Bank of the United States. He questioned the Bank's constitutionality, even though it had been upheld by the Supreme Court multiple times. He claimed the currency it minted was of poor quality.

Primarily, Jackson was opposed to the Bank on principle, distrusting the banking elite, who he thought didn't have average citizens' best interests in mind. The Panic of 1792, which was partly caused by the First Bank [see: 198], confirmed this view.

In July 1832, Jackson vetoed the bill for the renewing the charter of the Second Bank. The charter expired in 1835. Jackson also made several other reforms that limited the power of banks and central government in the financial industry.

The end of the Second Bank partially supported the growth of the private financial industry across the United States. Yet, the period between the closing of the Second Bank and the opening of the Federal Reserve Bank in 1913 was the most turbulent period in American economic history. The lack of a central bank was a key reason for that.

BORN TO COMMAND

OF VETO MEMORY.

HAD I BEEN CONSULTED.

KING ANDREW THE FIRST.

This cartoon portrays Andrew Jackson dressed in imperial robe, showing how he often overstepped the power usually allowed to the president.

Free Banking Era

213 1837 The Free Banking Era began in 1837 when four states adopted free-banking laws, and founding a bank no longer required legislative approval. By 1860, 17 out of the 28 states established free-banking laws (though in many states, banks could also be granted a government charter). At the time, private banks printed banknotes, but the state-by-state nature of the system disallowed banks from operating across state lines. Although banknotes would often circulate between states, they were accepted at less than face value outside the issuing bank's state. While some banks opened branches within the state, unit banking was the norm.

The Free Banking system had upsides and downsides. The system created flexibility, allowing banks to better adapt, scale, and offer services needed to better satisfy customers. It was essentially free-market capitalism for banks, much like we have for most other products. However, due to the widespread nature of unit banking, the system was highly fragmented and easily subject to panics and crashes. The ease of founding a bank let more unscrupulous businessmen into the system, too. These downsides ultimately swayed legislators to make changes. In 1863, the National Bank Act was passed, starting the National Banking Era [see: 233].

Wildcat Banks in US

214 1830s During the Free Banking Era, wildcat banks cropped up around the United States, primarily in remote areas. During this time, the requirements to found a bank were relaxed. For example, the General Banking Law of 1837 was passed in Michigan. It was modeled after a similar law in New York, and it required new banks to have a minimum value of $50,000 in capital and specie. This was a relatively low requirement.

Taking advantage of the low bar, unscrupulous businessmen created wildcat banks as get-rich-quick schemes. These banks were founded with insufficient capital, printed money in excess, and often lost depositors' money. A certain W. W. Brown, an escaped slave and novelist who supposedly founded a wildcat bank in a barbershop when low on cash, wrote "Many persons [wildcat bank-founders] borrowed money merely long enough to exhibit it to the bank inspectors, and then the borrowed money was returned, and the bank was left without a dollar in its vaults." Such wildcat banks were one of the things that contributed to the instability of the Free Banking Era.

Panic of 1837

215 1837 Optimism abounded in the 1830s United States. The US economy experienced hasty westward expansion, undertaking new railroad construction, along with excessive planting of cotton in the South and industrialization in the North. All of this activity created opportunities for financial mismanagement, allowed for by the closing of the Second Bank of the US and the start of the Free Banking Era.

Large scale crop failures and decreasing exports started the Panic of 1837. Jackson's Specie Circular order, requiring use of bullion for government-related payments, complicated all domestic and foreign payments. European money invested in America started moving back to Europe. Ultimately, a net negative specie flow out of US banks in early May 1837 forced them to suspend specie conversion for paper. Bank suspensions spread across the US, and bank runs followed.

A letter by Mr. Asa L. Shipman from New York shows the despair of the period. He wrote: "When the revolution of 1837 commenced … after a short time … work began to get short. … I spent every day in search of some kind of employment. … nothing could be got. … We often went with one meal a day." An 1840 estimate reckoned the damage from the Panic of 1837 at $6 billion. The depression caused by the crisis touched much of the country, before there were good economic protections, until at least 1843.

Branch Banking vs. Unit Banking

216 Branch banking is, as the name implies, when banks operate with multiple branches. Unit banking, on the other hand, entails each banking company operating out of a single building. Widespread branch banking is a somewhat recent change that has increased the stability of the banking sector. However, it has also contributed to wealth consolidation across fewer companies.

Some of the earliest banks, like the Medici, were branch banks. Historically, however, unit banking was more common. In 1784, seven out of 119 country banks in England had branches. By 1830, 75% had only one office, and half of the remainder had only one branch. In the US, branch banking was more common before the Civil War, as it was mostly prohibited by the National Bank Act in 1863. By 1900, only 119 bank branches existed in the US, most of which were state banks. The number of lone branches increased as banks switched from primarily printing banknotes to taking deposits.

Often, debates over which system is better revolve around cultural arguments about the appropriate size of companies. However, there are some statistics that suggest a clear winner. In cases where branch banking is widespread, there are usually more bank offices, which is beneficial for customers. A 1959 comparison between San Francisco, where bank branches were legal, and Chicago, where bank branches were not, showed that the number of bank offices was greater in San Francisco. Additionally, banks' profit margins increase as banks become larger and more concentrated, indicating that branch banking is more profitable. This may be because branch banks are also more efficient. One 1964 study found that banks in states that allowed branch banking had a median loan-to-deposit ratio of 72.9%, as compared with 67.3% in unit banking states.

Oriental Bank Corporation Founded

217 1842 While the foundational elements of the economy—coins, bonds, and credit systems—have long existed across civilizations, Western financial technology became standard internationally through the 19th century. The Oriental Bank Corporation (OBC), founded in 1842 as the Bank of Western India, is a key example of the spread of Western finance into Asia.

The bank moved its headquarters to London in 1845 and was granted a royal charter in 1851, allowing it to rapidly expand its international operations. The OBC was the first modern bank in China, establishing a Hong Kong branch in 1846. This laid the groundwork for future development in China. In India, OBC was one of the first British banks to challenge the East India Company's monopoly on financial transactions, facilitating foreign exchange and financing trade.

Despite its early successes, the OBC faced significant challenges. Overextension and substantial losses from loans, such as to coffee plantations in Ceylon and sugar estates in Mauritius, led to its decline. The bank ultimately closed in 1892. Despite its downfall, its impact on banking in China and India persisted, bringing Western banking into the regions.

Bank of England Modernizes

218 1844 The charter of the Bank of England was set to renew in 1844 [see: 164], but legislators wanted to make bank reform part of the renewal. That was the purpose of the Bank Charter Act of 1844, which intended to mitigate financial crises, tame inflation, and prevent the outflow of specie from the country.

The Act regulated the issue of banknotes by the Bank of England, disallowed newly-founded banks to issue banknotes, and established banknote issue as a government prerogative. To facilitate this, the BoE was split into a banking department and a note-issuing department.

The Act also reinforced the ability to convert BoE notes to specie. However, rather than mitigating financial crises, the Act exacerbated them by limiting the ability of the BoE to meaningfully respond to them. For example, the act stipulated that the BoE could only issue new banknotes if it expanded the supply of gold and silver reserves to back them up. These and other restrictions made conducting active monetary policy difficult. The Act exacerbated the Panic of 1847, the Panic of 1857, and the Panic of 1866.

Bank of England Monopoly on Banknotes

219 1844 Today, you do not see many people questioning the validity of the government's right to issue banknotes, something that used to be the prerogative of private banks. Governments have since taken over the job by giving themselves currency monopolies. Government involvement made banknotes more trustworthy. After Amsterdam gave its central bank a monopoly on banknote issue,

England followed.

The first attempt at giving a monopoly to the BoE occurred in 1697, five years after the Bank was founded. While the BoE was the only government bank in England, the currency monopoly failed to make it the only note-issuing bank. This continued to hamper its legitimacy, and strengthened bank competition diminished the public's trust in the BoE. Eventually, regional banks stopped issuing notes after 1826, when the Bank opened multiple branches outside of London.

The Bank Charter Act of 1844 finalized the BoE's monopoly, disallowing new banks from issuing notes and putting strong restrictions on existing banks. Government monopoly allowed the BoE to promote greater stability and took the job of the goldsmith bankers, who had by then been key to English banking for 200 years, contributing to their fall.

Telegraphs Used for Finance

220 1844 Difficulties of long-distance communication resulted in very speculative purchases of securities. If British investors wanted to purchase American treasury bonds, they would put an order on a ship that would take two weeks to cross the Atlantic for the order to arrive in New York. Processing the order would take a few days, and a receipt would then be sent on a ship returning to England. The telegraph, invented by Samuel Morse in the 1840s, facilitated nearly instant communication, solving this problem.

The first experimental telegraph line was set up between Washington and Baltimore in 1844. The first transatlantic cable, connecting telegraph signals from Ireland to Canada, was laid in 1866. The financial industry was quick to adopt the new technology. Before the telegraph, information asymmetries abounded. The prices of the same securities often varied between American cities, allowing arbitrage and inefficient markets. The advent of quick international communications increased financial market efficiency and reduced asset price volatility.

Panic of 1847

221 1847 The railroad industry around the world expanded through the 1830s and 1840s, leaving a large amount of Britain's capital locked up in railroad investments. During this time, American cotton prices were rising, the Irish Potato Famine was ongoing, and the European crop yield suffered. These global economic pressures would be expensive to resolve.

In 1844, the Bank Charter Act was ratified in the United Kingdom. As gold flowed out of the UK to pay for the rising prices of imported cotton and food for the Irish, the stipulations of the Bank Charter Act required that the BoE reduce the money supply accordingly. This effectively created a contractionary monetary policy that resulted in a liquidity crunch. The speculative bubble surrounding railroads burst as investors lost confidence. The BoE was ineffective at stopping the recession, as the

Act prevented it from generating sufficient cash to effectively act as the lender of last resort to banks.

On October 25, 1847, the Treasury temporarily suspended the Act, permitting the BoE to issue notes unbacked by gold. The BoE raised its discount rate to try to slow reserve depletion. Financial markets soon rebounded, but firms continued to suffer until 1848.

Gold Rush in California

222 1848 Gold was first found at Sutter's Mill near Coloma, California, on January 24, 1848. After James Marshall, a carpenter, made the initial discovery, more than 300,000 people from all over the world moved to the California territory to mine for gold. While average gold production in the US from 1792 to 1847 was estimated at 36 tons per year, this figure more than doubled to 76 tons from 1848 to 1857. It is difficult to estimate the total amount of extracted gold attributable to the California gold rush, though likely some 400–500 tons were mined.

For most of the 19th century, the US and Europe used a bimetallic coinage system, where money was backed by both gold and silver. The California gold rush, along with other gold rushes around the world, gave countries sufficient access to new gold that they could rely solely on a gold standard. Many argued that gold could provide more stable prices, particularly after silver was discovered in great quantities in the 19th century, devaluing it. Additionally, the discovery of gold contributed to a 30% rise in prices between 1850 and 1855. This inflation helped put an end to the Free Silver Movement [see: 242], helping seal gold as America's currency standard.

Sutter's Mill

Communist Manifesto Written

223 1848 In 1847, the international Communist League commissioned Karl Marx and Friedrich Engels to draft a manifesto outlining their principles. Marx and Engels composed the Communist Manifesto that was published in London in 1848. The manifesto begins with the declaration, "A specter is haunting Europe— the specter of Communism."

A specter was indeed haunting Europe, as money looked like it had gone astray. Industrialism meant laborers working 12-hour days in harsh conditions. Even children worked in factories instead of going to school. Revolutions broke out across

Europe in 1848, with people rebelling against current monarchies and established political systems.

Ultimately, the year brought little effectual change. The Revolutions did not establish more equitable governments, and their failure caused the Communist Manifesto to fall into obscurity. However, the Manifesto was revived within a few decades and became one of the most influential political treatises in history. It focuses on the notion that all human history is a history of one group oppressing another, and that the Capitalist system sows its own demise. While many see the Manifesto merely as a product of its time, many others see it as a true rendition of the present and future of capitalist society.

Marxist Economics

224 Marxist economics is the most broadly recognized alternative to traditional economic theory. The Labor Theory of Value (LTV), central to Marx's paradigm, states that the value of any good is determined by the amount of socially necessary labor time required for producing it. This labor time is the amount of time an average worker with average skill would take to produce something. As technology improves, goods can be produced faster, and the socially necessary time decreases. Thus, goods become intrinsically less valuable. This contrasts with the Subjective Theory of Value (STV), which states that the value of goods is based on economic factors, such as supply and demand.

How much labor is necessary? Marx says not as much as you might think. Marx's term *surplus value* is akin to the STV concept of profit: it is the extra value created in excess of the cost of production, which Marx defines as the labor effort involved in producing the good. The business owner keeps the excess. Marx writes, "the value of labour-power [wages/expenditures] and the value which the labour-power creates [revenue for the owner] in the labour process are two entirely different magnitudes." While a worker may have to work only four hours for the capitalist to break even, he is made to work all day, producing surplus value that the capitalist takes home.

Marx says Revolution—which may lead to Communism—is inevitable. He posits that as technology continues to improve, it will take less time for workers to produce the same quantity of goods, increasing the surplus value generated within the same length of a workday. Competition between capitalists incentivizes the implementation of more efficient means of production. While the LTV implies that goods prices should fall, Marx observed that market prices in capitalist society predominantly remain constant, allowing for the rich capitalists to get richer while the poor laborers remain at a low standard of living. The uneven distribution of wealth will anger the working classes, who will eventually stage a revolution. Thus, capitalism sows its own end.

First Currency Board Established

225 1849 The first currency board was founded in 1849 in the British colony of the Mauritius Islands, located off the east coast of Africa and east of Madagascar. These islands hosted many sugar plantations, meaning that a functional economy was needed there. Before the currency board was established, free currency-issue was permitted for commercial banks.

However, that created economic problems, as an ill-suited British banking law was imposed on the islands' economy, failing to create a stable money supply. The idea of allowing the colonial government to issue unrestricted money was shot down, as other colonies' governments had abused that power. Ultimately, a currency board

Currency Board or Central Bank?

226 Imagine you are running a country (or, as was often the case, a foreign empire now in the business of running a country that you've colonized). As all country-leaders know, one of your first priorities should be establishing a stable economy. You decide to create a central bank, until your finance minister keenly points out the downsides of central banks: they are complex, expensive, and quick to use discretionary action to make often wasteful decisions. He suggests that you create a currency board instead.

A currency board has two tasks: to provide a stable supply of domestic currency and to anchor its currency to a stable foreign currency—often that of its managing colonial power. Currency boards hold low-risk, interest-bearing bonds that are denominated in the anchor currency (and some gold). They hold reserves at a ratio of 100% or higher and do not engage in monetary policy—they only issue money. One author summarized economist David Ricardo's perspective, "There should have been no need for Central Banks. A Currency Board, working on a rule, should have been enough."

The first currency board was created in 1849, and this type of institution took off in the mid-20th century. It then almost entirely disappeared before regaining popularity in the late '90s when Argentina created one [see: 394].

Since currency boards do not make monetary policy, they do not have anything to be secretive about and usually post their balance sheets online. Conversely, central bank decisions are typically highly covert. With currency boards, the supply of money is determined by market forces. As a result, balance of payments problems tend to correct themselves, and speculative attacks often fail. Lastly, currency boards cannot succumb to the pressure of politicians, unlike how central banks do in many developing countries. Will you establish a currency board in your country?

was established in 1849 for the island colony. This effectively provided a stable money supply to the colony, and it became the world's first currency board. It was followed by the establishment of dozens of other currency boards throughout history.

Xianfeng Inflation

227 early 1850s As silver flowed out of China to pay for opium imports in the 1830s, copper was used to replace it. This resulted in copper becoming devalued under China's bimetallic system. Additionally, Emperor Daoguang made the salt tax the only tax that could be easily changed, inhibiting the government's ability to raise money. Further, the government had trouble replenishing funds stolen from the treasury in 1843. And the Taiping Rebellion broke out in 1850, the year Xian-Feng ascended to the throne. The rebellion cut off the supply of both copper for minting coinage and salt that the government could tax.

China started issuing copper "big coins" in 1854 with a higher face value than metal value. Forgers replicated them, making the coins even less trustworthy. Big coins were discounted as much as 20–40%. China also started reluctantly printing paper money. However, since people were allowed to only pay 50% of their taxes with the paper money, it wasn't considered as valuable as coinage and was discounted by as much as 60% in some parts of China.

These factors combined to generate massive inflation in China in the early 1850s. This undermined confidence in the Qing Dynasty's financial system, a problem that continued for decades even after inflation under Xianfeng subsided.

A cash note issued by the Ministry of Revenue under Emperor Xianfeng.

Panic of 1857

228 1857 In the early 1850s, global markets were relatively peaceful, and money was easily obtained. However, as gold extraction in California started to decline, bankers in the American West became nervous about their longevity. The railroad industry, primarily funded by East Coast banks, was booming through the 1840s and early 1850s, bringing settlers west.

Westward migration soon started to decline, partly due to a reduced crop yield in the northwest, declining international demand, and increasing uncertainty about the issue of slavery in the new American territories. The railroad expansion turned into a bubble, which burst in the summer of 1857. On August 24, 1857, Ohio Life, a bank with connections in New York, failed due to poor agricultural investments, throwing New York financiers into panic. Banks called in loans to stop runs on their gold. Some suspended currency convertibility. The newly adopted telegraph allowed the panic to spread across the country faster than any prior panic.

By 1859, the effects of the Panic started to subside. Multi-branch banks were able to resume specie convertibility, allowing them to recover more quickly than unit banks. In his State of the Union address after the Panic, President James Buchanan called for stricter banking regulations.

"Gilderfluke's perfected locomotive," a satirical nineteenth-century illustration of an over-engineered locomotive with absurd features, such as an X-ray headlamp that reveals train-robbers' thoughts and a boiling water cannon to scare hoboes and cattle off the tracks.

Banking for the Working Class

229 mid-19th c. Until about the middle of the 19th century, banking was mostly reserved for the wealthy. While banks are convenient for holding deposits of any size, they were generally used for investing or holding very large sums of money.

The most common type of financial institution for the poor in the UK were so-called "friendly societies," which operated more like insurance programs than banks. They were common before the arrival of banks. There were about 648,000 of such institutions in 1793. The first proper savings bank opened in 1810, and there were more than 400 in England by 1820. By the mid- to late 18th century, saving became possible for an increasing number of working class families. More and more of the not-so-wealthy started using banks to save small sums of money.

One bank, Limehouse Bank, had 1.5 million customers in 1875 with an average deposit of £29 per account. Another firm, Post Office Savings Bank, had about 300,000 more clients, with about £5.45 average savings per account—this bank was designed for smaller savers. Today, most people regardless of socio-economic class have a bank account, a precedent set by 19th century Britain.

Gresham's Law Coined

230 1858 When Queen Elizabeth took the English throne in 1558, she noticed a problem with the country's coinage: only debased coins were in circulation, while valuable coins were leaving the country. She called on one of the foremost financiers of her time, Sir Thomas Gresham, for assistance. Gresham's explanation became known as Gresham's Law, though that term didn't arise until 1858.

Gresham's Law argues that bad money circulates while good money is hoarded. This occurs in a country where legal-tender coinage is minted with precious metal that is required to be taken at face value. The debasement of some coins—often the newer ones—and not others results in some coins having lower intrinsic value. When a person is looking to buy something at a store and pay with many different coins claiming the same face values but different intrinsic values, the buyer has an incentive to give a more debased coin and retain the more valuable ones for himself. When the store owner uses his money to buy something, he will do the same, and soon only coins of lower intrinsic value will circulate readily.

Gresham explained his theory in a letter to the Queen, writing that "good and bad coin cannot circulate together." After the Great Debasement, England's coinage was left in an "unexampled state of badness," the result of which was that "all your fine gold was conveyed ought of this your realm." Though the Law bears his namesake, Sir Gresham was not the first person who noticed this. A line in the Greek play *The Frogs* reads "[Long ago the city provided coins of] Gold and silver, each well minted, tested each and ringing clear. / Yet we never use them! Others always pass from hand to hand." This trend was documented through the Middle Ages, too.

Greenbacks Issued

231 1861 The Panic of 1857 had taken its toll on the US economy. The succession of the southern states meant lost federal government tax revenue while needing to finance an expensive Civil War. In response, the US government issued both demand notes and United States notes.

The government issued $50 million worth of demand notes in July 1861. These notes could be used to pay taxes, but were not technically legal tender. They could, however, be converted to gold coins at the Treasury. Demand notes were printed with

A 1861 greenback note for $10.

green ink on the back and were thus given the name "greenbacks."

The issuance of demand notes proved insufficient to pay for the government's needs. In January 1862, Congress passed a law to introduce United States notes, which began circulating in April. Additional issues followed in 1862 and 1863. US notes were considered legal tender, and banks distributed them in place of coinage. The value of US notes often fluctuated based on how the men were doing on the battlefront during the Civil War.

This was the United States' first foray into unbacked fiat currency. Previously only ever printed in times of crisis, fiat money became standard in the country after the Civil War.

Inflation in the Confederacy

232 1861 The American Civil War cost the Confederate States $15.2 billion in 2008 dollars. Raising such an enormous sum was no easy task for any group of states at the time, but was especially difficult for the Confederacy. Most financial infrastructure and expertise resided in the North, and states' rights inhibited effective interstate monetary policy and taxation.

Banking regulation differed widely among states, and the lack of oversight and of a central bank resulted in frequent liquidity problems. States were reluctant to heed the requests for money from Jefferson Davis or treasury secretary Christopher Memminger. As much of the South was rural, agricultural, and poor, the country's tax-base was already small. For the entire war, the Confederacy only managed to take out one loan.

Memminger started printing notes, redeemable for gold two years after the Confederacy won the war—assuming it would win. Inflation of 10% per month set in as people spent their money quickly. In 1864, an act taking one-third of currency out of circulation was passed. But inflation continued to be buoyed by battlefield dynamics, and sped up. By the end of the war in 1865, prices in the South had multiplied by a factor of 92.

National Bank Act

233 1863 By the middle of the Civil War, the US government needed a more stable banking system and a consistent supply of paper money, which at the time was mostly issued by private banks. The state-by-state Free Banking system was simply not cutting it [see: 213]. The National Bank Act was ratified in 1863. It established the national bank system, allowing new banks to choose a national rather than a state charter. National banks issued banknotes backed by reserves of US bonds deposited in the US Treasury.

As part of the creation of the National Bank system, federal taxes were imposed on the note-issue of state banks, which led many state banks to close or convert to national charters. In 1863, there were 66 national banks and 1,466 state banks. By

1868, there were 1,640 national banks and 247 state banks.

A national charter, however, was not necessarily preferable. Originally, national banks experienced stronger regulations. Further, the minimum capital requirement for national banks was $50,000 when located in towns of less than 6,000 people, with graduations up to $200,000 for cities with more than 50,000 people. State banks could be chartered with as little as $10,000.

Latin Monetary Union

234 1865 The euro is not Europe's first attempt at currency union. In 1865, France, Belgium, Italy, and Switzerland (and later Greece) created the Latin Monetary Union (LMU). The term LMU was used sarcastically by the British press to stress that the union would only ever constitute southern European states.

As trade sped up in the mid-19th century, countries felt the need for a more integrated currency system to promote access to foreign capital and to boost national exports. Many European states already used French coinage or minted coinage to similar specifications. Under the LMU, participating countries adopted the French standard, were allowed to keep their coinage name and design, and were largely free to issue coinage as they liked. The LMU copied France's bimetallic standard of 1:15.5 ratio of gold to silver.

However, a few thorny problems brought the Union down. The instability of bimetallism resulted in arbitrage and an outflow of gold from the LMU. As paper money became more prominent, the LMU realized its inability to regulate it, and inflation took hold. Finally, a monetary union can only work if all countries' monetary policies are coordinated. Free coinage issue meant this was not the case under the LMU. The Union dissolved in 1926.

Panic of 1866

235 1866 From 1860, Overend, Gurney & Co., was one of the most well-respected and supposedly reputable banks in London. The fact that it was hemorrhaging money was kept secret. In 1865, the company went public, and its shares started trading at nearly 100% premium. Things turned around in May 1866 as a speculative investment fell through, and the company went bankrupt with liabilities totaling £18.7 million.

The failure threw London into panic. Twenty-one London banks closed with total published losses of about £50 million (about £4.9 billion in 2023), one of the worst financial panics in British history. This crisis was similar to the Panic of 1847 [See: PN74-0]. Banks had few ways to free up the cash necessary to meet their immediate liquidity needs. The only source available, the Bank of England Discount Window, was severely limited in its ability to lend or issue new paper money due to constraints created by the Bank Charter Act of 1844 [See: 218].

The Bank Charter Act was temporarily suspended, as it was in 1847, and the crisis subsided within a few days without the Bank of England exceeding its banknote issue limits. The Panic was partially responsible for the increased enfranchisement of working-class British, whose anger forced lawmakers to expand rights for the lower classes.

Ticker Tape Invented

236 1867 Thomas Edison invented a device that could print messages from telegraphs, improving upon earlier designs. In 1863, Edward Callahan, an employee at the American Telegraph Company, hooked up a modified form of Edison's invention and created the ticker tape, a device that prints stock quotes almost in real time. He demonstrated the ticker tape publicly in 1867. Edison made further improvements to Callahan's design and patented the ticker tape in 1871.

The effects of the high-speed communication allowed by the ticker tape are immense. The ticker tape allowed wider access to relevant information, closed price discrepancies and arbitrage opportunities, and helped markets run more efficiently. The ticker tape also changed the trading experience. It allowed traders (and news stations) to better understand what was happening in the market, rather than have to put together a mental image based on pieces of handwritten news that they could pick up. At the same time, the ticker tapes may have done more to allow for easy gambling, making markets possibly less efficient.

Thomas Edison gold sock telegraph, Henry Ford Museum

Black Friday Gold Panic

237 1869 James Fisk and Jay Gould befriended the brother-in-law of President Ulysses S. Grant to become privy to government economic policy. Prices on all commodities had been falling with the US Treasury's contractionary policy. The pair thought they could boost the price of gold and corner the market. Knowledge of the Treasury's gold-related plans and ability to sway the President's opinions would be beneficial. They persuaded the President that, if the Treasury sold its gold, it would hurt American agriculture.

Through mid-September, Fisk and Gould bought up gold as the price steadily increased. Wall Street was tense on September 24, 1869, later known as Black Friday. The opening bid for gold was at $150, 6% above the previous day's close. A little before noon, the price hit $164. The New York Times reported that the operators spoke like "outpourings of maniacs" and "pallor seemed to overspread the faces."

Grant realized what was happening. Just before noon, the Treasury showed up with orders to sell $4 million in gold. There were rumors of intentions to sell up to $15 million. Gold tumbled 20% as frantic operators sold as low as $130. This ended the careers of Fisk and Gould and hurt the country's gold market.

Bagehot's Rules

238 Bagehot's Dictum governs one of the more well-known jobs of central banks: acting as lender of last resort to failing banks. In his 1873 book *Lombard Street*, published in response to the 1866 crisis, Walter Bagehot gave three general rules to running a central bank:

I. Lend freely in times of crisis,
II. At penalty rates (high interest),
III. On good collateral to sound firms.

First, Bagehot realized that "in wild periods of alarm, one [bank] failure makes many." Thus, central banks must act as a lender of last resort for individual institutions to protect the entire financial sector. Central banks must also advertise that they will not be hesitant to step in when a crisis happens to instill confidence in the public.

Second, Bagehot argued that this lending should be at penalty rates to make sure that borrowing from the central bank is a last resort and cannot be abused. Commercial banks should first turn to cheaper markets.

Third, the central bank should accept sound collateral from sound firms. Bagehot suggests that most collateral is sound, even if its value is temporarily lower due to a crisis. Central banks should not stop all bank failures, just the failures of the banks that are otherwise sound.

Though well regarded, these rules do have some shortcomings. Bagehot wasn't specific about how to quickly determine if a failing bank is or is not solvent, and regulators still have not figured out how to do so. His rules also fail to account for the time required to determine if a bank is or is not solvent. In the real world, banks are often bailed out while their solvency is still in the process of being determined.

Japanese Yen Introduced

239 1871 In 1868, the warlord shogun lost his power in Japan and was replaced with a traditional emperor. The new man took the name Meiji, meaning "enlightened rule," in an event called the Meiji Restoration. As with many up-start governments, Japan was in a bad spot economically at that time. The new government enacted the New Currency Act in 1871, replacing the traditional ryo, bu, and shu currencies with a new yen, sen, and rin that were based on a decimalized system. The government started minting gold, silver, and copper coins using Western coin-manufacture technology. The yen, the largest unit, was set at 1.5 grams of gold and came in coin and paper form.

Today, the Japanese Yen is the third most traded currency on Forex exchanges and the third most widely held reserve currency, accounting for about 6% of reserves, behind the USD and euro and ahead of the pound sterling in both cases. It, along with the Chinese renminbi, are the only Asian currencies on the top 10 reserve currencies list.

Europe Moves to Gold Standard

240 1870s Britain was the first country to adopt the gold standard in the 18th century, and it remained an outlier for much of the 19th century [see: 173] . A global shift toward gold only became possible after gold was discovered in California in 1848 and in other parts of the world [see: 222].

Portugal was the first European country to follow Britain onto the gold standard in 1854, largely because of its close trade ties with the UK. It was not until Germany adopted the gold standard in 1871–73 that the shift gained momentum across Europe. Germany was prominent in European trade, and its adoption of gold practically forced its neighbors to follow suit. The Netherlands, despite initial reluctance, gradually moved toward gold between 1873 and 1877.

The Latin Monetary Union, which included France, Belgium, Switzerland, and Italy, initially operated on a bimetallic system, but began limiting silver coinage in the 1870s to maintain parity with gold. Countries abandoned bimetallism as more nations switched to gold and the value of silver declined. By the mid-1870s, gold was the precious metal of choice for European currencies. Gold dominated until World War I, during a period called the Classical Gold Standard.

Crime of 1873

241 1873 In the late 19th century, the United States was only slowly moving toward the gold standard due to resistance from those who supported silver. In 1873, a Coinage Act was ratified, and it listed all the types of coins that would be minted in gold and silver. A notable omission, however, was the silver dollar, meaning that it was essentially demonetized. Silver miners no longer had a place to sell their silver. The Act was one of the last battles in the debate of gold versus silver, and gold appeared to be winning. Despite this, there was concern that the switch from bimetallism to monometallism (gold exclusively) would create an unstable economy.

Many people thought the silver-demonetizing Currency Act was both damaging and unfairly passed. A conspiracy circulated that the law was passed by corruption. Ernest Seyd, a German-born British economist and supporter of bimetallism, was accused of bribing Congressmen for the law with money from England. In truth, he submitted an analysis of the Coinage Act to Congress advocating keeping the silver dollar. This Act was the beginning of a protracted debate over what type of metallic system the United States would use, called the Free Silver Movement.

THE CURRENT QUESTION

In this cartoon about the Crime of 1873, Silver tells Gold, "You need not hold yourself so high. I'm as good as you are." Gold responds, "You never were, and never will be, my equal."

Rise of Free Silver Movement

242 **1870s** If a nation is strapped with a large amount of debt and a serious bout of inflation hits, the real amount of debt to repay is reduced. If you are a lender to this nation, you have just lost a very large sum of purchasing power on the money that you are collecting from the loans.

After the Civil War and through the 1890s, this describes the situation of the United States. A dichotomy arose between the moneyed interests wanting sound-money policies and farmers of the West who had taken large loans to expand their farms and wanted inflation to help them out.

The US was legally on a bimetallic standard but practically operated on a gold standard for the latter half of the 19th century. The end of the Civil War turned national inflation into deflation, and farmers were becoming anxious about their debt.

Through the 1870s, Europe moved to the gold standard, reducing demand for

American silver. The resulting decline in price angered silver producers. Silver producers, however, were not a powerful political interest group. They conspired with the "cheap-money" farmers in 1878 and lobbied for a law that eventually passed, requiring the US to purchase between $2 to $4 million of silver a month for coinage. The new silver coinage would both increase the price of silver and create inflation, helping both parties. In the mid-1880s, falling agricultural prices further embittered farmers, motivating them to pass another silver purchase bill. This time, farmers partnered with manufacturers from the Eastern United States demanding tariffs and passed the Sherman Silver Purchase Act of 1890 [see: 252].

Gold started draining out of the country, setting off the Crisis of 1893 [see: 257]. The conflict between the wealthy and the farmers came to head in the election of 1896, when the populist William Jennings Bryant famously said, "You shall not crucify mankind upon a cross of gold." The Silverites' campaign ended when gold finally won America over, ending the Free Silver conflict.

Panic of 1873 in Europe

243 1873 The Panic of 1873 began in Europe. That May, the Vienna Stock Exchange collapsed by nearly 50% in just a few days, triggered by a burst in a speculative bubble of railroads and real estate. Many of these railroads were in the United States and didn't generate their expected returns. When confidence crumbled, so did the market. Over 100 Austrian banks and businesses failed in the aftermath.

Germany's market follows Austria's. The newly unified German Empire was flush with 5 billion francs in reparations from the Franco-Prussian War, and business boomed. But when Germany moved to the gold standard, credit tightened, deflation set in, and businesses went south. European banks, overleveraged and undercapitalized, started failing. In 1873 alone, over 20% of joint-stock companies in Germany failed. Britain, already struggling with a sluggish economy, felt the shock too, as its exports declined by nearly 25% between 1873 and 1879.

A depression set in, and industrial production across the European continent declined by nearly 15% over the next decade. Governments, reluctant to intervene, stuck to hard money policies, worsening the downturn. Word spread across the Atlantic, and the same forces brought the United States into the crisis.

Panic of 1873 in the US

244 1873 On September 18, 1873, Jay Cooke & Co., one of the largest investment banks in New York, failed. The next day, 19 more banks followed. On September 20, the New York Stock Exchange closed without plans to reopen for the first time in its history. New York and much of the western world headed into the Great Depression. (That is, until the term "Great Depression" came to mean the depression that happened in the 1930s).

Cooke failed because of speculation in railroads in the American West. Similar speculation engulfed the funds of European and American investors through the Gilded Age. Though railroad mileage doubled in the US in the previous eight years, much of it was fueled by European investment. The difficulty of consistent communications with the US, waning yields on railroad investment, and finally a severe financial crisis in Germany and Austria all combined to pull European money back home. The US was now out of cash.

Initially, little was done. President Grant intended to leave Wall Street to its own fate. The New York market was closed for 10 days. Bank reserves in New York City dropped from $50 million to $17 million. The Bank of England raised its discount rate to 9%. A depression set in that lasted until 1879.

Asian Trade Dollars

245 1873 By the mid-19th century, the Mexican dollar became entirely accepted in China and Japan as an international currency for trade [see: 156]. Western countries had to buy coins from Mexico to trade with China, paying for not only goods but for the right to pay. In San Francisco, Mexican dollars traded at a premium of 7.5% above their value in silver, while US silver was excluded from the market. In 1873, the US started minting trade dollars at the Mexican specifications: 416 grains silver, 7.5 grains more than the silver dollar.

Portugal, Germany, the Netherlands, England, and Japan followed, all minting their own coins for trade with China. The US trade dollars, slightly more valuable than the silver dollar, had limited application and no convertibility to gold like the silver dollar did. Trade dollars could not be used to pay public debts, yet had a higher value. To end this odd situation, the US trade dollar was discontinued in 1887.

First Private Pension Plan

246 1875 The first private pension plan was established by the American Express Company in 1875, around the same time that social security was implemented in Germany. Compared with modern plans, it had a few unusual provisions: it only applied to disabled elderly employees, and it was available to those aged 60 and older who retired after having worked for 20 years. However, the company's general manager had to recommend retirement, with approval by a committee from the board of directors. Annually, the program paid out 50% of employees' working wages, up to $500.

Pension programs spread to other companies. In 1880, the Baltimore and Ohio Railroad created a similar plan covering 77,000 workers. These programs gradually expanded and became more generous. By 1987, pension plans became widely available for those aged 55 and over after 5 to 10 years of service for a company. About a quarter of all US employees were covered. Since then, pensions have been phased out, replaced with less expensive and complex retirement alternatives, such as 401(k) s. Today, only 15% of employees are covered by pensions.

Bombay Stock Exchange Founded

247 1875 Through the 19th century, financial systems—particularly those de-signed in the West—proliferated around the world. By this point, the stock exchange had become a key part of finance. The Bombay Stock Exchange was the first exchange to open in Asia. It started in the 1850s, when five stockbrokers started meeting under the Banyan trees in front of the Bombay Town Hall. In a similar story, the exchange in New York originated under a buttonwood tree [see: 197].

As the Exchange grew, traders started meeting in different parts of the city. The Bombay Exchange was officially incorporated in 1875. It became known as the Native Share and Stock Brokers Association, and founded its own office. Fast forward to 1995, BOLT (BSE Online Trading) replaced on-the-floor trading with a computerized system. Since then, Mumbai has become the financial and trading center of India, with a market cap of over $5 trillion.

Stock Market Gets Telephones

248 1878 In 1878, the New York Stock Exchange (NYSE) installed its first tele-phones. This was a significant technological advancement for the time, and it facilitated faster trading. Prior to this, telegraphs were the primary means of transmitting orders to the exchange, which, while faster than earlier methods, still involved delays due to encoding, transmission, and decoding processes.

The introduction of the telephone allowed for direct, instantaneous voice communication between brokers and their clients. Investors from various parts of the country could now speak directly with traders on the NYSE floor, hastening trades. For example, a trade from Boston could be received and executed within approximately 30 seconds. Along with other innovations, such as the stock ticker [see: 236], telephones significantly increased market efficiency and contributed to the growth of US markets.

Illustration from 1872 showing parts of Alexander Graham Bell's telephone.

Germany Creates Social Insurance

249 1889 Today, governments pay out trillions of dollars in social insurance benefits, one of the largest expenses for nations' treasuries and taxpayers. The first of these systems was created under Otto von Bismarck of Germany in 1889 and was quite generous. It offered three categories of insurance: health insurance, accident insurance, and old-age insurance.

First, the health insurance portion required employers to pay for two-thirds of medical coverage for their employees. It also required other benefits, including 13 weeks of sick pay, support for childbirth, and funeral benefits. Second, the accident insurance operated through a system of nonprofit insurance funds. It not only paid partial salary and medical fees for injured workers but also paid out benefits to widows and orphans. In a contemporary example, a mason who made 1,392 marks per year was entitled 982 marks annually when he became disabled, and his widowed wife would get 835 marks if he were to die. Finally, people over 70 and those never able to work received old-age pensions. These pensions were smaller than other program benefits—about 18% of workers' average wages. These three systems applied to all blue-collar workers and only white-collar workers whose income did not exceed 2,000 marks.

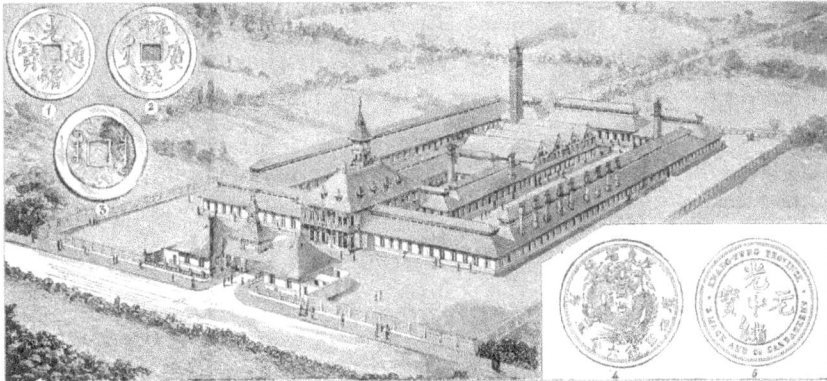

Drawing of the Canton Mint, 1888.

China Adopts Western-Style Coinage

250 1889 For much of the 19th century, China relied heavily on foreign coins acquired through trade, especially the Spanish and Mexican dollars [see: 156]. The Qing Dynasty, however, wanted to be more self-sufficient. Qing adopted Western coin-minting technology, as part of a larger push to adopt Western technology and governing methods, called Qing's Self-Strengthening Movement.

The first mint in China to produce Western style coins was the Canton Mint, led by Viceroy Zhang Zhidong, one of the key figures in the Self-Strengthening Movement. In 1887, Zhang secured a contract with the British firm Heaton & Sons to supply British minting equipment, as well as technical expertise. The Canton Mint was soon the largest mint in the world, with a production capacity of 100,000 silver coins per day.

Silver Dragon coins were the first coins to be minted, starting in 1889. They came in four denominations—dollar, half-dollar, 20 cents, and 10 cents—and were initially intended to compete. Another series of coins was produced starting in 1890, designed for broader distribution. These coins didn't gain immediate trust, and, having a higher silver content, were often melted down. However, the Canton Mint represents the West's triumph in financial technology in the modern world.

Sherman Antitrust Act Passed

251 1890 The United States has some of the best antitrust laws in the world, the first of which was the Sherman Antitrust Act of 1890. Intentions to make laws limiting monopolies, however, started long before that. Thomas Jefferson suggested that a line banning monopolies be put in the Bill of Rights.

The Sherman Act was akin to state laws banning monopolies that were already in place. The Act passed in the Senate with one vote of opposition and passed in the House with zero opposition. It describes a monopoly as "[Any corporate group] in the form of trust or otherwise that was in restraint of trade or commerce among the several states, or with foreign nations." One provision of the Act makes starting a monopoly punishable by time in prison, a sentence no longer given. More importantly, it established the basis for the government and competing companies to sue a monopoly and take it apart.

Standard Oil, IBM, Microsoft, and AT&T have all been brought to trial for monopolistic behavior under the Act. The financial industry, however, is not regulated by monopoly laws in the US.

Sherman Silver Purchase Act

252 1890 The Free Silver camp sprung up after the Crime of '73 [see: 241]. In 1878, they got the government to reverse the Crime of '73, but they really wanted virtually unlimited minting of silver into coins. On July 14, 1890, President Benjamin Harrison signed the new Sherman Silver Purchase Act, requiring the government to purchase 4.5 million ounces of silver per month, nearly the country's entire output.

The bill turned out to not benefit the Free Silver advocates. The quantity of silver to be purchased was measured in ounces, not dollars. This meant that a fall in silver price could undermine miners. Further, though the Silverites wanted to increase inflation, the government sought to avoid inflation and issued silver-redeemable Treasury notes. The notes were initially only redeemed in gold, limiting the physical amount of silver circulating.

There was another problem: the effects of Gresham's Law [see: 230]. Silver's market value was less than its official price, so it was used to pay government obligations while gold coins were hoarded. Silver coins returned to the Treasury as soon as they were sent out! Within three years, this issue boiled over into the Panic of 1893 [see: 257].

The 1889 cartoon "Bosses of the Senate" shows corporate lobbyists looking over Senators who are under their control. Industry names are printed on their shirts: steel beam trust, copper trust, Standard Oil trust, etc.

Baring Crisis

253 1890 On December 30, 1889, the Bank of England (BoE) sensed excessive euphoria in the air and raised its discount rate to a high of 6%. Over the previous two years, nearly £600 million (£62 billion in today's money) had been registered under joint-stock companies, with over 10% invested in Argentina. The speculation started to look excessive.

One British bank, Baring Brothers, was so well-established that it was once called the sixth European power (along with France, Britain, Russia, Austria, and Prussia). Yet, in early November 1890, cocky financial mismanagement (much of which was speculation in Argentina) forced Baring Brothers to declare bankruptcy.

The BoE was empowered to be lender of last resort. Together, with a group of private London bankers, including Nathaniel Rothschild, the Bank bailed out Baring Brothers. The group created a guaranteed fund that was to remain in place for three years. The fund totaled £6.5 million (£681 million today). About 15% was pledged by the BoE, nearly 8% was pledged by Mr. Rothschild, and the remainder originated from various other bankers.

Argentina went into a deep recession, and most banks closed by 1891. Argentina's GDP fell 11% that year, and the nation defaulted on £48 million of debt. The effects of Baring's failure also contributed to the 1893 Panic in the US.

First Trading Stamps

254 1891 Trading stamps are a marketing ploy using small paper stamps that are usually worth pennies each. They are given to customers for free when they make retail purchases, and customers can collect and use them for discounts at cooperating stores.

The first trading stamps were introduced in 1891 at Schuster's Department Store in Milwaukee, Wisconsin, United States. The first trading stamp company—a third-party company that prints the stamps, which are then issued by and redeemable at multiple different retailers—was founded in 1896, called the Sparing and Hutchinson Company. The popularity of these stamps greatly increased during the 1950s, by which point they were widely accepted at many supermarkets. They were involved in as many as 40-50% of all transactions. In 1957, trading stamps were a roughly half-billion-dollar industry. By 1960, nearly 40 million American families saved trading stamps.

Rising wholesale prices in the 1970s gave retailers an incentive to advertise reduced prices, instead of issuing stamps. Through the 1980s and 90s, loyalty programs, widely based on credit cards, became the norm. The last trading stamps company closed in 2008.

First Traveler's Checks

255 1891 Sometime between 1888 and 1891, American Express Company president J. C. Fargo took a trip to Europe and returned infuriated. He was only able to obtain cash with his letters of credit, an old type of credit guarantee, in a few major cities. Otherwise, he was out of luck. When he got back to the United States, he invented the traveler's check. American Express was not the first to attempt a system of globally accepted money for travelers. The railroad and travel company Thomas Cook issued "circular notes" in 1874. These notes were redeemable at certain locations overseas. However, they never took off.

The traveler's check is a money order—signed by an officer of the issuing company—for branches of the company to pay the amount of money indicated by the check. Unlike regular checks, traveler's checks are prepaid and printed with a denominated value, such that they can act as cash. They are printed on special paper and, after they are prepared by the issuer, are sent to agents around the world to sell on a massive scale. In 1964, 38,643 locations sold American Express checks. For a century, these types of checks made international transactions easier for travelers.

Banca Romana Scandal

256 1893 Between January 19 and 22, 1893, a handful of bankers of the Banca Romana of Italy were arrested. The Banca Romana, founded in 1833, operated in the Papal States and did all the things that banks do, including issuing banknotes. In the 1870s, it became one of a group of six banks to issue banknotes. In

1881, Bernardo Tanlongo was installed as governor of the bank.

Under Tanlongo, the Banca committed many offenses by taking advantage of Tanlongo's political connections. The bank made unsecured personal loans to politicians to help them win elections, printed two sets of banknotes reusing the same serial numbers, and allowed for 91% of the bank's total assets to be illiquid, just to name a few of the bank's wrongdoings.

In 1889, the bank was investigated, and major problems were found. However, Tanlongo covered up the bank's wrongdoings to hide the politicians' roles in the crisis and keep public trust in the bank. After the report of the investigation turned up in the hands of a political opponent, the scandal became public. People realized that the Italian banking system allowed for corruption, and the Italian government eventually increased banking regulation and created the Bank of Italy in August 1893.

Panic of 1893

257 1893 By the early 1890s, the Free Silver Movement was gaining momentum [see: 242]. This alarmed domestic and foreign investors, who feared that the US wasn't committed to its de facto gold standard. Investors began hoarding gold, and creditors started demanding repayment in gold or gold-backed obligations. Loans were called in, and banks became more reluctant to lend, helping trigger a rapid contraction in the banking system. Short-term interest rates skyrocketed, with some reaching as high as 74%, further exacerbating the credit crunch.

Financial instability in Europe led to a withdrawal of foreign investment from the US. This intensified the gold drain and deepened the Panic of 1893. US railroads were among the first casualties, followed by banks and other industries. Between 1892 and 1893, real gross national product fell by 4% and then 6% more from 1893 to 1894. By 1896-97, unemployment rose to between 12% and 14%.

The Depression of the 1890s had a major impact on American politics. Riots and labor strikes erupted as workers struggled under worsening economic conditions. The Panic also forced the US to recommit to gold, a move that culminated in the official switch to the gold standard in 1900.

Imperial Bank of China Founded

258 1897 In the 23rd year of Emperor Guangxu of the Qing Dynasty (1897), the Imperial Bank of China opened its doors in Shanghai. This bank makes it into the book as the first modern Chinese bank in history. China had seen a few banks of its own design [see: 210], but this one was the first modeled after Western banks.

Three things set the Imperial Bank apart from previous indigenous Chinese banks. First, the bank started with a capital of 4.9 million Qing yuan. Next, it was organized as a joint-stock company, which was less risky than the structure of the *piaohao* banks. Third, the bank pledged to operate on Western business practices and culture, which differed from traditional Chinese banks.

They put British banker Andrew Maitland in charge to carry this out. The bank was established by imperial edict and so was given many privileges. More important than the bank itself, though, was the role it played in beginning an era of modern, Western business in China.

Imperial Bank of China building, 1908.

US Adopts Gold Standard

259 1900 While much of Europe had officially adopted the gold standard by the 1870s, the United States took a little longer to come around. The US started moving away from silver in 1873 [see: 241] and adopted a de facto gold standard following the Resumption Act of 1875, which restored specie payments in gold that the Civil War had ended.

The move away from silver and toward gold was difficult, however. Farmers liked silver because they associated it with debt-lessening inflation, and they rallied behind the Free Silver Movement [see: 242]. Doubts about the US ability to maintain gold convertibility sparked the Panic of 1893, forcing the government to cement gold's dominance.

The debate over gold versus silver culminated in the 1896 presidential election. Democratic candidate William Jennings Bryan supported Free Silver. In his "Cross of

Gold" speech, Bryan argued that big business wanted to "crucify mankind [the poor] on a cross of gold." He was up against Republican William McKinley, who supported big business and the gold standard. McKinley won the election. In 1900, Congress passed the Gold Standard Act, formally committing the US to gold at a price of $20.67 per ounce. The US was now firmly a part of the international gold standard system.

This cartoon shows William Bryan holding a crown of thorns and a Cross of Gold while trampling the Bible, suggesting the exploitation of religious symbolism in his speeches.

Company Law in China

260 1904 A 1903 Qing Dynasty edict decreeing the need to create a commercial code for the country stated, "Of the many government functions, the most important is to facilitate commerce and help industry." The next year, the Company Law was enacted.

First, this law set China on a reasonable footing to start a modern economy. Leaders of the Qing Dynasty felt that the only way that China could compete with the West and Japan was to have legal corporate structures that would allow its companies to do business on the same level. The goal was not so much to compete internationally but for it to be Chinese companies that were selling goods to Chinese people.

Second, the Law attempted to remove China from under the thumb of the West and Japan. China needed a legal code up to "Western standards" to end extraterritoriality, a system whereby Westerners were granted immunity from the laws of a few Asian countries that were seen as barbaric. The United Kingdom agreed to end the system when it saw Chinese laws were fit to manage its citizens. Commerce was one of the areas that China felt it could step up its game in.

Chinese Concern About Western Influence

261 A key part of the financial development of the 19th century is the spread of Western financial technology. The many great cultures of the world were forced to adopt Western financial systems, which had advanced beyond the indigenous systems used everywhere else. During the 18th and 19th centuries, China's relationship with Western economic systems was complex. While China was initially cautious about Western financial influence, it also recognized the benefits of modernization and selectively integrated Western practices to strengthen its economy.

The Opium Wars and subsequent unequal treaties exposed China to foreign banking, currencies, and capitalist enterprises, disrupting parts of China's traditional system. The establishment of Western-controlled treaty ports and foreign banking institutions reduced China's economic autonomy—in some cases substantially—leading to anxieties about foreign control over trade and investment. People feared capitalism would primarily benefit Western powers and weaken China's own industries. Indeed, it often did.

However, despite these concerns, China also embraced many Western economic innovations. During the Self-Strengthening Movement of the 1860s to '90s, the Qing government and private Chinese entrepreneurs adopted Western-style banks, railways, and industrial enterprises. The creation of institutions such as the Imperial Bank of China reflected an eagerness to modernize financial structures. China adopted the Company Law, matching its business regulation with the West's.

Feng Guifen, a key proponent of the Self-Strengthening Movement, wrote, "When methods are faulty, we should reject them even though they are of ancient origins [e.g., traditional Chinese methods]; when methods are good, we should benefit from them even though they are those of the barbarians [Europeans]." By the early 20th century, Chinese reformers felt the need to adopt Western capitalism to compete globally, and by now, Asian growth has outdone the West in some respects.

First Central Bank in China

262 1905 Western-style banking solidified its presence in China after the founding of the Imperial Bank of China [see: 258]. The second Chinese bank to be founded on Western principles and the first central bank in China was the Great Qing Bank. Founded in 1905 and headquartered in Beijing, the bank was capitalized with 4 million tael up front and divided into 40,000 shares. Half were purchased by the Ministry of Revenue and the other half were sold to the public. Only Chinese people were allowed to invest—reselling stock to foreigners was prohibited. The bank's main business was issuing banknotes.

In 1908, the government renamed it Bank of Qing, and opened branches in every province to issue banknotes. The bank also exchanged money for the government, regulated prices, and cast silver ingots. In 1912, Bank of Qing was reorganized into the Bank of China under the new Republic of China.

1907 Financial Crisis

263 1907 On October 16, 1907, an attempt to corner the market on the United Copper Company stock forced its owner, Mr. Heinze, to resign. Heinze was a somewhat sleazy businessman who had made his fortune in speculative copper in Montana and was also president of the Mercantile National Bank.

A friend of Heinze was associated with the Knickerbocker Trust Company. On October 22, the day after the company's clearing house discontinued its services, there was a run on the trust, and it suspended operations. Knickerbocker, the third-largest trust company, was the first domino to fall. The next day, a run started on the Trust Company of North America (TCNA), the second-largest trust. The TCNA paid out $34 million in two weeks from its assets of $64 million.

Panic followed in New York City for a few days, soon spreading to regional cities. Many banks suspended payments and specie convertibility. The Dow Jones declined from 94 points in October 1906 to 55 in November 1907, making this one of the largest financial crises in US history. The market may have been unable to recover without the assistance of the financier J. P. Morgan [see: 265].

Other Causes of the 1907 Panic

264 1907 The reason that the 1907 Financial Panic happened may sound a little unconvincing. Can an attempt to corner the market on a moderately-important firm actually start one of the largest crises in history? While the cornering attempt is what set it off, other factors caused sufficient worry among investors to allow this panic to impart the considerable effects that it did.

In the 19th and early 20th centuries, between September and October of every year, many crops from the Midwest were transported to New York to be shipped to Europe. Because the money supply was rigid at the time—due, in part, to the lack of a central bank to adjust the supply as needed—the money needed to finance this transportation effort quite literally left New York City, raising short-term local interest rates in the City. Usually this was innocuous, as the higher local interest rates attracted money from Europe to fill the hole. However, over the previous year, European markets were in decline, and the Bank of England raised interest rates to keep money in Europe that otherwise would have gone to America. This meant the money supply in New York was uncomfortably tight in October 1907.

The recent expansion of trust companies also played a role. Between 1890 and 1910, trust companies grew 244% to $1.3 billion. By contrast, national banks grew 97%, all together worth $1.8 billion. While national banks were required to keep 25% reserves, trusts were only required 15%, with only 5% in the vault. Though they started as conservative institutions, by 1907, trusts did almost everything regular banks did but had a higher proportion of collateralized loans, which were considered risky.

Both of these circumstances—tight monetary supply and highly-leveraged trust companies—made New York finance risky in 1907, allowing a relatively minor incident to explode into a large crisis.

A Thanksgiving cartoon printed a month after the 1907 Panic subsided

J. P. Morgan Bails Out New York Banks

265 1907 The Financial Crisis of 1907 [see: 263] proved much larger than the limited amount of government intervention could handle. J. P. Morgan was called on to assist.

New York City lacked the cash to make its payroll, so Morgan and his friends bought $30 million in city bonds. Morgan also raised $25 million to loan to brokerage firms. Then, he got all of New York's bankers into his library. He put the commercial bankers in the east wing and the trust company presidents in the west wing, locked the doors, and left them to sort things out.

To save Moore & Schley, New York's largest investment firm, Morgan devised a monopolistic scheme. Morgan's company, US Steel, would buy Moore & Schley's Tennessee Coal. The trust company presidents would then give a $25 million bailout to smaller firms. While everyone finally agreed at 4:30 in the morning, Morgan knew the merger would violate the Sherman Antitrust Act. In order to go ahead with the merger, Morgan needed permission from President Theodore Roosevelt before the market opened the next morning. Two bankers in Washington got Roosevelt's agreement and rushed back to New York to share the news five minutes before the market opened at 10 am. The panic was averted, and Morgan briefly became a celebrity before his fame turned to suspicion that contributed to his death [see: 270].

The Rise of J. P. Morgan

266 mid-19th c. John Pierpont Morgan was born in 1837 in Hartford, Connecticut, to a wealthy family. He was educated in the arts, fluent in French and German, and even went to college in Europe. Morgan was born a businessman. At 12 years old, he put on a show for his friends and family called "A Grand Diorama of the Landing of Columbus." He charged for tickets and then wrote up a balance sheet reckoning the costs of the entire affair. By 15, he kept personal account books, listing his purchases and their prices.

Morgan was a key influencer in the world of late 19th century big business, controlling a large part of the American economy. He was a genius of corporate consolidations, often gobbling up smaller companies to make larger and more efficient ones. Morgan assembled General Electric, International Harvester, and U.S. Steel. He also bought up small railroads and reorganized them to maximize profit. By 1902, he controlled about one-sixth of all railroads in the US.

Morgan was also an avid collector of art. At the time, the great art of the West was located in Europe, while the United States had few works of note. Morgan looked to even things out and brought millions of dollars worth of art back home. Though in his work life he focused on mechanization and industrialization, he almost exclusively collected landscapes and narrative scenes of a long-gone world.

Morgan was a Gilded Age industrialist, exploiting the means of business available to him. He sits with the greats of Gilded Age business—with John D. Rockefeller and Andrew Carnegie. But like Rockefeller and Carnegie, the public distrusted—even despised—Morgan. To many, he was selfish and greedy, hurting the little guys for his personal gain. He retired to Europe in his later years. After a series of silent strokes, he died in his sleep in Rome in March 1913.

This 1903 cartoon shows J. P. Morgan and other industrialists caricatured as army men on Napoleon's retreat from Russia marching on horseback. Foot soldiers march in the distance carrying a flag of the "Army of Stock Holders."

Dollar Diplomacy

267 1909 How much influence the government should have in private financial affairs and how governments should use their financial status for political leverage overseas are debatable topics. Frederic Howe was a progressive reformer and, according to the Oxford English Dictionary, the first man to use the term "big business." Howe referred to Dollar Diplomacy as "the conversion of the State Department and Army and Navy into collection and insurance agencies for Wall Street interests."

Dollar Diplomacy was a policy created by President William Howard Taft and was designed to further American interests in Latin America and Asia using commercial rather than military power. This has been termed by some as a sort of "financial imperialism" and by others as both an idealistic and humanitarian way of promoting commercial aims and maintaining peace overseas.

Taft used the Department of State as a field agent for commerce. In one instance, the Department of State helped get a contract with Argentina in 1910 to build battleships and railroad equipment. In 1911, Taft reported a $300 million increase in exports over the previous years and $200 million more in 1912. The Taft administration attempted this policy in China, too, which failed. Dollar Diplomacy ended under President Woodrow Wilson.

Chosen Bank Set Up in Korea

268 1911 Japan's colonization of Korea in 1910 was done largely for economic purposes and as a means of expanding further into Manchuria and the rest of China. While European colonies were given currency boards [see: 225], Korea got its own more complex central bank, which remained in place until 1950 after its independence.

The Bank of Chosen was founded under the Bank of Korea Act of 1911. The bank was established as a joint-stock company with a capitalization of 10 million won. The Japanese government took 30% of the equity. Japanese citizens also traded shares, though the bank was under the control of the governor-general of Korea in practice.

As a central bank, it made economic policy, printed banknotes, and managed foreign transactions. It also acted as a private for-profit bank. One of the bank's biggest jobs was assisting Japan's expansion, and this may be why a central bank organization more complex than a currency board was needed. Operations in Korea only accounted for about 22% of Chosen Bank's total operations, compared with 37% in China and 24% in Manchuria.

Japan Takes Over the Korean Economy

269 1910s A satirical comic from 1887 depicts a Chinese and a Japanese man sitting beside a river trying to catch a fish labeled Korea. A Russian man stands angrily on a bridge over the river, having put his fishing rod down.

In the end, Japan caught the fish. Japan had a virtual monopoly of Korean trade since 1876, keeping China and Russia off the peninsula. By 1884, more than half of Korean imports were Japanese products, and 90% of its exports were sold to Japan.

Large economic changes came when Japan annexed Korea in 1910. Prior to this, Korea created a unified coinage system for the peninsula but otherwise did little in the way of financial modernization. Japan established a central bank in Korea and started making loans to Japanese businesses. Japan built roads and railroads for better transportation and streamlined the property ownership system. This increased Korean rice production, upon which Japan relied heavily.

Postmen of the Japanese resident-general of Korea

One economist noted that much of the development did not actually benefit Koreans, calling the changes "non-developing development." Even so, the changes were fast-paced, as annual GDP growth reached 5.4%. Agricultural and industrial production increased by 85% and 80% respectively. These developments set Korea up for its economic success in the later 20th century.

Pujo Hearings

270 1911 In the aftermath of the 1907 Panic, a conspiracy theory emerged: there existed a group of elite bankers known as the "Money Trust." Through interlocking agreements and board positions, the Money Trust, it was said, controlled giant swaths of US industry and banking with unparalleled power. In 1911, a Congressional hearing was called to investigate. The Committee analyzed financial data from 1905-12 and interviewed the Money Trust's three supposed kingpins: J. P. Morgan, James Stillman, and George Baker. These three men, however, were all in their 60s or 70s and spent most of their time in Europe collecting art—a sport not conducive to financial domination.

The Committee published its findings in 1913. It found that the Money Trust had connections with 341 directors in 112 corporations and a capitalization of $22.2 billion (nearly $700 billion today). The report went on to break down how much control the Money Trust had in each of the selected financial and non-financial industries. The chief attorney of the committee, Samuel Untermyer, thought the hearings painted Wall Street as secretly plotting for its gain, when in reality structural change was needed. The hearings motivated the passage of the Clayton Antitrust Act as well as the establishment of the Federal Trade Commission and the Federal Reserve.

Currency Boards in Africa

271 1912 The British Empire created currency boards for its African colonies to provide them with a stable money supply [see: 226]. The West, East, and Central African Currency Boards were established between 1912 and 1919, each covering specific portions of the Africa continent. The local currencies that were issued were fixed to the Pound Sterling or sterling-denominated assets at par, a common trait of currency boards. The boards had full control over most aspects of the currency and were organized such that colonial governments got a share of the profit of currency issue. The East African Currency Board replaced the Indian rupee, which was in wide use in the territory, with the East Africa rupee.

While these boards reliably provided money to the colonies, they had one key problem: they allowed the balance of payments to determine the money supply. That is, since there is no central bank increasing and decreasing the money supply as needed, the inflow and outflow of money in the country determines the money supply. After the colonies gained independence, they eventually established their own central banks.

VII

Money in a Modern World:
1910s – 1971

The period this chapter covers was one of remarkable change in the financial sector. By the end of the 19th century, most countries switched to using the gold standard, with the United States finally joining in 1900. By the end of this period, the gold standard was more or less forgotten. In 1913, the Federal Reserve was founded, which put an end to the turbulence of the 19th century. Turbulence came back in 1929, however, with the stock market crash and the beginning of the Great Depression, which sent waves of economic destruction across the world. From then on, the world changed. Every industry expanded. Increased materialism and personal consumption of the 20th century created massive economic expansion. To reap the benefits of and facilitate this increased production, financial systems advanced.

After World War II, 44 countries introduced the Bretton Woods system, making the US dollar the central reserve currency and increasing the US' importance in the world economy. This system was based on the gold standard, which helped keep prices stable.

The credit card was invented in the 1940s, making purchasing easier. The banking sector expanded, facilitating easier transfers of money and more personal debt. Innovations in computing allowed stock markets to speed up. The increasingly global economy created more opportunities for businesses to expand. The US, by this point, established itself as the world center of business and brought more money into the country, further boosting it as a world power.

Even with the increased importance of money, which one might think would result in more financial shenanigans and instability, central banks and lawmakers did an effective job of regulating the industry. After the 1929 market crash, the US created the Securities and Exchange Commission and passed regulations such as the

Glass-Steagall Act and the Truth in Lending Act. A period of remarkable financial stability followed the Great Depression. In fact, there were only two or three financial crises during this period. But the financial sector had become well-established enough by this point that crises did not have major implications in the long run. This was a sharp contrast to the unstable 19th century when a bank collapse could easily take down the entire system for months, with large sums of money simply disappearing. The most major disruptions in this period were caused by World War I and II, and even these crises were solved efficiently.

During this period, people started measuring the economy and financial system. The government first calculated the Gross National Product, along with information about consumer prices, jobs, and more. People from all walks of life started scrutinizing these numbers more closely.

Money, in general, became easier to come by for everyone, and a substantial increase in the standard of living followed. This period was one of innovation and expansion, which, by the next chapter, turned in some ways into over-expansion. The 20th century was markedly different from the 19th in terms of culture and living, and naturally the history of money changed, too, in this period.

Federal Reserve Founded

272 1913 Central banks proliferated around the Western world, but the US had no central bank since the SBUS [see: 212]. The lack of a central bank permitted the financial instability that characterized the 19th century, which culminated in the crisis of 1907 when J. P. Morgan acted as central banker [see: 265]. The country needed a real central bank.

Senator Nelson Aldrich, after taking a tour of successful European central banks, recommended that the US found one in 1912. His plan, however, received little traction, partly because of Aldrich's connections with some of the wealthy bankers who were attacked in the Pujo Hearings. In June 1913, the new President Wilson proposed the Federal Reserve Act to Congress, a bill based on the Aldrich plan but with some modifications.

The Act was controversial but passed in the House with 287–85 votes in favor. A few months later (after some talk of writing a whole new act for a central bank), the Senate finally approved the Federal Reserve Act, 54–34. Wilson signed the bill the same day, and the Fed began operations 11 months later.

How the Fed Works

273 20th c. The Fed, the United States' central bank, is a combination of private and public. There are three main parts of the Fed: the regional reserve banks, the Board of Governors, and the Federal Open Market Committee. Founded in 1913, the Fed was designed as a decentralized system. There are 12 Reserve Banks, which each operate in specific regions of the US. They are intended to operate in a way that is best for their respective regions. For example, each Regional Bank can set its own discount rate for its region. However, as markets have come to be better integrated, coordination is more important, and today the discount rate never differs between branches.

The Fed is run in Washington, D.C., by seven members of the Board of Governors. The Board sets nationwide policy and oversees the regional banks. It appoints the regional Reserve Banks' chairs and deputy-chairs. Each regional branch also has its own board. A key job of the Board of Governors is to change the interest rate and reserve requirement ratio [see: 165]. The Federal Open Market Committee, made up of 12 members, seven of whom are from the Board of Governors, makes and implements the Fed's monetary policy through open-market operations.

The Federal Reserve operates like a private company. It is not funded by the government but rather by profit it makes on fees for use of its services and interest on securities it owns. Net earnings are transferred to the Treasury. The Fed manages a giant amount of money and produces a large profit. After the 2008 financial crisis, the Fed increased its balance sheet by $2.3 trillion to $4.4 trillion. By 2022, it hit a maximum of $8.9 trillion. This means that, between 2011 and 2020, the Fed sent nearly $100 billion yearly to the Treasury.

US Establishes Permanent Income Tax

274 1913 In the late 19th century, industrial and technological innovation was making Americans wealthier. However, the country had a state-by-state patchwork of taxation systems that neither effectively nor fairly captured this newly-made money. This surge in innovation also created a new class of wealthy elites who were unpopular among the general public. The Pujo Hearings, antitrust acts, and a new federal income tax were seen as a way to keep the wealthy in check. Before the income tax, the federal government historically raised money with tariffs on imports.

Theodore Roosevelt, a Republican, publicly endorsed a federal income tax in 1906, but pushing new legislation also became of key interest to the Democratic Party. A Constitutional amendment would be needed to levy a federal income tax. The amendment was proposed in 1909. Many of the Republican legislators who were opposed to the amendment lost their seats in the 1912 election, and the amendment was ratified in 1913.

The new income taxation scheme only affected the wealthy, as most Americans did not make enough money to owe taxes. Indeed, less than 1% of the entire US population had to pay any federal income tax at first. Even in the northeast, the wealthiest part of the country, the income tax affected less than 5% of people.

World War I Ends Gold Standard

275 1914 The assassination of Archduke Ferdinand in 1914 sparked World War I—the war that ended the classical gold standard, the period from the 1870s to 1914 when many countries used the gold standard. (To be sure, the war had some other effects as well). All European countries found that they could not raise the amount of additional money needed to fight the War while maintaining the gold standard. Selling gold reserves, borrowing from quickly shrinking international financial markets, and collecting revenues from national taxation also proved to be insufficient to get the money countries needed.

Austria-Hungary, France, Germany, and Russia were among the first to suspend the gold standard and start printing paper money in large volumes. The United States effectively ended the gold standard by setting an embargo on US gold exports in order to stop the persistent outflow of gold to the United Kingdom for the purpose of arbitrage. The end of the gold standard strained markets and, after the War's end, countries wanted to return to the gold standard. However, the massive inflation that the War created complicated efforts. Through the late 1910s and '20s, countries tried to balance the economy—sometimes through forced recessions—to make the gold standard possible again.

Inflation Soars During World War I

276 1910s International inflation rates during and after World War I were some of the highest war-related bouts of price increases in history. The inflation was caused by both internal and external factors. Internally, many countries—France most notably—ran large budget deficits to finance the Great War. In 1913, France's debt-to-GDP ratio was 66.3%. By 1920, debt rose to 185.5%. The UK had a similar experience during this time: the debt-to-GDP ratio rose from 25% to 130%.

Externally, the war created uncertainty around international currency exchange rates, foreign and domestic debt repayments, and countries' borders. This instability made fully functional markets impossible to sustain. Germany's war-related reparation payments were another source of uncertainty. The Treaty of Versailles formally ended the War in 1919 and obliged Germany to pay for some of the damages, while also clearly stating that Germany simply didn't have the resources to pay. France wanted 226 billion marks ($94 billion). Germany offered 50 billion marks but finally agreed to pay 123 billion marks.

The scarcity of food, domestic supplies, and employment opportunities drove up prices across all economies. The highest rate of inflation was in Poland, of 66.4% yearly from 1914 to 1918. Hungary, Italy, and France faced 53.7%, 36.3%, and 30% inflation, respectively.

An armed blockade during the Paris Commune

USSR Takes Apart Banking System

277 1917 When the Bolsheviks started vying for power in Russia in the early 20th century, they thought a single national bank was a necessary tool for promoting their political ideals and keeping their revolution alive. Creating a single central bank was not a new idea in Russia. Unconnected from communism, Russians had been discussing the idea for a while. But Russian communists specifically looked back at the Paris Commune uprising of the 1870s. They saw that the Parisian communists failed to seize the banks, leaving their opponents with plenty of financial power with which to stop the spread of communism.

Immediately after the Bolsheviks seized power in October 1917, they effectively sacked all commercial bank employees and laid claim to all the gold in the country's vaults. Nationalization of the banking system became official as of December 14, 1917, when the People's Bank, later called Gosbank, was put in charge of all banking operations [see: 283]. All financial transactions ran through the Gosbank, and the Gosbank controlled the entire country's banking system. The central bank also regulated both company profits and the trade of precious metals. The Bolsheviks' next step was to summarily default on all "pre-revolutionary" debt.

Soviets Default on Debt

278 1918 Concerning the art of making loans, the banker J. P. Morgan famously said, "A man I do not trust could not get money from me on all the bonds in Christendom." Indeed, trust is sacred to lending. Defaulting on debt is the best way to break trust. Bolshevik-controlled Russia evidently was not too concerned about being trusted, though.

When the Bolsheviks overthrew the provisional Russian government in October 1917, Russian debt amounted to 13.2 billion rubles, most of which was held by France, the United Kingdom, United States, and Belgium. About 27% of the 13.2 billion owed were pre-war debts, and 48% were labeled as wartime loans. In early 1918, the Russian government declared that it would not service foreign debt, effectively repudiating it or defaulting. The Russian government also seized foreign assets located in Russia.

The default was a surprise. France was especially hurt. France called for the West to not recognize Russia or make any more loans to it. Sweden and the UK joined France in requesting that all gold shipments in and out of Russia be seized and that all payments involving gold be canceled. Russia's repudiation effectively cut her off financially from the rest of the world.

Europe Tries for Post-War Gold Standard

279 1918–'20s While the Great War ended the classical gold standard out of necessity, none of the belligerents actually wanted to end it. After the war's end, European countries wanted to return to the standard but could not do so easily. The difficulty re-enacting it stemmed from significant inflation, continuing wartime price controls, and simply not having enough gold. England was the first to try to return to the gold standard. However, overall prices had increased 115% during WWI and increased 41% more after the war as economic restrictions were relaxed. England was waiting for inflation to subside and its sovereign sterling to reach its pre-war exchange rate relative to the dollar. Conditions were finally right in 1925, and after a forced recession, England successfully rejoined the standard.

Thirty-nine countries either followed suit in reinstating the gold standard to back their sovereign currencies, or at least stabilized their currencies against the US dollar, helping mostly establish a de facto gold standard. Even so, markets remained uneasy through the late '20s. The resumed standard did not last long, as England abandoned it in 1931, and the rest of the world followed suit by the end of WWII [see: 297; 313].

A woman holds a flag for the gold standard while wearing a sign reading "I am starving."

Fedwire Founded

280 1918 Fedwire was founded to fix a large problem in financial transactions in the past: different exchange rates for gold that often existed between different regions within the US. This was mostly dictated by variation in the cost of shipping gold or cash to different parts of the country. The newly founded Federal Reserve eliminated this problem in 1918 by establishing a Morse code-based system to transfer money domestically. The system was named Fedwire and connected the 12 regional Fed banks, the Treasury, and all private banks in one system.

As communication technology became more advanced, the Fedwire system became more sophisticated. Standardization became increasingly important with the legalization of interstate banking, and automated computers were implemented as early as the 1960s. In recent years, the system started operating over the internet. Today, Fedwire only operates in the US, processing $1.6 quadrillion in 2022—about $4.2 trillion per day. This system not only fixes exchange rate problems. It also provides banks with a system to transfer large sums of money when, for example, one bank needs to help another bank resolve a short-term liquidity problem.

Ponzi Invents Ponzi Scheme

281 1919 Charles Ponzi was born in Parma, Italy, in 1883, and immigrated to the United States in the early 1900s. He worked many odd jobs before inventing the investment strategy that made him (in) famous: the Ponzi Scheme. In 1919, he started the Securities Exchange Company in Boston, which promised a 50% rate of return in only 45 days, or 100% in merely six months. He claimed he was participating in arbitrage involving International Postal Reply coupons, buying them cheaply in countries with favorable exchange rates and selling them at a profit in countries with higher exchange rates. Within six months, Ponzi had 20,000 investors and was managing $10 million. At the height of his operation, he employed 16 clerks and had a daily cash flow of $250,000.

After six years, investigators found that no more than $500,000 had actually been used on the Postal Reply stamps. Ponzi had engaged in what became known as a Ponzi Scheme. Instead of investing people's money in the stamps, he paid old investors fictitious gains with money entrusted to him by new investors. Investigators found he had $7 million of liabilities and only $4 million of assets. He was sentenced to jail but subsequently escaped. He was finally deported to Italy in 1934 and died poor in Rio de Janeiro in 1949.

DON'T BE
PONZIED

The Literary Digest recently quoted one of their numerous exchanges as saying "A Fool and His Money are soon Ponzied." Don't let the representatives of some Get-Rich-Quick firm or a Fly-By-Night Company get your hard-earned money.

SAFETY HAS ALWAYS BEEN THE FIRST CONSIDERATION in the conduct of this Bank. Deposit your savings here and they will receive the protection of the Mutual Savings Bank Law of the State of Washington — the strictest savings bank law in the country.

One Dollar will open an Account

Washington Mutual Savings Bank

810 SECOND AVENUE
Resources $12,600,000.00
Established 31 Years

A 1920 advertisement warning people about Ponzi schemes and advising they keep their money safe at Washington Mutual Savings Bank.

Depression of 1920–21

282 1920–21 Between January 1920 and March 1921, industrial production in the US dropped by 32.5% for a few reasons after the Great War. This was the largest drop in American economic history, save for the Great Depression. Unemployment jumped from 1.4–3% in 1919 to about 5% in 1920, and then to 8–11%. Eventually, unemployment fell to a historically normal 2–5% in 1923 and 1924.

In addition to using the newly established income tax system [see: 274] to fund the Great War, the United States relied on borrowing and expansionary monetary policy. With the War's end, however, expansionary policy had to end, but the transition was made too quickly. The Wilson administration cut monthly spending by 75% within a few months, balancing the federal budget by November 1919. The Fed raised the discount rate by 2.4 percentage-points over only eight months. These dramatic changes put the US into the Depression of 1920-21.

President Warren Harding chose to do essentially the opposite of what today's economists would think a prudent solution to the crisis. He took a laissez-faire approach. Harding reduced the national debt and cut the federal budget and federal taxes. He also told the Fed to sit back and relax. Surprisingly, this contractionary approach worked for debated reasons, and the recession ended by the middle of 1921.

Gosbank Founded

283 1921 After the nationalization of all banks in Russia, all previously private business operations were put in the hands of the State Bank, later renamed the People's Bank. However, Lenin became disillusioned with the People's Bank as the Soviet economy started to break down immediately after the country was founded. In January 1920, as the Russian Civil War raged on, the People's Bank was liquidated, and most of its functions were moved to the People's Commissariat of Finance. Additionally, Russian leaders thought that True Communism—the point at which the government dissolves and people live in utopian bliss—was right around the corner, and thus, there would soon be no need for a central bank at all. This prediction proved to be untrue.

In October 1921, a new State Bank of the Russian Socialist Republic was founded. After the Civil War ended in 1923, it was renamed Gosbank (meaning State Bank of the USSR). The Gosbank became the only bank in the country until the fall of the USSR in 1991, and it took care of all the financial work that otherwise would have fallen into the hands of the commercial system.

Consumer Price Index Published

284 1921 Quantifying something gives it a certain kind of legitimacy. Inflation has always existed, but it is much harder to talk about it without using the correct terminology and measurements. The Consumer Price Index (CPI) is one of the most widely used indexes to measure inflation in the United States. Similar indexes exist internationally.

The predecessor to CPI was created when the US had a large federal budget surplus at the end of the 19th century. The government cut the surplus by reducing tariffs—reducing the amount of money brought it. After the tariff law was changed, the Bureau of Labor Statistics (BLS) conducted a study on prices and cost of living between 1888 and 1890. Various other studies were conducted over the next few decades. In 1913, the BLS came up with the CPI and began using it in reports about price changes published annually starting in 1921.

Today, thousands of organizations and contractual agreements rely on the CPI. Gaining access to the information even a day early would give someone such a large advantage that, in the weeks before the data is published, the janitors in the BLS office are not even allowed to empty the trash cans in case a BLS employee threw away confidential papers.

How Economic Indicators Mislead You

285 The Consumer Price Index works by tracking the change in price of a basket of goods. The goods in the basket represent the things people buy in general. Some goods in the basket get more expensive over time, and some goods get less expensive, but the overall change in the price of goods in the basket represents the change in amount a consumer would spend in normal life. However, the CPI measurement has a key problem. The CPI is intended to measure the change over time of cost of living. The cost of living is the price a person must pay to maintain an equal level of material satisfaction. The change in price of maintaining an equal level of satisfaction may not follow the change in price of goods overall, however. This is for two reasons.

The first reason is substitution bias. When certain products get more expensive, people may start using cheaper substitutes. If the CPI continues to track the more expensive good, then it will show that the cost of living is rising. Using the substitute, however, likely will not result in a lower level of material satisfaction, but it will cost less. This means that the CPI will increase but the actual cost of living—of maintaining an equal quality of life—won't change. This problem arises when the basket of goods that the CPI is based on does not update for changes in what people actually buy. Substitution bias often overstates the cost of living.

The second way CPI can be misleading is when products improve. If a new bicycle is built with stronger metal and costs more, it wouldn't be accurate to say that the increased price is the result of inflation. Most goods were more expensive before the advent of mass production in the Industrial Revolution and recent outsourcing. This is also why it is so difficult to measure historical prices and create accurate inflation statistics for the past.

Hyperinflation Crisis in Germany

286 1923 War is an expensive endeavor—and it was particularly expensive for 1914 Germany, which had a weak taxation system. Because it could not raise enough tax revenue, Germany's government relied on borrowing to finance World War I, which created massive inflation. Germany thought that it could easily pay off the debt with the reparations it expected to demand after it won the war. However, Germany lost the war and was the one paying the reparations.

Employment increased, accompanied by quick inflation, during the few years after the end of the Great War. Between April and September of 1922, 99% of German trade union members were employed. Quick inflation turned to hyperinflation in early 1923. On November 12, 1923, one US dollar was worth 630 billion paper German marks. Eight days later, that number rose to 4.2 trillion. Trade union employment plummeted to 76.6%. Industry was decimated. That year, real national income in Germany was only 65% of the 1913 level.

By the end of 1923, anti-inflation measures, including creating a new currency, helped alleviate hyperinflation. Yet, the social damage was done. Hyperinflation pummeled the working class, allowing the Nazi party to gain recognition.

A Berlin banker counts stacks of hyperinflated German banknotes.

More Buying on the Margins

287 1920s In the 1920s, buying on margin—using leveraging to make larger investments—became pervasive in US stock markets. In the beginning of the 20th century, margin rates were usually between 20–30%, meaning that 70–80% of a stock's price would be paid for by a lender. If a stock bought on the margin loses value, the lender will force the investor to either put up more cash or sell the stock to repay the loan.

Buying on the margin was the biggest form of credit expansion leading up to the 1929 market crash. At the beginning of October 1929, investors had about $22 billion in margin loans. A government report wrote: "Excited by the vision of quick profits, [investors] assumed margin positions which they had no adequate resources to protect." Margins allowed investors to make more high-risk, high-reward bets.

Margin trading both contributed to the stock market bubble and created the risky market dynamics that led to the 1929 crash. Because a downturn in the market forces traders to sell their stocks to pay their margin contracts, margin trading can turn even a small dip in the stock market into a large downward spiral. In 1929, that is exactly what happened.

Production of cars like this Ford Model T expanded during the 1920s economic boom in the United States and Western world.

1920s Bubble Starts

288 1928 In 1922, the Dow Jones was at about 90 points. Over the next decade, new technologies spread, like mass-market automobiles, talking movies, AM radio, and electricity. The US' GNP growth was 4.2% yearly. The unemployment hovered between 1–2% for the entire decade. Industrialization spread, as the amount of farmworkers halved. More and more companies started IPO-ing. Consumer credit expanded, along with options to buy stocks on margin. Companies operated more efficiently. The market could not process such quick changes, and as a result, the economy started to overheat.

It is said that the 1920s bubble officially began on March 5, 1928—a Monday. RCA and General Motors were doing particularly well that day, and the Dow Jones was up to 204 points. Confidence was good across the markets. Economist Irving Fisher wrote, "The market went up principally because of sound, justified expectations of earnings, and only partly because of unreasoning and unintelligent mania for buying."

Economic expansion continued, while the Fed raised interest rates only modestly. By January 1929, the Dow hit 307 points as what became euphoria fully set in. In September, the Dow teetered at a record high of 381 before history's largest financial crisis started.

October 24: Black Thursday

289 1929 On Thursday, October 24, 1929, the bell rang in the New York Stock Exchange as usual to start the day of trading. The Dow Jones opened at 305.85 points. The stock market had been showing weakness since September, with the Dow falling from a high of 381 points, but this Thursday opened calmly. On the previous day, $4 billion was lost in the market. Were it not for the 24th, the 23rd of October would presumably be remembered as Black Wednesday.

Black Thursday's chaos began at 11 a.m. Stocks started falling. Almost every member of the Exchange was on the floor, with thousands of people anxiously crowded outside and around the Wall Street area. There were way more sellers than buyers. The ticker could not keep up. By 1:30 p.m., the ticker was 110 minutes late; by 2:30 p.m., it was 147 minutes late. The Dow hit a low of 272—a 9% decline in a few hours—at which point traders met at the J. P. Morgan house to try to do something. They helped somewhat. By the day's end, the Dow closed at 299 points—a loss of only 1.78% over the day—having processed a record-high 13 million orders. The tickers produced the final quote at 7:08 p.m., over four hours late. The 1929 Stock Market Crash had started.

Private Bankers Attempt to Bail out Market

290 1929 On October 24, known as Black Thursday, American stock exchanges tumbled after having shown weakness for the past month. According to Thomas Lamont, a prominent banker and senior partner at J. P. Morgan & Co., however, this was just a technical glitch arising from a very temporary lack of buyers. Investors had nothing to be worried about, he told the public. Even though Lamont claimed it was only a technical glitch, he, along with Charles Mitchell, Allan Wiggin, William Potter, and Seward Prosser, partners of some of the country's largest banks, must have been pretty worried.

The five bankers met at J. P. Morgan & Co. headquarters at noon on the 24th. Their goal was to bail out the market like J. P. Morgan had in 1907 [see: 265]. The group gave money to Richard Whitney, the brother of the vice-president of the NYSE, and told him to start buying stock. His first bid was for $2.05 million of U.S. Steel, at 15 points above the market value. Whitney's purchases soothed the market, and it soon started to recover. But the bail-out could not account for the underlying financial issues and ultimately did not stop the ensuing crisis.

October 29: Black Tuesday

291 1929 After Black Thursday, the markets briefly calmed Friday and over the weekend. However, the chaos soon returned. Over nine million trades were made on Monday, October 28. On Black Tuesday, the worst day of the crisis, that number reached 16.4 million. A large increase in traffic was felt on telephone and telegraph lines, as bankers and retail investors from around the United States and rest of the world desperately tried to keep tabs on their portfolios. Traffic over transatlantic lines increased by 100%, with domestic telegraph messages increasing by 300%. Some men sat in their offices anxiously watching spools of ticker tape unwind; others gathered around the stock exchange in New York, as sightseers of the historic event. One New York Times article criticized those who believed that "gambling on a margin was a better order of things than patient industry and legitimate earnings."

Recounting the previous week, the market became shaky on October 21, lost 31 points on the 23rd, 12 on the 24th, 49 on Monday the 28th, and now lost 43 more points this Tuesday. The NYSE governor decided not to halt trading. Black Tuesday may have been the worst day of the crisis, but it was not the end of the decline.

Men crowding in Wall Street on October 24, 1929

Margin Calls

292 **1929** With the onset of the 1929 crash, the New York Times wrote, "About the busiest persons in brokerage offices in the last few days have been the margin clerks." This likely was not meant literally but points to how margins trading impacted the 1929 market crash. With stock values declining, brokers hastily sent out margin calls requiring the liquidation of securities bought on the margin. Sent out overnight, margin calls may have contributed to much of the mania consuming the trading floor and the 1.6 million orders made in the first half hour of trading on Black Thursday.

Margin calls may have impacted the market more severely than the underlying factors that actually started the panic. Margin requirements were raised right before the crisis started, which was supposed to make the market safer. However, the raise instead made investors more susceptible to margin calls. The Dow declined by 2.8% on the average day between September 16 and November 14, a period when many margin calls and other forced sales were recorded. Margin calls went out on seven of the worst 10 days after Black Thursday.

Herbert Hoover Fails to Stop Great Depression

293 1929–30 Hoover had been president for only seven months when the market crashed in 1929. A political novice, he rose through the government ranks by appointments, not by elections. His response to the crisis turned him from the winner of a landslide victory in 1928 to one of the most disliked presidents in American history.

Hoover limited federal government intervention, advocating instead for locally administered aid. He supported promoting economic recovery through federal funds carefully allocated to assist banks, railroads, and influential companies. Hoover strongly opposed government hand-outs, worrying they would create government debt and hurt the entrepreneurial spirit of the country needed to prompt a vigorous recovery.

The public held high expectations of Hoover when he entered office, given his past accomplishments. Hoover, however, was a poor speaker. While Hoover stressed the importance of confidence-inducing rhetoric to help resolve the crisis, he was unable to give it. He shied away from public speaking, worrying he would just make things worse. This allowed his opponents to openly criticize him, painting him as a failure at solving people's problems. One analyst wrote, "No president had ever made his mistake so thoroughly advertised as Hoover."

Great Depression Hits

294 1930 The market crash of 1929 and the Great Depression are not the same thing, and their causal connection is debated. The market crashed in October, but other economic metrics suggest that the start of a depression was actually in August of 1929. The depression ended by the late '30s, while the stock market did not recover until the 1950s.

One opinion claims that the loss of personal wealth due to the 1929 market crash created heightened income insecurity and disincentivized spending, turning the crash into the Great Depression, the worst period in American economic history. Unemployment rose to an all-time high of nearly 25% in 1933. GDP declined from $104 billion to $57 billion between 1929 and 1933. The S&P composite price index fell from a base level of 100 in 1929, to only 15 in 1932.

The Depression also had non-economic effects that affected people's everyday life. Life expectancy started declining in 1933 and troughed in 1937. Marriage rates in Niagara Falls, New York, nearly halved, but divorce rates also declined. Homelessness increased, as people moved into "Hoovervilles," living in shelters constructed of wood scraps and repurposed trash. Hollywood boomed as people turned to movies to escape their dreary reality.

The 1929 Crash and the Great Depression: Causal or Coincidence?

295 Though it is taken to be the cause among non-experts, the 1929 stock market crash was not in fact the lone cause of the Great Depression. A depression had started a few months before the market crash and ended within a few years. However, the stock market did not rebound to its original levels until the mid '50s. The start of the Great Depression has many plausible causes, some of which give more credit to the crash than others.

The Smoot-Hawley Act of 1930 raised import tariffs on all US trading partners. These trading partners then raised tariffs against the US, reducing the supply of goods available in the US and tax revenue generated from tariffs. President Hoover, in trying to balance the federal budget, refused to lower domestic taxes. He did not try to run a deficit to boost demand.

Excess capacity for production was built up through the 1920s. That is, not only did the stock market expand into a bubble, the real economy did as well. There was an estimated 17% excess capacity, some of which was Great War military equipment.

Some economists focus on the international monetary system. Commodity producers were unable to sell enough due to unfavorable terms of trade and protectionism, meaning that manufacturers using those commodities were in a fragile position. Some even say that the Depression in the US was triggered by crashes in other countries, such as the 1931 German crisis.

The economist Kindleberger wrote that a country in depression needs to lend more and promote international investment to stop the crisis from spreading. The Great War weakened the UK, making it unable to do so, and the United States did not fill the gap. Another perspective blames the US government for letting the money supply decline too much.

Some economists do primarily blame the market crash, which contributed to uncertainty about the economy. The crash motivated many to keep their money under the mattress and not invest it. Additionally, the crash simply reduced people's wealth enough to severely cut household consumption. Most likely, all of these factors conspired to start the Great Depression.

European Banking Crisis of 1931

296 1931 The German banking system had been weakening since the '20s. Inflation, foreign competition, and limiting regulation were taking a collective toll on many German banks. Germany was heavily indebted to other countries (16 billion reichsmarks in 1930), and the government struggled to sell long-term domestic debt to German citizens. On May 11, 1931, the Vienna Creditanstalt bank did not publish its annual reports, causing general anxiety in German markets. This anxiety soon turned into bank runs.

On June 6, the German government announced that it refused to pay any further war reparations. That same day, Hoover announced a year-long moratorium on Germany's payment of political debts, allowing Germany to relax. Yet, runs on German banks continued. Foreign investors started taking their money out of Germany, including gold, forcing Germany to end its gold standard in mid-July. The central Reichsbank created financial restrictions to try to keep money inside the country.

Eventually, Germany's major banks either collapsed or were restructured due to bank runs. German currency was withdrawn, and the payment system's operations were limited. By the end of July, an agreement was reached to pause foreign creditors in Germany. As banks decreased their reserve ratios, consumers restored their deposits, and the money supply started decreasing more slowly. This facilitated a slow recovery of Germany's banking system.

A Hooverville shanty town

England Ends Gold Standard

297 1931 The UK was the world's foremost center of a gold standard and, after reinstating the standard in 1925, was firmly resolved to maintain it. When the pound's value started quickly declining in the summer of 1931, British authorities intended to keep the gold standard at all costs. However, on September 18, 1931, the Bank of England abruptly and unilaterally ended the standard.

Ending the gold standard was a shocking, unexpected move—at least at the time. In retrospect, however, it was more or less unavoidable. The reason for the UK's capitulation was very similar to the United States' 40 years later [see: 353]. The country was experiencing high levels of foreign capital withdrawals. During that time, the macroeconomic costs of staying on the gold standard would have been higher than ending it. Gold would start flowing out of the country faster, and maintaining the pound's peg to gold would become more expensive. Policymakers saw that leaving the gold standard would make for a quicker recovery from the Great Depression, as the government would be able to better control the supply of money. England's end of the gold standard hastened the international move to fiat currency.

Banking Panics of 1931

298 1931 Worrying that the US would end its gold standard as the UK had in September 1931, foreign central banks started converting US dollars into gold, which was allowed under the US's gold standard. Within two months, the US lost $725 million of gold. American depositors, having already pulled $2.7 billion from banks since the start of the year and deeply skeptical about the health of domestic banks, started withdrawing money even faster. As US banks already had underlying liquidity problems with failing investments, the withdrawals sparked a series of banking panics, solidifying the haze of the Great Depression.

Banks closed in modest numbers in the US since 1929, but the industry took a bigger hit in 1931. Between June and December of that year, 2,000 out of 21,000 commercial banks closed their doors. By June 1933, only 13,900 U.S. banks remained. This was the darkest period of the Depression, even after the Dow hit 41 points in June 1932.

In 1932, the federal government created the Reconstruction Finance Corporation and made $900 million of loans to help U.S. banks stay solvent. Congress passed a number of economic subsidy acts, including Glass-Steagall, and the Fed stepped in with open-market operations. These efforts were, however, insufficient and did not stop the Depression.

Great Depression Spreads Worldwide

299 early 1930s Every single industrialized country around the world was affected by the Great Depression, though the US market crash was not the instigator in all of them. For most of the world, the downturn started between May 1928 and November 1929. Most European countries, including Germany, France, and the UK, were experiencing recessions during the mid '20s—after the end of World War I—but their economic declines hastened after the 1929 crash.

On indices measuring economic production, most European countries fell from a baseline of 100 in 1929 to a level between 60–70 by their troughs in 1932–3. This drastic economic decline made all goods harder to come by. Italy, for example, escaped a large economic contraction; Germany, Austria, Latvia, and the United States all fared worse during the Depression.

Hitler was elected chancellor of Germany in 1933, and his administration began large projects to reduce unemployment in Germany. The government started significant infrastructure projects, such as large and expensive freeways, housing, and railroad projects, and passed many tax breaks. Hitler also shunted much of this economic stimulus into his many and growing military departments (many in violation of the Versailles Treaty), which became significant only a few years later.

How the Depression Helped the Nazis

300 The rise of the Nazis can be partly explained from an economic perspective, as a reaction to Germany's ongoing economic turmoil after World War I. The Great Depression added to Germany's already large economic problems and made the liberal, free-market system look like a failed institution. Economic hardships created social unrest, channeling energy into alternative political and economic ideologies, such as Communism and Nazism. One historian wrote: "One can observe a causal relationship between the severe depression, the disintegration of the democratic system, and the rise of first a military and then a fascist, dictatorial regime."

Indeed, Nazi wins in Germany's parliament tracked changes in civilian unemployment. With an unemployment rate of 14% in 1930, Nazis won 18% of the votes. Their vote-share rose to 57% in early 1932 but dipped later that year as unemployment fell. With an unemployment rate of 52% in 1933, the Nazi party received 64% of all parliamentary votes. Hitler was made chancellor of Germany later that year.

Hitler saw the Jews as affecting the German economy in two rather contradictory ways. He thought Jews were pushing Communism in Russia and that they also controlled finances on Wall Street. Hitler wrote, "Jews control the financial forces of America on the stock exchange. Year after year the Jew increases his hold on Labour in a nation of 120 million souls." Second, Hitler thought that unemployment was high in Germany because Jews were taking German jobs and displacing true German citizens. He thus gave many jobs held by Jews to Germans, which, of course, did not actually lower unemployment but did facilitate the political goals of the Nazi party.

Economics can have giant social impacts. It may be sheer luck that other economic convulsions, such as the 2008 crisis, didn't have the devastating ramifications that the Depression brought about in Germany.

Hitler at a Nazi parade

March 1933 Bank Holiday

301 1933 The Great Depression hit its low point. On February 14, 1933, the state of Michigan declared an eight-day-long banking holiday to relieve pressures on banks in the state. A number of other states followed suit, rekindling depositor fears and restarting a series of bank runs. Franklin Roosevelt became president on March 4 of that year. Two days later, his administration enacted a four-day-long national bank holiday, which also closed all stock exchanges. Four days later, the bank holiday was further extended.

While the banks were closed, Congress passed the Emergency Banking Act on March 9, 1933, giving the federal government (and the President himself) considerable power to investigate all the banks in the country and determine if they were sound enough to reopen. The Act also allowed the government to issue an unbacked emergency currency and gave banks a 100% guarantee of solvency.

Roosevelt wanted to make sure that, when the banks reopened, the runs would not resume. He went on the radio with his Fireside Chats, touting the importance of trust in the US banking system. Banks reopened on March 13, and on March 15, the Dow jumped 15.34% in one day. The Depression seemed to be slowly fading away.

Gold Standard Ended for Americans

302 1933 The Fed had trouble bringing the United States out of the Great Depression in part due to the gold standard. While offering good monetary stability, the gold standard made it difficult for the country to use expansionary monetary policy to combat recessions. If interest rates across the economy were lowered, investors would be motivated to send their money overseas to countries where rates were higher. If the US Treasury printed more money, foreign investors would question the US' ability to maintain gold backing and exchange their dollars for gold. Either way, gold leaves the country. The more gold that flows out of the country, the more difficult it is for the government to maintain the dollar's peg to gold.

When Franklin Delano Roosevelt took office, he suspended the gold standard and nationalized all gold holdings. US citizens had to hand over all their gold to the federal government at the current value of $20.67 per ounce. Americans could no longer convert paper dollars for gold. While the United States continued to peg the dollar to gold, only other countries could exchange dollars for gold in official transactions. Fiat currency was becoming the new international standard.

"Phew! That's a nasty leak. Thank goodness it's not at our end of the boat."
This 1932 cartoon satirizes the shortsightedness of wealthy nations seeming
unconcerned about economic collapse elsewhere.

FDIC Insurance

303 1933 Between the market crash of 1929 and 1933, a total of 9,000 banks became insolvent and closed their doors. U.S. citizens lost $1.3 billion in personal wealth. While the US government historically tried to keep its hands off of the private sector, the events of the Great Depression made the Roosevelt Administration rethink this approach. They decided it was time to intervene.

In 1829, the state of New York had created the country's first bank insurance program, and a few states followed suit [see: 209]. On the federal level, 150 bills relating to deposit insurance were proposed to Congress between 1886 and 1933. All of these bills either did not pass or were purposefully weak and had little effect.

As part of the New Deal, Roosevelt created the Banking Act, which was signed into law in 1933. The Act opened the Federal Deposit Insurance Corporation (FDIC) the next year. The FDIC insured bank deposits up to $2,500 per depositor when it first opened. Today, it insures deposits up to $250,000. Because of the FDIC and other types of government insurance for banks, bank runs have become (mostly) non-existent in the US and in other countries with similar programs.

Great Depression's Macroeconomic Crash

304 early 1930s Looking at basic economic data, we can better understand the devastation experienced by citizens of the world's economies during the Great Depression. We can create a more complete understanding of what life was like during much of the '30s.

GNP in the US fell from $105 billion in 1929 to a low of $57 billion by 1933. While the size of the economy nearly cut in half, unemployment rose from less than 1% to over 20% during this same period. The American economy didn't fully recover until World War II. Between 1931–33, the currency-to-demand-deposit ratio increased by 20 percentage points, indicating a sizable fall in the relative supply of money, causing deflation of as much as 10% in 1932. The Fed was largely passive, save for some limited open-market operations.

Furthermore, politicians were reluctant to undertake fiscal expansion to boost aggregate demand, inclined instead to balance the federal budget. Even so, the federal government ran a deficit of a little over 2.5%, meaning that it didn't fully achieve its goal. Things started improving between 1933–37, as gold flowed in from Europe, allowing the money supply to gradually increase while the New Deal was getting off its feet. During that period, unemployment fell by 5–10 percentage points, and the GNP nearly recovered by 1940. Inflation resumed at normal levels.

The experiences of the rest of the world's economies were mixed. Sweden and Britain, which suffered significantly in the '20s, managed to ride the economic growth of the 1930s. By 1933, Germany's GNP fell by 30%. After the Nazi regime took over in 1933, government spending rose to 33% of GNP. German tax rates, however, remained relatively constant as employment recovered. Nazi economic policy worked, and by 1937, German GNP surpassed the US.

GDP Calculated

305 1934 The concept of gross domestic product (GDP) was first developed by William Petty. Born in 1623, he was an inventor of things of all sorts. In addition to theorizing about economics, he created ways to survey land and designed a rudimentary copy machine. He also briefly sat in the English Parliament. The actual structure of the GDP statistic that we use today was created by Simon Kuznets, who won a Nobel Prize for his modern version of Petty's idea in 1971.

Kuznets created the GDP statistic to better understand the effects of the Great Depression. He outlined the statistic in a document titled "National Income, 1929-32," which he sent to the US Congress. The GDP is the total value of finished products produced within a country's borders. GDP measures an economy's health and, by proxy, people's quality of life. However, many argue that since the GDP only tracks the monetary value of production, it does not fully represent people's happiness. For example, Kuznetz wrote, "The volume of services rendered by housewives and other members of the household toward the satisfaction of wants must be imposing indeed."

But since familial relations receive no wages, they—along with other people who do important work—are not accounted for in the GDP.

Invention of "The Economy"

306 1930s In the 2016 State of the Union Address, President Obama used the word "economy" 19 times, said "inflation" once, and "unemployment" four times. In the 1864 State of the Union Address, Abraham Lincoln used economic terms zero times. This is because the economy is a new concept. While taxes, expenses, and treasury receipts are an age-old concern for all countries—and Lincoln certainly had a lot to say about them in his speech—the idea of gauging the economic health of an entire country as a cohesive unit using a few key statistics originated during the Great Depression.

While depressions had happened before, the Great Depression was the first large-scale event to affect the entire country—and a sizable portion of the world. Americans wanted to know why. The GDP statistic was invented in 1934, lumping the whole country into a single number. Similarly, though unemployment was first measured in the US in the 1880 census, it was not until 1940 that this metric was defined in its modern sense.

The public and private sectors became increasingly reliant on these statistics. Under the Bretton Woods System, GDP was the main measure used to gauge the economic health of countries [see: 313]. One author wrote, "The first thing you do in the 1950s and '60s if you're a new nation is you open a national airline, you create a national army, and you start measuring GDP."

So is the economy real? If it really is just these numbers that bind a country—an "economy"—together, then, an economy is only as real as the numbers are. The people who calculate the numbers decide what should and should not be counted based on a somewhat arbitrary definition. However, if the idea of an economy represents a very real state of economic interconnection present in the modern world, and these statistics reflect that information correctly, if a little vaguely, then, yes, the economy is real.

Keynes Publishes Theories

307 1936 Disillusioned with the existing state of economic thinking that was incapable of explaining the causes of the Great Depression (and of addressing it), John Maynard Keynes developed his own theory of how a national economy works. He outlined his novel model in his 1936 book, The General Theory of Employment, Interest and Money, which he wrote while he was a fellow at King's College at Cambridge. Before he wrote General Theory, Keynes produced many books and articles about current politics and math in addition to economics.

General Theory sparked a "Keynesian Revolution" in economic policy. Most economists and government leaders soon became Keynesians and created fiscal policy based on Keynes' theories. Even Nixon is purported to have said, "We're all Keynesians now." Ironically, he said this right before Keynesianism started failing due to its limitations.

Keynesians thought that the Phillips curve—the relationship between inflation and unemployment, where higher inflation leads to lower unemployment—was stable over time. The 1970s and '80s, when both unemployment and inflation were high at the same time, proved this model wrong. Further, Keynes' recommended methods for ending recessions started to look more like a recipe for inflation. Though still important today, Keynesianism is no longer considered the all-true economic theory it was once thought to be.

Keynesian Economics

308 Existing economic theory fell flat during the Great Depression. Bagehot's Rules, one of the best contemporary theories for solving banking crises, could explain how banks ought to be bailed out but could not help with an enduring depression. John Maynard Keynes's new theories of macroeconomics offered governments a solution to the Great Depression. Keynes' motto was, "Demand creates its own supply." In order to boost the economy, the government has to use fiscal policy to create demand, which then attracts suppliers to the market.

First, Keynes argued that prices and wages are "sticky downwards" in the short run. That is, prices and wages generally stick in place, so to speak, and respond slowly to changes in market supply and demand, particularly when market pressures push wages and prices lower. This means that changes in aggregate demand fail to produce large changes in overall prices and instead tend to affect total output in the economy. In contrast to traditional economic theory, Keynes claimed that a decrease in demand does not mean that prices will fall, which means that a decrease in aggregate demand won't motivate more demand. Keynes thought that economies aren't inherently self-balancing in the short run. In order to solve a depression, the government must boost aggregate demand in place of the private sector.

Keynes argued that because aggregate demand determines an economy's health, and only the government has the capacity to increase aggregate demand, the government should optimally adjust aggregate demand using only fiscal policy. As a result, while classical economics advocates for the government taking a hands-off approach and letting the market work itself out, Keynesians contend that the government should take activist policies to fix short-run problems with aggregate demand. Importantly, the government does not need to keep its budget balanced, as Keynesians advocated for the government running peace-time deficits to keep the business cycle in check.

Securities and Exchange Commission Founded

309 1937 After the stock market crash in 1929, the public's confidence in the operations of the financial industry was lost. Before the SEC was founded, the United States had poor financial regulation. Between 1911 and 1933, every state except Nevada created "blue sky laws" designed to reduce fraud. These laws, however, were ineffective. In 1915, the Investment Bankers Association told its members they could avoid blue sky laws by trading across state lines by mail. Interstate stock trading was barely regulated. The state-by-state system came under criticism after the stock market crash of 1929.

As part of the New Deal, Congress ratified the Securities Act of 1933, which regulated interstate commerce and required that securities be registered before they can be traded in markets to reduce fraudulent trading. Originally, the power to enforce this law was vested in the Federal Trade Commission. In 1934, another Securities Act was ratified. This act regulated secondary markets, founded the Securities and Exchange Commission, and gave the Commission the power to oversee these newly regulated markets. Since then, the job of the SEC has expanded to make it one of the central regulator bodies in the financial sector.

Japanese Military Yen

310 1937 While the European colonial powers established currency boards for their territories [see: 225], the Japanese Empire issued a new currency in 1937 called the "military yen" for its empire. This currency was forced on most of the countries in East Asia and the Pacific that were under Japanese control. Only a few colonies kept their own currencies. The banknotes featured a standard design. The value of the currency was printed in the corner in either numbers or Japanese characters. It included a portrait of the Emperor and phrases denoting its authenticity. Some of these banknotes featured serial numbers. However, as more and more notes were issued, the serial numbers were eventually dropped, and inflation ensued.

In 1999, a group of 17 plaintiffs from Hong Kong sued the Japanese government, demanding that they be allowed to exchange the military yen that they still had for 700 million modern Japanese yen (which included compensation for their economic difficulty). Presiding judge Seiichiro Nishioka threw out the case, pointing out that the Japanese government ended convertibility in September 1945.

Eugenicists Advocate for Minimum Wage

311 early 20th c. Today, the minimum wage is regarded as a means to ensure a somewhat livable wage for workers with little bargaining power. However, some people's original reasons for wanting the minimum wage was quite the opposite. Progressive economists who studied eugenics, a movement focused on breeding undesirable characteristics out of the population, saw the minimum wage as a means to put undesirables out of work. The mechanism here is that if the minimum wage is higher than what the work of undesirables is worth, employers won't hire them, and they will remain unemployed and slowly disappear from the population.

Progressive economists thought that the required standard of living determined wages. Standard of living was determined by race and need. The "low-wage races" could tolerate a lower standard of living and would thus fill the workforce, as employers want the cheapest labor. The minimum wage worked to protect superior races. Indeed, Progressive economists saw unemployment as a social benefit. Sidney Webb wrote, "Unemployment is not a mark of social disease, but actually of social health. [O]f all ways of dealing with these unfortunate parasites ["unemployables"], the most ruinous to the community is to allow them to unrestrainedly compete as wage earners." Minimum wage was designed to create unemployment and keep inferiors out of the labor force. It was designed to do the opposite of what it is supposed to do today.

These black workers were paid $1 (about $22 today) to work from 6 a.m. to 7 p.m. in cotton fields in Mississippi in 1937.

Minimum Wage in US

312 1938 As part of the New Deal, Congress enacted the first federal minimum wage in the United States under the Fair Labor Standards Act of 1938. This law passed a few decades after New Zealand passed the first minimum wage law in the world in 1894. The US federal minimum wage was set at 25 cents per hour and was to increase by 5 cents per year until it reached 40 cents. Previously, all minimum wage laws were determined on a state-by-state basis. Massachusetts enacted the first such state law in the US in 1912. Around that period, most states' minimum wage laws only applied in specific cases, or only to female workers.

Initially, the Fair Labor Standards Act was only somewhat effective. Many employees were exempt due to their profession, as coverage extended mostly to those working in goods production. Particularly in the South, employers simply ignored the law. Many economists today argue that the minimum wage is a little bogus. Most states' minimum wages—the legally required minimum payments—are well below the present average national wage of about $35 per hour, which is the average amount that people are actually making. Additionally, only about 1% of employees earn at or below the minimum wage. Thus, the minimum wage is misleading as few people are actually paid according to it—most people are earning substantially more.

Bretton Woods System Created

313 1944 On July 1, 1944, the Bretton Woods Conference convened in Bretton Woods, New Hampshire, to create one of the most important global, multi-lateral economic agreements in history. Though World War II was still ongoing, 730 delegates from 44 countries set out to design the system that would control the world's economy after the war's end.

The Bretton Woods system was multifaceted, but the most significant part was member countries' currencies were all fixed to the US dollar. The reliance on the US dollar made international trade easier. The dollar, in turn, was pegged to gold at $35 per ounce. Countries could exchange gold with each other and could convert dollars to gold, but seldom did—at least for the first two decades. In fact, the system ended in a large part because countries eventually tried to actually exchange dollars for gold [see: 353].

The Agreement also established the International Monetary Fund (IMF) and World Bank. The two organizations had the job of improving and maintaining the world's financial system. The framers of the Bretton Woods Agreement underesti-mated how long it would take for all member countries to ratify it. By 1952, only six countries could fully comply with the treaty. Six years later, the major European countries agreed to maintain convertible currencies.

World Bank Formed

314 1944 The World Bank and the International Monetary Fund (IMF) were both established at the Bretton Woods conference and formally began oper-ations in 1946. Harry Dexter White, a key designer of the bank, wanted to create an international organization where every member had a say in its operations. The origi-nal purpose of the World Bank was to lend to poor countries—particularly those in post-war Europe. Since those war-torn nations had little to put up as collateral and were a huge credit risk, it was hard for them to obtain money from private banks. They needed a bank that could handle unusual risk. The World Bank made its first loan of $250 million to France in 1947. That year, it also gave loans to the Netherlands, Den-mark, and Luxembourg.

Over time, though, the World Bank's job has changed. In 1948, the US Marshall Plan took over the job of helping rebuild Europe and, in the 1970s, the World Bank started to focus on the big-picture goal of reducing extreme poverty and establishing future global trade opportunities. The World Bank is an example of a key humanitarian organization that came out of an agreement that did not initially have such charitable aims.

IMF Founded

315 1944 The IMF was founded at the Bretton Woods conference along with the World Bank. The original goal of the IMF was to oversee the fixed exchange rate agreements under the Bretton Woods system between countries and to make loans to help with balance of payments crises, which were particularly problematic as they made it harder for countries to maintain their currency peg to the dollar. Additionally, a balance of payments surplus or deficit could indicate financial mismanagement, something the IMF intended to stop.

After the fall of the Bretton Woods system, the implications of balance of payments issues became less clear-cut. If a nation has a balance of payments deficit, it does not necessarily reveal itself if its economy is being mismanaged or if it is simply experiencing a short-term macroeconomic fluctuation. This eventually caused the IMF to switch from solving balance of payments deficits to monitoring counties' overall macroeconomic performance. Additionally, the IMF took on the job of lender of last, last resort. The IMF steps in to bail countries out when the countries cannot afford to help themselves. The designers of the post-war economic order decided that the world needed a large economic regulatory body that continues to operate today.

CFA Franc Created

316 1945 The CFA Franc, or Franc of the Financial Community of Africa (FCFA), is the currency of 14 west- and central-African countries. While it is technically two currencies, the West African CFA Franc and the Central African CFA Franc, they are both valued at par and are essentially interchangeable. During the 1930s and '40s, French Africa colonies each minted their own currency, backed by a French-sanctioned financial organization. After France signed the Bretton Woods Agreement in 1945, all the African colonies consolidated their currency in one FCFA currency.

The creation of the CFA Franc has been lauded for stabilizing the economies of participating countries. However, its relative lack of fungibility across the world's economy is also criticized for acting as a barrier to economic expansion and development. France made a provision requiring African states to keep 50% of their CFA Franc reserves in the French treasury in order to receive financial backing from France. The currency benefitted African states from the 1960s to the '80s, keeping inflation low and promoting GDP growth. However, various economic factors from 1989 to 1993 caused misalignment between the value of the currencies, which resulted in price surges in Africa followed by political upheaval.

World War II Drives Inflation

317 late 1940s Similar to the World War I era [see: 276], the United States and Europe experienced rapid inflation during World War II. Between 1939 and 1941, the money-supply in the US increased by 29% while wholesale prices increased 23%, largely driven by exports to the United Kingdom. When the United States entered the war in December 1941, it financed 59% of the expenses with domestic borrowing in the form of war bonds. Prices rose 16% from 1941 to 1946 as the money-supply more than doubled.

The War hammered European economies. National income essentially halved in both France and Italy between 1938 and 1945. Prices in France more than tripled between 1946 and 1950 and doubled in Italy. England escaped high inflation. Germany, the epicenter of the war, had an unusual situation. The economy completely collapsed. After the war, Germany did not have any productive capacity, raw materials, or really a functional government. The currency became worthless. Before the war, a cigarette cost 0.033 reichsmarks; after the war, it cost 10. However, German law required financial reporting as if the currency was stable, ignoring inflation. Business was done in barter until West Germany introduced a new currency unit in June 1948, returning to stability.

Demolished buildings in Ukraine or Russia

Hungary Hyperinflation

318 1946 In 1946, Hungary experienced the worst recorded instance of hyperinflation in world history. Following World War II, very little of Europe was in a good place economically. Much of Hungary's infrastructure was destroyed, and it had to pay massive reparations to the Soviet Union. The government couldn't raise tax revenue and couldn't secure a loan, resorting to the printing press to pay its deficits.

Hungary's currency, the pengö, collapsed completely. Prices in Hungary doubled approximately every 15 hours at the peak of the crisis, with the daily inflation rate exceeding 200%. From August 1945 to July 1946, the cumulative inflation rate was 41.9 quadrillion percent. The largest denomination note that Hungary issued was for 100 quintillion pengö. But the banknote held almost no purchasing power.

Shopkeepers stopped quoting prices in pengö, and economic activity shifted to barter and hard currencies. The black market flourished, and wages failed to keep up with daily increases in the cost of living. Stabilization only came with the introduction of a new currency, the forint, on August 1, 1946. Hungary established stricter monetary policy along with it. One forint was set equal to 4×10^29 (400 octillion) pengö, demonstrating the total collapse of the old monetary system.

First Venture Capital Firm Founded

319 1946 During World War II, the US government invested broadly in new, speculative technologies. Many of the government's investments failed, but some succeeded and made a profit for the government. Private investors observed the government's success and thought they could do the same thing. MIT president Karl Compton, Harvard Business School professor George Doriot, and a few other businessmen were the first to attempt this strategy. They founded the American Research and Development Corporation (ARDC) in 1946 to make high-risk investments in small, promising companies that were innovating with technology developed for the War effort. Doriot later wrote, "A commercial bank lends only on the strength of past successes and proven assets. I want money to do things that have never been done before."

The company operated as a publicly traded closed-end fund. This financial structure is a type of mutual fund that raises capital up-front by selling shares that can then be traded by investors. Because actual cash never had to be returned to investors, ARDC could invest in illiquid assets, like companies. As the first venture capital firm, ARDC's success was mixed. Almost half of its profit came from a $70,000 investment made in 1957 in Digital Equipment Company, which grew into $355 million.

"Dollar gap" in Europe After World War II

320 1940s Dollar gaps were a problem in both World War I and II. They hampered effective development and recovery. The essential issue was that global trade operated in US dollars, but since the end of World War II, the US exported twice as much as it imported. More dollars were entering the US than leaving. US exports amounted to $12.5 billion after the war, whereas imports amounted to only $6 billion. The greater European economy did not have enough US dollars and, having been destroyed by war, did not have enough goods to export in order to earn enough US dollars. European countries badly needed dollars to import materials to rebuild themselves. The dollar gap hit its worst in 1947, totalling $11.5 billion.

The United States solved the dollar gap by giving loans and grants to Europe, which included the Marshall Plan. The United Kingdom helped, too. This imported money helped the dollar gap end as post-war reconstruction matured in the mid 1950s.

People's Bank of China Founded

321 1948 The Soviet Union was a model for Communist states around the world. The People's Republic of China was no exception and modeled its central bank, the People's Bank, on the Soviet Union's central Gosbank [see: 283]. The

People's Bank was established in December 1948—about a year before the Communist government took full control of China—through a merger of Huabei Bank, Beihai Bank, and Northwestern Farmers' Bank. Like the USSR did, the Chinese government closed all private banks or folded them into the People's Bank within a few years, making the People's Bank the only bank in China [see: 327].

With the beginning of the Cultural Revolution in 1966, the People's Bank came under attack from the political leadership. The Bank was absorbed into the Ministry of Finance, and its scope was significantly cut back, leaving China without an independent banking system until the liberalizations implemented in 1978 following the end of the Cultural Revolution. After these new, freer policies were created, a few private banks opened. But until 1978, the existence of the People's Bank meant that the economies of two of the largest countries in the world—the USSR and China—were controlled by two government institutions alone.

People's Bank of China Headquarters in Beijing

First Hedge Fund Founded

322 1949 The hedge fund was invented by Alfred Jones. Jones earned a PhD in sociology at Columbia University in 1941. His dissertation, Life, Liberty, and Property, examined the history of class distinction in the US. After graduating, Jones worked for Fortune magazine while gaining an interest in finance. An article he wrote about technical approaches to stock forecasting convinced him that he could make a living on investment.

In 1949, he and four friends founded A. W. Jones & Co. with $100,000 of start-up capital, $40,000 of which Jones put up himself. Jones dabbled with different investment methods before coming up with the idea of "hedging." In his first year, Jones made a 17.3% rate of return. In the 5 years from 1960 to 1965, his firm made a 325% rate of return—more than the highest-earning mutual fund at the time, Fidelity Trend Fund, which earned 225%. As of 1966, $44.9 million was invested with Jones' fund, and the company was managing a portfolio of $70 million.

Suddenly wealthy, Jones founded a philanthropic organization, Foundation for Voluntary Service. He made trips with the Peace Corps and continued a lifelong fight against global poverty.

How the First Hedge Fund Worked

323 Traditionally, investors offset the risk of losing money by placing only a portion of their investment portfolio in risky stocks, leaving the rest in conservative bonds. Alfred W. Jones, the inventor of the hedge fund, came up with an investing strategy that is still in use by companies today to manage well over $5 trillion: "hedging," as Jones called it. To hedge, Jones' firm bought short positions that rise in value when the market goes down, as well as long positions that rise in value when the market goes up. With this strategy, Jones' firm wins whichever way the market goes, though the decrease in risk means that the potential rate of return is lower than that of a firm using the traditional strategy.

Here is how hedging works. As a point of comparison, imagine that a traditional investor with $100,000 puts $80,000 in the stock market and the remaining $20,000 in relatively safer bonds. Jones, on the other hand, would use the $100,000 to borrow $50,000 (different permitted leverage rates allow for different amounts of risk and profit). With this total of $150,000, Jones then puts $110,000 into stocks that he thinks will make money (long positions) and also spends the remaining $40,000 on short positions on stocks that he thinks will fall in value.

In this way, the $40,000 functions as a hedge for risk and an underlying $70,000 is the part of his $100,000 investment that is exposed to risk. The hedged position exposes 70% of the total investment to risk. This compares to the $80,000 that the traditional investor considers to be at risk, which comprises 80% of his total investment. If the value of the stocks fall 10%, Jones' hedged portion of the total investment will be unaffected, and the unhedged portion will lose $7,000. The traditional investor, on the other hand, will lose $8,000. If stocks fall, Jones loses less than traditional investors. If stocks rise, Jones makes less than the traditional investor, too. That is the trade-off of hedging.

Diners Club Invents Credit Card

324 1950 Frank McNamara was having a business dinner at a restaurant in Manhattan. When the check came, he realized he had forgotten his wallet in another suit. He got to thinking about how he could streamline the process of making payments at restaurants to avoid this embarrassing situation in the future. With his associate, Ralph Schneider, McNamara founded the Diners Club. This was the first credit card company, created with $1.5 million of start-up capital. Initially, 14 restaurants agreed to accept his cards.

Frank's awkward situation must have been a common occurrence as, after only a year, over 42,000 people opened Diners Club credit card accounts. McNamara's system was handling $3 million annually, making an estimated $60,000 in profit. Of that, $18,000 per year came from the card's membership fee. The rest came from the 7% fee charged on every transaction, which translated into about 70% of the company's profit coming from merchants. By 1956, Diners Club cards could be used at 9,000 establishments, many of which were not restaurants.

Competition soon started moving in: the BankAmericard launched in 1958 [see: 331]. Plastic was now pushing out paper as the preferred means of payment.

Specialized Banks Emerge China

325 1951 The People's Bank of China soon realized it was in over its head trying to manage rural activities itself and was unable physically (and likely also culturally) to reach the vast number of far-spread peasant farmers. The Chinese government founded two types of institutions to supplement the People's Bank.

The first was a special bank designated for the agriculture sector. In July 1951, the Agricultural Cooperative Bank was founded, the first attempt to establish such a bank. Constructed as a replica of a Soviet agricultural bank, it never got off the ground. The second attempt came in 1955, with the creation of the Agricultural Bank of China. This bank promoted investment in agriculture and managed farmers' finances.

China also created credit cooperatives. The earliest was founded in 1933 in a part of China that was already under Communist control at that point. These cooperatives were run collectively based on geographic districts, taking deposits from and making loans to its members.

This expansion of banking services meant that more people had access to banks in China than ever before. A stronger banking sector allowed for more efficient economic expansion and better allocation of financial and thus physical resources, something China desperately needed at the time.

Quantitative Investing Developed

326 1952 Harry Markowitz was interested in physics and philosophy as a boy but eventually turned toward economics in graduate school. He became particularly interested in using mathematics to more accurately predict stock movements. In his research, Markowitz found that then-current models lacked a systematic analysis of risk. He developed what became known as Modern Portfolio Theory and published his findings in the Journal of Finance in March 1952 under the title "Portfolio Selection." He later expanded his article into a book published under the same title.

Markowitz's thesis was that a stock portfolio's returns were based on the mean and variance of the returns of the portfolio's underlying assets. A higher mean value results in higher expected returns, but a higher variance means the returns come with more risk. By holding the variance constant, investors can maximize expected returns; while holding expected returns constant (the mean), investors can minimize variance. He developed this relationship into the efficient frontier of financial returns on a graph where standard deviation is on the x-axis and expected returns is on the y-axis. The frontier is a somewhat elongated bullet-shaped curve that shows the correlation between risk and return. Efficient portfolios lie on the bullet's edge.

Communist China Closes Private Banks

327 early 1950s When the Chinese Communist government took over in 1949, there were around 900 private or semi-private banks in the country that were founded under the previous government. None of these banks lasted long once the Communist government took power, as the new government imposed stricter regulations on all such private banks. These banks were made to answer to the new People's Bank and keep reserves with it. The government also limited private banks' basic function of lending by setting the reserve requirement ratio as high as 50%. For reference, about 10% is standard. The government also prohibited private banks from owning stock and participating in certain types of speculation.

The government also started slowly giving more jobs to government-funded banks, and the People's Bank became more competitive in both the public and private sector. Soon, the People's Bank set monetary policy in ways that hurt private banks. In 1952, five semi-private banks, which had been consolidated from many smaller banks, consolidated into the Joint Public-Private Bank. The Joint Public-Private Bank became an agent of the People's Bank. This ended private banking in China and assisted the government in modeling its financial sector after the USSR's, further pushing the institution of socialism onto its people.

AFL-CIO Founded

328 1955 The AFL-CIO was formed in 1955 through the merger of the American Federation of Labor (AFL) and the Congress of Industrial Organizations (CIO), uniting two major labor federations that had long been rivals. Today, the AFL-CIO is the largest trade union in the United States, with over 15 million members. The AFL was established in 1886, primarily organizing skilled craftworkers, while the CIO, formed in 1935 after splitting from the AFL, focused on organizing industrial workers across entire industries. The two unions' differences created competition, conflict, and disputes over membership and organizing strategies.

The two organizations recognized that their rivalry was counterproductive by the 1950s. In response, leaders from both sides initiated discussions to reunify the organizations. A unification would give them more power to negotiate fair labor practices. The merger was finalized at a joint convention in New York City on December 5, 1955, resulting in the creation of the AFL-CIO.

The merger agreement included provisions to address civil rights, emphasizing non-discrimination in union practices. It shows the rise of labor power during the mid-20th century to combat attempts at exploitation. The joint union has led a number of strikes, including the 1970 Great Postal Strike for mailmen.

AFL-CIO strike in Texas, 1967

European Economic Community Created

329 1957 In an effort to integrate European markets and to protect Europe from future war, six European countries signed the Treaty of Rome in 1957 to create the European Economic Community (EEC). The EEC was broader and longer lasting than previous attempts at union in Europe, like the European Coal and Steel Community of 1951. Remnants of the EEC continue to exist today.

The Treaty established the so-called Four Freedoms: free movement of goods, capital, labor, and the freedom to establish and provide services. It required that member nations eliminate trade barriers between themselves. This agreement is similar to today's European Union. The Four Freedoms still apply. The EEC established a single set of external trade barriers, as well as a number of new institutions to operate as arms to manage and govern the EEC. These included the Commission and the European Investment Bank. The EEC expanded to 14 members, which have all since joined the European Union.

European Investment Bank Founded

330 1958 After the Treaty of Rome established the EEC, the European Investment Bank (EIB) was founded to help fund development in Europe. The bank's goals and functions are similar to the World Bank. The EIB was capitalized with one billion units of account, defined as totaling that same number of dollars. At the time, it was equivalent to about 980 tons of gold. Member states were required to make loans to the bank on demand.

Today, the Investment Bank is one of the largest banks in the world, having invested over 1.1 trillion euros in its first 60 years of operations. It has served about 160 countries around the world. The EIB tries to further the European Union's policy and social goals. This often means investing in various humanitarian causes. Recently, the

EIB has been working to fight climate change. Between 2012 and 2019, it invested 550 billion euros in projects that will reduce fossil fuel emissions and help countries adapt to changing environments.

BankAmericard First General Credit Card

331 1958 On Thursday, September 18, 1958, every Bank of America customer in Fresno, California, opened their mailbox to find a not-so-shiny BankAmericard (the early ones were made of matte paper). The first BankAmericards came with a credit limit ranging from $300–500, and they required bank approval for purchases above $260. Retailers had to pay a 6% fee for every purchase plus $25 per month. Initially, there were 300 retailers. This was the start of the first true, all-purpose credit card.

By the end of 1959, the BankAmericard program spread across California. Twenty-five thousand retailers and two million households had a card. Early in the program, however, there was ample fraud, many unpaid accounts, and not enough retailers. The company did not turn a profit until 1961.

The most important feature of the invention of the credit card was its effects on the amount of borrowing by the middle-class. Credit cards democratized borrowing, such that by 1945, borrowers amassed roughly $2.5 billion of consumer credit. By 1970, that figure reached $105 billion. The easier it is to borrow, the easier it is to buy. The credit card allowed for the expansion of the economy of consumer goods.

Bretton Woods System Becomes a Reality

332 1958 Though the Bretton Woods agreement was ratified in 1944 [see: 313], it took 14 years to sort out the post-war obstacles standing in the way of its implementation. In Europe, there were many pre-existing economic agreements and a dollar shortage [see: 320]. The International Monetary Fund (IMF) was unable to do its job at the necessary scale to be effective. The United States took its place, running itself into a balance of payments deficit to supply a sufficient amount of dollars to Europe.

When the Bretton Woods System was finally implemented, it looked different from what its framers had originally agreed upon in New Hampshire. The dollar replaced the pound sterling as the global reserve currency due to England's burgeoning government debt, large current account deficit, and subsequent devaluation of its currency. The scope of the IMF's job was shrunk, and the exchange rate system switched from using an adjustable peg to a de facto fixed exchange rate to gold.

Even with the system's complex financial problems—such as promotion of current account deficits and European resentment that the US could pay its debt using its own currency—the system maintained some of the best economic stability seen in the past 150 years.

Bernie Madoff Gets His Start

333 1960 In 1960, a 22-year-old Jewish boy from Queens started a market-maker firm with $5,000 that he saved from working as a lifeguard and selling sprinkler systems. The boy's name was Bernie Madoff. His firm, Bernard L. Madoff Investment Securities LLC, started trading over-the-counter stocks using pink sheets. Madoff was an early adopter of computers and even helped design the Nasdaq stock exchange. Madoff's operations grew, eventually becoming the largest market-maker on the Nasdaq exchange. At this point, Madoff moved his offices to the 19th floor of the Lipstick Building in Manhattan.

However, two stories below, on the 17th floor, things were looking different. Known as the hedge fund floor, this was the location of Madoff's Ponzi scheme, which started in the 1990s. While he claimed to employ an investment strategy called "split-strike conversion," he in fact deposited investor money that he received into an account at Chase Bank, which held $3-5 billion at any given time [see: 480]. Madoff was able to raise such large sums of money through the many feeder funds with which he worked, as well as from his personal connections of wealthy friends and many non-profit organizations. Madoff ultimately swindled billions of investor dollars until 2008, when the scandal came crashing down [see: 455].

Gold Pool

334 1961 In October 1960, the price of gold spiked, which was bad news under the Bretton Woods System. The US and the UK started working together to keep gold prices stable, but when in mid-1961 gold prices spiked again, the two countries were unable to maintain price stability. In November, the US and seven European central banks agreed not to buy gold on certain exchanges above a price that they would determine collectively. The Bank of England was the agent for this agreement, dubbed the Gold Pool.

The countries set their agreed-upon gold price at $25 per ounce, but the BoE could raise it to as high as $35.20. The BoE would buy gold and either distribute it among the member nations of the Gold Pool or sell it. The original limit of $270 million was soon raised to $2.5 billion.

The devaluation of sterling in 1967 shook the financial system. Inflation rose in the US, and the gold market was under a severe speculative attack. Worrying about gold draining from UK coffers, the London market was temporarily closed, and the Gold Pool ended in mid-March 1968. The former members then agreed to trade gold among themselves at the set price of $35 per ounce.

African Central Banks Open

335 1960s As African countries gained independence in the 1950s and '60s, they began to establish their own central banks. These banks replaced the colonial currency boards that managed much of the African continent's money since the beginning of the 20th century [see: 271]. The central bank for countries that use the West African CFA Franc originated in 1955, when the right to issue notes in what was then called the French West African Federation was transferred from a commercial bank to a public bank. The public bank's jobs were expanded in 1962 to operate as a full central bank, the Central Bank of West Africa.

The Democratic Republic of the Congo created its central bank in 1961. The Bank of Central African States was founded in 1972. The expansion of central banking in Africa shows the triumph of European financial institutions and prepared the new African states to become full-fledged economies with the tools to participate in global trade. From a historical perspective, the creation of African central banks is a product of a key development of the 20th century: one of the government's key jobs is managing the economy.

Bretton Woods System Becomes Precarious

336 1964 The Bretton Woods system's biggest problem was built into its very design. The United States was expected to have enough gold in reserve to cover all countries seeking to exchange dollars for gold at $35 per ounce. In 1959, the United States had $19.5 billion in gold stock but a precariously close $19.4 billion in total liabilities, with $10 billion in official liabilities. By December 1964, official liabilities equaled gold stock, at about $15 billion.

This parity meant that, if all countries converted their dollars to gold, the United States would be unable to pay. In fact, this tenuous situation incentivized countries to cash out to make sure that they get their gold, fearing they would lose the gold they were entitled to if other countries cashed out first.

The United States could do nothing to solve the problem. New gold was not being dug up, the United States could not unilaterally revalue gold and, since dollars were used for all international trade, the federal government had to keep printing more and more money. The Bretton Woods system put the country into a decades-long contradiction that ultimately brought the system down.

Great Inflation

337 1965 The Great Inflation was a period of long-term inflation that, broadly speaking, lasted from 1965 to 1982, though it was centered in the 1970s. The US inflation rate reached a high of 14% in 1980, and prices tripled over the 17-year period.

Like the Price Revolution of the Renaissance, the causes of the Great Inflation are debated [see: 133]. But there are two primary explanations: unintentionally bad monetary policy and high government spending, from both rising social services spending and attempts to avoid a recession. One of the questionable monetary policies was the "stop-go" approach, where the central bank would aggressively raise and lower interest rates to alternate between lowering inflation and lowering unemployment. Another perspective claims that the Fed was pursuing expansionary monetary policy causing inflation due to a misinterpretation of the economy's performance, which, once understood, was corrected.

High federal government spending was also a contributor to inflation. US President Johnson's "War on Poverty" injected a substantial amount of money into the economy. Additionally, factors such as the ending of the gold standard, the energy crisis [see: 353; 359], and the period's quickening economic growth contributed to the Great Inflation.

What is Stagflation?

338 Inflation can be beneficial to an economy because it usually accompanies economic growth. Stagflation, however, is when price levels rise without economic growth, and unemployment remains high or increases. Stagflation is hard to control, as governments cannot use typical contractionary policy as such policies would exacerbate unemployment and hurt the economy. They cannot use expansionary policy because that will create more inflation.

There are various causes of stagflation. Supply chain shocks can create unexpected shortages of goods and services. When aggregate supply suddenly drops, prices broadly rise without any economic growth—stagflation. The 1973 Oil Crisis is a good example of a supply shock.

Another cause of stagflation is when most people's expectations of future prices increase, whether for rational or irrational reasons. Labor unions and workers in general will all require higher wages today, even if growth is coming tomorrow. This creates what is known as "cost-push" inflation, where production costs for goods and services increase without increases in aggregate output, spurring inflation without economic growth.

Economists have proposed many solutions to stagflation. The most obvious is to somehow stop the supply shock that is causing higher overall prices without increases in aggregate output. Government intervention may or may not be able to solve domestic labor or capital market failures or resolve international issues that are limiting the supply of vital productive resources. Another solution is to minimize the regulations governing market activity. This allows the fastest and most effective free-market response to unanticipated supply shocks. It allows employers to allocate labor and physical capital to their most efficient uses, decreasing unemployment, and promoting overall price stability.

When implementing any of these solutions, the government is often battling against a ticking clock of popular resentment. The economist Wassily Leontief said, "The long-standing claim of economists that they know how to control inflation is an empty pretense." Stagflation defies traditional inflation-stoppers.

Inflation caused high gas and food prices in the West that contributed to social unrest.

Market Data System Introduced

339 1966 In May 1966, on the third floor of the New York Stock Exchange building, four computers started operations. Before these computers were introduced, employees moved paper tapes with stock information between offices all around the building. These tapes were then typed up onto the ticker tape to display the latest available market data. Now with this computer system, employees only had to scan special paper cards at a trading post to enter the same data into the computer system and then onto the ticker tape in mere seconds.

Computerization was important for both the NYSE and the Securities and Exchange Commission. The NYSE was looking to remove human interference in the process of disseminating market information. The SEC was looking to increase information transparency in the market to reduce information asymmetry. By the end of the 1960s, the system not only managed the ticker tape but also double-checked human data entry work and sent data around Manhattan via a web-like connection. Humans still played an important role in entering information into the machine. But this market data system helped start the computer take-over of stock trading.

Visa Founded

340 1966 With the success of BankAmericard [see: 331], other countries created similar consumer credit card systems. Barclays launched a credit card program in 1966 with the same business model and corporate organization. Banks in Mexico, Spain, Canada, France, Japan, and other countries followed. By 1974, there were 35 million cardholders, 9 million of whom were outside the US, and 5,700 banks worldwide.

All the international banks were built on the original Bank of America model, and each had bilateral agreements with certain US banks. The cost and complexity of keeping track of all these agreements soon became unsustainable. National BankAmericard Inc. was created to unify domestic banks, and IBANCO was created for international banks. Both companies were renamed VISA in 1977, and international banks started issuing new Visa cards under a unified standard.

The names may be simple, but the details were not. A proliferation of different card companies and banks followed. In the 1970s, Business Week magazine reported: "An estimated 60% of the 55 million holders of national bank cards [in the US] do not know which bank issued their cards."

World's First ATM

341 1967 On a particular weekend in the 1960s, John Shepherd-Baron was at his home in Surrey, England, when he found himself without enough cash for his activities. The banks were closed, leaving Shepherd-Barron motivated to invent a machine that could dispense cash automatically. So goes the story, giving Shepherd-Baron the often-challenged title of inventor of the ATM.

The idea was based on a chocolate bar-dispenser, replacing the chocolate with cash. It does not matter which chocolate bar a machine dispenses, but it does matter from which account a machine dispenses money. Shepherd-Baron realized that authenticating the person withdrawing cash from an ATM was a challenge. His employer, De La Rue, had already been using cards impregnated with carbon-14 as an employee verification method since 1962. Shepherd-Baron decided to use carbon-14 in the cash machine card.

The first ATM went into service on June 27, 1967, in Enfield, a small town in England. It was known as Barclaycash and was connected with Barclays bank. Computers started encroaching on another part of banking.

Ginnie Mae and Freddie Mac Founded

342 1968 Together, Ginnie Mae and Freddie Mac manage nearly $6 trillion in mortgages today. Founded in 1968 and 1970 respectively, the US government created these two government-subsidized enterprises (GSE) to help make housing more affordable. Back before the 1930s, buying a house was expensive. The down-payment on a home loan was often half of the house's price. The loans were commonly paid over only 10 years.

As part of the New Deal, the US government pushed mortgages that required less cash up front. The National Housing Act of 1934 established the Federal Housing Administration that made long-term mortgages safer for lenders. Fannie Mae was established in 1938 as a secondary market for FHA-insured mortgages to add liquidity to the mortgage market, making it easier for lenders to lend.

In 1968, Fannie Mae was turned into a private company and Ginnie Mae (Government National Mortgage Association) was founded, which made it easier for lenders to sell mortgages to investors, incentivizing lenders to lend more. Freddie Mac was created in 1970 and started buying mortgages from savings and loan banks, allowing S&Ls to fund more mortgages. Both Ginnie Mae and Freddie Mac make it easier to buy houses and both issue and guarantee mortgage-backed securities, making them a viable investment [see: 350].

Magnetic Stripe on Credit Card

343   1969 Before magnetic stripes were put on credit cards, the process of paying by card was a little complicated. A clerk would place the customer's credit card into a small press containing carbon paper. The raised numbers on the card would impress the cardholder's information onto the carbon paper, which would be taken to the bank later. Alternatively, the clerk would read the card information over the phone to an employee at the bank. In the 1960s, Forrest Parry at IBM first attached a magnetic stripe to a card in order to identify CIA agents. It was not a complex operation: he simply taped the metal strip to a piece of cardboard with clear tape.

The first credit card to use magnetic stripe technology was the Air Travel Card issued by American Airlines in 1969. The magnetic stripe made credit cards feasible for quick, everyday transactions and a default for payments. Today, $6 trillion a year are processed with credit cards; however, credit cards with the magnetic stripe have mostly been replaced with smart-cards, making payments more secure [see: 378].

An early magnetic stripe plastic credit card

Master Charge Card Introduced

344   1969 In June 1966, Marine Midland, a bank in upstate New York, applied to be part of the BankAmericard (Visa) network and issue cards under the brand [see: 340]. Bank of America worried that the bank was too large to participate and declined the application. Karl Hinke, a vice president at Marine, was not happy with the response. He decided to create his own credit card network to compete. Marine and eight other banks—with the later addition of four of the five largest banks in

New York—founded the Interbank Card Association in 1966, later renamed Mastercard.

Soon, Mastercard was the largest credit card association in the US, with 2,000 offices and 175 member banks by 1968. The firm went national in 1969 when it consolidated with the Western States Bankcard Association. While both Mastercard and Visa issued consumer credit cards directly linked to banks, they each managed their networks differently. Visa used a franchise approach, making contracts with banks individually. Mastercard, on the other hand, worked more closely with its banks. In 2020, Mastercard processed $6.3 trillion, coming a long way from Karl Hinke's dispute with Visa.

Special Drawing Rights Created

345 1969 The US dollar being the world's reserve currency caused a complex problem under the Bretton Woods system [see: 313]. Since international trade was financed in US dollars, any need for an increase in world liquidity required an increase in the total number of US dollars. This tended to create a balance of payments deficit for the US, undermining global confidence in the dollar. This scenario was known as the Triffin Dilemma.

To overcome this problem, the IMF created a synthetic reserve asset, known as Special Drawing Rights (SDR). Initially, SDRs were defined in terms of a fixed quantity of gold (equivalent to 0.888671 grams of gold, the same as one U.S. dollar at the time). On January 1, 1970, SDRs were redefined as a basket of major international currencies, weighted based on the currencies' relative importance. While SDRs are not actually a currency, they can be exchanged among IMF member countries to address any balance of payments issues. Initially, three billion units of SDRs were created and allocated among IMF member central banks. After the fall of the Bretton Woods system, SDRs lost their original purpose and today constitute less than 1% of the world's reserves.

First ECN Founded

346 1969 An electronics communications network (ECN) is defined by the SEC as an "electronic system that widely disseminates to third parties orders entered therein by an exchange market maker or OTC market maker, and permits such orders to be executed." Basically, orders are sent in, and the ECN matches buyers with sellers at the best price, outside a physical stock exchange.

The first ECN was called Institutional Networks Corporation (Instinet). For its 50th anniversary, it published a graphic novel detailing its history. According to the book, Instinet was founded in 1969 by Jerome Pustilnik and Herbert Behrens. It was designed to solve problems created by inefficiencies resulting from evolving demands for making stock trades outside the traditional market locations, as such trades were limited by a lack of financial innovations up to that point.

In 1993, ECNs processed 13% of share volume on the Nasdaq exchange. In 1997, ECNs were deregulated by the SEC after it found that Nasdaq market makers were colluding over stock-price spreads. Since then, Nasdaq-owned ECNs, including Instinet, have come to process three-quarters of all trading volume on the exchange.

Nationalization of Indian Banking

347 1969 While Communist China and the USSR are known for nationalizing their banking sectors [see: 327; 277], the less overtly socialist India actually also did the same. By the 1960s, the Indian government realized both the significance that its banking sector had in promoting domestic economic development and the fact that the sector was also a very large employer. Nationalization could allow the government to promote development and protect jobs. While the State Bank of India was nationalized in 1955, an order in 1969 gave the government control of the 14 largest banks as well. Six more banks were nationalized in 1980, with the goal of allowing the government even more control of credit delivery.

Nationalization proved beneficial. The banks grew at about 4% a year. Deposits at branches rose 800%, and bank advances jumped 11,000%. However, bankers were not working as hard or as efficiently as they could. In the 1990s, a new prime minister liberalized the banking sector, allowing new private banks to run alongside state banks. The government relaxed banking regulations, particularly regarding foreign investment. These changes made the

Regional State Bank of India office, 2024

banking industry more competitive, and bankers no longer worked the so-called "4-6-4 method": borrow at 4%, lend at 6%, go home at 4 p.m.

Money Laundering Made Illegal

348 1970 It is estimated that money laundering is an $800 billion to $2 trillion business annually. This is about 2-5% of the world's economic output. The US was one of the first to try to stop money laundering, passing the Bank Secrecy Act of 1970 (BSA). The BSA requires created standards that financial firms must follow when recording where money came from and where it is going. The BSA requires banks to report all domestic deposits over $10,000 to the Financial Crimes Enforcement Network (FinCEN), a bureau of the US Department of the Treasury. Banks must keep track of who deposited the money, as well as where the money came from and for what it is being used. The US added to the BSA in 1986 with the Money Laundering Control Act. This Act made money laundering a crime and tried to patch loopholes in BSA reporting.

Money laundering became a crime in the UK with the Financial Action Task Force in 1989 and the money laundering directive of 1994. The European Union passed its first anti-money laundering directive in 1990. These laws, however, do not effectively stop illegal financial activity.

How Money Laundering Works

349 Money laundering is not new. Chinese merchants laundered money to hide their profit from the government as long as 2,000 years ago. Modern money laundering was developed during the 1920s to legitimize profit from illicit alcohol sales during the years of Prohibition. However, the term "money laundering" likely originated around the time of the Watergate Scandal in the early 1970s.

Here is how money laundering works. Let's say you are a criminal, and you just made $1 million on drug sales. If you try to deposit your million dollars in the bank, you are going to have to tell both the bank and the government the source of the money. That would give your operations away. Instead, you must pretend the money came from legitimate sources. There are three steps to launder money. The first is to get it into the legal economy. You can use a legitimate restaurant that you own, for example. If your restaurant takes in $30,000 a month, you can, say, deposit $50,000 at the bank monthly, adding $20,000 from your illegally-earned million. It will take 50 months to move all $1 million dollars into the bank, $20,000 dollars at a time.

Step two is layering. To further hide the source of the money, you need to invest it in other legitimate businesses or assets. The more layers, the better. You can buy real estate, invest in stocks, use it in other businesses, or ideally move it through many different countries. You can buy international assets or exchange currencies. You can also put the money through a shell company or leave it in an offshore tax haven.

Step three is to use the money. At this point, your million dollars is legal.

First Mortgage-Backed Security

350 1970 In 1968, the Housing and Urban Development Act was passed in the US. It did two things to make mortgage-backed securities possible: the Act created Ginnie Mae and allowed firms to make mortgages and sell them to other firms. Ginnie Mae was important because it backs mortgage-backed securities; the ability to sell mortgages made it possible for a firm to buy sufficiently large amounts of mortgages to assemble them into mortgage-backed securities.

Ginnie Mae introduced the first mortgage-backed security in 1970. In 1977, Bank of America introduced the first private MBS. Importantly, these BofA MBSs were so-called "non-agency," meaning that they were not backed by a government agency like Ginnie Mae or Freddie Mac. While agency MBSs are guaranteed by the government, non-agency MBSs are private and broken intro tranches for different risk levels. Through the 1980s, the MBS market expanded as investors looked for security amid volatile interest rates. In the early 2000s, non-agency MBSs really took off. The volume of available MBSs hit 50% of US GDP by 2008 when non-agency MBSs contributed to the financial crisis. The MBS market has not fully recovered since the 2008 crisis, but is still strong. By 2021, 65% of residential mortgages were bundled into MBSs.

How CDOs and MBSs Work

351 Imagine a steak. Now imagine you chop up the steak, mix it around, add salt, pepper, vinegar, oil, mold it into an interesting shape, and refrigerate. Now you have steak tartare!

The steak is a regular type of security, such as stocks or bonds. The mortgage-backed security, or steak tartare, is a reworking of traditional investments to make a new, better type of security: one that pays fixed interest rates monthly that are higher than US government bonds and yet are a very safe investment with diversification built in.

Mortgage-backed securities (MBS) and collateralized-debt obligations (CDO), which are very similar, work as follows. People buy houses with a mortgage loan (or, in the case of CDOs, any other type of debt-financed, cash-flow producing asset). To create an MBS, a bank that created a large number of mortgage loans can bundle them into a "package." The bank can then sell shares of the package—that is, the mortgage-backed security—as an investment security. When an investor buys an MBS, he is essentially lending money to all the borrowers—at times thousands of borrowers—whose mortgages are bundled in the one mortgage-backed security. In many cases, when the borrowers make payments on their mortgages, the money goes through to the MBS share owners. Often, these MBS pools are also allocated into tranches based on their underlying risk.

As so many mortgages covering a large geographic area are bundled into one security, and as people usually pay their mortgages, MBSs can be a very safe and profitable investment. If a borrower defaults on his mortgage, since his house was pledged as collateral, the investors get an asset (the house) that can be sold off. The MSB shareholder has little exposure to risk. In fact, MBSs are only ever a risky investment in the case that too many of the underlying assets (mortgage loans) are bad on a multi-billion dollar scale.

Decimalized Currency in the UK

352 1971 England's coinage system before 1971 was confusing. Prices were list-ed in pounds, shillings, and pence. There are 20 shillings in a pound, and 12 pence in a shilling, making a pound worth 240 pence [for this system's history, see: 73]. Coins were denominated in often unusual values of these subunits. In the millen-nium prior to 1971, paying at the till meant that you could employ any coin from a long list of options, including: the mite, mark, penny, farthing, florin, noble, sover-eign, crown, half-crown, three-pence, six-pence, angle, half-pound, unite, triple unite, laurel, broad, guinea, twopence, and about two dozen more.

The confusion was put to an end on Decimal Day, February 15, 1971. The pound, shilling, pence system was replaced with a decimal system of currency: one pound was one hundred pence. The shilling was soon forgotten about. The change was carried out smoothly. The UK introduced new coins three years before the switch, and set up the Decimal Currency Board two years in advance. Banks closed four days before the switch date to prepare. The plan was to completely phase out the old system within 18 months, though the coins denominated in the old system ceased being minted by the end of the year. Today, only two countries in the world continue to use non-decimal currencies: Mauritania and Madagascar.

Nixon Nixes Gold Standard

353 1971 In 1968, after the Gold Pool ended, the market price of gold was al-lowed to diverge from the government-sanctioned price [see: 334]. At the beginning of the 1970s, currencies started to appreciate against the dollar, which led to speculation that the dollar would be officially devalued against gold. Additionally, countries became increasingly annoyed with the US's unreliability in converting dol-lars for gold, and some just did not like US dominance. In 1965, France started con-verting its dollars to gold, which may have been motivated more by resentment of American political power in Europe than by real economic goals.

Matters came to head in August 1971 when the United Kingdom requested to convert US$3 billion into gold, amounting to 25% of the US' gold reserves. That month, the Nixon Administration announced that the government was ending its policy of convertibility. This was meant to be a temporary measure, designed to put pressure on other countries to revalue their currencies against the dollar. In 1972, the Smithsonian Agreement was created, changing gold-related currency valuation dynamics. The US ultimately never resumed convertibility, and within the next two years, the dollar was floated.

Smithsonian Agreement

354 1971 The Bretton Woods System ended by barely avoiding what could have been a very large debacle. A new system was expected to replace it to keep the world's currencies tied together. In December 1971, delegates from the Group of Ten countries met at the Smithsonian Institution Castle in Washington, D. C. They worked out a new system that was essentially the same as the Bretton Woods system, save two important aspects. The United States agreed to change the dollar's value from $35 per ounce of gold to $38, amounting to a 7.89% devaluation. Additionally, the US treasury would no longer let foreign central banks exchange dollars for gold, as under the Bretton Woods system.

Within a week, participating countries pegged their currencies to the dollar at new rates that reflected changes in purchasing power. The Smithsonian Agreement allowed currencies to fluctuate within a margin of up to 2.25%. While participating countries were lauded for their amiable diplomacy, the problem remained that the system required no coordination of monetary policy among countries. The newly agreed-upon exchange rates lasted for less than 14 months. By 1973, the Smithsonian Agreement was abandoned, and most of the formerly participating countries floated their currencies.

VIII

The Rise of Financialization: 1971 – 2008

Since the 1970s, money and financial systems have become more abstract, complex, and important in society. Increasingly, these systems—and the people who control them—rule the world. The financialization of the world economy has come to take many forms over the past half century. An ever larger and more diverse array of traders, investors, and lenders have emerged, using ever more complex financial instruments. They operate in more countries, moving around more money at faster speeds thanks to new technologies. Their actions impact more people, industries, and communities, in ways good and bad, often in ways that ordinary citizens don't understand.

A key feature of financialization is greater access to credit within an increasingly efficient, global financial market. Easier credit has allowed companies to adopt better technologies, expand their scale of production, and produce products ever more cheaply. Along the way, the nature of money has changed. Cash money has been in steady decline over recent decades, while bank money—including credit cards—starts to be used for more and more transactions.

Growing financialization brought benefits as more ordinary investors shared in stock market returns through investing vehicles like mutual funds, index funds, and 401(k)s. But it also brought new risks. Collateralized debt obligations, which looked like completely safe investments, were among the innovations of this period that would turn out to have unintended consequences. Hedge funds, developed to offset risks for investors, also brought instability to markets in unexpected ways. When one of these investment firms, Long-Term Capital Management, failed, it required a multi-billion dollar bailout.

Financial market deregulation, largely motivated by neoliberalism, gave the system room to expand. The repeal of the Glass-Steagall Act in the United States allowed commercial banks and investment banks to merge and money to be put to more efficient use, helping expand the financial industry and the economy as a whole. But deregulation also exposed investors to more risks and increased the dangers posed by financial crises. These developments complicated the challenge of ensuring stability and fairness in an increasingly complex financial system. The term "too-big-to-fail" was first used to describe the government bailout of Continental Illinois Bank in 1984. A few decades later, it would become a phrase known to millions of people amid a near-meltdown of the global economy.

Index Funds Launched

355 1971 People were becoming dissatisfied with the performance of mutual funds as investments because they were often underperforming the broader market [see: 185]. John Bogle, the founder of The Vanguard Group and the man who helped popularize the index fund, wrote: "Investors as a group cannot outperform the market, because they are the market. [. . . They] must underperform the market." That is, at best, investors as a whole can only break even if they play smart. But after taxes and fees, their real take-home sum ends up underperforming.

From here, the solution was obvious—create a fund merely made up of stocks in a given market sector. This removes the need for active account managers and dramatically reduces the fees needed to manage the fund. Fewer fees means higher net profits. In 1971, the first index fund was created by Wells Fargo for institutions. Retail investors first got access in 1975 with Bogle's broad-market fund. By 1976, Wells Fargo expanded its offerings, making an index fund to track the S&P 500. By 1981, it created another fund to track the entire market. Index funds have since become one of the most popular types of investments.

An 1971 computer system illustrating the size and complexity of the kind of early technology initially used for the Nasdaq exchange

Nasdaq Founded

356 1971 The National Association of Securities Dealers Automated Quotations (Nasdaq) launched in February 1971, a spin-off product of the National Association of Securities Dealers (NASD). The NASD founded the Nasdaq in response to the SEC's request to create an automated service for over-the-counter traders. The new Nasdaq trading service was entirely digital. Prices were quoted on retro, foot-deep CRT monitors. Orders could be made by computer on a digital system that connected market makers. The Nasdaq was ahead of its time, as most exchanges, such as the New York Stock Exchange, were making only limited forays into computer trading systems [see: 339].

One of the biggest advantages of Nasdaq was that it could offer more transparent trades and competitive prices than exchanges that were operated by hand. On the NYSE, a trader on the floor and a trader in his office would see different prices at the same time. By allowing more equitable access to market price information, Nasdaq claimed to offer better prices for the same stocks. Nasdaq later created a system that worked on a regular desktop computer. The Nasdaq also made high-frequency trading possible [see: 436].

First Money Market Fund

357 1971 In 1971, Henry Brown and Bruce Bent created the Reserve Fund, Inc., a mutual fund established to address unpredictable cash flows associated with mortgage loans. Short-term investors started using the Reserve Fund as an alternative to traditional money market instruments like Treasury bills or certificates of deposit. Reserve Fund's structure eliminated many of the mechanical issues investors faced with these instruments, such as canvassing markets for the best rates or scheduling maturities. Investing with very low risk, the Reserve Fund became the first money market fund.

The Reserve Fund distinguished itself with a fixed unit price, and "dividends" (which were simply interest) paid in fractional shares. The highly liquid fund offered same-day redemption deposits, making it easy to move money in and out, and required a minimum investment of $1,000. Founded with assets of about $1 million, by 1977 the Reserve Fund managed $1 billion. Its ease and efficiency allowed the fund to challenge traditional banking and investment approaches, making it easier for small, risk-averse investors to grow their money.

Automated Clearing House

358 1972 Before 1972, the physical process of cashing a check in the United States was complicated. After handing over a check at the bank, the piece of paper would be bounced around the country through various processing facilities before being executed. By the mid-20th century, the number of checks was piling up quickly—soon to be too many for the technology available. In 1968, the Special Committee for Paperless Entry was founded to research the problem, and in 1972, the first Automated Clearing House (ACH) was created in California. By 1978, many ACHs were created and linked nationally with the Federal Reserve System.

The system was designed for small recurring payments, such as payroll and mortgages. ACH does not actually process checks but makes electronic transactions that replace checks. Initially, many transactions used punch-cards or magnetic tape and were settled through a regional Federal Reserve Bank or private bank, though the system is entirely digital today. Today, 93% of Americans receive their salary via the ACH system.

1973 Oil Crisis

359 1973 About a fortnight after Egypt and Syria led a surprise attack on Israel on Yom Kippur of 1973, the Organization of Arab Petroleum Exporting Countries (OAPEC) cut the production of oil. It subsequently set an embargo against the United States and a few other countries, hoping to pressure them into reducing aid to Israel. Oil was a key source of American and European energy in 1972, making up 45.6% of American energy consumption and 59.6% in Western Europe. The West Texas Intermediate crude oil prices index clocked in a 183% price rise, from $3.56 in July 1973 to $10.11 in January 1974. Secretary of State Henry Kissinger threatened military action against the Arab states, but the Arab states threatened to destroy their oil-producing machinery if the US chose to attack.

US President Nixon tried to create a consumer group to bargain more effectively with the OAPEC, and in March 1974, the embargo ended as the US helped negotiate a ceasefire agreement between Israel and its adversaries. This embargo contributed to the Great Inflation of the 1970s [see: 337].

An oil facility in Libya, an OAPEC country

1973 Stock Market Crash

360 1973 The 1970s was a decade of economic pain, as the Western World was hit with a series of economic problems, which culminated in one of the largest market crashes in history. World markets peaked in late 1972 during a period of rapid GDP growth. But the Great Inflation was an ongoing problem. The Bretton Woods system, which allowed for remarkable economic stability, ended in 1973 and was replaced with the Smithsonian Agreement that barely lasted two years [see: 353]. This threw the world economy into disarray.

In 1973, stock prices fell drastically. Overall, stock values in Western Europe,

Canada, and Japan fell 34-52%. US stocks fell by 48%, and in the United Kingdom, which was hit the worst by the crisis, markets plummeted by 68.5%. The world's stock markets hit their trough at the end of 1974, and world economies did not rebound quickly. While countries recovered in nominal terms by the end of the decade, in real terms, the economies did not recover until the end of the 1980s. The crash of 1973 contributed to the economic hardship of the 1970s.

SWIFT System Created

361 1973 Before the invention of the Society for Worldwide Interbank Telecommunication (SWIFT), bank-to-bank transactions would be typed up and sent across a telegraph. The process was subject to much human error. By the 1960s, people started talking about creating a standardized system.

SWIFT was founded in 1973, headquartered in Brussels to avoid the New York-London rivalry. However, the system did not begin operating until 1977, at which point it had an initial membership of 239 banks from 15 countries. Two years later, the SWIFT system was processing 120,000 messages a day. That number grew to about 43.5 million messages a day in 2021.

The SWIFT system is made up of a computer system to manage transactions and a standardized message format. The bank identification code (BIC) consists of eight to 11 digits. It includes the bank code, country code, location code, and branch code. The head office of J. P. Morgan-Chase, for example, is identified as "CHASUS33XXX." "XXX" is the code for a head office. This BIC is included in a larger code that also encodes more information about the transaction and information to help guide the computer system processing it.

IRA and 401(k) Created

362 1974 An article from 2003 claimed that the number of people retiring and expecting Social Security benefits will increase so much that the Social Security program will become insolvent by 2023. That prediction has not come true as of the publishing of this book, but may come true in the near future.

A provision for a retirement plan funded by individuals, the IRA, was created in 1974. The 401(k), which is funded by both employers and employees, was first created by the 1978 Revenue Act. Both of these investments gained popularity ever since because pre-tax contributions from income made to either of these funds are not subject to federal income tax. However, the money is taxed when withdrawals are made during one's retirement years.

In the US, $11.5 trillion was held in IRAs in 2022, amounting to about one-third of the $37.8 trillion total held in retirement accounts. In the United Kingdom, the self-invested personal pension is the closest equivalent of the 401(k), created under the Finance Act of 1989. In Europe, individual countries have their own plans. For example, as of 2018, 90% of Danes had money in such retirement plans.

Program Trading

363 1974 Program trading entails using computer algorithms to quickly trade entire portfolios—possibly hundreds of stocks. Program trading emerged after Congress passed the Employee Retirement Income Security Act of 1974 and was originally employed for portfolio insurance. It enabled institutional investors to hedge against market declines by dynamically balancing stock and futures positions. It also allows investors to capitalize on market opportunities and execute complex trading strategies on a large scale.

Program trading gained wide recognition during the 1987 Black Monday crash [see: 387], when it intensified market volatility as automated "sell" orders flooded the market. In the 1990s and 2000s, high frequency trading (HFT) emerged, which is similar in many ways to program trading, sharing benefits and downsides [see 436].

Concerns about program trading's impact on market stability were reignited when the Dow Jones Industrial Average dropped nearly 1,000 points in minutes during the 2010 Flash Crash [see: 464]. Today, some 10–30% of trades are executed with program trading. Because program trading adds liquidity to the market, many see it as beneficial, even as concerns abound that computerization makes markets riskier.

Consolidated Ticker Tape Ticks

364 1975 While New York has always been the center of finance in the US, there were indeed many other stock exchanges around the country, known as regional exchanges. Stocks listed on the NYSE could often be traded at these exchanges as well. However, regional exchanges typically quoted different prices for the same stocks, making trading more complicated.

The consolidated tape, based on Callahan's 1867 ticker tape [see: 236], was introduced in 1976 to record all the trades made on regional exchanges and the NYSE in one place. This made it easier for traders to coordinate and find the best prices. Today, the consolidated tape aggregates data from all online brokerage services and is available over the internet. Europe did not create a consolidated tape until 2025.

DOT Trading Introduced

365 1976 Designated Order Trading (DOT) was an early electronic order-routing system used on the New York Stock Exchange (NYSE) to facilitate the execution of trades. Introduced in 1976, DOT was developed to streamline the trading process and reduce the NYSE's reliance on manual recording. DOT allowed brokers to electronically send small orders directly to the trading floor for execution. Orders were routed to a designated market maker or specialist responsible for helping trade a particular stock.

DOT primarily handled smaller, marketable orders (retail trades, for example), while larger and more complex orders often required manual intervention. Super-

DOT replaced DOT in 1984, which expanded on DOT's functionality. The Super-DOT system enabled the handling of larger orders, enhanced order-routing capabilities, and allowed direct communication between brokers and specialists. These two order processing systems helped make the NYSE more efficient for all traders. They contributed to the rise of high-frequency trading and other computerized investment.

Grameen Bank Gives Microloans

366 1976 As this book shows, money's uses in the late 20th century became abstracted from the medium of exchange's original purpose: to make trade (and thus life) easier. Muhammad Yunus, a Bengali economics professor, believed that banks should actively try to better people's lives. In 1976, he started a research project on how to use banking to help the poor. He came up with the Grameen Bank. The bank would make small loans to rural poor—mostly farmers—who own under one acre of land and do not have other assets to put up collateral. Grameen Bank made "micro-loans" to help these borrowers improve their station. The bank believes that, even though no collateral is required, borrowers will nevertheless pay back their loans on time out of goodwill. The pay-back rate is 98%.

After proving itself in one part of Bangladesh, Grameen Bank was given a charter in 1983, with partial government ownership. As of 2021, the bank had 9.5 million members and made $2.2 billion in loans. About 96% of borrowers are women, living in 81,000 villages. Professor Yunus is quoted as saying: "In the future the question will not be, 'Are people credit-worthy,' but rather, 'Are banks people-worthy?'"

A Grameen Bank office in Kolhui, India

1976 Sterling Crisis

367 1976 By 1976, the pound sterling was looking too strong. On March 4, the Bank of England (BoE) quietly intervened to devalue it. While the BoE wanted to avoid popular commotion, the slight devaluation still caused the market to respond quickly. People were not used to the BoE acting this way, and private traders became worried. The value of the pound started falling. The BoE thought it had succeeded and cut the minimum lending rate, helping push the pound down. But the pound soon started losing value a little too quickly. On March 8, the pound fell 5% against the dollar in only one day. This was the biggest single-day drop since the pound was floated in 1972.

The BoE changed course, selling reserves to keep the pound from falling too fast and overspending the $2.4 billion in reserves that it had collected. By November 1, the BoE had spent $5.5 billion. On September 29, the United Kingdom applied for a loan from the IMF. The UK received $3.9 billion, the largest loan ever made up to that point. However, the British economy already started rebounding and ultimately only half of the loan was utilized.

China Allows Commercial Banks

368 1978 After Chairman Mao died, the Cultural Revolution ended in 1976. The PRC's only bank, the People's Bank of China [see: 321], realized it was unable to manage the new "socialist market economy" on its own. Between 1979-84, the PBC delegated many of the jobs it did to four new commercial banks.

These four banks, though nominally autonomous, were merely arms of the government designed to do specific tasks. Over the '80s and '90s, China continued to permit more of such commercial banks to open. However, this banking liberalization was essentially a political artifice. Bureaucrats, not bankers, were put in charge of the new banks. As the bureaucrats were poor bankers, they racked up tons of non-performing loans.

In 1998, the national government orchestrated a $33 billion bailout and set up a few asset management companies to purchase $168 billion of non-performing loans to shore up the Big Four banks. In the early 2000s, China decided to restructure the system as a government-controlled version of the US financial system. The People's Bank was redesigned as a clone of the Fed, and the Big Four went public in Hong Kong and Shanghai.

European Monetary System Created

369 1979 The European Monetary System (EMS) was established in 1979. It was an adjustable exchange rate agreement whereby European currencies were linked together using pegs that permitted slight deviation. Europe had already had one currency union, the Latin Monetary Union, which ended in the 1920s [see: 233]. This new union had similar objectives: stabilizing and promoting international commerce in the highly interconnected European continent. The system based its exchange rates on a basket of 12 participating European countries' currencies, called the European Currency Unit (ECU).

One of the EMS's key goals was reducing the volatility of exchange rates. While the exchange rates under the EMS actually caused a financial crisis in England [see: 396], European currencies did in fact become somewhat more coordinated. Since Europe's currencies were pegged to the ECU, a weighted average of other currencies, rather than to an outside point (such as the US dollar), there was no tangible "anchor" to set monetary policy to. The EMS helped create closer cooperation among European countries and paved the way for future cooperation among European states. The EMS was eventually replaced with the European Economic and Monetary Union [see: 392].

European Currency Unit Introduced

370 1979 The European Currency Unit (ECU) came into existence on March 13, 1979, to serve as the reserve currency under the European Monetary System. The currency was defined by a basket of nine European Economic Community currencies [see: 329], which were weighted based on each country's share of trade within Europe, their GNP, and their economic standing in the Community. Three more currencies were later added.

In the beginning, the ECU was unattractive to banks and not widely used privately. Few computer systems could render the ECU's currency symbol, a linked capital C and E. The currency was only ever a unit of account, despite attempts to make a physical version of it. However, as the '80s progressed, the ECU became increasingly useful. ECUs helped countries with weaker currencies borrow capital. Further, many investors found the ECU more attractive than national currencies, as it was less costly to use when taking into account changes in national currencies' exchange rates and interest rates. The ECU was eventually replaced with the euro in 1999 [see: 426].

European Currency Unit symbol

Silver Thursday

371 1980 Three brothers, Nelson, William, and Lamar Hunt, were simply concerned about inflation and sought to create an effective hedge. In 1970, the price of silver was only $1.50 per ounce. By 1979, with the help of a few financial firms, the brothers bought up 92 million ounces of silver, worth $4.5 billion. At this point, one ounce of silver traded for $45. Inflation was not getting any better, and the Hunts attempted to corner the market on silver.

The Hunts bought on the margins and used the silver they purchased as collateral for taking loans to buy more silver. By January 18, 1980, silver was trading at $49.45 per ounce, and the brothers were in control of 69% of the world's silver supply. However, they soon ran into some problems. Buying silver on the margins exposed them to the risk of falling silver prices (similar to buying stocks on the margins in 1929; see: 287). Silver prices would soon decline. Additionally, regulators started noticing their holdings. On January 21, 1980, commodities exchanges enacted tougher rules, forcing the Hunts to sell some of their silver. The subsequent margin calls forced them to sell even more. On March 27, known as Silver Thursday, an ounce of silver hit $10.80 per ounce. The Hunts declared bankruptcy.

Junk Bonds Created

372 1980s During the 1970s and '80s, Micheal Milken, an employee at Drexel Burnham Lambert investment bank, invented the market for junk bonds. What makes junk bonds "junk" is that they have not been rated by a major credit-ranking agency, making them appear riskier. Because of this risk, junk bonds offer much higher interest rates than investment-grade bonds.

Milken argued that junk bonds can be good investments, even though investors may lose money in them. If the higher interest rates junk bonds pay (at least from the ones that do pay) can cover whatever investors lose when unreliable firms go bankrupt and fail to pay interest, the investors come out ahead.

However, this principle did not pan out in the way Milken expected. Savings and loan institutions in particular lost much money to junk bonds. Some of these losses were bailed out by the federal government, costing American taxpayers billions of dollars. Later, Michael Milken was found guilty of conspiracy, securities fraud, mail fraud, market manipulation, and tax fraud. He was sentenced to 10 years in jail, though he only served two, and he was fined $600 million.

First Airline Rewards Program

373 1981 After the Airline Deregulation Act of 1978 was passed, commercial airfares were no longer regulated by the government. Because one of their biggest price protections was removed, US airlines had to get more competitive to survive. They introduced what has now become one of the most important parts of the money-spending economy: credit cards with airline rewards.

Technically, the first airline rewards card was created by Texas International Airlines, but that program didn't last long. The real credit goes to American Airlines' AAdvantage program. Opening in May 1981, the AAdvantage program tracked how many miles you flew and gave you certain discounts after attaining different mileage tiers. At the top tier of flying 75,000 miles in the first year, you could get two free first-class round-trip tickets. The introduction of these new rewards programs incentivized more people to use credit cards, helping consumer credit become an increasingly integrated part of the economy.

Reaganomics

374 early 1980s The term Reaganomics was coined by supporters of supply-side economic policies espoused by President Ronald Reagan during his term from 1981 to 1989. Reagan believed in creating an economy that rewarded individualism, hard work, and relied on free markets with limited government intervention to more efficiently allocate productive resources and spur economic growth. Rather than continue with traditional Keynesian economic policies that focused on augmenting the demand side of the economy, Reagan's policy goals focused on the supply side, espousing lower taxes, smaller government, and reduced inflation—all of which had burdened the US economy for two decades.

Reagan's greatest success was in lowering income taxes. When he took office, the highest marginal income tax rate was 70%, which was cut to 28%. The corporate tax rate was cut from 48% to 34%. Despite these lower tax rates, total federal tax revenue remained relatively stable.

Reagan also preached cutting the federal budget. However, federal spending only fell from 22.9% of GDP to 22.1% by the time he left office. Yet, his supply-side policies spurred one of the longest periods of peacetime growth in US history. Growth in real GDP per working-age adult increased to 1.8%, and unemployment fell from 7% to 5%. Inflation hovered between 3–4% through Regan's term, down from nearly 14% in 1980.

However, Reagan's policies left the country with some real problems. Unable to slow the growth of government spending amid tax breaks, the federal debt-to-GDP ratio increased from 22% to 38%. Trade barriers were increased, and the focus on deregulation weakened the government's response to the Savings and Loans Crisis. Ultimately, many of the economic problems Reagan set out to solve went unresolved. While the country's economic state improved, the government was not greatly downsized, and Americans still complained about burdensome taxes. Reagan's influence did, however, usher in a new age of political conservatism and neoliberal economics.

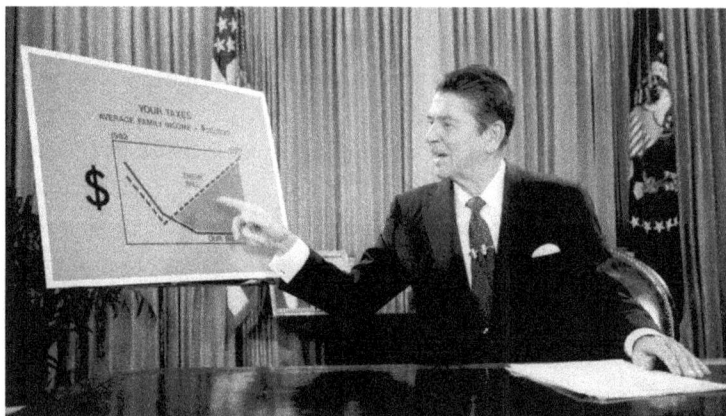

Reagan showing how he will cut taxes. The poster shows "their bill" increasing taxes and "our bill" decreasing them.

Renaissance Technologies Founded

375 1982 After earning his bachelor's degree from MIT in 1958, Jim Simons continued studying mathematics, getting his PhD from the University of

California, Berkeley. Simons then went on to become a codebreaker for the National Security Agency. However, he left in 1968 to pursue the academic track, becoming head of the mathematics department at Stony Brook University in New York. After holding that position for 11 years, he eventually got bored. He soon started assembling the pieces for his investment firm, Renaissance Technologies, which he founded in 1982.

Compared with other firms, Renaissance Technologies appeared to be operating a modest business. Unlike the offices of many Wall Street executives, Simons' office was 300 square feet, located on Long Island, 50 miles away from Midtown Manhattan. Yet, the firm is one of Wall Street's most successful. For example, in 2008, Renaissance Technologies' portfolio profited 98.5% net of fees. No information on the firm's trading strategy is currently available to share, as Renaissance keeps its methods top secret.

Later in life, Simons turned to philanthropy. He founded the Simons Foundation, which funds scientific research and Math for America, which supports math and science teachers in New York City.

eCash Created

376 1982 Online financial transactions can be tracked and are not anonymous, unlike cash. In 1982, cryptographer David Chaum, worried about financial anonymity, introduced the concept of eCash. Chaum, who got his PhD in computer science from the University of California, Berkeley, based eCash on his idea of blind signatures. Blind signatures essentially mean that someone can sign something without seeing its content. The signature can then be publicly verified against an unblinded message. The method can be used to disguise the message content from a signer or disguise the signer himself.

Chaum's eCash system worked by allowing banks to issue digital tokens, which users could spend without revealing their identities. When a transaction occurred, the recipient could verify the validity of the digital money with the issuing bank, but without linking it to the spender as a credit card would. To make real-world transactions with eCash possible, Chaum founded DigiCash in 1989. The company let users withdraw digital currency from their bank and spend it at participating merchants. A few key European banks signed with DigiCash. Chaum wasn't, however, able to strike a lasting deal with any major companies. DigiCash filed for bankruptcy in 1998. Though short-lived, eCash laid the groundwork for future cryptocurrency.

Online Banking Booms

377 early 1980s In the early 1980s, New York banks were the first to utilize the new dial-up internet to offer banking services from home. The now-defunct Chemical Bank released Pronto, which allowed customers to check account balances, create budgets, transfer funds, and make online payments with 17,000 businesses. This service cost $12 a month, and Chemical Bank also offered a business version. However, the product failed to last through the decade.

Chase developed its own system that cost $10 per month for individuals and $50 for businesses, plus dial-up service fees. Banc One launched two systems but was not able to gain enough subscribers for the company to break even. Bank of America also created a system, but customers found that the load-time was just too slow to use effectively.

Most of these early online banking systems ran on 300 or 1200 baud (bits per second). The user experience was poorly designed. Customers had to go through many complex menu pages that made more sense to a banker than to a customer. Going through these pages often required complex verification procedures—each one loading at 300 baud—and made early online banking torturous.

A 1985 AT&T home banking console

Smart Card Introduced

378 1984 The magnetic stripe revolutionized the credit card but was not a very secure technology. Anyone who can read the magnetic stripe can steal the card's information. Fraudsters easily installed devices on credit card readers that surreptitiously transmit a card's information when used for an otherwise legitimate transaction. As early as 1968, the first patent on a "smart card," a credit card with an integrated computer chip, was filed in Germany. The technology was first used in telephone cards and then as credit cards in France. Smart cards use a custom Europay, Visa, and Mastercard (EMV) chip [see: 404], which generates a unique code for every transaction based on an algorithm, making it nearly impossible to steal credit card information from a reader. The unique code is also why it takes so much longer to make a transaction with a smart card than using the magnetic stripe.

Smart card technology did not garner wide usage among merchants until the late '80s, when the chips became smaller and cheaper. By the mid-'90s, the EMV specification was broadly instituted, and smart cards were widely used across Europe. The US did not fully adopt smart cards until 2010 because the country had less fraud and lacked regulation incentivizing the switch.

Back of a smart card chip with eight pins

Continental Illinois Failure

379 1984 The phrase "too big to fail" was coined in May 1984, after the federal government determined that Continental Illinois Bank, the US' eighth-largest bank at the time, could not be permitted to fail. In the '70s and early '80s, Continental was trying to grow rapidly, but Illinois state law banned banks from opening multiple branches. This pushed Continental to start aggressively acquiring oil and gas loans, invest in riskier securities, and hold deposits from other banks.

Ultimately, only 15% of Continental's deposits, about $3 billion, were insured by the FDIC. The bank took small blows from US monetary policy changes in the late '70s. It then suffered a major blow when Penn Square Bank, where Continental Illinois got most of its oil loans from, failed in 1982. A run on Continental Illinois started on May 7, 1984. Ten days later, the FDIC announced that it would guarantee all the bank's creditors. Next, it loaned Continental $2 billion, and finally agreed to ensure all of Continental's further liquidity requirements. This did not fully end the bank run, and the FDIC took an 80% equity position in the bank. Operations finally returned to normal, and Continental was purchased in 1994.

Savings and Loan Crisis

380 1980s Savings and Loan (S&L) banks had inherent problems that were exacerbated in the inflationary environment of the late '70s and early '80s. The interest rates that S&Ls could pay on deposits were set by the government. When inflation pushed up all interest rates, the S&Ls lost customers who took their business to banks that chose their own interest rates. Further, the S&Ls were unable to pursue profit from elsewhere because their business model was supplying long-term, fixed-rate mortgages financed by short-term loans (customer deposits).

Soon, S&Ls started failing at a scale too large for the government to address. In 1980, 11 S&Ls failed with assets of $1.3 billion and required a $150 million bailout. By the height of the crisis in 1988, 190 S&Ls failed with assets of $98 billion, costing the government $46 billion. Net income for S&Ls fell from positive $0.8 billion to negative $17.6 billion.

Ultimately, it would cost $25 billion to pay off the failed firms' insured deposits, but the Federal Savings and Loan Insurance Corporation had only $6.3 billion in reserves. The clean-up was protracted—in fact, it lasted about as long as the crisis itself.

The Creation of "Too Big to Fail"

381 The concept of "too big to fail" emerged in the US after the government bailed out Continental Illinois Bank, even though many of its depositors were not FDIC insured. The idea behind the phrase is that certain financial institutions are so large, interconnected, or important in the economy that the government is obligated to save them, lest their collapse cause catastrophic ripple effects for financial markets.

Once the eighth-largest bank in the US, Continental faced insolvency due to several bad oil and gas loans. The federal government intervened by guaranteeing all depositors (including those above the FDIC-insured limit) and injecting capital in the bank to help it stay solvent. Since the Continental Illinois bailout, people have come to expect the government to save important banks. However, the Bank of England set the precedent of saving struggling banks as far back as the 19th century, as per Bagehot's rules [see: 238].

The phrase "too big to fail" gained further popularity during the 2008 global financial crisis. The 2008 crisis highlighted the fragility of the entire US financial system, something that could be exacerbated if important firms disappeared. Saving major institutions became the US government's policy. In the wake of the crisis, the Fed disbursed billions of dollars to hundreds of banks and financial companies [see: 444; 447].

Critics argue "too big to fail" incentivizes large banks to exercise reckless behavior, as many can expect government rescues if something goes wrong. This "moral hazard" prompted reforms like the 2010 Dodd-Frank Act, which sought to reduce systemic risks through stricter capital requirements, stress tests, and resolution plans ("living wills") for big banks [see: 465]. When push comes to shove, however, governments often feel an obligation to their citizens to save important institutions, as unfair as it may seem.

Response to Savings and Loans Crisis

382 1980s The response to the S&L crisis was as protracted as the crisis itself. Many thought that S&Ls were only insolvent on paper due to temporarily high interest rates. They assumed that once interest rates went back to normal, the S&Ls would recover. The government needed only to sustain S&Ls for a short time.

Deregulation was the chosen solution. In 1982, the number of insured S&Ls and the total amount of insurance both increased while the requirements to qualify for insurance were lowered. Further, the interest rate cap placed on deposits was also removed, allowing S&Ls to compete with other banks.

This strategy worked, if only a little too well. The S&L industry's decline slowed between 1982-5, and assets increased by 56%. However, many insolvent S&Ls continued to operate, incentivizing the pursuit of riskier investments. If these investments paid off, the bank could be saved. If they failed, the government would pay. However, many investments were not even intended to pay off. Thus, many S&Ls moved from investing in mortgages to investing in everything. Attempts to reform the system filled the mid '80s, until the whole system was overhauled in 1989.

Plaza Accord

383 1985 The Plaza Accord was significant for two reasons. First, it contributed to Japan's asset price bubble of the late '80s. Second, it is one of the last major government interventions of its type, marking the recent movement toward market privatization.

The US dollar was quickly appreciating in the early 1980s, largely due to a combination of expansionary fiscal policy under the Reagan Administration (in the form of tax cuts rather than increased spending) and tight monetary policy from the Fed, driving up long-term interest rates. The combination attracted overseas capital into the US, making the dollar appreciate against other currencies.

The G7 countries wanted to devalue the dollar and pushed the US to take action. After a research paper was published in 1983 showing that government intervention may not be all that helpful, the US dollar continued to appreciate. In 1985, a meeting was called at the Plaza Hotel in New York. The United States, United Kingdom, West Germany, France, and Japan all agreed on a 10–12% depreciation of the dollar. The plan succeeded, but the resulting change in currency values among the major trading partners contributed to Japan's economic bubble .

Japanese Asset Price Bubble

384 1985 As early as 1982, a bubble began to form in Japan's economy, which then accelerated in 1985–6. The bubble was marked by staggering increases in asset prices. The Nikkei stock index tripled between 1985 and its peak in 1989. Land prices nearly quadrupled during that time, and goods prices followed. The real

GDP growth was also at a fast-paced 2–6% yearly for most of the period. Additionally, between 1985 and 1990, the money supply increased at a rate of between 8–12.5% yearly.

The bubble had a few causes. First, the Japanese yen appreciated significantly after the signing of the Plaza Accord, hurting the export-driven economy. Second, companies became more optimistic, and financial firms started acting more aggressively. Finally, the government enacted widespread financial deregulation, weakening oversight on firms' aggressive moves. Monetary policy was also relaxed, making credit easier to come by. Underpinning this was a generally confident attitude. The bubble hit its peak around 1990–1, before Japan subsequently slid into a decade-long recession: the Lost Decade [see: 409].

Big Bang in the Stock Market

385 1986 The Big Bang is a term for a series of financial liberalizations created from 1984 to 1986 in the UK under Margaret Thatcher. These new policies were put into effect on October 27, 1986, and they created a massive increase in stock trading volume—a big bang in the markets. The policies that created the Big Bang came out of an antitrust suit of the London Stock Exchange brought to court by the Office of Fair Trading, pertaining to restrictive practices on trading.

The Big Bang included a few primary changes. First, fixed commissions on trading—charges for a broker making trades on an investor's behalf—were eliminated. Fixed commissions were seen as monopolistic and replaced with negotiable commissions. Foreigners were allowed to trade on the London Stock Exchange, which had previously been British-only. Another restrictive regulation that was removed was the separation between brokers and market-makers, known as jobbers, who match investors' buy and sell orders. Brokers and jobbers could not simultaneously be part of larger financial institutions. This meant that the London Stock Exchange was under-capitalized, stunting the UK's role in international exchange. The Big Bang allowed London to strengthen its place in international finance.

London Stock Exchange building

CDO Constructed

386 1987 The first collateralized debt obligation (CDO) was constructed in 1987 by Micheal Milken, known as the Junk Bond King [see: 372]. A CDO is very similar to a mortgage-backed security (MBS) but can be made up of all sorts of debt, not just mortgages [see: 351].

Early CDOs were made of junk bonds, as it was the Junk Bond King that was making them. In the late 1990s, investment firms realized they could include even more and different kinds of cash-flow-generating assets in CDOs. These new CDOs included leases for all sorts of vehicles, mortgages (and even mortgage-backed securities), mutual fund fees, and other assets that paid predictable interest yields. While the underlying assets of MBSs provide built-in protection, the diversification of these CDOs was designed to protect investors even more.

In the early 2000s, CDOs started to perform poorly. Investors thought that diversification was actually hurting CDOs, as the investors who assembled highly-diversified CDOs could not possibly be experts in such diverse types of investments. Because of this realization, CDOs increasingly became made up only of mortgages. Thus, they were easily roped into the mortgage crisis of 2008.

Asset Type	Description	Avg. Value ea.	% of Portfolio
Subprime Residential Mortgages	Loans to high-risk homeowners	$200,000	40%
Prime Residential Mortgages	Loans to low-risk homeowners	$250,000	20%
Commercial Real Estate Loans	Office, retail, and industrial property loans	$1,000,000	15%
Auto Loans	Car loans, often bundled by lenders	$20,000	10%
Credit Card Receivables	Bundled unpaid credit card balances	$5,000	5%
Home Equity Lines of Credit	Second mortgages or credit lines on homes	$75,000	5%
Small Business Loans	SBA-backed or private small business debt	$150,000	5%

A hypothetical breakdown of what is in a collateralized debt obligation

1987 Stock Market Crash

387 1987 On October 19, 1987, known as Black Monday, the Dow Jones fell 22%, the S&P fell about 20%, and the stock market was thrown into chaos for approximately a week. This was the worst market crash in history, and trades were made in such volume that the world's financial infrastructure was strained. In the years leading up to the crash, the market grew quickly, and spectators worried that it had become overvalued. Indeed, in the five years between 1982 and 1987, the Dow Jones grew by 350%. Meanwhile, computerized trading, including program trading, became increasingly mainstream [see: 363].

Panic selling in volume started when the market opened; however, not all stocks were trading. There was such a great imbalance of sell orders to buy orders that some market makers didn't open for business. By 10 a.m., one-third of the S&P 500 was not trading. When stocks finally did open, their prices nose-dived. Computer systems dumped their holdings as their algorithms triggered sell orders. Many panic orders were recorded more than an hour late.

Even though the scale of the 1987 crash was giant, the crash had limited effects. The Fed's quick actions ensured that markets rebounded Tuesday.

Market Recovers Quickly After Crash

388 1987 To help the market recover from the October 19, 1987 crash, the Fed quickly responded by making four key moves. First, it made a single-sentence proclamation reading, "The Federal Reserve, consistent with its responsibilities as the Nation's central bank, affirmed today its readiness to serve as a source of liquidity to support the economic and financial system." The Fed was attempting to instill confidence in the market—the true key to stability. Second, the Fed supplied more US Treasury bonds as investors fled stocks to buy such bonds. The Fed suspended key restrictions on loaning US Treasury securities. It loaned Treasury bonds that were in high demand to investment firms, using bonds that were not in high demand as collateral. Third, the Fed lowered the federal funds rate from 7.5% to 7%, with talk of lowering it further. Finally, by suspending a regulation, the Fed allowed Continental Illinois to aid a key subsidiary company. When Continental Illinois purchased this subsidiary, First Options of Chicago Inc., regulators limited the amount Continental could lend it. Removing that limitation allowed Continental to inject funds into First Option and save it. These four actions contained any fallout from the 1987 crisis.

Stock Market Circuit Breakers Installed

389 1988 After the Black Monday stock market crash of 1987, a US presidential task force was put together to analyze the causes of the crash and determine how such a crisis could be avoided in the future. Of the several recommendations the task force made, one of them was to create "circuit breakers" in stock markets.

Circuit breakers are triggered to temporarily stop all trading whenever markets fall precipitously. These new circuit breakers would be triggered if the S&P 500 fell by an amount corresponding to one of three levels: level one is triggered by a 7% decline, level two at 13%, and level three at 20%. A level one or two decline freezes trading market-wide for 15 minutes. A level three fall freezes the market for the remainder of the day. The NYSE also uses a Limit Up-Limit Down system, which limits trading at unusually high or low prices using continually updating price bands. The stock market circuit breakers were first triggered on October 27, 1997, during the Asian financial crisis [see: 413]. The market crash caused by the Covid-19 pandemic was the only other time that market-wide circuit breakers were used [see: 491].

Banknotes Printed on Plastic

390 1988 On Christmas Eve 1966, the Australian mint realized that the new series of banknotes that it just issued had already been forged, despite the mint having bought the latest, highest-tech banknote-printing technology. In 1969, the mint enlisted the Commonwealth Scientific and Industrial Research Organization, an Australian government agency responsible for scientific research, to help develop an even better type of banknote.

By 1972, they had a proof-of-concept design. This new note was very different, however, from old ones. It was made of plastic. The Australian mint was understandably reluctant to accept the new product, as it had been whipped up in just a few years. The new plastic notes, however, were more durable and harder to counterfeit than paper notes. In 1982, a new governor took over the central bank and insisted that the polymer banknotes be put to use. He set the release date to January 1988, the bicentennial of the landing of the First Fleet at Botany Bay by Captain Arthur Phillip. Since then, over 45 countries have adopted polymer banknotes.

Macedonian polymer banknote

Argentina Literally Runs Out of Money

391 1989 Argentina started having financial troubles in the 1980s. The country's debt had risen from US$46 billion in 1983, to US$65 billion in 1989. By then, inflation reached 3,000% annually. On April 28, 1989, the country ran out of money—literally.

There was no paper to print money on. A dock strike stopped workers from unloading the paper that the government used to mint its money. A printers' strike stopped the mints. Banks started offering 100% interest rates to obtain any money that anyone would give them. Businesses stopped accepting credit cards because it took at least 20 days for transactions to clear. Some banks simply closed because they did not know how much interest to charge. The government managed to end the strike and declared a bank holiday. The mint pledged to work through the weekend to print 4 billion australs of notes, worth about US$53 million.

European Economic and Monetary Union

392 1990 The European Economic and Monetary Union is the most recent iteration of attempts to integrate European countries' economies. It is the successor to the Latin Monetary Union and European Monetary System (EMS).

Because the EMS had some in-built shortcomings, the question of creating a stronger union emerged in 1988. The Delors Report, which outlined three stages for creating the Economic and Monetary Union, was put together in 1989. Stage one, launched in 1990, brought the member countries' economic policies closer together. This made their performance on economic indicators match and removed many of the economic barriers between the countries. In stage two, which started in 1994, the European System of Central Banks was set up and began to take charge of making monetary policy that was previously left to individual countries [see: 419]. Stage three began in 1999. Currency exchange rates between countries were locked in place. Ultimately, national currencies were replaced with a single currency, the euro [see: 426]. From there, the number of member countries in the Economic and Monetary Union expanded to now include most of Europe.

1991 Indian Economic Crisis

393 1991 By the late 1980s, India faced mounting fiscal deficits, with government expenditures consistently outpacing revenues. The gross fiscal deficit grew from 9% of GDP in 1980–81 to 12.7% in 1990–91. Simultaneously, the current account deficit grew from increased imports and sluggish export growth. Foreign exchange reserves dwindled to less than $1 billion by mid-1991. This was barely sufficient to cover three weeks of imports. Investors lost confidence in India and started taking money out of the country, causing a crisis.

In response, India essentially revamped its economic system. India had been operating under a so-called Permit Raj, whereby the government controlled many parts of the economy. In response to the crisis, the Permit Raj was dismantled, and domestic trade was deregulated. India secured a $2.2 billion loan from the International Monetary Fund (IMF), pledging 67 tons of gold as collateral.

India's GDP growth accelerated, foreign exchange reserves rebounded, and the country became more integrated into the global economy. The liberalization policies attracted foreign investment and spurred the growth of the services sector. However, the rapid changes also led to increased income inequality and concerns over labor rights. Nonetheless, the reforms that came in the wake of the 1991 crisis and subsequent reforms are seen as key to setting India on a path to quicker growth.

Argentina Currency Board

394 1991 The Argentine government decided it had enough of inflation and economic instability and thought it was time to turn things around. The government came up with a new plan, the most notable aspect of which was the strict peg of one peso for one dollar. The country was attempting a hard mindset switch, seemingly of the sort advocated for by motivational speakers.

The plan took effect in April 1991, and with it, the Argentine financial system seemed to be quickly restored. Inflation slowed, and the financial sector expanded. The new-found political stability allowed the government to reform itself. The country experienced 6.4% annual GDP growth between 1991–98. One of Argentina's goals was to establish its currency as internationally reputable, which it only partially managed to do.

Dollarization increased, with ever more transactions being carried out in dollars. This greater reliance on dollars meant that maintaining the peg was crucial for Argentina's economy. As Argentina entered a depression in 1998 [see: 423], the president announced a growth plan. The expenditures necessary for the growth plan, combined with a more relaxed approach to maintaining the peg, resulted in lost confidence in the currency and forced the government to end the peg in 2001.

BCCI Collapses

395 1991 The Bank of Credit and Commerce International (BCCI) was founded in 1972 by Agha Hasan Abedi. It was capitalized by the ruler of Abu Dhabi, five other Middle Eastern royal families, and Bank of America, which owned about a quarter stake by 1978. Headquartered in Luxembourg, BCCI quickly gained credibility and grew to manage assets of $20 billion, with 400 offices in 73 countries.

However, the bank was insolvent almost from the start. Bank executives manipulated the books, hid losses and illegal investments, and created non-existent profits. The bank made loans to Middle Eastern shipping companies that were larger than its capital base. Further, it was accused of providing banking services to people in illegal industries, along with paying government officials (including US presidents) to allow it to skirt laws and expand.

Though the bank started quietly reorganizing in the late 1980s, it was eventually dragged into the spotlight. The bank pleaded guilty to money-laundering in the US in 1990, and on July 5, 1991, investigators raided multiple BCCI offices around the world in what was called Operation C-Chase. Within months, the entire bank came down. A number of its bankers were arrested and fined, and the BCCI was forced to close.

Black Wednesday

396 1992 The United Kingdom joined the European Monetary System (EMS) in 1990 [see: 369]. Membership required each country to frequently revalue its own currency against other countries' currencies. The system was relatively stable from 1985 to 1992, so the currencies did not seem to need much realignment. However, because the EMS did not standardize monetary policy, the currencies' real exchange rate fluctuated against each other, making currency speculation rampant.

On September 13, 1992, the Bank of Italy realigned its currency and suggested that the pound sterling should also be realigned. The pound's value soon fell to the bottom of its permitted rate bracket. On September 15, the president of Germany's central bank publicly commented that England would have to realign its currency. The next morning, investors started selling pounds.

The UK government responded by buying pounds to maintain the currency's value but was unable to buy enough to offset the selling. At 11 am, the Bank of England agreed to raise the interest rate to 12%, later discussing raising the rate further to 15%. Later that evening, the UK government suspended membership of the exchange rate mechanism. The BoE had sold $28 billion of its reserves that day. This marked one of Europe's many failed attempts at a currency union before the euro.

In 1989, the USSR government exchanged 17 warships for Pepsi Cola concentrate due to currency controls. Pepsi immediately sold the ships for scrap.

USSR Economy Resorts to Barter

397 1990s The first event in this book talks of the earliest form of trade: barter and the gift economy. Trade was financed not through cash payments but through informal agreements between people. Since then, the financial system evolved to provide an intermediary between buyers and sellers to facilitate transactions: money. When the financial system disappeared after the fall of the USSR, the ancient barter system returned.

There are three reasons why people resorted to bartering after the USSR fell. First, extreme inflation hit the country, which meant cash money quickly lost its value. Next, a nuance of Russia's taxation system meant that though barter trades were taxed, the tax was not owed until the cash money was exchanged. The longer you waited to hand over the cash, the more inflation ate into the real sum of money you owed in taxes. Lastly, there simply wasn't enough cash in banks across the country, and banks couldn't provide much needed liquidity to the economy.

In 1992, an estimated 5% of sales were done through barter. By 1998, that number jumped to 50%. Even in the modern, technologically advanced world, old means of exchange still have not lost their place.

The Soviet Field of Economics

398 Someone educated in "economics" in the West has quite a different conception of the field than someone who learned economics under the now-fallen Soviet Union. Here is a crash course on Soviet economics. In the USSR, the study of economics was broken into two fields: political economy and mathematical economics. Most of those who studied economics studied political economy.

Political economy is certainly an important part of the field of economics in the West, but the Soviet version was very different from its Western counterpart. Soviet political economists made heavy use of Marxist terminology, making their work sound more like that of some unusual brand of political theorist. A sentence from one 1990 journal article analyzing the effects of Perestroika reads, "The revolutionary mass proletarian consciousness is characterized by authoritarianism, hyperideologization, simplification all the way to the primitivization of relations with culture and religious morality, pseudo-rationality based on the primacy of labor relations, and their reduction to a universal form of social community." This mumbo jumbo essentially means that the proletariat is highly motivated by ideology and sees things in a simple, class-based way. This sounds more like social science than economics. Articles about political economy didn't use mathematics and rarely tried to create formal models. Instead, articles focused on influencing current events more than entertaining a theoretical discussion. This is in sharp contrast to political economy studies outside of Russia.

Soviet articles about mathematical economics used incredibly complex math with little explanation or justification. Rather than using formal behavioral models of economic actors, such articles often utilized non-behavioral models based on the Kondratiev wave, which treats development as a cycle with high and low rates of growth. Another important branch of mathematical economics was the "System of Optimal Functioning for a Socialist Economy," a theoretical basis for optimal planning that focused on optimizing production efficiency, analyzing information flow within the system and calculating shadow prices. The field was designed to make the Soviet command economy more efficient.

Soviet Republics Disagree on Economic Policy

399 1991–93 After the fall of the Soviet Union, there was a tense period of negotiation between the countries comprising the Ruble Zone (former Soviet states using the ruble) over domestic economic policies. In 1991, the heads of former Soviet Republics' central banks met in Uzbekistan but were unable to come to any meaningful agreements. A few weeks later, Russia announced that it did not want a multilateral agreement. It instead wanted each state that intended to keep the ruble as its currency to enter a bilateral agreement with Russia. The Central Bank of Russia (CBR) would be the central economic authority.

The countries that intended to remain in the Ruble Zone (most former Soviet republics, initially) wanted two things. First, they wanted a better supply of banknotes from Russia; the lack of which created trade and economic problems for them. Second, they wanted larger loans from Russia, something the CBR cracked down on. However, these countries also worried about yielding too much power to Russia. Further, there was much disagreement inside Russia over the continuation of the Ruble Zone. By 1993, former Soviet republics started moving away from the ruble, and at this point Russia seemed happy to assist them.

Dissolution of Ruble Zone

400 1991–95 Though the USSR was falling apart, the government in Moscow intended to maintain influence over the Soviet states, and the Russian central bank continued to mint their money. After the Soviet Union collapsed, the 15 new countries neither adopted new currencies right away nor necessarily intended to. They continued using the ruble, forming the Ruble Zone.

Concern about the future of the ruble pushed countries away from the currency, however. Russia's inability to ship enough banknotes to the Soviet states made the ruble unattractive. Additionally, after Ukraine and a few other countries announced their leaving the Zone, rubles flowed out of these countries, creating inflation for the remaining countries still using the ruble.

Russia was insistent that it would keep control over the ruble, against the will of most other former Soviet countries. Five such countries left the Ruble Zone before July 1993—Estonia, Latvia, Lithuania, Ukraine, and Moldova. When Russia eventually demonetized the ruble, it pushed four more countries to leave, while five decided to work with Russia but ultimately created their own national currencies due to economic policy disagreements. Tajikistan was the last country to leave the Zone, in 1995.

Demonetization of Russian Ruble

401 1993 In July 1993, while the Ruble Zone was coming apart, Russia abruptly demonetized all rubles minted before that year—active immediately. By

October, electricity supply companies realized there was no money in banks to be withdrawn from customers' accounts and stopped paying their suppliers. A number of rudimentary trading systems cropped up, like ruble-denominated IOUs and barter [see: 397].

Demonetized rubles flooded into those countries that were still using them, particularly from former Soviet states that introduced their own currencies, like Ukraine. Millions ended up in Kazakhstan, pushing it and five other countries to agree to join Russia in a monetary union. Russia wanted the countries to print their own rubles that would be interchangeable with the Russian notes. Kazakhstan wanted Russia to ship them new, non-demonetized rubles. Russia made intentionally unreasonable demands, such as asking for "collateral" for these banknotes, seemingly with the goal of forcing these countries to adopt their own currencies, while also wanting them to stay connected to the Russian economic system. The former Soviet countries soon all adopted their own currencies, ending the union of states that made the first socialist country.

Credit Default Swap Invented

402 1994 The credit default swap (CDS) is a type of financial instrument that hedges against defaults on loans. When a lender makes a loan to a borrower, the lender is on the hook if the borrower defaults. Using a CDS, the lender can swap the risk with another investor, who will, in the case that the borrower defaults, reimburse the lender. This is not a free ride for the lender, though—he must pay a premium to the other investor. Investors are betting that the borrower will not default, in which case they make a profit on the premium that the lender pays them.

The idea of a CDS first emerged in 1991, when a group of J. P. Morgan investors were looking for a way to free up capital that J. P. Morgan bank was legally required to hold on its books to ensure its liabilities. They created the first CDS in 1994. The tool has since become incredibly popular with large investors. CDSs look smart but are not always. As they are widely-used, risky, and not regulated by the government, Warren Buffett once called them "financial weapons of mass destruction."

Interstate Banking Legalized in US

403 1994 In 1994, banks were, for the first time, fully allowed to operate across state lines within the United States. Historically, the US banking system had been highly geographically-fragmented.

Before interstate banking was legalized, bank holding companies (BHC) would simply skirt the law by owning what were technically multiple banks legally chartered in different states but treating them as branches of one company. The McFadden Act of 1927 and the Bank Holding Company Act of 1956 prohibited BHCs from operating in this way, unless a bank's home state permitted it. Though many states permitted it, only a few large banks took advantage of it. The 207 BHCs in 1994 managed two-thirds of the country's deposits but constituted only 3.8% of the total number of banks.

In 1994, the Riegle-Neal Act was passed, permitting bona fide interstate banking and eliminating the need for BHCs. This change made banking in the US more integrated and efficient. However, the change also allowed for more financial power that was previously dispersed around the country to be concentrated in Wall Street.

EMV Released

404 1994 The first iteration of the Europay, Mastercard, Visa (EMV) standard debuted in 1994. Because previous credit card authentication methods required the retailer to call the issuing bank to make a transaction, European stores were plagued with expensive phone bills, often for international calls. The EMV standard was designed to fix that. By 2005 in Europe, and 2015 in the United States, there was a "liability shift" making merchants or card-issuers—not customers—liable for certain fraudulent transactions. This helped the EMV standard reach a dominant position in the credit card market. Today, 12 billion EMV cards are in use, accounting for 90% of in-store transactions.

The chips in EMV credit cards generate non-reusable codes for transactions, making it impossible for fraudsters to steal card information from credit card readers. The system, defined in a series of books spanning more than 2,000 pages, works in four steps. First, the card and reader exchange basic information, such as the name of the issuing bank. Second, using a complex set of codes, the reader verifies the card's authenticity. Third, the customer must verify the transaction with a pin number or a signature, although not all banks require verification. Fourth, the transaction is approved or declined offline (a decision the card makes based on presumed risk), or sent to the bank online for approval.

Long-Term Capital Management Founded

405 1994 Long-Term Capital Management (LTCM) was founded in 1994 by a group of 11 partners, including a half-dozen ex-traders from Solomon . Brothers, three ex-Harvard professors, the vice-chairman of the Federal Reserve, and a co-author of the Black-Scholes model, the basis for LTCM's trading scheme.

LTCM was formed as a hedge fund with an initial capitalization of $1.25 billion, receiving investments from many large banks. Between 1994 and 1996, LTCM made between 19.9% return yearly on the low end and 42.8% on the high end. The firm used leverage at a rate of as much as 40-to-1. In 1997, the firm's capital was $6.7 billion, but it held $126.4 billion in debt.

LTCM's trading method was a type of arbitrage based on convergence trading. When two assets are mispriced relative to each other, the company bought futures on one asset and shorts another similar asset, profiting when the prices move closer together. This method only makes a small amount of money per trade, requiring many trades and necessitating high leverage. Things soon turned south, however, and LTCM eventually had to be bailed out by the government to avoid taking the whole financial system down when it collapsed [see: 421].

What Are Shadow Banks?

406 A shadow bank is a type of financial institution that does many things that traditional banks do but is not registered as a bank and therefore not subject to strict banking regulation. Shadow banks do not necessarily operate in the shadows—in fact, many types of firms such as hedge funds, private-equity firms, investment banks, and mortgage lenders are considered shadow banks. These types of firms are technically called nonbank financial companies (NFBC). In June 2008, the shadow banking industry had amassed about $22 trillion in liabilities, making these non-bank banks larger than actual banks, which had total assets of about $14 trillion.

Shadow banks come with a number of pros and cons. The pros are that shadow banks provide more liquidity to the economy through relaxed loan-making laws and by providing access to higher-yielding securities. The cons are that shadow banks are unregulated and not subject to government oversight, making the firms risky themselves and introducing systemic risk into the economy. Furthermore, shadow banks do not have access to government assistance, such as Federal Reserve bailouts (except for Long-Term Capital Management in 1998).

Because of the benefits and complexity of shadow banking, shadow banks have remained a significant part of the financial industry despite creating clear financial risks. This increased risk was more widely recognized after shadow banks played a role in exacerbating the effects of the 2008 crisis by contributing to the scale of unregulated and risky securities investments and introducing systemic risk. Yet, the size of shadow banking internationally has ballooned to over $60 trillion today.

Mexican Peso Crisis

407 1994 On January 1, 1994, a Mexican militant group took control of the state of Chiapas. Over the previous few years, Mexico was liberalizing its economy and remaking its image internationally. Mexico joined NAFTA and investor confidence in the country soared, providing it with much foreign capital. After the attack, however, investors fled Mexico.

The peso, which was pegged to the dollar, came under attack. The government started using dollars to buy pesos. Its dollar reserves stood at US$30 billion in March 1994. By November, they were down to US$17 billion. Early attempts at propping up the peso worked well, incentivising imports and creating a balance of payments deficit. However, things eventually got worse. Dollar reserves stood at US$11 billion on December 19 and were down to US$6 billion just three days later. If Mexico kept buying pesos to maintain the peg, it would go bankrupt. Mexico abruptly floated the currency.

When developing countries float their currencies, it often signifies that they are running low on money and can't afford to maintain the peg. In 1995, the nation was hit with 52% inflation, a 3–5% contraction of GDP, and interest rates surpassing 100%. The peso lost almost half of its value against the dollar, and the United States intervened with an enormous bailout.

US Bails Out Mexico

408 1995 With the Mexican economy in shambles after Mexico floated the peso, the country was on the verge of bankruptcy. The nation had barely US$6 billion in the bank and needed to pay nearly US$800 million per week on dollar-denominated bonds. On January 3, 1995, the government announced a plan with emergency relief measures, which no one took very seriously.

With its southern neighbor in disarray, the United States stepped in. On January 12, President Clinton proposed a relief package of nearly US$40 billion to Congress. Approval was not forthcoming, and Mexico spent into negative dollar reserves. On January 31, Clinton made an executive decision to put together a US$53 billion bailout package with the help of the IMF.

As per the agreement, Mexico had to pay interest on part of the loan, using oil exports as collateral, and had to adhere to IMF policy recommendations. Mexico met these requirements by enacting unpopular austerity measures designed mostly to raise tax revenue and reinstate investor confidence. Mexico took an economic blow from the crisis, but it could have been much worse.

Japan's "Lost Decade"

409 1990s Japan's economy was booming throughout the 1980s. Televisions, radios, cars, and more were flying out of the country left and right. Average annual GDP growth was nearly 4% during this period. But the '80s turned out to be a bubble [see: 384]. And the bubble did what bubbles are known to do: burst. Between 1989 and 1992, the economy turned south. Between 1991 and 2003, annual GDP growth fell to 1.14%. This period became known as the Lost Decade. Stock prices fell 60%, and land values fell 80% by 1999 from their peaks in 1990.

The Lost Decade was caused by a liquidity trap, in which a stagnant economy persists despite a prevailing low interest rate. Since stimulatory fiscal and monetary policy relies on lowering interest rates, policymakers can do little to stimulate the economy.

As a result, the Japanese government created stimulus packages, which had little effect. The Bank of Japan was also ineffective. The yen deflated, further hurting GDP growth. After a major earthquake, the public started hoarding cash, which resulted in further appreciation of the yen in the mid '90s, creating a liquidity shortage and drop in demand. The economy finally started to stabilize by 2003.

A Japanese-made Sony HiFi system from the 1980s. Products like these came out of Japan's economic bubble.

The Evolution of Contactless Payment

410 1995 As of 2024, 85% of transactions made at grocery stores and 38% of transactions made at retailers are done with contactless payment. These payment systems use radio-frequency identification (RFID), an umbrella term that includes near-field communication (NFC). In the 1980s, RFID technology was initially used for access control systems and toll payments, like the contactless transit cards used in public transportation systems.

The first contactless payment system was created in South Korea in 1995, to be used on the Seoul metro system. In the 1990s, the Europay, Mastercard, and Visa (EMV) consortium standardized the protocol for processing credit cards [see: 404]. NFC capability was later added to the EMV standard.

Major payment networks like Visa (PayWave) and Mastercard (PayPass) introduced contactless credit and debit cards in the early 2000s. NFC chips were first put on smartphones in 2014. Driven by convenience, speed, and enhanced security, contactless payment makes buying things even easier.

Dot-Com Bubble Starts

411 1995 The Dot-Com Bubble is one of many speculative bubbles inflated by innovative technology. By the mid-1990s, the potential profit the internet could offer was obvious. Backed by venture capitalists (VC), tech start-ups used a strategy whereby they would run into the red for years with heavy investment in order to grow, grab market share, and gain a first-mover advantage.

Netscape was the first example of this. Receiving an initial $5 million investment in 1994, it controlled three-quarters of the web browser market by 1995. Netflix went public in August of that year, with its evaluation immediately soaring to over $2.2 billion, up from $21 million a year prior. This legitimized the VCs' strategy and set off the dot-com craze. The Nasdaq was at about 800 points in 1995, while VC investment was $7 billion yearly. By 2000, VC investment jumped to $100 billion yearly, 80% of which went to internet companies, and the Nasdaq passed 4,600 points.

During the bubble, 24,000 internet companies raised a combined $256 billion. VCs started investing 10 times more in companies than in the past. Bubbles do not last forever, though, and this one burst within five years [see: 427].

An airplane owned by Amazon, one of the most successful companies founded during the Dot Com boom

Thai Baht De-Pegged from the Dollar

412 1996 By 1996, Thailand's economy had experienced an average of 8% annual GDP growth for a decade. Projected growth for 1997 suffered, as the economy was overheating. Foreign debt was more than half of Thailand's GDP. In an effort to secure the financial industry, the government increased the reserve requirement for financial companies, unintentionally starting a run on banks.

A speculative attack on the Thai baht began in early 1997. Some blame speculative investor George Soros for initiating it, as he had bet against the baht. But he likely did not cause the crash. Panic hit baht owners, and they quickly sold their holdings, forcing the Thai government to buy back the currency to maintain its peg to the US dollar. Thailand had $39 billion in reserves and spent $6.8 billion, pledging $23 billion more. Eventually, the government finally gave up and floated the baht on July 2.

The baht immediately lost 20% of its value, eventually losing 77% more. Over 1997, the Thai stock market halved, and two-thirds of Thai financial companies disappeared. The crisis in Thailand spread to the rest of Asia, as international financial contagion set in. The 1997 Asian financial crisis had begun.

October 27, 1997 Mini Crash

413 1997 Coming after an extended bull market period, the October 27, 1997 Mini Crash was set off in international markets by the devaluation of the Thai baht. Before the crash, interest rates and inflation were low, and corporate earnings were high. In the fall of 1997, growth started to slow, but interest in mutual funds kept it going. The average daily trading volume on the NYSE rose from 200 million to 500 million shares between 1991 and 1997.

The October 27 crash is called a mini crash because it was rather small. On this day, the Dow Jones declined 554.26 points. It fell 350 points by 2:36 p.m., and the stock market circuit breakers halted trading for the first time [see: 389]. The market reopened 30 minutes later, but stocks continued to fall, tripping the next circuit breaker and ending the day's trading early. In that week, the markets of other countries suffered. Between October 20-22, Hong Kong was down 14% over concerns about if it would maintain its peg to the dollar. On October 28, the Nikkei 225 fell 4%, and Hong Kong's market fell 10% more, while London's FTSE fell 9%.

Other Causes of the 1997 Crisis

414 1997 While the depegging of the Thai baht incited the 1997 Asian financial crisis, many other factors were at work. This includes the legitimate weakness of the economies involved, and the prevalence of large debt among Asian countries.

Asian exchange rates were likely overvalued, becoming a greater problem as the dollar kept getting stronger. Large amounts of foreign investment was flooding into Asian countries, which had poorly regulated financial markets and already well-financed sectors, like real estate, that did not produce meaningful returns. Finally, the undercapitalized banking sector began deteriorating.

High debt in Asia created a self-fulfilling prophecy. If foreign lenders openly worried that new lenders would not roll over a country's short-term debt, and if the country did not have enough foreign reserves to pay off all its debt when it comes due, lenders would stop lending to avoid being stuck with a default when the country must choose who to pay with its limited reserves. In 1996, foreign short-term debt as a percentage of international reserves was extremely high in some countries: 340% in Korea and 176% in Indonesia. The start of panic tipped the first of these debt-dominoes.

Asian International Contagion

415 1997 Once Thailand's decline started, international contagion carried the 1997 crisis around Asian financial markets. The many existing loans between banks created systemic risk. When one bank is short of cash, it calls back loans from other banks, which then call back loans from still other banks. During financial crises, foreign lenders are reluctant to defer repayment of loans, making the calls for repayment of loans ripple through the system. In December 1997, Korea's short-term debt jumped to 751% of international reserves, meaning many interbank loans may have to be called back.

As countries' currencies are realigned during a crisis, the price of imports changes. In Thailand's case, this doubled the price of buying foreign goods. Other countries racked up a current account deficit, making investing in those countries even riskier.

Private capital flows through Asia dropped from $38 billion to $1.5 billion, and direct investment dropped by $15 billion between 1997 and '98. Dollar reserves declined substantially in the affected countries, making them look less stable. Investors pulling out of some Asian countries spread fear about the stability of all developing countries, allowing the crisis to spread as far as Brazil and Russia.

Asian Financial Crisis: the Numbers

416 1997–9 The significance of the Asian financial crisis can be seen in the numbers. The epicenter of the crisis was in Indonesia, Korea, Malaysia, the Philippines, and Thailand. In 1998, the GDP of these countries dropped by 13.7%, 5.8%, 6.7%, 0.5%, and 9.4%, respectively. That year, inflation hit 77% in Indonesia, inciting the May 1998 Riots that ravaged the country.

The real exchange rates for these countries fell from a base of 100 in 1990 to around 70-80 in January 1998. Indonesia's exchange rate, however, fell below 40. This meant they were paying higher import prices while earning less from exports, which were key sources of national income. The crisis spread around the world, particularly to Brazil, Argentina, and Long-Term Capital Management in the US [see: 422; 423; 421].

Many world stock markets fell from a base of 100 in 1997 to a value of 30-40 in January 1998. By the end of 1998, the spread on dollar-denominated sovereign bonds in Indonesia increased 2,000 basis points and increased as much as 1,000 points in other countries, indicating greater risk. In 1999, the IMF had to step in to bail out many of the Asian economies.

IMF Provides Assistance Packages

417 1998-9 Indonesia, Korea, and Thailand fared the worst in the 1997 crisis. In August 1997, the IMF pledged separate bailouts worth $42, $58, and $17 billion to each of these countries, respectively. Though the pledged amounts did not fully cover the amounts needed, it was expected that IMF-involvement would instill confidence, and foreign creditors would resume rolling over loans. This proved to be true, as less than half of the pledged money was ultimately used.

By December, Korea appeared to be on the verge of default. Creditors converted short-term debt to medium-term debt, and the IMF increased disbursements, helping to turn things around. The Korean government restructured $22 billion of its own debt early in 1998. However, Indonesia's government was unable to do the same, and its economy did not recover as quickly. Much of Thailand's debt was owed to foreign banks, whose owners simply decided to wait out the crisis.

The IMF helped close insolvent financial institutions across Asia as people moved to more secure banks. It also mandated stronger financial regulation. Asia started a slow but sure recovery from one of the largest crises in history.

The Korean boy band Sechs Kies debuted in 1997. It was one of the first K-pop groups to combine singing, dancing, and attractive young men.

Countries Respond Negatively to IMF Aid

418 1998 onward The IMF bailout of 1997-8 was a huge embarrassment for Asian countries. This was particularly true for South Korea, which labelled the day of the bailout as the "Day of National Humility." In her book, The Birth of Korean Cool, Euny Hong tells how strongly Koreans felt about the financial panic. President Kim Yong-Sam was apparently "whipping himself every day" for accepting the bailout. Many of South Korea's chaebol companies did not weather the crisis. Daewoo, the fourth-largest company, went bankrupt in 1997, losing $35 billion. Hyundai, which had held the number one spot, lost $28 billion in 1999. Samsung and LG managed to grow during the crisis, rising to account for 60.3% of Korea's GDP in 1998. They were forced to reorganize as part of the IMF bailout, though their capitalization remained relatively unchanged.

Kim Dae-Jung became president in 1998. He soon created a plan to rebrand

South Korea, seeking input from Edelman, a public relations company. Part of the solution was inventing K-pop. With limited national resources and regulations on Korea's tech sector (and envious of the success of American pop culture), Korea decided that pop culture was the thing it would specialize in exporting to help recover from the financial crisis.

European Central Bank Founded

419 1998 The European Central Bank (ECB) was established in June 1998. It replaced the temporary European Monetary Institute, which was founded to facilitate the transition to stage three of the European Economic and Monetary Union [see: 392].

The Bank's governing method is unique. Unlike most central banks, the ECB must coordinate its policy with the policies of the EMU's member countries' national central banks. Together, the individual nations' central banks make up the European System of Central Banks (ESCB). Each national bank prints and manages the euro [see: 433]. The ESCB creates stable monetary policy and works to avert financial crises, playing a role in the European Debt Crisis.

The ECB is not lauded from all sides. While the Bank consistently kept the inflation rate below the target 2% and arguably established the euro as second only to the US dollar internationally, it has not necessarily benefited all European countries. Many claim that the European Union contributed to Greece's significant and ongoing financial problems [see: 429].

Russia Financial Crisis

420 1998 After the fall of the USSR in 1991, Russia faced a large economic challenge. The country's inefficient industries and outdated economic institutions, designed and implemented under the Communist government, started to weigh heavily on the country's economy. In particular, the lack of private property rights, combined with the absence of developed business law, left the government without the essential tools to create a free-market system. The 1997 Asian financial crisis did not help.

Russia's debt burden was quite high. Servicing the debt accounted for one-third of total government spending. Foreigners could purchase Russian bonds, called GKOs. The interest rates on these bonds hit 100% as the Russian economy waned, making it harder for private banks to take out loans. The resulting liquidity squeeze caused the government to pay ever higher interest to finance its debt, resulting in triple-digit inflation. Russia now struggled to borrow from foreign banks.

The IMF, World Bank, and Japan all arranged a $17 billion bailout in July 1998. This arrangement included inflation controls, a moratorium on the GKOs, conversion from short-term to long-term debt, and other standard austerity measures. Russia was the first outside of Asia to struggle in the wake of the Asian financial crisis.

Long-Term Capital Management Collapses

421 **1998** Five days after the Russian default in 1998, Long-Term Capital Management lost $553 million in a single day. According to LTCM's investment formulas, this loss was simply impossible. Yet, there were a few reasons why Russia's default had such a big impact on the company. First, the default caused general fear in the markets. Second, LTCM held a considerable portion of Russia's debt. Third, LTCM's formula relied on market convergence of bond interest rates—the crisis made interest rates start moving apart.

Because the firm was so highly leveraged, small losses could wipe out all of its capital and take the company down. In an unusual move, the Federal Reserve stepped in to bail out LTCM. While in general the Fed only acts as lender of last resort for commercial banks, if LTCM were allowed to fail, it could take the entire economy down with it.

Initially, Warren Buffett, Goldman Sachs, and AIG offered to buy the company for $250 million and inject billions of capital. The deal didn't land. Ultimately, the New York Fed arranged for 13 large banks to buy 90% of LTCM for $3.75 billion. While the Fed's decision remains controversial, it certainly helped avoid a broader financial catastrophe.

Brazilian Real Crisis

422 **1998** As the economies of Asia and Russia suffered [see: 416; 420], investors started pulling money out of developing countries around the world. Brazil came under attack. Brazil had pegged its currency to the US dollar since 1994, and with increasing national debt, lenders became wary of Brazil's situation, offering fewer long-term loans. The pegged currency did not help bolster global trust in the Brazilian economy. Throughout 1998, Brazil spent about $35 billion to maintain the dollar peg.

Near the end of 1998, the government shot down multiple expenditure-cutting measures. Meanwhile, nervous investors were taking nearly $350 million out of the country's economy every day. Brazil's reserves were drying up. The last straw was when the governor of the state of Minas Gerais announced that his state would withhold its debt payments to the Brazilian federal government for three months. In January 1999, the Brazilian real was taken off the peg and its value dropped almost 36%. The next month, Brazil agreed to an economic austerity program to qualify for a $41.5 billion rescue package from the IMF, World Bank, and a consortium of other countries.

Argentine Great Depression Starts

423 **1998** The introduction of a fixed-exchange regime in Argentina in 1991 pegged the peso to the US dollar. This stabilized the prior hyperinflation of the peso, setting the Argentine economy on an upward trajectory [see: 394]. Ten percent annual GDP growth followed, which slowed to a not-so-slow 6%. But dark financial clouds were forming around the world. After pawing at Russia and Brazil, the instability let loose by the Asian financial crisis came after Argentina.

As the value of the dollar increased, the pegged Argentine peso became more expensive, and the price of Argentine exports increased. Political instability led to a lack of trust in government policy. When government debt grew precipitously, taxes were raised in 2000. The higher taxes burdened the economy and stifled economic recovery. The currency peg was eventually abandoned, letting inflation continue.

These factors sent Argentina into a Great Depression. Bank deposits were frozen, reducing annual economic activity by 15.5%. Riots broke out, and officials of all sorts resigned. Real GDP fell by 28% from 1998 to 2002. Unemployment hit 24% in 2002. Real wages fell by 24%, and the poverty rate rose by 20 percentage points. The year 2002 was the low point of the Great Argentine Depression. However, recovery was soon on its way [see: 434].

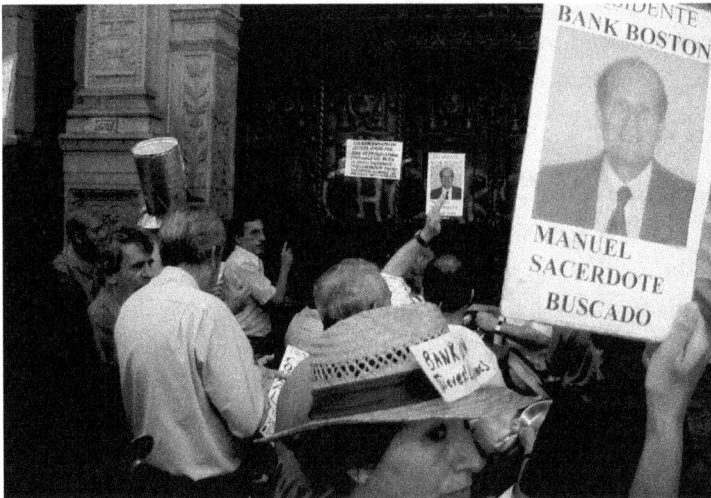

A 2001 protest against the Argentine government for freezing bank withdrawals and creating other monetary controls at the height of the Argentine Great Depression

Glass-Steagall Repealed

424 1999 Today, the largest commercial banks invest deposited money into stock and securities markets in addition to loaning it out. This was not always the case, as the Glass-Steagall Act of 1933 (GSA) prevented banks from using depositors' money in such risky markets.

By the late 1990s, US financial institutions faced increased competition from foreign banks that were not bound by similar investment restrictions, putting them at a perceived disadvantage in global markets. Further, the global financial landscape was evolving, and large conglomerate investment banks offered a full range of services, including banking, insurance, and securities, which the GSA restricted.

Major banks and financial firms lobbied extensively to repeal the GSA, arguing that it would allow them to diversify services, reduce costs, and better serve customers. The repeal of the GSA had significant bipartisan political backing. However, the repeal of the GSA may have contributed to the 2008 crisis. Allowing banks to invest deposited money incentivized them to take more risks with money that is supposed to be considered safe. The repeal of the GSA also allowed banks to consolidate, giving more power to fewer people and creating more institutions that are "too big to fail."

Deregulation of Wall Street

425 1999 Imagine if, by repealing a few pesky laws, you could create 200,000 jobs, reduce economic inequality, and modernize the entire financial sector to make it more efficient and competitive.

Under US President Bill Clinton, the government tried to do just that by taking broad action to deregulate the financial sector. Parts of the New Deal era Glass-Steagall Act were removed, liberalizing the rules governing bank mergers. Clinton signed the Gramm-Leach-Bliley Act in 1999, which also removed many merger-related restrictions placed on financial firms but did not give additional authority to the SEC to regulate these now-larger firms. The Commodity Futures Modernization Act of 2000 exempted over-the-counter derivatives from regulation.

These changes were intended to increase efficiency without increasing risk. Clinton said that the Gramm-Leach-Bliley Act "[will] stimulat[e] greater innovation and competition in the financial services industry. America's consumers, our communities, and the economy will reap the benefits of this Act." He was generally correct about increased efficiency. The promises of reducing income inequality also turned out to be true. However, risk ultimately did increase, and this deregulation allowed for the shenanigans that led to the 2008 financial crisis.

Euro Introduced as Unit of Account

426 1999 Stage three of the adoption of the European Economic and Monetary Union required that participating countries adopt the euro [see: 392]. Denmark and the United Kingdom opted out. Sweden refused to join the required Exchange Rate Mechanism program, and Greece failed to meet the annual government budget deficit limit of 3% of GDP. Ultimately, 11 EU member countries were prepared to join the Eurozone.

The 11 countries' currencies were fixed to the euro based on their exchange rates as of December 31, 1998. The euro began existing on January 1, 1999. The financial sector made the switch quite efficiently, and all tradable securities were denominated in euros almost immediately.

However, no physical euro banknotes or coins yet existed. National currencies became subdivisions of the euro, and people were permitted to use their national currencies for a three-year transition period from January 1, 1999 to December 31, 2001.

The first euro banknotes were printed in 2002 [see: 433], by which point most of the European continent was using a single currency.

Dot-Com Bubble Bursts

427 2000 On March 10, 2000, the Nasdaq closed at 5,048 points, just as the Dot-Com Bubble was at its height [see: 411]. The Dot-Com Bubble certainly was a bubble, as exhibited by the market taking great swings in value without any changes in the fundamentals of the underlying economy. The market valuation seemed unrealistic, as the 1,000% return on equity of the internet sector between 1998 and 2000 far exceeded rational expectations of future returns.

From its peak on March 10, the market took a plunge. By April, it had fallen 34%. The Nasdaq hit its bottom of 1,114 points on October 9, 2002, having fallen 77%. The market did not fully recover until 2014.

This wasn't just a bubble—many Dot-Com companies simply weren't making profit. Dot-Coms relied heavily on investor capital to pursue a strategy that focuses on gaining market share, not increasing revenue. Soon, the tech sector's growth started slowing. Once investors and venture capitalists realized this growth model couldn't go on forever, they pulled the plug. Microsoft was later found to be a monopoly by the FTC, further hurting investor confidence in the industry. Tech may have revolutionized how dog food is delivered, but it couldn't shake traditional market dynamics.

Company	Date	Quote (Fractional)	Decimal Equivalent
Ford Motor Co.	Q3 1997	46 1/8 – 38 3/16	$46.0625 – $38.1875
Ford Motor Co.	Q1 2000	55 3/16 – 40 1/4	$55.1875 – $40.25
Exxon Mobil	Dec 31, 1999	19 1/8	$19.125

Examples of stock prices quoted in fractions

Stock Prices Listed in Decimals

428 2001 In June 2000, the SEC ordered exchanges to use the decimal system rather than fractions to report stock prices. Previously, American exchanges listed prices in 1/16ths of dollars. This use of fractions followed the historical conventions of Spanish dollars, which were traditionally broken into eighths. The switch to the decimal system meant that the smallest possible change in stock prices was now 1 cent rather than 6.25 cents. This event may sound like a minor issue, but this small change was very important for many financial firms.

By reducing the spread—the minimum amount by which a price can vary—the switch reduced possible losses in trading. With a 1/16th-dollar spread, you lose over six cents whenever the value of the stock decreases; with a one-cent spread, you only lose money one cent at a time. Similarly, the decimal system allows for smaller profits to be made more easily. This created opportunities for all sorts of new trading methods that profit enormously on very large numbers of very small gains. This change matters most in computerized trading and was key for the development of high-frequency trading, which has come to increasingly dominate the stock market since.

Goldman Sachs Helps Greece Hide Debt

429 2001 Now part of the European Union, Greece was required to adhere to certain economic policy rules and show improvements on various economic indicators if it wanted to adopt the euro. Greece was unable to meet these standards of economic health. Instead, Greece lied about its financial performance to reap the benefits of being part of the Eurozone sooner. Goldman Sachs investment bank helped by giving Greece a sort of "cash advance" that took 2% off of Greece's debt, which was about 130% of GDP at the time.

The cash advance worked as follows: Goldman Sachs provided Greece with a 2.8 billion euro loan in the form of over-the-counter swaps (a type of derivative contract). Importantly, EU regulations did not require that anyone report this type of loan. Cross-currency swaps were used between dollars, yen, and euros to be exchanged back later. The exchange was made at a fictitious rate, providing Greece with 1 billion euros more value than it otherwise could have raised on its own.

Goldman Sachs is said to have profited about 600 million euros for providing these services. Of course, Greece's problems were not solved. By 2005, it owed $5.1 billion in off-the-books debt.

Enron Goes Bankrupt

430 2001 Kenneth Lay founded Enron in 1985 by merging Houston Natural Gas with Internorth. The company owned 37,000 miles of natural gas pipelines. After its founding, Enron's operations expanded dramatically. During the 1990s, it started investing in and trading natural resources (and, in one unusual scheme, broadband internet capacity). Enron stock rose by 311%.

Though much of its business was legitimate, at its core Enron was a fraud. The diversity of Enron's ventures made its accounting processes complex. Enron used mark-to-market accounting to evaluate its long-term contracts. This allowed Enron to essentially unilaterally determine the value of its own assets and create profits. Enron also used numerous special-purpose entities to keep important financial transactions off its public books. Enron's employees—and its auditors—were compensated heavily enough to turn a blind eye.

In October 2001, Enron announced its first quarterly loss of $1 billion. Soon, it was forced to publish other losses. Investors started losing confidence, and the SEC started paying attention. Enron's business model could only make money if investors continued buying stock, which now abruptly stopped. In November, Enron restated its profits because of accounting errors, reducing them by 90%. The company filed for bankruptcy in December, making one of the largest bankruptcies in American history.

How the Enron Scandal Worked

431 Between 1993 and 2000, Enron's revenue from domestic pipelines increased from $1.4 to $2.9 billion, and revenue from international pipelines increased to $22 billion from $900 million. But much of this expansion was facilitated by fraud. By misusing mark-to-market accounting, exploiting special-purpose entities (SPE), and employing old-fashioned bribery, Enron artificially inflated its earnings and stock value in what became one of the largest financial scandals in recent history.

With mark-to-market accounting, Enron's could profit immediately from the projected future profits on long-term contracts. When the profits actually materialized—if they materialized—Enron could count them again. However, many of Enron's ventures were risky and never did make a profit. In 2000, Enron recorded a profit of over $110 million from a 20-year contract with Blockbuster Video for an on-demand streaming service. When Blockbuster later withdrew from the deal, Enron kept the upfront profits on the books but actually incurred a loss.

SPEs helped Enron leverage assets without reporting the debt on its balance sheets, such as buying a company while hiding the debt required to finance the purchase. While these SPEs were often capitalized with legitimate assets, Enron failed to disclose that it was exposed to some of these SPEs' risks.

At the turn of the millennium, Enron announced a number of asset write-downs. In 2000, the company changed its income from $979 million to $99 million, reducing shareholder equity by $1.7 billion. Enron's CEO Jeff Skilling quit four months before Enron's bankruptcy but was still found guilty of 18 counts of fraud and one count of insider trading. He spent 12 years in prison. Kenneth Lay was found guilty of six counts of fraud and conspiracy and four counts of bank fraud. Enron's stock price fell from a high of almost $90 per share, to 21 cents per share on December 2, 2001, the day it filed for bankruptcy.

Argentina Does Largest Default in History

432 2001 Argentina was in the throes of a depression [see: 423] when, in 2001, it defaulted on $132 billion of debt, with $81.3 billion owed to private creditors. This was the largest sovereign debt default in history. Going back, the Argentine government, taking advice from the IMF, started an economic austerity program. However, this did not help the depression. In late 2001, bank deposits were frozen to stop capital flight. This also didn't help. The president resigned, and in the next 10 days, five different men filled his office.

On December 23, Adolfo Rodríguez Saá stepped up to the presidency. On the next day, he announced the default. While defaulting was bad, keeping the debt may have been worse. Assuming a 12.5% interest rate, Argentina would have had to pay over $12 billion a year to service its debt. That was 10% of its GDP, an unfeasibly large burden.

The default left Argentina with a competitive exchange rate and some extra cash, allowing it to recover more quickly than it otherwise could have. In 2005, Argentina restructured $81.8 billion of debt. By 2008, unemployment had dropped to 7.9% from 21%. However, this was certainly not the end of Argentina's problems.

Euro Begins Circulation

433 2002 Three years after the euro was created, the first euro banknotes and coins entered circulation on January 1, 2002. National currencies acting as temporary subdivisions of the euro were ended, and all national currencies of countries participating in the euro were demonetized by the end of February of that year. The euro became the sole legal tender. The nearly 12-year-long switch, which had started with the founding of the European Economic and Monetary Union [see: 392], was complete.

Recovery from Argentine Great Depression

434 2002 The lowest point of the Argentina Depression was in 2002. From that year on, the economy started recovering. The real economy recovered first. Depreciation of the Argentine peso against the dollar incentivized exports, accounting for 71.3% of GDP growth in the first six months of 2002. Economic growth ensued, with GDP rising 8% annually by 2003. Such growth came primarily from the construction, manufacturing, and trade sectors. By 2005, GDP returned to pre-crisis levels. The unemployment rate fell to 9.6% in 2007 from a previous high of 21.5%. The country started running a current-account surplus, helping increase national revenue.

Aggressive and controversial stabilization policies that the Argentine government created helped recovery. The government stabilized the currency by restricting the flow of pesos out of the country. It also seized dollars earned from exports to rebuild its dollar reserves, which were then used to maintain the peso's value. The 2001 default [see: 432], though it caused three months of hard depression, ultimately allowed Argentina to restructure its economic policy. Argentina managed to reduce its national debt from 127% of GDP to 62% in 2007, by which point the depression was officially over.

Mutual Fund Scandals

435 2003 In September 2003, the state of New York filed a complaint accusing the New Jersey-based Canary Capital Partners (CCP) of fraud in mutual fund markets. Later, investigations found 20 mutual fund companies that participated in similar fraudulent trading.

CCP employed two fraudulent trading methods. First, the firm practiced late trading. Mutual funds' prices are evaluated at market close at 4 p.m. EST. If a share is bought afterward, it must be sold at the next day's price. Canary, however, bought shares after the market was closed but paid that same day's price. CCP was acquiring shares at higher current prices based on new market information but was paying a lower prices based on old information. The firm also practiced "timing," which is the repeated buying and selling of mutual fund shares over a short period of time, exploiting small changes in share prices and the mechanism mutual funds used to price shares.

The SEC individually charged firms with manipulating the share prices of 145 funds with assets of $277 billion. The scandal revealed that major mutual fund companies, including Janus Capital, Bank of America, and Strong Capital Management, had all facilitated or turned a blind eye to illegal practices.

High-frequency Trading Develops

436 2005 High-frequency trading (HFT) is an investment method that uses computer programs to carry out buy and sell orders within milliseconds. Made possible by 30 years of technological advancement and legal changes, this speed enabled tiny gains from large numbers of trades, adding up to large profits. The founding of Nasdaq in 1971, the first electronic stock exchange, allowed for trading entirely by computer [see 356]. The installation of designated order turnarounds in the NYSE allowed orders to be processed electronically and faster [see: 365].

By the 1980s, program trading allowed computers to buy lists of stocks without human oversight [see: 363]. The widespread introduction of electronic communications networks in the 1990s computerized the entire trading process, making fast trades possible [see: 346]. When the stock market switched from listing stock values in fractions to decimals, firms could profit from trades across even smaller price differences [see: 428]. In 2005, the SEC enacted the Regulation National Market System, which created rules for how to match buy and sell orders in a way favorable for HFT traders. Today, most trades are carried out with HFT systems.

SEC Fails to Investigate Bernie Madoff

437 2005 Between 1992 and 2008, the SEC received six different complaints that Bernie Madoff was operating a Ponzi scheme [see: 281]. The SEC investigated his operations five times. The first time, the SEC sent a small and inexperienced team to investigate Madoff himself after receiving a complaint about a firm called Avellino & Bienes, a feeder fund to Madoff's fund. The team did little and found nothing.

In 2000 and 2001, the SEC received a few more complaints. An article published in the popular investment magazine Barons provided a very well-reasoned explanation of how Madoff's firm could not possibly work. Initially, the SEC ignored these complaints, but eventually initiated another investigation in December 2003. It uncovered numerous red flags that were then ignored, and some potentially indicative information went unpursued.

In March 2005, the SEC finally conducted an on-site investigation and found Madoff uncooperative. He even tried to control the investigation himself. In May 2006, Madoff testified in front of the SEC. He was highly evasive and criticized those who doubted him, yet gave obvious clues to his participation in a Ponzi scheme. The SEC did not follow up on these clues and never found out that he had fabricated $68 billion.

High-Frequency Trading: What it Is

438 High-frequency trading (HFT) is a term for computer stock trading technology that executes orders at very high speeds. As of 2017, 60% of trades in the US and 30% in the UK were executed with HFT algorithms. HFT employs multiple strategies. One such strategy takes arbitrage trades to a new level. A delay exists when digital information travels between stock exchanges, even if it is only a few milliseconds. HFT traders exploit this delay, buying a certain security on one exchange and immediately selling another security whose price is affected by that purchase on a different exchange before the prices on the two exchanges can synchronize. This makes a small profit for the investor. Some algorithms are designed to interpret the intentions of other algorithms and make trading decisions based on that.

Order types also matter. The market order (an order to buy or sell immediately) is the most common type of order. But it is risky due to these millisecond delays. Thus, stock exchanges invented over 200 types of orders to attract HFTs, to whom many markets give preferential treatment. Additionally, HFT requires infrastructure. HFT firms install new and faster cables to transfer data and try to locate their computer systems as close as possible to stock exchanges to gain millisecond advantages over competitors.

HFT is controversial. On one hand, letting computers manage markets is risky and can create unusual market dynamics, like the 2010 Flash Crash [see: 464]. It also allows those who already have money an unfair advantage. As to the positives, HFT adds liquidity to the market, allowing people to more easily trade assets without affecting the assets' market price. Proponents argue that HFT limits short-term volatility, making markets more stable. As with many changes brought by tech, HFT requires a trade off.

Rise of the CDO and MBS Market

439 mid-2000s Reduced regulation and savvier investors in the early 2000s made mortgage-backed securities (MBS) and collateralized debt obligations (CDO) more attractive investments [see: 351]. In 2001, Wall Street issued $87 billion of subprime and $11 billion of Alt-A private-label MBSs. By 2005, that number jumped to $465 billion and $332 billion, respectively. By 2005, almost all BBB-rated tranches of MBSs were bought by the creators of CDOs, and half of all CDO collateral was composed of MBSs. During 2006, $225 billion of these CDOs were sold.

Adam Smith stated, "When the profits of trade happen to be greater than ordinary, over-trading becomes a general error." On the eve of the 2008 crisis, investors held over $2 trillion of private-label MBSs, with a couple trillion dollars of government-secured MBSs in circulation too. Many of the underlying subprime mortgages within these MBSs used "teaser" rates, where home-buyers pay a lower mortgage rate for the first few years of their loans. Many mortgage holders could not afford their monthly payments when their interest rates reset to the full market rates, and they defaulted on their loans. This brought down the MBS and CDO market, starting the 2008 financial crisis.

IX

From Crisis to Crypto: 2008 – Present

The near-meltdown of the global economy in 2008 was possibly the largest financial crisis in history, and it certainly was the largest since the Great Depression. Born of a complex web of mortgages, the crisis was hard to solve and contributed to years of economic stagnation in North America and Europe. Countries responded to the crisis by increasing financial regulation, which had largely been reduced in the years leading up to the 2008 crisis as it was deemed unnecessary.

Few parts of the advanced world have been spared from instability. The European Sovereign Debt Crisis followed shortly after the 2008 crisis. Greece suffered from a protracted bout of excessive debt, and the European Union and IMF had to bail it out. Ireland and Portugal also needed bailouts because of excessive debt, while other European countries struggled to pay their debt. The crisis in Cyprus, caused in part by the Sovereign Debt Crisis, also affected the health of both the European Union and the euro. The Eurozone, which had proven one of the greatest feats of international unification, started to look like a failed system. Debt problems were not limited to Europe, though. Argentina faced persistent debt issues, which the IMF has struggled to address.

While financial systems built on traditional money were struggling, in 2008, an anonymous coder created Bitcoin. In 2021, El Salvador made Bitcoin a sovereign currency, while other countries and a growing array of entrepreneurs and traders also experimented with crypto. The failure of the crypto-trading firm FTX in 2022 made crypto look less like what it was intended to be: a currency secure and stable because big banks were not managing it. In short, the story of recent years has been familiar through financial history, as new and more advanced financial tools have emerged, creating both new opportunities and new risks.

Throughout this period, finance and banking increasingly moved online. Telecommunications companies rolled out technologies that have turned phones into de facto banks, transforming people's relationship to money in places with limited access to formal banking, like Africa and India. Markets became increasingly digitized and efficient. Culture also became increasingly financialized, and financial systems continued to become more important in society.

Housing Bubble Bursts

440 2007 In the early 2000s, low interest rates pushed house prices 31.6% higher between 2002 and 2006. Subprime mortgages—mortgages given to people with poor credit history—constituted 9% of all mortgages in 2002, rising to 25% by 2006. Some home buyers with good credit received "Alt-A" loans, which had higher loan-to-value ratios, making them just as risky as subprime loans. Together, these borrowers comprised 40% of all mortgage loans issued at the peak of the 2007 bubble.

Why were so many bad loans issued? Mortgage issuers made money regardless of how the loans performed, as they usually resold the loans in the secondary market. Appraisers abetted the problem by creating inflated house values to get more business from mortgage issuers. Banks bought mortgages from the secondary market and bundled both risky and safe loans into tradable mortgage-backed securities. Since so many mortgages made up MBSs, banks did not necessarily care about individual bad loans. Combined, these changes created the perfect storm.

From 2006 to 2007, the mortgage bubble began to deflate. Homeowner vacancy rates increased from 1.7% in 2005 to 2.8% in 2007. Delinquency rates were under 2% in 2005 and jumped to 11% by 2010. This was the spark for the 2008 crisis.

Bear Stearns Merges with J. P. Morgan

441 2008 In the fourth quarter of 2007, Bear Stearns reported its first ever loss of $379 million. A long and complex series of events required the firm to take a few billion dollars of unexpected debt onto its books after two of its hedge funds failed in July 2007. Investors lost confidence, wondering what Bear Stearns was doing. Bear Stearns had to scramble to stay afloat.

On January 30, 2008, Bear Stearns had less than $5 billion in liquidity, despite holding $36.7 billion in mortgage-backed security (MBS) products, two-thirds of which were either Alt-A (over-leveraged) or subprime. On Thursday, March 13, the company announced that it would be "unable to operate normally on Friday." The company needed credit—and fast.

J. P. Morgan would not help without government-backing, fearing exposure to Bear Stearns' risky MBSs. The Fed loaned Bear $12.9 billion on Friday, but the firm's debt was downgraded to BBB, and its stock fell by 47%. If Bear Stearns did not find a buyer before Asian markets opened Sunday night, it was done. J. P. Morgan and the New York Fed gave Bear a $29.97 billion loan, and Sunday night J. P. Morgan agreed to buy Bear Stearns for $2 per share, which was later raised to $10.

Bear Stearns office, 383 Madison Ave., New York

Fannie Mae and Freddie Mac Nationalized

442 **2008** Mortgage lenders started dropping out of the market in mid 2007. Fannie Mae and Freddie Mac were among the only remaining lender organizations. These two government-sponsored enterprises (GSE) had to keep giving out loans to keep the market moving, but it was unclear if they could continue to do so. In December 2007, Fannie reported that it had $44 billion in ready capital with which it could absorb losses on $875 billion in assets and $2.2 trillion of guarantees on MBSs. In other words, if losses exceeded 1.45%, Fannie would be insolvent. Freddie would be insolvent if losses exceeded 1.7%.

Officials began talking about loosening regulation on GSEs to allow Freddie and Fannie to raise their capital. In June 2008, the companies' stocks suddenly dropped sharply. By September, the Treasury decided that the companies had to be put into conservatorship. The Treasury purchased $1 billion in preferred stock of each GSE, with permission to purchase 79.9% of their outstanding shares. This move worried the market, may have accelerated the decline, and eventually cost the government more than $300 billion. But at least the $5.5 trillion institutions did not fail.

Lehman Brothers Collapses

443 **2008** After the fall of Bear Stearns in early 2008, many worried that Lehman Brothers was next. The firm had $197 billion of short-term repossession loans in Q1 of 2008 (meaning ample systematic risk), with $90 billion in mortgage-related exposure. By the second quarter of 2008, companies were trying to distance themselves from Lehman, which tried to recapitalize with more conservative sources. For example, Lehman made a deal to invest in Korea Development Bank. The deal fell through on September 9. Lehman stock fell 55%, to $7.79.

Two tense meetings in early September, one with the Fed and one with J.P. Morgan bank, provided Lehman with little aid. On September 10, Lehman announced Q3 losses of $3.9 billion. That day, Bank of America decided it would not buy Lehman without government help, and J. P. Morgan said it would stop offering Lehman credit without more security. A few days later, Barclays agreed to purchase Lehman Brothers, but the UK government stopped the deal unless the US government agreed to step in. The firm was out of options.

On September 15 at 1:45 a.m., Lehman filed for bankruptcy, failing to secure government assistance. This threw the market into chaos. As of September 2010, some 66,000 claims had been filed against Lehman Brothers, exceeding $873 billion.

AIG Bailed Out

444 **2008** American International Group (AIG) had $1 trillion in assets, which proved insufficient to weather the 2008 crisis. AIG suffered from multi-billion-dollar losses on investments, high near-term liabilities, and its potential inability to meet collateral calls if its credit rating was downgraded. A rating downgrade would cost the company $33 billion. AIG held only $12–13 billion in cash and had limited revolving credit options. The federal government was reluctant to lend to AIG, as it would be unfair, seeing as it did not lend to Lehman Brothers. The government also worried that it would not be of much assistance anyway.

On September 15—the day Lehman Brothers declared bankruptcy—the Fed tried to organize a syndicate of banks to lend $75 billion to AIG. That afternoon, rating agencies downgraded AIG. This triggered $13 billion in cash collateral calls, which then jumped to $32 billion. The syndicate fell through. AIG stock fell 61% to $4.76.

The Federal Reserve, with only a few hours to act, decided to bail out the company and offered it $85 billion. This amount was later increased to $182 billion. A day later, AIG stock traded at $1.99. The company lost $99.3 billion in the year 2008 alone.

Year	Return (%)
2008	-99.95
2007	-16.77
2006	20.30
2005	46.58
2004	13.29
2003	40.55
2002	-18.02
2001	2.87
2000	71.07
1999	82.86
1998	-12.96
1997	68.60
1996	47.65
1995	44.07
1994	-15.71

Lehman Brothers stock performance from 1994 to 2008

US Congress Rejects Bailout Bill

445 2008 Two weeks after the collapse of Lehman Brothers, the Emergency Economic Stabilization Act was drafted and brought to the US House. The bill authorized the US Treasury to use $700 billion to stabilize the financial system. It created the Troubled Asset Relief Program, allowing the government to purchase toxic assets from struggling banks to restore liquidity and confidence in the economy. The act also included measures to increase oversight, protect taxpayers, and assist homeowners facing foreclosure.

Voting started on Monday, September 29. The Dow Jones had closed at 11,143 the previous Friday. President Bush and many Congressional leaders pushed the bill, but many Congressmen, knowing the bailout was unpopular among voters, did not want to take the risk of supporting it only five weeks before the upcoming election. At a little past two o'clock, voting concluded with 205 yeas and 228 nays. Two thirds of the Republicans voted against the bill. Following the vote, the Dow plunged 778 points, causing the largest single-day decline up to that point. It closed at 10,365. Legislators planned to reconvene later that week.

Stock Market Crash in US

446 2008 The Dow Jones peaked in October 2007, at just above 14,000 points. Between May and July 2008, the Dow lost about 2,000 points before leveling off between July and September that year. However, some market turbulence persisted throughout. The day Lehman Brothers failed, the market closed 200 points down, and $700 billion in value of investment portfolios disappeared. The market fell another 700 points when the Emergency Economic Stabilization Act fell through in the House. The passage of the Act a few days later did not stop the decline—the Dow hit a low-point of 7,773 on October 10, before rebounding temporarily, then continuing its downward spiral. The S&P 500 did not fare any better, falling to 680 points from a high of 1,500.

Macroeconomic indicators took some time to catch up. The unemployment rate, which hovered around 5% for the past few years, peaked at 10% in October 2009. This meant that over 15 million people were unemployed and looking for work. The GDP fell about $500 billion during the period.

Congress Approves Bailout

447 2008 After the bailout bill failed in the House on September 29, 2008, the Senate made some amendments, and a new bill was passed a few days later. It was not only the threat of economic meltdown that helped push the bill. The bill also included provisions for the expansion of solar and wind power and reduced federal income tax burdens. Still, not everyone supported the bill. Marilyn Musgrove, Republican representative of Colorado, summed up the opposition: "Some things have changed in this bill, but taxpayers will still be picking up the tab for Wall Street's party."

The bill created the Troubled Asset Relief Program (TARP), allowing the Treasury to purchase up to $700 billion of mortgage-related assets and other assets that would contribute to financial stability. The Capital Purchase Program allowed for up to $250 billion to be injected into financial institutions. Compensation for executives was limited.

The act helped stabilize the financial system. It restored a degree of investor confidence, kept several major banks from failing, and made credit more available in the months that followed. However, it did little to stop foreclosures, and many homeowners continued to lose their homes. The program prioritized large financial institutions while offering limited support to small businesses. The TARP program finally closed in 2023, having distributed $443 billion

Iceland Financial Crisis

448 2008 When measured as a proportion of the size of the economy, the Icelandic financial crisis of 2008 was the largest crisis in world history. Further, it was the third-largest series of bank failures in history. At the turn of the millennium, banking sector assets totaled 15.6 trillion Icelandic króna, or $155 billion. This was nine times Iceland's GDP, and assets were growing quickly. By 2007, however, Iceland's economic growth was starting to slow. In the wake of the 2008 crisis on Wall Street, three highly-leveraged Icelandic banks—Glitnir, Landsbanki, and Kaupthing—were unable to finance their debt. They collapsed in September 2008.

The Central Bank of Iceland, with only $2 billion in assets, was forced to nationalize the banks. Glitnir went first. Money started flowing out of the country over fears of further nationalization, forcing Landsbanki to follow suit on October 7. Icelander's deposits at these banks were safe, but it was unclear whether the rest of Europe's depositors were similarly protected. On October 8, the UK imposed anti-terrorist sanctions on Iceland and seized those assets it had access to, effectively cutting Iceland off from the rest of the world. Kaupthing fell next. Iceland needed help quickly.

Scene from the "Kitchenware Revolution" in November 2008, a protest that followed the Iceland financial crisis

Iceland's Recovery from its Financial Crisis

449 2008 Iceland nearly financially capsized from its crisis in 2008. The country took $4 billion in loans from its neighbors. The IMF gave the country $2.1

billion under a few conditions.

First, the three nationalized banks had to be reorganized. Creditors received either shares in the new banks or payments from the insolvency estates of the old banks when assets were liquidated. Second, the national banking regulations had to be changed to prevent similar problems in the future. Senior bank executives were prosecuted for financial misconduct—unlike in the United States, where no one was punished after the 2008 crisis. Additionally, the IMF forced Iceland to ensure all foreign deposits in the same way it protected its citizens' deposits. Lastly, Iceland had to find additional financial help from other countries to subsidize the IMF's stabilization package. Denmark, Norway, Finland, and Sweden provided a combined $2.5 billion. Poland also provided a loan of 200 million euros. This worked. While Iceland's GDP fell from $21 billion in 2007 to $13 billion in 2009, it fully recovered by 2017.

European Bailouts

450 2008–17 While bank bailouts in response to the 2008 crisis mostly occurred in the US, Europe spent almost as large a sum bailing out its own banks. Between 2008 and 2017, the European Commission approved 1.5 trillion euros of capital-assistance aid and 3.7 trillion in liquidity aid, though not all of these funds were used. Of this, some 213 billion euros were permanently lost.

While Americans were primarily concerned with the moral implications of picking up Wall Street's tab, Europeans noticed reduced funding for welfare programs. This came amidst concern about the stress that immigrants were already placing on Europe's welfare programs. This could have been one of the motivators behind Europe's move to the political Right, which gained votes in the 2017 elections.

Conflicts of interest were also a concern. The rescue package was designed by a group of four consulting firms, while financiers held several EU government positions. Importantly, both the extra debt taken on by financial institutions and the increased scrutiny they came under after 2008 contributed to the European Debt Crisis.

Crypto Conceived

451 2008 In October 2008, Satoshi Nakamoto, which is a pseudonym for an unknown person or group of people, published a white paper outlining a new idea for a decentralized payment system: cryptocurrency. One journalist figured that an American Nick Szabo was involved. Szabo denied that he was Nakamoto himself. He is just one of many people suspected of creating Bitcoin, the world's first cryptocurrency.

The concepts behind cryptocurrency are certainly not new. Online government-control-dodgers, often called Cyberpunks, had developed some ideas for anonymous payments in the 1990s. These early ideas garnished little attention. Yet, coders, often motivated by Libertarian political ideals, continued attempting to develop untraceable payment technologies.

The instability caused by the 2008 financial crisis motivated Nakamoto to invent cryptocurrency, money that is controlled neither by the government nor by banks. The first block in Bitcoin's chain is a headline from Britain's *The Times*, reading "Chancellor on brink of second bailout for banks." As a peer-to-peer payment system, Bitcoin does not require third party verification, and is "robust in its unstructured simplicity," as Nakamoto put it.

How Blockchain Works

452 When paying with cash, a transaction is made from a buyer directly to the seller. The transaction is irreversible and anonymous. When paying with a credit card, however, the transaction goes through a bank. The transaction is not anonymous and can be reversed at the bank's discretion. Cryptocurrency is computerized cash. Like most other cash, it is a fiat currency.

The cryptocurrency system makes transactions trustworthy by using a peer-to-peer, distributed ledger of proof. The ledger shows that transactions were made and shows the work necessary to make them. Each crypto coin is a "chain of digital signatures" that retains all the signatures from all previous transactions facilitated by the coin (or, portions of the coin).

Before each coin can be realized, a computer must calculate its proof-of-work—some highly complex math that requires a good deal of CPU power. The proof-of-work is included in the block's signature, which is then included in any successive blocks. This means that, to change one block, you must change all of the blocks before it and their proof-of-work. This requires that you have more CPU power than the rest of the people in the entire network.

New blocks are added to the chain by being broadcast to the other computers (called "nodes") within the network. The system is decentralized, so each node has its own chain that could be different from other nodes' chains. When a node receives another block, it will calculate the proof-of-work and accept it. Nodes always accept the longest chain, and they know which is longest because the length is encoded in the proof-of-work in each block. Nodes show their acceptance of the longest chain by creating a new block with the signature of the last block on that chain. This new block is a transaction.

Zimbabwe Inflation Hits Sextillion Percent

453 2008 Zimbabwe, a country located in southern Africa, was once the richest country in the region. However, by the early 2000s, political tensions that had persisted for decades eventually impoverished the nation. President Robert Mugabe was in office from 1987 to 2017. He was lauded by some as a hero of Africa liberation and criticized by others as a dictator who allowed for human rights abuses and genocide. His party participated in several sparring matches with the opposition, the Movement for Democratic Change. As is often the case with political instability, economic instability followed.

Zimbabwe first hit hyperinflation levels in March 2007. From there, it got worse. The government eventually stopped reporting inflation data as Zimbabwe hit a high of 79.6 billion percent month-to-month inflation in November 2008. That came out to 89.7 sextillion percent year-over-year, coming in second for highest inflation in his-

Hyperinflation

454 Inflation is a tough issue. Some price inflation is not bad, as many developed governments try to maintain a 2% annual inflation rate. Yet, when inflation is too low, it can quickly lead to deflation, where prices are *falling* over time. This scenario motivates companies to reduce output, making it harder for the government to stimulate GDP via lower interest rates. When inflation is too high, it can create hyperinflation, where prices rise over 50% annually. Widespread panic often follows, as workers and consumers try radical solutions to combat their quickly declining buying power.

Hyperinflation has many causes. It can occur when people lose trust in their nation's sovereign currency. While gold and silver maintain their value, the value of paper fiat currency, like the US dollar, is based solely on the trust in the sovereign government issuing the currency. This means fiat money can lose its value quickly if the government cannot operate effectively, like in times of war, severe financial or political instability, or persistent corruption. Indeed, countries like Zimbabwe and Argentina suffered hyperinflation due to their highly unstable governments.

Hyperinflation can also occur from printing too much currency. The government's ability to adjust the supply of money can assist in moderating changes in its economic output. However, if the money supply grows substantially faster than the economy's output, consumers start spending more money on the same quantity of goods. This increases the price of every transaction, and regular inflation can quickly turn to hyperinflation. During the American Civil War, the Confederate government started printing money because it couldn't get the Southern states to contribute to the war effort [see: 231]. Hyperinflation also happens when the supply of goods decreases drastically but the supply of money does not. This often happens during or after wars, when goods are in short supply.

tory [for first, see: 318]. In response, the government just added zeros to its currency. It ordered 100 trillion Zimbabwe dollar notes, which were worthless by the time they made their way into circulation. It stopped printing notes in 2009, and people started using foreign currency instead of local currency. To help with this transition, the government created a program to exchange Zimbabwe dollars for US dollars, at a rate of ZW$175 quadrillion to US$5.

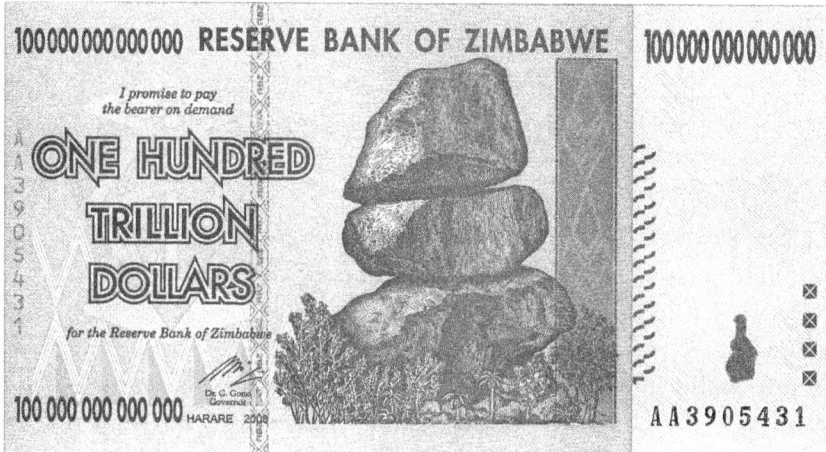

A 100 trillion Zimbabwe dollar banknote

Bernie Madoff Exposed

455 2008 The collapse of the Madoff Ponzi scheme resulted in some of the largest losses of the 2008 crisis. Sort of. Investors lost $64.8 billion of non-existent gains on never-invested money. People from all walks of life were invested in the firm: hedge fund managers, charities, pension funds, retirees, and regular citizens. Some investors had millions or billions with Madoff.

The run on the Madoff investment bank started during the 2008 crisis, as investors were trying to take their money out of the market. Madoff's firm, however, continued showing gains. Problems hit the firm in mid-December. Over the previous month, $1.2 billion had been withdrawn from the fund, and Madoff was unable to secure a loan or get more money from feeder funds as aid. By December 10, he realized his days were numbered. That morning, he cashed $173 million out of the accounts of his friends and family. At about noon later that day, Madoff told his wife and his sons that his hedge fund was a fraud.

One of Madoff's sons turned him in, and the FBI raided his office the next day. On March 12, 2009, Madoff pleaded guilty to 11 criminal charges and was sentenced to 150 years in prison.

How Madoff's Ponzi Scheme Ran

456 The Madoff scheme, which started in the '80s or '90s, involved the money of over 40,000 investors, creating $64.8 billion in fictitious gains. Here is how Bernie Madoff did it. His firm, Bernard L. Madoff Investment Securities LLC, was actually two companies. On the 19th floor of the Lipstick Building—his head office in Manhattan—he operated a legitimate trading firm, run by his two sons, Mark and Andrew. Two stories down, on the 17th floor, was where the Ponzi scheme operated, run by Bernie's long-time right-hand man, Frank DiPiscali, and a few others. Madoff gave important jobs to people he knew for a long time and trusted. Annette Bongiorno and Joanne Cupi were his other top employees, and they worked for Madoff for 40 and 30 years, respectively.

Frank's job was to create fictitious trading records showing 10–17% annual returns. To get this rate-of-return, the firm traded retroactively. They found stocks that went up in the past and claimed they had bought those stocks, when no money was actually invested. Madoff avoided adopting computer systems as long as possible. Into the 2000s, the Madoff fund had no website and mailed account statements that were printed on DotMatrix printers. It was easier to create fraudulent transactions by hand. Madoff did eventually hire two coders to put together a computer program to create fraudulent documents.

When asked about his investment strategy, Madoff told the public he used a "split-strike conversion strategy." According to him, an investor makes three purchases to establish a position: one, a basket of securities that correlate with the S&P 100 index; two, an out-of-the-money S&P 100 Index put option; and three, the sale of an out-of-the-money S&P 100 Index call option. This strategy is meant to balance itself and have a safe, constant rate of return, and other firms used this strategy, even if Madoff did not.

US Interest Rate Hits All-Time Low

457 2008 On December 16, 2008, the Fed effectively reduced the federal funds rate to 0–0.25%, the lowest rate in US history (at least until 2020). The federal funds rate is the rate at which banks charge other banks for loaning out money on a very short-term basis, usually for only a day. This interest rate has limited implications for the interest rates that businesses and individual consumers actually pay when taking out loans. Mortgages, car loans, and credit cards all maintained much higher rates, as they are often calculated as a multiple of the federal funds rate. This means that even though the government set interest rates at nearly zero, most consumers still paid interest on goods.

A concern with extremely low interest rates is that, if the economy deteriorates further, the Fed will have no room to lower interest rates further in an attempt to stimulate economic output and recover from a recession. However, in this case, the lower interest rates were deemed necessary and, ultimately, did not mean the Fed had thrown out a key tool for creating expansionary monetary policy to boost the economy.

Stock Market Hits Bottom

458 2009 After the 2008 crisis, the Dow Jones hit its lowest point of 6,547 points on March 9, 2009. The crisis started with the sale of Bear Stearns on March 16, 2008. From that point, the Dow fell 5,425 points, or 45.3%. The market capitalization of US companies fell from $19.9 trillion in 2007 to $11.6 trillion in 2008, before rebounding somewhat to $15 trillion in 2009. As a percentage of GDP, the market cap fell from 137% to 78%, then rose back up to 104%. This resulted in a loss of $3.9 trillion of US retirement assets between 2007 and 2008.

On February 17, 2009, a few weeks before this bottom point, a recovery bill was passed. It allocated $787 billion for economic stimulus, providing money to over two dozen government departments, with the goal of boosting GDP and creating 3.5 million jobs. The wide-ranging provisions of the act addressed nutrition assistance programs, administration of justice, funding for sciences, and more. They say that, when a country hits rock bottom, the only way to go is up. The US, however, stayed at this low point for over a year.

The Huge Scale of the 2008 Crisis

459 2008–10 It can be difficult to appreciate the sheer scale of the losses resulting from the 2008 crisis. Here are some of the numbers. By 2007, $1.3 trillion outstanding subprime mortgages existed, with $265 billion of teaser rate loans scheduled to reset to higher interest rates in 2007—rates as high as 12%. Resetting loans resulted in a delinquency rate of 12.6%, and the financial stress shook the stock market for an $8 trillion loss in stock value between 2007 and 2009.

Tri-party repo borrowing is a type of borrowing designed to ease repossession and ensure smooth settlement between the borrower and lender. This type of borrowing was thought to be safe. However, it created systemic risk, the risk of widespread financial instability due to the failure of a key firm. Tri-party repo hit a daily volume of $2.8 trillion by 2008.

Bear Stearns, the first firm to collapse in the crisis, managed a balance sheet of $400 billion. Mortgage securitization was its biggest business, generating 45% of the firm's revenue. Lehman Brothers was the largest firm that failed in the crisis. In 2008, the firm had $28 billion in shareholder equity, as well as about $90 billion in real estate assets on its books. In Q1 of 2008, Lehman used $197 billion of repo borrowing and its $54 billion in liquidity proved insufficient to weather the 2008 crisis.

Fannie Mae and Freddie Mac, which were both government-sponsored, guaranteed $5.3 trillion in mortgages. These firms each had portfolio caps of over $700 billion. They lost a combined $229 billion between 2008 and 2010.

In all, it is estimated that US banks and brokerages alone experienced losses of $1.8 trillion in loan and securities write-downs due to the 2008 crisis. This amount is equivalent to the size of the entire Polish economy today. Indeed, the GDPs of only 19 countries worldwide exceed this amount.

Great Recession

460 2007–9 Just as the 1929 market crash contributed to the Great Depression, so too did the 2008 crisis contribute to the Great Recession. However, the Great Recession technically started before the crash in December 2007, due to a general downturn caused by the factors that ultimately caused the crash. According to the National Bureau of Economic Research, it lasted until June 2009, though its effects continued to linger a few years longer.

US unemployment hit 10% in October 2009 and did not return to its pre-crisis level until 2016. That statistic, however, does not account for the fact that 16% of workers lost their job at some point during the Recession. Median family income dropped by 8%. One-fourth of all households lost at least 75% of their wealth between 2007 and 2011. By 2013, housing prices—a measure of demand—were 30% below their 2006 peak. The stock market did not recover until 2013.

The 2008 bailout package and 2009 stimulus bill—which together cost the country over $1.4 trillion—may appear to have not really worked, as things immediately got worse. However, economists have put together counterfactual models for an economy without these packages, finding that the unemployment rate would have been over 11%, and 7 million more people could have descended into poverty.

A poster advertising a tour of houses foreclosed on in the wake of the 2008 crisis

Great Recession Internationally

461 2007–9 The Great Recession impacted Europe and North America the most but had limited impact on Asia. Even so, China announced a plan in November 2008 to spend over 4 trillion yuan ($586 billion) on the nation's infrastructure, shortly after the southwest region of the country was hit by an earthquake. China's annual economic growth dipped below 10% for the first time in five years in 2008, and its exports as a percentage of GDP fell from 36% in 2006 to 24.7% in 2009.

Internationally, most countries fared better than the US on unemployment. The Netherlands' rate, for example, barely hit 5%. However, while the US GDP dropped from $14.8 trillion down to $14.3 trillion, the EU GDP measured in current US dollars dropped from $16.2 trillion to $14.7 trillion. In May 2008, output fell 1.9% in the European Monetary Union, while in 2009, Greece's GDP fell 4.3% and Italy's fell 5%.

While the US mostly recovered by 2016, the rest of the world did not catch up as quickly. The Asian Miracle stopped by the end of the Great Recession, while Europe moved into a debt crisis.

The Men who Made Billions During 2008

462 2008–9 The losses from the 2008 crisis and its aftermath are estimated to be somewhere between $2–10 trillion. However, some astute individuals profited from the crisis. Michael Burry, a 32-year-old hedge fund manager, was obsessed with mortgage-backed securities (MBS). He read dozens of the multi-hundred-page-long documents detailing how these investment devices worked. In 2004, he realized that the underlying mortgages making up many MBSs were of very poor quality. In 2005, he predicted that it would only take three years for mass defaults to occur, and he bought the first of many credit-default swaps (CDS) against MBSs, effectively shorting them.

Steve Eisman, who worked at a hedge fund called FrontPoint, also picked up on the problems in the MBS market. He started buying similar CDSs. By April 2006, he had bet $1.9 billion against MBSs. However, by the end of 2006, he had a problem. Of the $555 million invested with him, $302 million became eligible for withdrawal by his clients. He decided to keep the money. His client contracts stipulated that if money was invested in stocks that could not be sold, the firm was not required to give investors their money back. His investors threatened to sue. It did not help that in 2006, while the S&P had gained 10%, his firm lost 18%.

By the start of 2007, the mortgage market started to appear to be having trouble. But large Wall Street firms simply ignored it. The month-over-month delinquencies, foreclosures, and bankruptcies on mortgages that Burry and Eisman had bet against began rising, hitting 16% by May and 37.7% by August. Michael Burry and Steve Eisman's plans worked, though with a slight delay, and they soon profited $100 million and $1 billion, respectively. A handful of other investors profited billions of dollars as well. These events were retold in the book-turned-movie, *The Big Short*.

Steve Eisman realized the housing market was a bubble after meeting a stripper who told him she owned five houses purchased with little or no collateral.

Goldman Sachs's Computer Algorithm Stolen

463 2009 Imagine if the global economy could be derailed with the push of a button. This fear permeated investor sentiment after the highly proprietary high-frequency trading (HFT) computer algorithms developed by Goldman Sachs were stolen in 2009.

HFT algorithms react to each other, making trades in mere milliseconds. People feared that a single, malevolent HFT program could exploit the interconnectedness and speed of HFT systems and instantly propagate errors or shocks across international markets, creating a systemic, global financial crisis. The 2010 Flash Crash is an example of such extreme market movements. HFT algorithms contributed to a plunge in the Dow Jones Industrial Average of nearly 1,000 points within mere minutes.

Sergey Aleynikov, who immigrated to the United States from Russia in 1990, was the man behind the theft. He worked for Goldman Sachs as one of its highest-paid programmers, making an annual salary of $400,000 helping develop Goldman's HFT code. He was arrested in July 2009 and spent 11 months in prison, a reduced sentence from a possible 10 years. Speculators noted that the effort put in to convict Aleynikov was a step forward in prosecuting intellectual property theft.

2010 Flash Crash

464 2010 On May 6, 2010, US financial markets experienced one of the most turbulent moments in their history. For 36 minutes. The flash crash started at 2:32 p.m., and within the next 36 minutes, the Dow Jones lost about 1,000 points. Other markets were severely affected, too. Then, almost as quickly, stock prices rebounded.

Algorithm-based computerized trading was the primary cause of the 2010 Flash Crash. In the days leading up to May 6, the markets experienced some unusual volatility. In response, the HFT algorithms [see: 436] at a group of mutual funds decided they had to sell 75,000 E-mini S&P 500 futures contracts. Evidently, the computer systems were not very forward-thinking, as this one sale order triggered sales orders on many other HFT programs, starting a downward spiral. Markets plunged for about 13 minutes. Prices then rose for the next 23 minutes, returning roughly to pre-crisis levels. The 2010 Flash Crash crisis showed the possible dangers arising from computerized HFT trading. New regulation was developed, but computerized HFT trading continued, starting yet another flash crash in April 2015.

Dodd-Frank Act

465 2010 Financial regulation sometimes goes in circles. After a financial crisis, more restrictive regulation is developed. A few decades later, the regulation is thought to be excessive, and it is relaxed. Soon, another crisis happens, at which point new regulation is demanded, and the circle of regulatory life continues.

The Dodd-Frank Act, passed in 2010, restarted the loop following the 2008 crisis. The Act raises financial management standards. It provided a clear way for the Fed to handle failing institutions, including banks that are "too big to fail." The Act also boosted transparency in risky markets, such as derivatives markets.

These provisions appear beneficial, but the Act is not entirely favorable. It requires that the Fed make emergency loans to entire categories of institutions, rather than to individual ones. Further, it must get permission from Congress to make certain types of emergency loans. These two provisions appear to limit the timing and scope of the Fed's crisis-prevention abilities.

Scholarship is still inconclusive about whether increased government oversight is beneficial to finance markets. One perspective blames the U.S. government itself for exacerbating the 2008 crisis by encouraging risk-taking and eroding the rule of law by using excessive discretionary federal power.

IMF Bails Out Greece

466 2010 In 2009, a new government in Greece inherited a budget deficit that was almost double what the government had thought it was, contributing to a 115% debt-to-GDP ratio. Within months, credit opportunities for Greece dried up, investors fled, and the country's debt ratings were downgraded. This happened just as Greece needed money to recover from the 2008 crisis.

Borrowing had been easy for Greece since it switched to using the euro in the '90s. Now unable to borrow, Greece quickly enacted economic austerity measures, but doubts remained about its future solvency. There was concern that Greece's continued debt could hamper the economic recovery of other EU states, possibly bringing down the entire EU system.

Saving Greece was important for the global image of the euro and would require one of the largest international bailout packages. A plan was struck between Greece, the IMF, and the EU. The EU countries would lend a total of 80 billion euros, and the IMF would lend another 30 billion. Despite the agreement to significantly cut Greece's deficit, the debt-to-GDP ratio increased to 180% by 2017. It became clear that Greece would need ongoing assistance rather than a one-time bailout.

A bank branch burned in 2010 during a protest against austerity measures

European Financial Stability Facility

467 **2010** The European Financial Stability Facility (EFSF) was created in May 2010. Originally intended to make loans to Greece, Ireland, and Portugal, the EFSF was financed and backed by Eurozone member countries. Though it had a public role, the EFSF was incorporated as a private entity in Luxembourg that was owned and jointly managed by 17 EU member states. This meant it was under the control of the member countries and the European Central Bank, but not the European Parliament.

The EFSF had 440 billion euros of its own money, plus 310 billion euros more from the IMF, allowing it up to 750 billion euros to support countries. The EFSF contributed a part to bailing out the Irish and the Portuguese, providing about one-quarter and one-third of the total packages those countries received, respectively. The EFSF also disbursed 130.9 billion euros to Greece, making it Greece's largest creditor.

The EFSF pooled the money it collected from European countries, meaning that no one country was responsible for the whole of any given bailout. The organization was replaced in 2012 with a permanent entity, the European Stability Mechanism.

Ireland and Italy Bailout

468 2010 The Irish housing bubble burst in 2007. Although the government injected over 60 billion euros into its banking system, the crisis-induced decline in GDP made it difficult for Ireland to pay back the debt used to finance the injection. Ireland applied for a bailout on November 21, 2010. The EU provided Ireland with 85 billion euros, 35 billion of which went to the Irish banking system, and the remaining 50 billion went to helping with government expenses. The package came with three conditions: Ireland must strengthen its banking system, reduce its deficit to 3% of GDP by 2015, and promote economic growth, particularly in the labor market.

Portugal's economy had been in decline for a decade. The country found itself in crisis when its bond rates rose. In May 2011, the EU provided Portugal with 78 billion euros. As part of the package, Portugal agreed to government reforms, privatizing its healthcare system, assisting its banks, and cutting its deficit to 3% of GDP by 2013. The package also required a tax increase and government spending cuts. Unlike Greece's deal, the package did not require the politically-unpopular cuts to public sector payrolls or any change in the retirement age for public pensions.

European Countries' Debt Downgraded

469 2011–12 As a symptom of the debt crisis, the sovereign debt ratings of European countries were downgraded. This had the effect of raising their borrowing costs, making it harder for them to recover from the 2008 crisis. By September 2011, Standard and Poor's Ratings Agency downgraded Italian debt from A+ to A. Italy's SPRA rating was downgraded further to BBB+ in 2012. The justification cited was the uncertainty surrounding the effectiveness of Italy's 60 billion euro austerity measures and the growth-hampering effects of the tax increases used to decrease the national debt.

The ratings of Austria and France were also decreased from AAA to AA+, while Portugal and Cyprus were given junk-bond status. Even the European Financial Stability Facility (EFSF) was downgraded, as rating agencies noted its guarantor nations may have difficulty backing EFSF loans. Germany's rating remained at AAA.

The rate on Spain's 10-year government bonds hit 6.8% in 2012, up from around 4% a few years earlier. The cost to Italy rose one-third of a percentage point, and in France, it rose 0.04%, while the downgrade of the EFSF may have impaired its operations. Of course, making it harder to borrow did not help the debt crisis.

European Economies Contract

470 2011–13 For Europe, the European Sovereign Debt Crisis dragged out the Great Recession. By April 2013, Greece's unemployment rate hit 27%, and Spain's hit 26%. Portugal was also doing poorly, with an unemployment rate ranging from 14–15% from 2011 to 2013. Greece's GDP fell by 7.1% in 2011, Portugal's fell

1.6%, and Spain's rose by a paltry 0.4%. Greece's debt was the highest, hitting 170% of GDP in 2011. Italy's debt was at 120% of GDP, and Portugal's was 108%.

Poor macroeconomic indicators were not the only effects of the Sovereign Debt Crisis. After the May 2010 bailout was announced, riots broke out in Greece. Protesters—many of whom were associated with left-wing political parties—rallied and sparred with police. Politicians came under heavy criticism, and union workers went on strike. (All certainly of aid to the GDP!) "They say the only way of salvaging our economy is more austerity, but that's a total lie," one Greek shipyard worker participating in a Communist-led demonstration told reporters, summing up the protesters' complaints. "These latest measures have been cooked up by outsiders [and] are aimed not at the rich but at the poor."

Euro Under Attack

471 After the Eurozone Crisis, many questioned whether the euro was fit to be an international currency. The naysayers had been critical since the euro's adoption, and now they were garnishing more attention. William Hague, a conservative member of the UK Parliament, who led the Save the Pound campaign in 2001, described the euro as a "burning building with no exits." He claimed that the system "will be written about for centuries as a kind of historical monument to collective folly."

Hague's comments may have been a little aggressive, but he points to the presence of legitimate shortcomings in the Eurozone system. Unlike the United States—which has an economy about the same size as the EU and similarly uses a single currency to span diverse regions—the EU does not have a central institution that coordinates economic policy, as does the US Fed. Since a central institution is not making a unified policy, individual countries must implement policies that do not necessarily reflect the best interests of the monetary union as a whole. At the same time, individual countries cannot run their own expansionary or contractionary policy without running into balance of payments troubles. Thus, the use of a single currency leads to issues unless the economies of the participating countries are synced. Since EU countries are very different, keeping them in sync is difficult.

Greece suffered most. Discussions of Greece leaving the Eurozone started in 2010, termed "Grexit." Greece's prime minister at the time, George Papandreou, denied that Greece had plans to leave. Arguments against leaving claimed that if Greece left, the unemployment rate would jump to 34%, and inflation would jump to 30%. These concerns never became a reality, even though supporters for Grexit re-emerged through Greece's three bailouts.

Debt Ceiling Crisis

472 2011 In 2011, the United States federal government had a $14.3 trillion debt ceiling, though the budget already exceeded that amount. If the debt ceiling was not raised, the government would be breaking federal law. Whenever the debt ceiling was reached in the past, Congress simply raised the cap without debate. But this time, Republicans refused to raise the ceiling without extracting spending cuts from Democrats. The consequences of not raising the ceiling would be disastrous. Not only would the government have to close—it would be defaulting on its debt.

August 2, 2011, was the deadline set by the Treasury Department. On that day, the US government would be out of money. Officials realized the impending problem in December 2010, but no real steps were taken until July 2011. On July 31, then-President Obama and a group of Congress members agreed on the Budget Control Act. The Act raised the debt ceiling by $2 trillion and cut federal spending by $2.4 trillion. The crisis was averted. This incident, however, made investors worry that politics threatened US financial security, and US bonds were downgraded for the first time.

US President Obama and Vice President Joe Biden shaking hands after the resolution of the debt ceiling crisis

US Bonds Downgraded

473 2011 A debt-ceiling crisis was narrowly averted on August 2, 2011. While Fitch, a large credit-rating agency, kept US bond ratings at AAA, the S&P Rating Agency (SPRA) downgraded the United States' sovereign credit rating on August 5, changing US bond ratings from the top ranking of AAA to the second-best rating, AA+. This meant that the SPRA had less confidence in the US' ability to pay back its debt. The SPRA's stated justification was that political controversy undermined the government's ability to act in the best interest of its creditors. The agency was also concerned about the ability of the US Congress to effectively enact economic policy in the future. This is the first time the US' creditworthiness was downgraded.

While the US no longer being considered a completely risk-free borrower was a symbolic blow to the country's image, it is unclear if the downgrade had any real implications. Since poorly rated debt is perceived as riskier, lenders require a higher interest rate, making borrowing money more expensive. However, US government borrowing continued to be as strong as ever, and the stock market rebounded within two weeks of the debt-ceiling crisis.

First Altcoins

474 2011 The launch of Bitcoin in 2009 opened the door for a proliferation of different cryptocurrencies [see: 451]. These new cryptocurrencies were based on Bitcoin's technology, but offered different services with various improvements. They were termed alternative cryptocurrencies, or "altcoins." The first altcoin, Namecoin, was introduced in 2011. It aimed to provide decentralized domain name registration, reducing the risk of censorship by governments and corporations. Namecoin was based on Bitcoin's code but added the ability to store data within its blockchain.

Another early altcoin was Litecoin, launched in October 2011. Litecoin modified Bitcoin's code to offer faster transaction times and used a different hashing algorithm, Scrypt, which made mining (creating new coins on the blockchain) more accessible to individual users. It was often referred to as "the silver to Bitcoin's gold." In 2012, Peercoin introduced a proof-of-stake system, where users in the crypto network validate transactions based on the amount of Peercoin they hold, rather than by solving math equations as is the case in proof-of-work. Proof-of-stake is more energy efficient than proof-of-work, as it requires less computing power.

Other notable early altcoins include Ripple in 2012, which focused on fast and low-cost cross-border payments, and Feathercoin in 2013, which sought to improve Litecoin's design. These altcoins contributed to the spread of crypto technology.

European Stability Mechanism

475 2012 The European Financial Stability Facility (EFSF) was set to operate for only three years and was originally limited by a "no bailout clause" in the Treaty of the Functioning of the European Union [see: 467]. Before those three years expired, the Treaty was amended, and the European Stability Mechanism (ESM) was founded in February 2012. The ESM was to permanently replace the EFSF.

An intergovernmental agreement created the ESM, meaning it is not a traditional legal entity bound by normal EU laws and not overseen by EU organizations. The ESM is also not fully a government organization and is not designed to assist in economic reform programs or surveillance. The organization is empowered to lend up to

500 billion euros.

After replacing the EFSF, the ESM managed to help Europe out of the Sovereign Debt Crisis. Its first operation was making a loan of 41.3 billion euros to Spain in July 2012 to help recapitalize its banks. In 2013, the ESM loaned 9 billion euros to Cyprus and continued to help Greece. The ESM must take its permanent designation very seriously, as it is set to be collecting debt from Greece until 2060!

Argentina Kicked Out of IMF

476 2013 In 2007, Nestor Kirchner, the president of Argentina, fired two officials at Argentina's national statistics agency. He was looking to replace them with folks who could "improve operations." Within a few months, new inflation statistics were published that were substantially more attractive than those created by the old officials. The official cumulative annual inflation rate reported by the government for the period between 2007 and 2011 was 39%, even though the unofficial rate was 120%. The relationship between Argentina and the IMF was strained since Argentina's crisis in the '90s, and the IMF was not happy to hear about Argentina's incorrect reporting of its macroeconomic data.

In September 2012, the IMF issued an order to Argentina to correct its data. Argentina did not comply, and on February 1, 2013, the IMF released a censure on Argentina, allowing until September for the country to correct its statistics. Argentina lost its voting privileges and aid, until the censure was revoked in 2016. In 2023, the IMF caved and started to organize another $44 billion bailout for the country.

Robinhood Gamifies Investing

477 2013 In 2013, Vladimir Tenev and Baiju Bhat, two entrepreneurs looking to democratize the stock market, founded Robinhood. Using Robinhood, people could trade on their phone without a traditional brokerage account. By 2014, 340,000 people put their name on the waitlist to use the app. In 2021, the app hit 21 million users, though the number of users backslid in the following years. Part of Robinhood's popularity comes from how it gamified investment. The app shows animations when stocks are traded and offers lottery games to win free stocks. However, the app also lacks technical features pertinent to trading, including legal information, and it emphasizes popular stocks, which are not necessarily the best investments.

Robinhood makes money using payment-for-order flow. Robinhood's market-maker—the company that actually processes the trades made on the Robinhood app—pays Robinhood a very small sum per trade that Robinhood directs to it. The market-maker makes money from the difference between the bid and ask price for stocks it processes. Thus, Robinhood makes money when its users make trades—be they good or bad. As other financial services moved onto people's phones, Robinhood helped investment switch, too.

Cypriot Financial Crisis

478 **2013** In the 2000s, Cyprus' banking sector was quickly expanding. The sector's assets increased from 286% of GDP to 600% between 2004 and 2010. In 2011, Greece lowered the value of its debt, much of which had been lent by Cypriot banks. Concurrently, non-performing loans were piling up as Cyprus' politics looked increasingly unstable.

Eventually, credit rating agencies downgraded the debt of Cyprus and its banks. Additionally, Cyprus' second-largest bank, Laiki, lent an extra 5.5 billion euros to the Greek government that it had received from the EU Emergency Liquidity Assistance program. Soon, a general run on Cypriot banks started. Though the ELA program turned its attention to helping Laiki itself, it did not prove to be of much assistance as Laiki was liquidated on March 25, 2013.

Debt from Laiki and other firms was transferred to the Bank of Cyprus (BoC), the country's largest bank. However, the BoC had insufficient capital to absorb this extra debt, so it converted the cash of 47.5% of unsecured depositors with over 100,000 euros into BoC shares in August 2013. The Bank felt there was little alternative. Meanwhile, Cyprus' debt-rating was further downgraded to CCC. Cyprus was now in the midst of a full-blown crisis.

Bank of Cyprus regional office

Cyprus Rescued with Bail-In

479 **2013** After the 2013 Cypriot Financial Crisis set in, it was decided that the country needed a bail-in, the opposite of the more common bailout. Unlike a bailout, where the government rescues a bank by paying off its debt, a bail-in occurs when the government cancels a bank's obligations to debtors and creditors or converts the obligations into bank shares. Instead of the government giving money to a bank to pay its debt, the bank uses its deposits to restructure its debt. Bail-ins are preferable when the government cannot afford a bailout or wants creditors to pay rather than taxpayers.

In March 2013, Cyprus received 17 billion euros from the European Central Bank, the IMF, and the European Commission. This amount looks small in absolute terms but was equal to Cyprus' annual GDP. Of that, 10 billion euros went to rolling over expiring debt and budget deficits. The rest went to helping Cyprus' two largest banks. Capital controls were imposed, meaning that the euro was essentially devalued within Cyprus. Between 2011 and 2015, the GDP declined 10%, and unemployment rose 84%. As Cyprus began recovering after 2015, some economists suggested that Cyprus leave the euro. Cyprus ultimately did not leave.

JPMorgan Chase Found Helping Madoff

480 2014 In 2014, it was discovered that the money managed by the Madoff investment advisory Ponzi scheme—the money that should have been invested in the stock market but was not [see: 456]—was actually just sitting in a bank account at JPMorgan bank. And the bank knew about it all along.

Madoff first opened his account in 1986. Up to his demise in 2008, he deposited and withdrew a total of $150 billion from the account, keeping an average balance of $3–5 billion. The government regulation aimed at stopping this type of fraud evidently was not enforced and did not work, as JPMorgan ignored numerous red flags and even recommended its clients to Madoff's feeder funds.

The government fined JPMorgan bank $3 billion for being complicit to fraud. However, the bank received a deferred prosecution agreement. Under the condition that the bank made certain compliance-related reforms, the charges would be dismissed.

Mt. Gox Collapses

481 2014 Mt. Gox was launched in Japan in 2007. Originally founded as a trading platform for Magic: The Gathering cards, Mt. Gox transitioned into a Bitcoin exchange in 2010. By 2013, it handled about 70% of all Bitcoin transactions worldwide. However, it did not reign for long. Mt. Gox collapsed in 2014 after losing approximately 850,000 BTC, worth around $450 million at the time.

Almost since its start, security flaws and poor management plagued the platform. In February 2014, Mt. Gox abruptly halted withdrawals, citing technical issues related to transaction malleability, an exploit allowing attackers to alter transaction details before confirmation. Soon after, the exchange shut down completely and filed for bankruptcy in Japan with debts of 6.5 billion yen (over $60 million). The exchange had, in fact, been losing Bitcoin for years due to undetected hacks and mismanagement. Although 200,000 BTC were later recovered, over 20,000 customers lost money in the collapse. The price of Bitcoin fell from over $1,100 down to as low as about $450 shortly thereafter.

Following the collapse, Mt. Gox's former CEO, Mark Karpelès, was charged with fraud and data manipulation. In 2024, the firm began to return nearly $9 billion of crypto to customers.

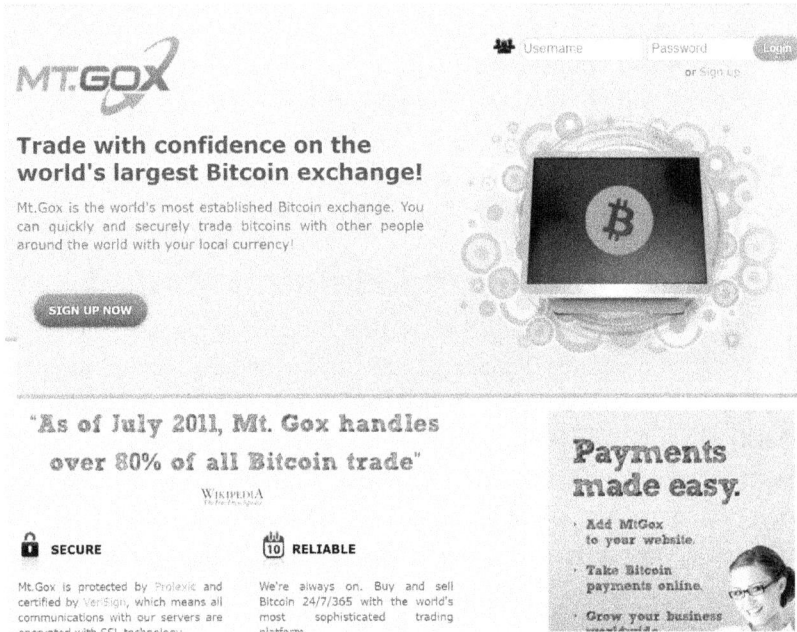

The Mt. Gox website home page, January 2013

Payment on Phones

482 **2014** In September 2014, Apple launched Apple Pay. The next year, Samsung added payment technology to its phones, too. These services use near-field communication (NFC) technology, a way of wirelessly transferring data across four centimeters or fewer, to allow cellphones to be used like credit cards at check out. NFC chips are tuned to 13.56 Mhz and can send 106–848 kib/sec, along with the electricity necessary to power the chip.

This wireless, contactless payment is just as secure as using a credit card's magnetic strip or chip. Credit card information is not stored on the phone but saved inside the phone company's servers as a secure token. For each payment, a unique dynamic security code is generated to authenticate the token and transaction. Further, your phone requires a password to make a payment, while a credit card does not.

As of 2022, mobile payments comprise half of all retail transactions and are used by over 2.8 billion people. Not only does NFC make transactions easier and faster, it also makes digital payment more accessible. Unbanked people who cannot get credit cards can still use their phones to make transactions, accessing the ease of non-cash payments that would otherwise not be available to them.

Purchasing Power Parity

483 Purchasing power parity (PPP) relies on the "law of one price," where the price of a good will be the same in all locations if it is quoted in the same currency. Applying PPP reveals how much a currency is worth compared to others, based on its current purchasing power. It differs from the market currency exchange rate, which is influenced by what traders will pay to buy and sell currencies.

The price of a McDonald's Big Mac is an often-used example. If a Big Mac costs £2 in London and $4 in New York, then the pound is worth twice the value of the dollar according to the PPP rate. Of course, a hamburger is not representative of all goods in a country, so a basket of goods is used instead to calculate PPP.

The earliest versions of PPP traces back to 17th century Spain. Many classical economists of the 19th century endorsed PPP views. Swedish economist Gustav Castell brought the theory to mainstream attention. In 1916, he published an article looking at prices in the US and Sweden. He noted that, though market exchange rates changed during World War I, PPP exchange rates stayed the same. He also used PPP to argue that countries like Britain needed major deflation to remain on the gold standard. Castell argued that PPP will only occasionally diverge from market exchange rates and should not diverge dramatically.

The relationship between PPP and market exchange rate was later developed by Keynes, who wrote that "purchasing power parity deserves attention, even though it is not always an accurate forecaster of the foreign exchanges." Interest in PPP resurged after international exchange rates had to be realigned after World War II, and the measure continues to be used as a tool by international agencies today.

China's GDP Surpasses US

484 2015 This claim sounds a little misleading: As of 2025, US nominal GDP was over $30 trillion, while China's was about $20 trillion. So what is going on?

Nominal GDP measures the value of all final goods and services produced within a country's borders in a certain period of time. The value of nominal GDP is counted using the value of a country's currency in contemporary dollar terms at the time (not inflation-adjusted values). Thus, nominal GDP is heavily influenced by the specific exchange rate between the country under analysis (China) and the country doing the analysis (US).

Measuring real GDP using purchasing power parity-adjusted (PPP) tells a different story. PPP GDP is measured in international dollars, which is an imaginary unit that would buy the equivalent amount of goods in a foreign country that a dollar would buy in the US. When adjusting GDP for PPP, China has come out ahead since 2015. As of 2022, the US PPP GDP is $25.5 trillion while China's is $30.3 trillion. This means that, though the nominal measure of GDP is higher in the US than in China, the lower relative prices in China make GDP in PPP terms bigger in China than in the US.

Ethereum Created

485 2015 Ethereum, introduced in 2015 by Vitalik Buterin, expanded on the design of Bitcoin [see: 451] to make blockchain more versatile. Most notably, Ethereum introduced smart contracts—self-executing agreements with the terms directly embedded in code. While traditional contracts often require a trusted third party to manage a transaction, smart contracts automatically and securely execute on their own.

Smart contracts make decentralized finance safer. They facilitate the creation of tokenized derivatives, the values of which are derived from underlying assets. This allows complex financial instruments to be managed on the blockchain. Ethereum can be used to create platforms where users can lend, borrow, and trade assets without traditional financial institutions.

Ethereum also pioneered the concept of tokenization through standards like ERC-20 and ERC-721. ERC-20 allows for the creation of fungible tokens, which can be exchanged one-to-one with other tokens that represent interchangeable assets, rights, or money. ERC-721 supports non-fungible tokens (NFT), which represent individual unique assets. This can include art, real estate contracts, and other specific items. Additionally, Ethereum allows developers to build and deploy decentralized applications on the blockchain. Ethereum was the first tool on the blockchain to make financial instruments other than money decentralized.

Greece Misses Debt Payment

486 2015 After Greece's first bailout [see: 466], the country received two more rescue packages: the second in 2012, and the third in 2015. Greeks complained the 2010 and 2012 packages went to repaying debts, not to helping the underlying problems of the economy. Exasperated creditors complained that Greece was not "following the rules."

In the 2015 Greek election, a far-left, anti-austerity campaign won seats in the parliament. In June of that year, the Greek government and its creditors were unable to come to an agreement and move forward, while Greece was running out of cash needed to make payments on its debt. On June 26, a referendum was opened as to whether Greece should accept austerity measures demanded by its creditors in exchange for a 7.2 billion euro bailout.

As concerns that Greece would leave the EU abounded, people withdrew deposits from banks, many of which closed. On June 30, the Greek government missed a 1.5 billion euro payment to the IMF, and a few days later, the austerity referendum was shot down. About a week later, Greece agreed to stay in the Eurozone, accept a new rescue package of as much as 86 billion euros, and make large economic reforms. No final solution was proposed, however.

A protest for voting "no" on the 2015 austerity referendum in Athens, Greece

Indian Banknotes Demonetized

487 **2016** On November 8, 2016, the Indian government demonetized the Mahatma Gandhi series 500 and 1,000 rupee banknotes and revoked their legal tender status. The goal of the demonetization effort was to reduce the amount of counterfeit notes in circulation, as most counterfeits at the time were 500 and 1,000 rupee notes. The Indian government opened offices at which people could deposit their money in bank accounts or exchange it for non-demonetized banknotes. Digital transactions were unaffected. The demonetization, however, ultimately turned out to be a mess.

The Gandhi series 500 and 1,000 rupee banknotes made up 86% of India's money supply. As digital and bank-to-bank payment methods, such as credit cards, were not used nearly as widely in India as in more developed countries, reducing the money supply by removing so much currency from circulation had disastrous effects. Citizens had difficulty making payments for everyday transactions for lack of access to legal currency. Further, the insufficient money supply stifled India's rapid rate of economic growth. At the end of the year, actual GDP growth was lower than the growth predicted before the demonetization. The Sensex index fell 1,700 points, or a little over 6%.

How Governments Stop Counterfeiting

488 The US Treasury reports that there is $70–200 million of counterfeited money in global circulation. Governments put a lot of effort into creating more secure notes and stopping counterfeiting. Today, banknotes have become remarkably complex. Let's look at some of the ways governments create more secure notes and coins.

The most basic security feature of banknotes is what they are made of. Banknotes are not paper; in most countries, they are made with paper-like cloth. US banknotes are 75% cotton and 25% linen. Many countries use polymer banknotes, which require more expensive and sophisticated technology to produce [see: 390]. Raised or textured text, micro text, and watermarks are other oft-employed security measures.

However, these basic features are not the end of modern banknotes' protections. The US $100 bill also features color-changing ink, clear embedded security threads (with micro-printing on it), an embedded blue 3D ribbon, holograms, and blue and red cloth fibers woven into the banknote's "paper." Some banknotes from other countries have clear plastic parts, portions that respond to black lights or chemicals, or multicolored ink. Since 1996, most banknotes also feature a EURion constellation, which is a graphic design that disables photocopiers and photo editing softwares, making it harder for counterfeiters to take advantage of easy banknote-copying technologies.

The edges of coins are often marked with parallel grooves (called "reeding"), which makes it easy to spot attempts at clipping. Some coins, such as the one and two euro coins, are made of multiple, combined metals. In similar fashion to banknotes, some coins are painted with fluorescent pigments that respond to UV light or are engraved with micro designs.

Wells Fargo Makes Fake Accounts

489 2016 Imagine you are a banker in a town of 20,000 people. Management has just given you and your five colleagues the goal to open five accounts per day. If you hit the goal, you will be rewarded with a bonus of 15–20% of your salary. Achieving this goal would mean that everyone in town is going to have a bank account in under three years.

Wells Fargo management handed down similar orders to its employees starting in the mid-2000s. If a customer had a savings account, a banker would offer them a checking account, credit cards, a 401(k), a mortgage, and more. This is called cross-selling and is the easiest profit-boosting strategy for banks. Ultimately, Wells Fargo opened 1.5 million new bank accounts and 565,000 credit cards—many without customers' consent—which likely brought in tens of billions of dollars in revenue for the company.

The scandal broke in late 2016. Wells Fargo promptly took out ads attempting to reinstate confidence in the bank and fired 5,300 of its employees. The bank was found in violation of the Consumer Financial Protection Act, fined $185 million dollars, and hit with $3.7 billion in lawsuits. That year, 40% fewer new accounts were opened.

Spices in an Indian market

Iran Switches from Dollars to Euros

490 2018 In April 2018, Iran was looking to move away from the US dollar primarily for political reasons. That is, heavy US sanctions against Iran leaves even foreign companies liable to sanctions if they make transactions with Iran in USD. This makes the euro a more appealing currency to trade in and resulted in Iran improving relationships with European countries.

This is important in the history of money, as it illustrates another purpose of money other than trade and provides a real-world example. Previous events have shown how physical coins can spread propagandistic messages. The heads of emperors and presidents adorn coins to remind the citizens of their rulers. Rejecting the use of a strong world currency to avoid undesired trade restrictions both minimizes the country's exposure to financial risk but also can be used to show political rejection of the world currency's issuing country. This event reveals the non-transactional benefits and the social implications of using one currency or another.

2020 Stock Market Crash

491 2020 This book has shown stock market crashes caused by poor harvests, war, and financial mismanagement. Recently, financial mismanagement has been the main cause of crashes. The 2020 financial crisis, however, broke this trend. The crisis was caused by the threat of economic contraction due to the spread of the Coronavirus disease.

The market became shaky in February, and over the four worst days, March 9, 12, and 16—deemed Black Monday I, Black Thursday, and Black Monday II, respectively—and March 23, the Dow Jones fell 26% to a bottom of 18,000 from a high of 28,000 only a month earlier. Japan's Nikkei 225 fell 30% in that same period. Of course, there was not the usual on-the-trading-floor chaos, as everyone was in quarantine and trading from home.

The economic impact of the crisis was large, and it was not caused solely by the market crash. The markets merely reflected how the quarantine and lockdown requirements stifled the economy. US GDP fell by 8.9% in the second quarter of 2020, while UK GDP fell 21.4%, and Europe's fell 12.4%. The crisis's long-term effects were limited, and by the end of 2020, the Dow reached its pre-crisis level, having grown 66% over the year.

NYSE Goes Virtual

492 2020 On March 23, 2020, the New York Stock Exchange (NYSE) floor closed temporarily while electronic trading on the Exchange continued. This was the first time that a major exchange closed without stopping trading. The closure officially marks what was slowly becoming a reality for decades: humans do not need to physically be at the exchange to trade stocks.

After two employees tested positive for Covid-19, the NYSE closed to stop it from spreading. This was not the beginning of online-only trading. However, even though the number of traders on the floor had been steadily decreasing in the decades leading up to the March closure, the NYSE insisted on keeping the floor in use. Sure enough, the floor reopened on May 26, eight weeks later.

The NYSE is an outlier among the world's exchanges for keeping the physical floor open for so long. The Nasdaq became the first all-electronic exchange in 1971 [see: 356]. The London and Tokyo exchanges followed in 1986 and 1999. Because of this widespread shift, even though there are some benefits to on-the-floor trading, the NYSE closing its floor in 2020 did not have a major impact on world finance.

Bahamas Sand Dollar

493 2020 The first digital currency was the Bahamian sand dollar. This currency is not, however, a cryptocurrency, as might be expected. The Bahamas took a different approach to digitizing money than El Salvador did when it made Bitcoin legal tender [see: 494]. Sand dollars operate like a traditional currency—they are just accessed through your phone.

The Bahamas' geographical and political situation motivated the invention. Spanning more than 700 islands, many Bahamian citizens do not have access to physical banking services, and disruptions caused by hurricanes do not help. On the political side, reliance on three Canadian banks limited the Bahamas' economic independence. Many undocumented immigrants are unbanked and therefore disenfranchised from buying things easily. Further, crypto was an unpopular solution as it makes money laundering easier.

Sand dollars were launched in late 2019. By October 2020, there were 100,000 mobile users and $350,000 in circulation. While no bank account is required to keep small balances, the currency can be integrated with traditional bank accounts. The Bahamas' central bank partnered with MasterCard and Island Pay. Sand dollars now work as any other legal tender, both in the Bahamas and internationally.

NYSE officials ringing the opening bell to celebrate 24/7 subway service returning to New York City after Covid lockdowns ended

El Salvador Makes Bitcoin Legal Tender

494 **2021** On September 7, 2021, El Salvador's government made Bitcoin legal tender, making it the first country to officially use cryptocurrency. In order to be taken seriously, a currency must universally (at least within a country) be taken as a medium of exchange. El Salvador making Bitcoin legal tender meant forcing digital currency upon its citizens. The El Salvadoran government pushed the currency by launching the Chivo Wallet app. To encourage people to use it, El Salvador gave $30—nearly four days of work at minimum wage—to anyone who signed up.

It remains an unanswered question as to whether cryptocurrency will work in El Salvador—and if it will be implemented in other countries. Crypto's biggest benefit is that it allows unbanked people access, save, and make easy transactions. However, a study conducted a year after the law took effect found that, in fact, educated people who already have bank accounts were the most likely to adopt Bitcoin. Interestingly, El Salvador's crime rates improved, taking the country from the worst in the world to the best in the Americas after Bitcoin became legal tender. Cryptocurrency has not made money laundering easier.

MasterCard and Visa Suspend Russian Cards

495 2022 Who controls people's money? Since the value of money is determined by if it is accepted as a medium of exchange. In a sense, people control the value of money. However, since governments always control the quantity of money in any economy, governments also determine the value of money. Today, most money transactions are processed by large financial companies. This can make the private sector appear to be dictating who can use their money and how.

The private sector took control in 2022 when the US government effectively forced Mastercard and Visa to suspend cards issued by Russian banks outside of Russia and cards issued internationally inside of Russia, after the Russian invasion of Ukraine. The suspension initially only affected cardholders outside of Russia, as the country uses its own payment processing system, resulting from its prior trend toward financial independence. The Russian national banking system continued to operate normally.

Further disenfranchising Russia from the international financial system, Switzerland froze about 7.7 billion Swiss francs-worth of Russian bank accounts in 2023. This was only a small part of the 150 billion francs held in Switzerland by Russians.

SWIFT Sanctions Russia

496 2022 After Russia invaded Ukraine in 2022, the US and the EU pushed to have Russia removed from the SWIFT system [see: 361]. At that time, 300 Russian banks and half of all Russian credit institutions used the SWIFT system. In fact, the US was the only country with more SWIFT users, suggesting that an exclusion from SWIFT would make it extremely difficult for the Russian government and Russian businesses to participate in international financial transactions. Removal from SWIFT could stifle the Russian economy.

However, some European countries, including Italy, Hungary, and Germany, refused to support the embargo. Their refusals were largely driven by the fear of economic retaliation. Russia supplied over half of Germany's natural gas and about 40% of Italy's.

Finally, on March 2, the EU made the decision to kick seven large Russian banks out of the SWIFT system. However, they allowed the largest Russian bank to remain in the system to allow gas and oil transactions with Europe to continue. Still, the World Bank estimated Russia's GDP contracted by 4–5% in the following year, largely due to SWIFT-related trade and financial disruptions.

FTX Goes Bankrupt

497 2022 While cryptocurrency was designed to avoid big bank involvement, the traditional bank-like crash of the crypto trading firm FTX reveals how risks associated with big banks are not totally avoidable even with systems designed to be decentralized like crypto.

In 2017, Sam Bankman-Fried founded a cryptocurrency firm called Alameda Research. Two years later, he founded FTX as a crypto futures trading firm, headquartered in the Bahamas. FTX's market value quickly shot up to $30 billion. Things changed when on November 2, 2022, an investigation revealed that 40% of Alameda's assets were in the form of FTT, which was FTX's crypto token. This indicated a concerning level of cooperation between the two companies.

After FTX lost $5 billion the next week, Bankman-Fried sought an acquisition deal with Binance, a Chinese crypto trading firm. The deal fell through over suspicions of fraud. On November 8, FTX froze its withdrawals, and the Bahamian SEC froze FTX's funds. FTX declared bankruptcy on the 11th.

Reports surfaced that FTX had committed fraud by secretly lending money to Alameda, lying about the company's financial state to create a better public image, and employing a poor auditing process to hide its relationship with Alameda. In 2023, Bankman-Fried was found guilty of fraud and conspiracy, fined $11 billion, and sentenced to 25 years in jail.

Sign for the Silicon Valley Bank headquarters in Santa Clara, California

Silicon Valley Bank Fails

498 2023 The bank run is now a relic of the days before the Federal Deposit Insurance Corporation (FDIC) was created to insure US bank depositors.

However, the FDIC only secures the depositors of member banks and only insures a maximum amount per depositor. At Silicon Valley Bank (SVB), only 6% of deposits were insured. This allowed for the second-largest bank run and failure in US financial history.

While SVB had been practically insolvent on paper for a few years before its 2023 failure, it became technically insolvent on March 8, 2023, when the bank announced it sold $24 billion of book value securities at a loss. The bank's assets were valued using a mark-to-market accounting basis, and the asset sale meant losses were now fully realized. SVB depositors worried their money could be lost.

On March 9, depositors withdrew $42 billion—25% of SVB's deposits. Withdrawals continued the next day, and the FDIC stepped in that morning, putting SVB into receivership. Panic spread to similarly structured banks, with Signature Bank losing $10 billion of its total $110 billion in assets. And First Republic Bank lost $25 billion of its $213 billion in assets.

Government Bails Out SVB

499 2023 The FDIC had to save depositors of SVB and was required to do so at the "least cost." Usually this meant that the FDIC would find another bank and negotiate with them to take on the obligations of the failed bank. With the speed of the SVB failure, however, there was no time to find another bank. There did not appear to be a "least cost" option to secure all of SVB's uninsured depositors. And 94% of SVB depositors were uninsured. On March 12, two days after SVB's failure, the FDIC invoked the "systemic risk exception," ensuring all uninsured depositors.

The Fed also introduced the Bank Term Funding Program. The Program raised the collateral value of certain securities that banks owned that could be used to borrow funds directly from the Fed. If the program had been in place before the SVB failure, SVB may have been able to survive, as the program helped First Republic Bank survive for a few more weeks. Signature Bank did not have the correct collateral agreement with the Fed and thus was unable to access the emergency discount window. It was put into receivership on March 12. Without insurance, bank runs are still possible.

Global Integration Challenged

500 2025 Although the financial developments that occurred in this and the last chapter have offered wide benefits to society, they have not improved the lives of everyone. Globalization, a product of recent financial and technological innovation, has meant many working class people in the developed world losing jobs to people whose labor is less expensive in the developing world. In 2016 and in 2024, Donald Trump was elected President of the United States, in part by people wanting to reverse this trend.

In April 2025, Trump established the so-called "Liberation Day" tariffs to force businesses to return to the US and subsidize tax cuts. He imposed a 10% blanket

Arial view of shipping facilities in Los Angeles

tariff on most imports and higher reciprocal tariffs ranging of 20–50% on a handful of targeted countries. China, which took many manufacturing jobs from Americans, faced up to 54% tariffs, with threats of raising them to 125%.

The problem, however, is that these tariffs would increase the price of many goods since many goods are manufactured in China. Businesses didn't have an incentive to move manufacturing back to the United States, as the tariffs didn't seem permanent. The S&P 500 declined nearly 19% from a high of 6,100 in late February 2025 to 5,400 in early April, before recovering.

Looking into the future, financial development may continue as it has for the past few centuries. However, if the populist ideology Trump represents continues to spread, the next 500 events in the history of money may well undo much of the liberalization achieved over the last 500. They might also reverse some of the inequality and unrest that liberalization helped produce. I leave it to you, my diligent reader, to decide whether that would be a step forward or a step back

References

Citations listed by event number.

1: Ashley, 1895, p.337; Strauss, 2016; Graeber, 2011, p.22-6

2: Davies, 2002, p.50; Robson, 1998, p.2-3; "Wedge-shaped writing", n.d.; Garbutt, 1984, p.86-87; Faure, "Money Creation: Genesis 3", 2013, p.3

3: "Taxes in the Ancient World", 2002; Mark, 2017; Muhs, 2016, p.14-15; MacDonald, 2015; Jarus, 2015

4: Powell, 1996, p.226-229; Dilke, 1987, p.46

5: Stepien, 2009, pp. 84-9

6: Davies, 2002, p.50-1

7: Hudson, n.d., p.1-2; Renger, 1994; Garfinkle, 2005, p.2-5

8: Sandor, 2016, pp.59-64

9: King, n.d.; Davies, 2002, p.51

10: New International Version: Deuteronomy 23:19-20; Exodus 22:25; Ezekiel, 18:13; Luke: 6:34-5

11: Vincent, 2014, section I.1, 2.a, b

12: Davies, 2002, p.57; Xinhua Publishing House, 1983, p.2-4; Cribb et al., 2007, p.136; Swann, 1950, p.10

13: Davies, 2002, p.36; Yang, 2011, pp. 1 ff

14: Wang, 1951, p.69-76

15: "Viking Weights and Measures", n.d.; Thompson & Skaggs, 2013; Ialongo & Lago, 2021, p.3; Kruse, 1988 p.285-6

16: Fu, 1981, pp. 7-9

17: Borrell, 1840, p.216; Middelkoop, 2016, p.18; Davies, 2002, p.62-4; Mundell, 2002, p.21; Encyclopedia Britannica, "Lydia", 2023

18: Porteous, 1969, pp. 179-82; Bean, 1994, pp.27-9

19: Schaps, 2007, p.282-4

20: Metcalf, 2012, p.61-4

21: Scheidel, 2006, pp. 5-11; Gordon, 1961, p. 608; Skultety, 2006

22: Wunsch, 2007, pp. 236-45

23: Zhang, 2006, p. 8-10

24: Geotzmann & Rouwenhorst, 2005, p.32-7

26: Fleckner, 2014, pp. 6-8; Verboven, 2011

25: Starr, 1977, p.112; Martin, 1996, p.257-262; Meadows & Shipton, 2001, p.24

27: Pankenier, 1998, p.29; Yu & Yu, 2004,

p.8; Xinhua Publishing House, 1983, p.6

28: Cohen, 1992, p.194-5; Fawcett, 2016, p.154-5/190-2

29: Fateh, 1928, pp. 725-6

30: Cohen, 1992, p.6-10/23

31: Cohen, 1992, p.12-16

32: Cohen, 1992, p.61

33: Morkholm, 1991, p.8; Kallet & Kroll, 2020, p.148/150

34: Cohen, 1992, p.215-9

35: Bernard, 2016, pp. 329-30; Vishnia, 2012, 86-7

36: Meikle, 1994, pp. 1-6; Svizzero & Tisdel, 2019, p. 3; Ashley, 1895

37: Mattingly, 1945, pp.65-8; Davies, 2002, pp.88-9; Frank, 1919, pp.314-5, 318-9; Elliot, 2018, p.7; Encyclopedia Britannica, "as", n.d.

38: Faure, 2013, "Money creation: genesis 3", p.4; Davies, 2002, p.54

39: Sydenham, 1918, pp. 157, 184; Sydenham, 1919, p. 115

40: Davies, 2002, p.79-87

41: Hobler, 1840; Abir, 1966, pp.1-2

42: Das, 1925, pp. 174-5; Rajisha, 2019, p. 466

43: Das, 1925, pp. 171-4

44: Faure, 2013, "Money creation genesis 1"; Faverio, 2022

45: Moshenskyi, 2008, pp. 40-2

46: Collins & Walsh, 2014, pp. 184-5, 189, 193-5

47: Geotzmann & Rouwenhorst, 2005, pp.38-9; Ligt, 2007, pp.17-8; Davies, 2002, p.93

48: Xu, 2017, 518, 526-8

49: Pickering, 1844, p.137-8; Baidu Encyclopedia, "pibi", n.d.; Coal miners' wages from Fred "Average Daily Earnings, Coal Miners for France (A08148FRA303NN-BR)"

50: Bian, 2012; "中国货币史", n.d.

51: Bodde, 1946, p.413-5; Ban, 111/n.d., chapter 24a

52: Davies, 2002, pp. 90-1; Ehrenberg, 1964, p.149; "A new honor", n.d. Encyclopedia Britannica, "Senate", n.d.; Art Institute Chicago, "Denarius coin…", n.d.

53: Burnett, 1977, pp. 60-2; Sydenham,

1918, pp. 182-4

54: Clark et al, 2003, pp. 25-7

55: Davies, 2002, pp. 88-9

56: Stephens, 1982, p. 53; Pulliam, 1924, pp. 546-8; Southern, 2007, p. 73; Dilke, 1987, p. 51

57: Dubs, 1940, pp.233-9; Qilu Evening News, 2013

58: Sanders, 1993, p.249-56; Gospel of Matthew 21:12–17; Mark 11:15–19; Luke 19:45–48; John 2:13–16

59: Frank, 1935, p.336-41; Thornton & Thornton, 1990, p.655-62

60: Sakuraki et al, 2010, p. 17; "Money gallery", n.d., pp. 66-8

61: Kopf, 1927, pp. 231-3; Pechter, 2008, p. 10

62: Wassink, 1991, p.465; Kent, 1920, p.39-40; Davies, 2002, p.101-2

63: Morton, 1995, pp. 95-6; Holcombe, 2001, p. 136; "bei wei", n.d. p. 5

64: Rovelli, 2018, pp. 69-77

65: Hussain et al, 2015, p. 7; Rammal, 2003, p. 107

66: Hussain et al, 2015, pp. 6, 11

67: Tan, 2017, pp. 49-51

68: Spufford, 1988, p.9; Davies, 2002, pp.188-22

69: Horesh, 2012, p.68; Twitchett, 1970, p.73

70: Nezhad, 2004, pp. 53-4; Abdullah, 2020, pp. 3-5

71: Sakuraki, 2010, pp. 17-8; Lazar, 2022, pp. 46-50, 53-5

72: Woods, 2018, pp. 94-8

73: Miskimin, 1967, p.35-6; Johnson, n.d.; "Coin Reform of Chrlemagne", n.d.; "Sing a Song of Six Pence", n.d.

74: Feavearyear, 1963, pp. 7-8; Weale, 2000, pp. 78, 81-2

75: Mork & Yang, 2010, p.13; Baidu Encyclopedia, "feiqian", n.d.; Graeber, 2011, p.269; Ramsden, 1911, p.5

76: For Weber's thesis: Ajl, 2012, p. 143

77: Abdur-Rashid, 2021, pp. 50, 54-5, 57-9

79: Davies, 2002, p.130; Attenborough, 1922; Foot, 2011, page unknows, but using end-note 111 of Writing a Medievil Life; Dolley, 1961, p.72-5

80: Xinhua Publishing House, 1983, p.49; Gan, 2006

81: Chen & Kung, 2023, pp. 6-16; McEvedy & Jones, 1978, p. 167

82: Ebrey et al, 2006, p. 156; Onge, 2017, p. 235

83: Jones, 2018, pp. 4-6, 9-11

84: Western History II lecture, David Byrne at SMC; Fernihough & O'Rourke, 2021, p. 1137; "Historic coal data...", 2013; "Coal production for France", n.d.

85: Kozo, 1973, pp. 438-46, 454-7

86: Richardson, n.d.

87: Cazel, 1989, pp. 116-21

88: Davies, 2002, pp.154-4; Setton, 1969, pp.130-1; Gourdin, 1855, p.22

89: Davies, 2002, p.148-51; Baxter, 1989, p.44; Littleton & Yamey, 1952, p.229

90: Cazel, 1989, pp. 125-6; Kedar, 1974, p. 339

91: Pryor, 1977, pp.5-8, 13; Lopez, 2001, pp.174-6

92: Le Goff, 2012, p.63; Tanner, n.d.; "Lateran III Complete", n.d., p.1-2, sect.25

93: North & Thomas, 1971, pp. 795-9

94: "Chapter 2: A History of Merchant...", n.d., p. 9; Craig, 2001, pp. 29-30; Davies, 2002, pp. 345-6

95: Cipolla, 1967, pp. 38-51

96: Sigler, 2012; Suplee, 2000

99: Passant, 2016, pp. 69-70

100: Curtis, 1961, pp. 165-6

101: Davies, 2002, p.182; Goodrich, 1969, p.174

102: Guan et al, 2022, pp. 1-2, 7-10, 13-4; Von Glahn, 2023, pp. 58, 61

103: Pezzolo, 2005

104: Pickering, 1844, p.136

105: Meggs & Purvis, 2006, p. 51; Mockford, 2014, p. 123; Muller, 2021

106: De Roover, 1999, pp. 99-102; Munro, 2003, p. 520

107: Feavearyear, 1963, pp. 8-9; Gordon, 1939, p. 153

108: Hunt, 1990, p. 149; De Roover, 1963, pp. 2-3; Hunt & Murray, 1999, pp. 103-6

109: Sodhi, 2021, p.98-100; Nair, 2019, p.1-3

110: Ray, 2016; Hunt, 1990, p.149-160; Prestwich, 2005, p.273-5

111: Bell et al, 2017, pp. 138-9, 141-4

112: Hunt, 1990, pp. 149-160

113: Jedwab et al, 2020, pp. 8-10; Routt, 2008

114: de Roover, 1946, "The Medici Bank Financial and Commercial Operations", p.155-8; de Roover, 1946, "The medici bank organization and management", p.24-30; Ghosh, 2006, p.542-3; Ferguson, 2008, p.42-9; de Roover, 1947, p. 75

115: See sources for the Medici founded event

116: Le Goff, 2012, pp. 68-70

117: Roberds & Velde, 2014, pp. 28-31

118: Lahaye, n.d.; Hanley & Paganelli, 2014, p. 192

119: Chan, pp. 29-31

120: Arp, 2022; Harris, 2007

121: Day, 1978, p.3/6-8/12; Pamuk, 2000, p.43; Sussman, 1998, p.127/129

122: Jacobsen, 1964, pp. 222-7

123: Ovunda, 2015, pp.132-3; First Republic Bank, 2022

124: Littleton, 1926; Garbutt, 1984, pp. 89-91; Littleton, 1927; Guo, 1989, p. 9; Oldroyd, 1995, 120

125: Lopez & Miskimin, 1962; Cippola, 1964

126: Davies, 2002, p.39-40; Ingersoll, 1883; Snyderman, 1954, p.469-470

127: Davies, 2002, pp.194-6; Heldring, 2021, pp. 15-7

128: Grytten, 2020, pp. 192-3, 196 ff

129: Challis, 1967, p.441, 444; Gould, 1970, p.1-2; Li, 2009, pp.7-9; price rise calculation based on: https://www.bankofengland.co.uk/monetary-policy/inflation/inflation-calculator

130: Arce-Burgoa & Goldfarb, 2009, p.7; Lane, 2021, pp.23-4, 29-30, 36-7

131: Porteous, 1969, pp. 177-9

132: Baron, 1978, pp.565/80; Willan, 1954, pp.604-5

133: Fisher, 1989, pp. 883, 886; Gould, 1964, pp. 250-1; Bernholtz & Kugler, 2007, p. 2

134: Drelichman & Voth, 2011, pp. 1207-11

135: "'Slave trade' bracelets", n.d.; Caley & Shank, 1966, p. 331-2

136: Oner, n.d.

137: Morio, 1996, pp. 4, 10, 15

138: Birtles, 1999, pp. 77-81; Kunze, 1971, pp. 9-12

139: Ferguson, 2008, pp. 127-30; Gelderblom et al, 2013, pp. 1053-5; Petram, 2011, p. 2

140: Goetzmann & Rouwenhorst, 2005, pp. 165 ff

141: Petram, 2011, pp. 1-7

142: Poitras, 2006, pp. 45-6; Pauletto, 2012, p. 7

143: Quinn & Roberds, 2005, pp. 4-10; Ferguson, 2008, p. 48

144: Roberds & Velde, 2019 pp. 38-9

145: Feinman, 1993, p. 2; Hulsmann, 2003, p. 412

146: Lydon, 2009, pp. 251-2

147: Kindleberger, 1991, p. 158-61; Kindleberger & Aliber, 2005, p. 127-8

148: Wilson, 1941, p. 13; Poitras, 2009, pp. 493-5

149: Garber, 1989, p.537, 543-4; Hirschey, 1998, p.11-14; Thompson, 2007, p.99-101

150: Davies, 2002, p.249

151: Clarke, 1937, p.668-72, 674, 681. 683

153: Riksbank, 2009; Marmefelt, 2018, p. 152

154: Riksbank, 2009

155: Nichols, 1971, pp. 98-9; Richards, 1930, p. 51; Milevsky, 2017

156: Bailey & Zhao, 2009, pp. 1-2

157: Borrego, 2023, pp. 4-5; Schenk, 2009, pp. 4-6;

158: Fritz, 2003

159: Davies, 2002, p.253-5; Burnett, 1823, p.532-3; Richards, 1930; Browning, 1966, p.352

160: Powell, 2005, pp. 4-5; Newman, 2008, pp. 157-9

161: Poitras, 2009, pp. 498-500

162: Goldberg, 2009, p. 1092-1100; Davies, 2002, p. 462-3; Michener, n.d.

163: Cardozo, 1946, pp. 137-8, 140; Boxer, 1969, p. 456; Lamim-Guedes, 2012

164: Andreades, 1909, pp. 45-73;

165: Horsefield, n.d.

166: Kynaston, 2017, p. 12; King, 1945, pp. 68-9; Broz, 2001, p. 2

167: Davies, 2002, pp. 280-1

168: Smith, 2012, pp. 211-5; Larkin, 2006

169: Gilmore, 2007; Vaughn, 1978, pp. 312-6

170: Kintgen & Moss, 2010, p.1, 5-8

171: Kintgen & Moss, 2010, p.1, 5-8

172: Roberds & Velde, 2014, pp. 61-4

173: Craig, 1945, pp. 228-9

174: Fay, 1935, pp. 109-12

175: Roberds & Velde, 2014, p. 65; Velde, 2007

176: "The South Sea Bubble", 1840, p. 98; Dale et al, 2005, pp. 234-6; Hoppit, 2002, p. 144

177: Dow, 1971, pp. 196-201;

178: Koph, 1927, pp. 250-2; Poterba, 1997, pp. 7-8

179: Schnabel & Shin, 2004, pp. 930-1, 945-6; Quinn & Roberds, 2015, p. 1150; Schnabel & Shin, 2003, pp. 25-6

180: Connelly & Rowell, 2012; Marshall, 1976

181: Ernst, 1965, p.33-36; Greene & Jellison, 1961, p.485-6/489-90-1

182: Munro, 1997, p. 555; Arnold, 1937, pp. 4-5

183: Rajput, 2018, p. 51

184: Sheridan, 1960, p.162/170-1; Rockoff, 2009, p.18-20/43-44; Andrews, 2013; Kosmetatos, 2014, p.3-4; Wilson, 1939, p.124-5

185: Rouwenhorst, 2004, pp. 1, 6, 17

186: Baack, 2001 pp. 640-9

187: Rae, 1895, pp. 1-5; Bussing-Burks, 2003, pp. 37-55

188: Rae, 1895, pp. 285-94

191: Rothschild, 1994, p. 319; quotes from the Wealth of Nations

191: Davies, 2002, pp. 287-9; Ashton, 2013, p. 179; Clapman, 1945, pp. 157-8

191: White, 1995, pp. 229-34

192: Hawtrey, 1918, p.300-311

193: Edling, 2007, pp. 287-9; "The assumption bill", n.d.

194: Morgan, 1956, p.472/480; "The First Bank of the United States", 2015

195: Bruno, 2019, pp. 2-4; Cannadine, 1998, pp. 95, 100-1

196: Davies, 2002, p.462-7; Constitution Annotated, "Art1.S8.C5.1...", n.d.; Seiber, 2012, p.7; Eagle, 2021

197: Statista Research Department, "Largest stock exchange oporators...", 2023; Kenton, 2022; Waxman, 2017; "New York Stock Exchange", 2023; Banner, 1998; Painting described at the end https://irp.cdn-website.com/ed6fb230/dms3rep/multi/1792-buttonwood-mural.webp (mural info: mural reimagining the signing of the Buttonwood Agreement at 1792, the bar and restaurant at the New York Stock Exchange)

198: Cowen, 2000, pp. 1041-4; Sylla, Wright, Cowen, 2009, pp. 77-8; Sylla, Wright, Cowen, 2006, pp. 15-8

199: Speer, 1906

201: "The US dollar as the. . .", 2022

203: Cheng, 2003, pp. 14-6

204: Hilly, 1984, pp. 416, 420-1; Comstock, 1920, p. 489

205: Alberts, 1969, p. 423; Davies, 2002, p. 347; Potter et al, 2003

206: Hammond, 1953, p.80-83

207: Davies, 2002, p. 304

208: Dangerfield, 1952, pp. 88-9, 176; Wilentz, 2005, 206-9

209: FDIC, 1998, pp. 3-12; Golembe, 1955

210: King, 2014, p.92; Mork & Yang, 2010, p.2

211: Morck & Yang, 2010, pp. 3-6

212: Hammond, 1947, p.5-11; Knodell, 2006, p.542

213: Dwyer, 1996; Economopoulous & O'Neill, 1995

214: Gorton, 2015, pp. 10-12; Dunbar & May, 1995, p. 223

215: "Reflections of the 1837 panic", 1933; Siles et al, 1986, p. 92; Reznek, 1935; Glasner, 1997, pp. 512-3;

216: Pakonen, 1969; Federal Reserve Committee, 1930, pp. 1-6; Davies, 2002, pp. 290-1

217: McGuire, 2004, p 2; "Banks and banknotes", n.d.

218: Maux, 2020, pp. 1-2

219: Andreades, 1909, pp. 110-1; "The bank of...", 1969, p. 213

220: Silber, 1978, p.819-832; Scott & Zechariadis, 2012, p.3-4

222: Bancroft et al, 1884, p. 33; Blakley & Barnette, 1985, p. 31

221: Ward-Perkins, 1950

223: Engels & Marx, 1848; Heilbroner, 1953, p.136

224: Munro, 2008

225: Stukenbrock, 2004, p. 54

226: Hanke, 2002, pp. 88-92; Stukenbrock, 2004, pp. 54-5

227: Chen, 1958

228: Calomiris & Schweikart, 1991; Fulfer, 2022

229: Perriton & Maltby, 2015, pp. 414-5,

425; Davies, 2002, pp. 323-6

230: Mitchell, 1903, p. 5; Officer, 1981, pp. 631-3; Mitchell, 1898, p. 147

231: Daggett, 2008; Nielsen, 2005

232: Million, 1894; Grossman, 2010

233: Fendel & Maurer, 2015, pp. 93, 96-8, 101, 103-10; Einaudi, 2000, pp. 284

234: Andreades, 1909, pp. 357-61; Xu, 2022, pp. 2118-2120

235: Federal Reserve Bank of Richmond, 1975

236: Handel, 2021, pp. 858-9; Dahlquist & Kirkpatrick, 2010, p. 201

237: Timberlake, 1964, p. 34; "The gold excitement", 1869

238: Bank of Japan, n.d.; "The Meiji Restoration and Modernization", n.d.; Eagle, 2021; Bank for International Settlements, 2013

239: Eichengreen, 2008, pp. 15-18; Shaw, 1896, pp. 263-71

240: Selgin, 2010; Murray, 1908, pp. 56

241: Friedman, 1990, pp. 1159-66

242: Comstock, 1953

244: Wells, 1937, pp. 238-9; Nitschke, 2018, pp. 224-9;

245: Garnett, 1917; Zheng, 2012, pp. 40-1; Allen, 2001, pp. 282-3

246: Seburn, 1991, pp. 16, 22

247: Malepati, 2015, p. 2

248: "The history of NYSE", n.d.

249: Guinnane & Streb, 2021, pp. 9-11

250: Xinhua Publishing House, 1988, pp. 36-7; Wright, 1976, p. 180

251: Khan, 2011, p.758-9; Dickson & Wells, 2001, p.3-4; "Sherman Anti-Trust Act", 2022; Twin, 2023

252: Allen, 1999, pp. 251-2; Socolofsky, 1987, pp. 58-9

253: Andreades, 1913, pp. 362-368; "Official bank rate history from 1694", n.d.; White, 2018, p. 25

254: Clapp, 1962; Stowell, n.d.

255: Hawkland, 1966, pp. 501-3

256: Pani, 2017, pp. 7-8, 26-8; Pohl, 1994, p. 564

257: Glasner, 1997, pp. 516-8; Witten, 2001

258: Cheng, 2003, pp. 25-7; Ma, 2012, p. 11

259: Selgin, 2012, pp. 6-7; Elwell, 2011, pp. 6, 8

260: Kirby, 1995, pp. 43-4

262: "银行发展史", 2022

263: Sprague, 1908

264: Moen, 2001

265: Constitutional Rights Foundation, 2012; Chernow, 1990, pp. 126-8

266: Allen, 1948, p.8-13; Encyclopedia Britannica, "J. P. Morgan", 2023; Mall, 2021; Strouse, 2000, p.17-20/51-5

267: Howe, 1916, p. 312; Coletta, 1973, pp. 184-6

268: "Joseon eunhaeng", n.d.

269: King, 1975, pp. 1-10; Cho, 2017, p. 4

270: "Say money trust is now disclosed", 1913; "The 'Money Trust'", 1911; Frydman & Hilt, 2017; Pujo, 1913

271: Furness, 1975, p.51/68-69; Stukenbrock, 2004, p.29; Newlyn, 1954, p.46

272: Johnson, 2010, pp. 18-32

273: Federal Reserve. 2021, pp. 1-4, 7-12; Craig and Millington, 2017

274: Buenker, 1981, pp. 1-12

275: Crabbe, 1989, pp. 423-6

276: Lopez, 2018, pp. 4-10, 38

277: Moscow Financial Institute, 1966, pp. 76-7; Garvy, 1977, p. 18

278: Pasvolsky & Moulton, 1924, pp. 20-2; Toussaint, 2022; James, 1920

279: Crabbe, 1989; Pasvolsky, 1931

280: "Fedwire Funds Service - Annual Statistics", 2023; "The Fedwire Funds Service: Assessment of Compliance", 2014; Gilbert et al, 1997

281: "Ponzi dies in Rio in charity ward", 1949; "Charles Ponzi: a pyramid of postage", 1986

282: Kuehn, 2012, pp. 156-7; Romer, 1986, p. 31

283: Garvy, 1977, pp. 18, 20, 23-30

284: Rippy, 2014; "Consumer Price Index: history", 2023

285: OpenStax, 2022, p. 227

286: Southern, 1979, pp. 1029-32; Balderston, 1989, p. 222; Hill et al, 1977, pp. 300-2, 337

287: Smiley & Keehn, 1988; Borowiecki et al, 2022, pp. 17-9, 24

288: White, 1990, pp. 69-76; Smiley, 2004; "Dow-Jones industrial...", n.d.

289: "Financial Markets", 1929; James, 2010, pp. 133-4; "Ticker prints last...", 1929; Bell, 1929; "Brokers in uproarvvvv", 1929

290: James, 2010, p. 133; "Financiers ease tension", 1929; Rothman, 2014

291: James, 2010, p. 134; Houck, 2000, p. 163; "Phone, radio, cable...", 1929; "The stock market", 1929; "Proposal to halt...", 1929; "Crowds see market...", 1929

292: Borowiecki et al, 2023, pp. 815-6, 824; "Topics in...", 1929; Klein, 2001, p. 209

293: Houck, 2000, pp. 155-6, 160-4; Carcasson, 1998, pp. 350-1

294: Romer, 1990, pp. 597-8, 600-2; Dombusch & Fischer, 1981, p. 312; Granados & Roux, 2009; "Depression cuts...", 1933; "Depression hits...", 1933; "Gross domestic product", n.d.

295: Barber, 1978, pp. 432-6; Romer, 1990, pp. 600-1

296: James, 1987, pp. 71-82; Schnabel, 2004, p. 822

297: Morrison, 2016, pp. 175-8

298: Friedman & Schwartz, 2008, pp. 313-6, 319-22; Board of Governors of the Federal Reserve System, 1943, p. 19

299: Albers & Uebele, 2015, pp. 19-20, 22-3, 30-3; Garraty, 1973, pp. 909-11

300: Schweitzer, 1947, p. 347; Weck & Frey, 1983, pp. 406-7; quotes taken from Mein Kamph: https://greatwar.nl/books/meinkampf/meinkampf.pdf

301: Silber, 2009

302: Elwell, 2011, pp. 9-11

304: Fisher & Hornstein, 2001, pp. 33-6; Dornbusch, 1981, pp. 312-5; "Consumer price index, 1913-", n.d.; "Unemployment rate for the United States", n.d.; "Gross national product", n.d.;

305: Kuznets, 1934; "Petty impressive", 2013; Dickinson, 2011

306: Card, 2011; Goldstein, 2014

307: Friedman, 1997, pp. 2-5

308: Jahan, 2014

309: "THE FTC DURING THE ADMINISTRATIONS OF...", n.d.; Seligman, 1982, p. 45

310: "Court rejects H.K. residents' claims on military yen", 1999

311: Leonard, 2005, pp. 212-5

312: Brown, 1988, p. 134; Levin-Waldman, 2015, pp. 9-18

313: Elwell, 2011, p. 11; Ghizoni, 2013; Mason & Asher, 1973, pp. 1-4; Williamson, 1985, p. 74

314: "Getting to know the World Bank", 2012; NPR Staff, 2015; Clemens & Kremer, 2016, pp. 54-5; Gavin & Rodrik, 1995, pp. 329-31

315: Jensen, 2004, p. 196

316: Taylor, 2019; Signe, 2019;

317: Friedman & Schwartz, 1980, pp. 129-140, 144; Casella & Eichgenreen, 1991, table 1 and figure 1; Holzer & Schonfeld, 1963, pp. 277-8

319: Gompers & Lerner, 2001, pp. 146-7

320: Bell, 1954

321: Chiu & Lewis, 2006, pp. 188-9; Liu, 2023, pp. 37-9

322: Loomis, 1966

323: Loomis, 1966

324: Klaffke, 2003, p.22; Evans & Schmalensee, 2005, p.54-6; "Diners | cards", n.d.

325: Hsiao, 1971, pp. 31-8, 41, 50-1

326: "Harry Markowitz", n.d.; Elton & Gruber, 1997, pp. 1744-5

327: Hsiao, 1971, pp. 24-7

329: Toepke, 1981, pp. 640-5

330: Batiz-Lazo & Angel, 2016, pp. 16-29; Stearns, 2011, p. 122

331: Dillenbeck, 1962, pp. 568-72; "EIB - promoting EU...", 2017; "The EU bank...", n.d.

332: Evans & Schmalensee, 2005, pp. 56-7; Nocera, 1994

333: Bordo et al, 2017, pp. 8-10

334: Weiner, 2007, pp. 188-9; "The Madoff files...", 2009; Henriques & Berenson, 2008; Merced, 2008; Berkowitz, 2012, p. 194; "Plea allocution...", n.d., p. 2

335: Bordo et al, 2017, pp. 16-20, 29-31, 46-9

336: Bordo & Eichengreene, 1993, pp. 55-7; Board of Governors of the Federal Reserve System, 1976, pp. 899, 932

337: Banks, 1977, pp. 47-8; Collard & Dellas, 2007, pp. 713-5; Bryan, 2013

338: Bhatia, 1985, pp. 5-6; "40 ANS D'HISTOIRE DE LA BEAC", n.d.

339: Bronfenbrenner, 1976

340: Kennedy, 2017, p.889

341: Batiz-Lazo & Reid, 2008

343: "Magnetic stripe technology", n.d.; Bowman, 2022

344: Douglas, 2018, pp. 129-32

345: Williamson, 2009, pp. 1-2

346: Barclay et al, 2003, p. 2641; Mizrach & Neely, 2006, p. 532

347: Khanna & Kaushal, 2014, pp. 38-9

348: "History of Anti-Money Laundering Laws", n.d.; Edmonds, 2018, p.6; "Money Laundering", n.d.; Forgang, 2019, p.2

349: Zhou, 2014, 106-9; Morris-Cotterill, 2001; Levi, 2002, p. 182; Eads, 1991, pp. 1478-9; "Money laundering and...", 2002

350: Kagan, 2023; Dunnan, 1989; Tempkin, 2013

351: ibid

352: Johnson, n.d.; Bullion By Post, "UK coins", n.d.

353: Elwell, 2011, p.11/13; Manly, 2021; Lioudis, 2023; Simard et al, 1994, parag. 1-2

354: International Monetary Fund, 1996, pp. 553-6; Eichengreen, 2012, pp. 61-3

355: Maginn et al, 2010, ch. 7.4; Bogle, 1997

356: Mackintosh, 2021

358: Bradford, 2007; McAndrews, 1994, pp. 16-9

359: Painter, 2014, pp. 189-93

360: Davis, 2003

361: Scott & Zachariadis, 2012, p.4-6; "Swift History", n.d.; "Chase Bank Swift Codes in the United States", n.d.

362: Schrager, 2018; Laumakis, 2003

364: Silber, 1978, p.828-832; Chen, 2022

363: Gastineau, 1991

365: Kenton, "Designated Order Turnaround", 2021

366: Kandker et al, 1995, pp. 9-11; Barua, 2006, pp. 1-2; Grameen Bank, 2021, pp. 8-9

367: Naef, 2022, pp. 190-203;

368: Roach, 2022, pp. 225-6; Turner et al, 2012, pp. 54-5

369: Alogoskoufis, 1991; Liberto, 2021

370: Bordo & Schwartz, 1987, pp. 1-6

371: Pusey, 2019; Kleit, 2018, pp. 41-2

372: Kindleberger & Aliber, 2005, pp. 74-5; "Micheal Milken's guilt", 1990

373: Grimes, 1981; Hayward, 2023

374: Niskanen, 1988; Jacob, 1985, p. 10

375: Tomkiw, 2024; Teitelbaum, 2008

378: Effing & Rankle, 2004, p.2-5; "Why are chip cards more secure than swiping?", 2023

377: Cronin, 1998, pp. 41-3

379: "Continental Illinois", 2023; Doti, n.d.; Swary, 1986, p.451

380: Federal Deposit Insurance Corporation, 1997, pp. 168-9; "Savings and Loans Cri-sis", 2013; Congressional Budget Office, 1992, pp. 7-8

382: Federal Deposit Insurance Corporation, 1997, pp. 178-81; Oshiro, 1990, p. 5

383: Frankel, 2015, pp. 3-7

384: Okina et al, 2001, pp. 397-418

385: Lawson, 2006, p. i-1; Plender, 1986, p. 39

386: The Financial Crisis Inquiry Commission, 2011, pp. 129-30

387: Carlson, 2006, pp. 3-10; United States General Accounting Office, 1988, p. 14;

388: Nygaard, 2020, pp. 124-6

389: "U.S. equity market resiliency...", n.d.; Greenwald & Stein, 1988, p. 3

390: Kamp & Hunter, 2019, pp. 321-3

391: Lissardy, 1989; Ferguson, 2008, p. 112

392: Committee for the Study of Economic and Monetary Union, 1989, pp. 8, 30, 33-5; "Economic and monetary union - a timeline", n.d.

394: Torre et al, 2003, pp. 46-63

395: Passas, 1996, pp. 57-62; Kanas, 2005, p. 102; Adams & Frantz, 1992, pp. IX-XIII

396: Inman, 2012; Sevilla, 1995, pp. 1-3, 22; James, 2020, pp. 296-301; "The cost of black wednesday reconsidered",1997, p. 2

397: Bold, 2004, pp. 2, 11-15

398: Alexeev et al, 1992, pp. 138-42

399: Hill & Jewette, 1994, pp. 32-6; Odling-Smee & Pastor, 2001, pp. 3-10

400: Odling-Smee & Pastor, 2001, pp. 3-10

401: Hill & Jewet, 1994, pp. 32-3; Oliker & Charlick-Paley, 2002, p. 27

402: Philips, 2008

403: Aguirregabiria et al, 2016, pp. 532-3; Dunnan, 1985, p. 54

404: EMV Migration Forum, 2015; EMCco, 2022; Stax, n.d.; Basin et al, 2021, pp. 1768-9

405: Guo, 2008, p. 2; Ferguson, 2008, pp. 322-4

406: Pozsar et al, 2010, pp. 2 ff, 8-9

407: Springer & Molina, 1995, pp. 57-68; Sharma, 2001, p. 60

408: Springer & Molina, 1995, pp. 65-7; Sharma, 2001, p. 72

409: Horioka, 2006, pp. 3-4, 15-6; Okina et al, 2000, p. 3; Makin, 2008, pp. 2-4

410: Visual Korea, 2020; Flugge, 2017, p. 161

411: Crain, 2021, pp. 75-9

412: Leightner, 2007, pp. 62-4; Punyarata-bandhu, 1998, p. 161

413: "Trading analysis...", 1998

414: Berg, 1999, pp. 3-18

415: Berg, 1999, pp. 8, 15; Walker, 1998, pp. 4-8; Seth et al, n.d., pp. 3-8; IMF staff, 1998

416: Berg, 1999, pp. 4, 24; Himawan et al, 2022, pp. 242-3

417: Berg, 1999, pp. 19-27

418: Lee, 2000, p. 8; Kim, 2013, pp. 2, 7-9; Hong, 2014, pp. 91-8

419: "Information guide", n.d., pp. 2-5; Dominguez, 2006, pp. 67-8

420: United Natons Conference on Trade and Development, 1998, pp. 1-12

421: Jickling, 1999, pp. 5-6; Slivinski, 2009

422: Gruben & Kiser, 1999; Anderson & Cavanagh, 2000, p. 12

423: Saxton, 2003

424: Heakal, 2023; Amadeo, 2022

425: "Bill Clinton on...", n.d.; Beck et al, 2010; Clinton, 1999

426: Scheller, 2004, pp. 25-6

427: Laffey, 2004, pp. 183, 186-7; Delong & Magin, 2006, p. 8; "Nasdaq composite index", n.d.

428: McGowan, 2010; The Record, 2000

429: Hass, 2013; Sucic, 2011, pp. 6-7;

430: Healy & Palepu, 2003, pp. 1-11; Moncarz et al, 2006, pp. 28-9; Benston, 2003, p. 12

431: Stevens & Haag, 2019; Barrionuevo, 2006; Healy & Palepu, 2003, pp. 9-12; Moncarx et al, 2006, p. 24

432: Guzman, 2016, pp. 3-4; Krauss, 2001; Delivorias, 2023, p. 4

433: Scheller, 2004, pp. 27

434: Weisbrot & Sandoval, 2007, pp. 3-10

435: Spitzer, 2003, pp. 2-3; McCabe, 2008, pp. 1, 8-9

436: McGowan, 2010

437: "Case no. OIG509", 2009, pp. 1, 6-7, 12-19

438: Gomber et al, 2011, pp. 1-2; Lange, 2017, pp. 101, 105-111

439: The Financial Crisis Inquiry Commission, 2011, pp. 123, 130, 169

440: Baker, 2008, pp. 73-7; "Delinquency rates", n.d.; "homeowner vacancy", n.d.

441: The Financial Crisis Inquiry Commission, 2011, pp. 280-91

442: The Financial Crisis Inquiry Commission, 2011, pp. 309-29

443: The Financial Crisis Inquiry Report Commission, 2011, pp. 325-40

444: The Financial Crisis Inquiry Report Commission, 2011, pp. 344-50

445: Associated Press, 2008; "Final vote results", 2008

446: Stock market values obtained from Wall Stree Journal advanced viewer, and other indicators from FRED

447: Webel & Murphy, 2008; "Troubled Asset Relief Program", n.d.; Herszenhorn, 2008

448: Centonz, 2011, pp. 140-5; Benedoksdottir et al, 2017, pp. 191-3; Glitnir, 2008; Kaupthing Bank, 2008; Landsbanki, 2008

450: Vila, 2017; European Court of Auditors, 2019, p. 4

451: Nakamoto, 2008; Derman, 2015; Popper, 2015

452: Nakamoto, 2008

453: Hanke & Kwok, 2009, p.354-355; Jafari, 2004, p.105; Frisby, 2016

455: Henriques, 2011, pp. 1-14

456: Turgeon, 2020, pp. 16-8; Barnard & Boyle, 2009, pp. 62-3

457: "Fed slashes interest rates", 2008; "Fed slashes key rate", 2008

458: Congressional Research Service, 2009, p. 6; "Market capitalization of listed domestic companies (current US$)", n.d.; "Market capitalization of listed domestic companies (% of GDP)", n.d.; Brady & Holden, 2009

459: Financial Crisis Inquiry Commission, 2011, pp. 280-1, 283-4, 309, 312, 322, 324-6; Associated Press, 2007

460: Danziger, 2013, pp. 6-7, 10, 14

461: Evans-Pritchard, 2008; Barboza, 2008; economic statistics from World Bank and Fred

462: Lewis, 2010, pp. 185-198; Lewis, 2010, "betting on the blind side"

463: Lattman, 2010; Stempel, 2019; McGowan, 2010, parag. 32-4

464: Kirilenko et al., 2014, p.1-5; Weinberg, 2015

465: Twight, 2015, pp. 198-9; Baily et al, 2017, p. 21

466: Bilefsky & Thomas, 2010; Ardagna &

Caselli, 2014, pp. 293-5; Nelson, 2017, pp. 2-4;

467: "European Financial Stability Facility", 2016

468: Wearden, 2011; BBC, 2011; BBC, 2010; "European financial stability facility", 2016, pp. 5-6, 8

469: "Italy's sovereign debt...", 2011; "France loses AAA...", 2012; "Standard & Poor's downgrades...", 2012;

470: Smith, 2010; Statistics obtained here: https://www.bbc.co.uk/news/business-13361934

471: Tagaris, 2012; "William Hague...", 2011; Elliott, 2010; Godley, 1992

472: Cooper & Story, 2011; Associated Press, "Budget office warns about debt", 2011; Associated Press, "Short-Term Increase in Debt Limit Suggested", 2011; Hulse & Cooper, 2011; "Timeline of debt negotiations", 2011

473: Appelbaum & Dash, 2011; "United States of America Long-Term Rating Lowered...", 2011; Hauser, 2011; Reuters, 2011

475: Rovekamp, 2020, pp. 2-4

476: IMF, 2013; Wroughton, 2013; Barionuevo, 2011

477: Gallow, 2023; Lacapra, 2023

478: Brown et al, 2018, po. 71-86

480: Morrissey, 2016, p.2-

482: Statista, "Mobile payments worldwide", 2023; "Apple Announces Apple Pay", 2014; "Samsung announces launch dates...", 2015; Jeffries, 2014; Leitgeb et al., 2007, pp.1-2

483: Dornbusch, 1985, pp. 3-9

486: Nelson, 2017, pp. 5-7

487: Killawala, 2016; Saikia, 2016

489: Corkery, 2016; Venable, 2017; Morgenson, 2023; Davidson, 2016

490: Reuters Staff, 2018; Norman, 2020

491: Mazur et al, 2021; "Economic Report of the President (2022)", 2022, pp. 100-1; "Dow-Jones...", n.d.; "Nikkei stock...", n.d.

492: Lin, 2020; "The history of NYSE", n.d.; Li, 2020

493: Belgen et al, 2024, pp. 2-5;

494: Alvarez et al, 2023, pp. 1-2

495: Revill, 2023; Paybarah, 2022; McCrank, 2022

496: Macias, 2022; RFE/RL, 2022

497: Ery et al, 2022; Cohen & Godoy, 2023

498: Metrick, 2024, pp. 143-6

499: Metrick, 2024, pp. 144-6

Bibliography

"1972-2012: 40 ANS D'HISTOIRE DE LA BEAC." n.d. *BEAC*. https://www.beac.int/beac/la-beac/1972-2012-40-ans-dhistoire-de-beac/.

A Concide Encyclopedia of Economics. 2009. "NYSE Cuts Order Execution Time to 5 Milliseconds from 105." https://web.archive.org/web/20121012053452/http://www.nyse.com/press/1246442836537.html.

"A New Honor: The Image of Caesar on Coins." n.d. http://www.humanities.mq.edu.au/acans/caesar/Portraits_Coins.htm.

Abdullah, Adam. 2020. "The Islamic Monetary Standard: The Dinar and Dirham." *International Journal of Islamic Economics and Finance Studies* 1 (1). https://dergipark.org.tr/en/download/article-file/1030977.

Abdur-Rashid, Khalil. 2021. "Financing Kindness as a Society: The Rise and Fall of the Waqf as a Central Islamic Philanthropic Institution (Awqāf)." *Journal of Muslim Philanthropy & Civil Society* 5 (1). https://scholarworks.iu.edu/iupjournals/index.php/muslimphilanthropy/article/view/3565/316.

Abir, M. 1966. "Salt, Trade and Politics in Ethiopia in the 'Zämänä Mäsafent.'" *Journal of Ethiopian Studies* 4 (2). https://www.jstor.org/stable/41965738.

Adams, James Ring. 1992. *A Full Service Bank: How BCCI Stole Billions around the World*. Pocket Books.

Aguirregabiria, Victor, Robert Clark, and Hui Wang. 2016. "Diversification of Geographic Risk in Retail Bank Networks: Evidence from Bank Expansion after the Riegle-Neal Act." *The RAND Journal of Economics* 47 (3). https://www.jstor.org/stable/43895656.

Ajl, Max. 2012. "The Origins of Divergence: China, Europe, and the Future of Development." *McGill International Journal of Sustainable Development Law and Policy* 8 (1). https://www.jstor.org/stable/24352542.

Albers, Thilo, and Martin Uebele. 2015. *The Global Impact of the Great Depression*. Working Paper No. 218. LSE. https://eprints.lse.ac.uk/64491/1/WP218.pdf.

Alberts, Robert. 1969. *The Golden Voyage: The Life and Times of William Bingham, 1752-1804*. Houghton Mifflin.

Alexeev, Michael, Clifford Gaddy, and Jim Leitzel. 1992. "Economics in the Former Soviet Union." *Journal of Economic Perspectives* 6 (2).

Allen, Frederick Lewis. 2016. *The Great Pierpont Morgan*.

Allen, Larry. 1999. *Encyclopedia of Money*. ABC-CLIO.

Allen, Larry. 2001. *The Encyclopedia of Money*. Checkmark Books.

Alogoskoufis, George. 1991. "Review: Limiting Exchange Rate Flexibility: The European Monetary System." *Economica, New Series* 58 (230). https://doi.org/10.2307/2554656.

Alvarez, Fernando E., David Argente, and Diana Van Patten. 2023. *Are Cryptocurrencies Currencies? Bitcoin as Legal Tender in El Salvador*. Working Paper No. 29968. National Bureau of Economic Research. https://www.nber.org/system/files/working_papers/w29968/w29968.pdf.

Amadeo, Kimberly. 2022. "Glass Steagall Act of 1933: Its Purpose and Repeal." https://www.thebalancemoney.com/glass-steagall-act-definition-purpose-and-repeal-3305850.

Anderson, Sarah, and John Cavanagh. 2000. *Bearing the Burden*. Institute for Policy Studies. https://web.archive.org/web/20120327050935/http://actrav.itcilo.org/library/english/05_Globalization/unfair/bearing_the_burden.pdf.

Andreades, A. 1909. *History of the Bank of England*. Translated by Christabel Meredith. P. S. King & Son, Orchard House.

Andrews, E. 2013. "Peter Koudijs: Risk Analysis or Risk Paralysis?" *Stanford Business*. https://www.gsb.stanford.edu/insights/peter-koudijs-risk-analysis-or-risk-paralysis.

Appelbaum, Binyamin, and Eric Dash. 2011. "S. & P. Downgrades Debt Rating of U.S. for the First Time." *The New York Times*.

"Apple Announces Apple Pay." 2014. https://www.apple.com/newsroom/2014/09/09Apple-Announces-Apple-Pay/.

Arce-Burgoa, Osvaldo R., and Richard J. Goldfarb. 2009. "Metallogeny of Bolivia." *SEG (Society of Economic Geologists) Newsletter*, no. 79. https://web.archive.org/web/20150402122145/http://www.dim.uchile.cl/~lsaavedr/archivos/joseline/pdf/Metallogeny%20of%20Bolivia.pdf.

Ardagna, Silvia, and Francesco Caselli. 2014. "The Political Economy of the Greek Debt Crisis: A Tale of Two Bailouts." *American Economic Journal: Macroeconomics* 6 (4). https://doi.org/10.1257/mac.6.4.291.

"Aristotle's Doctrine of Barter." 1895. *The Quarterly Journal of Economics* 9 (3). https://www.jstor.org/stable/pdf/1883583.pdf.

Arnold, Arthur. 1937. *Banks, Credit, and Money in Soviet Russia*. Columbia University Press.

Arp, Claire. 2022. "Labor and Power in the Incan Economy." Michigan Journal of Economics. https://sites.lsa.umich.edu/mje/2022/12/19/labor-and-power-in-the-incan-economy/.

Art Institute Chicago. n.d. "Denarius (Coin) Portraying Julius Caesar." https://www.artic.edu/artworks/5588/denarius-coin-portraying-julius-caesar.

Ashton, T. S. 2013. *An Economic History of England: The Eighteenth Century*. Routledge.

Associated Press. 2007. "Will Subprime Mess Ripple Through Economy?" *NBC News*. https://www.nbcnews.com/id/wbna17584725.

Associated Press. 2008. "House to Meet Thursday After Rejecting Bailout." *NBC News*. https://www.nbcnews.com/id/wbna26884523.

Associated Press. 2011a. "Budget Office Warns About Debt." *The New York Times*.

Associated Press. 2011b. "Short-Term Increase in Debt Limit Suggested." *The New York Times*.

Atlas, John, and Peter Dreier. 2007. "The Conservative Origins of the Sub-Prime Mortgage Crisis." *The American Prospect*. https://web.archive.org/web/20080411171345/http://www.prospect.org/cs/articles?article=the_conservative_origins_of_the_subprime_mortgage_crisis.

Attenborough, F. L. 1922. *The Laws of the Earliest English Kings*. Cambridge University Press.

Baack, Ben. 2001. "Forging a Nation State: The Continental Congress and the Financing of the War of American Independence." *The Economic History Review* 54 (4). https://www.jstor.org/stable/3091625.

Baidu Baike. n.d. "飞钱 (fei qian)." https://baike.baidu.com/item/%E9%A3%9E%E9%92%B1/5351072.

Baidu Dictionary. n.d. "皮币 (pibi)." https://baike.baidu.com/item/%E7%9A%AE%E5%B8%81/9159386.

Bailey, Martin Neil, Aaron Klein, and Justin Schardin. 2017. "The Impact of the Dodd-Frank Act on Financial Stability and Economic Growth." *The Russell Sage Foundation Journal of the Social Sciences* 3 (1). https://www.researchgate.net/publication/318048349_The_Impact_of_the_Dodd-Frank_Act_on_Financial_Stability_and_Economic_Growth.

Bailey, Warren, and Bin Zhao. 2009. "Familiarity, Convenience, and Commodity Money: Spanish and Mexican Silver Dollars in Qing and Republican China." *SSRN*. https://papers.ssrn.com/sol3/papers.cfm?abstract_id=1424070.

Baker, Dean. 2008. "The Housing Bubble and the Financial Crisis." *Real-World Economics Review*, no. 46. https://www.files.ethz.ch/isn/57117/Housing_Bubble_0508.pdf.

Balderston, T. 1989. "War Finance and Inflation in Britain and Germany, 1914-1918." *The Economic History Review* 42 (2). https://doi.org/10.2307/2596203.

Bancroft, Hubert Howe. 1970. *The Works of Hubert Howe Bancroft, Volume 23: History of California, Volume 6*. Wallace Hebberd.

"Banks and Banknotes." 2011. https://web.archive.org/web/20110605054801/http://www.info.gov.hk/hkma/eng/exhibition/1-3.pdf.

Banks, Stephen J. 1977. "The Great Inflation:

Its Origins and Its Effect on Investment Value." *Financial Analysts Journal* 33 (3). https://www.jstor.org/stable/4478035.

Banner, Stuart. 1998. "The Origins of the New York Stock Exchange." *The Journal of Legal Studies* 27 (1). https://doi.org/10.1086/468015.

Barber, Clarence L. 1978. "On the Origins of the Great Depression." *Southern Economic Journal* 44 (3). https://doi.org/10.2307/1057202.

Barboza, David. 2008. "China Unveils Sweeping Plan for Economy." *The New York Times*. https://www.nytimes.com/2008/11/10/world/asia/10china.html.

Barclay, Michael J., Terrence Hendershott, and D. Timothy McCormick. 2003. "Competition among Trading Venues: Information and Trading on Electronic Communications Networks." *The Journal of Finance* 58 (6).

Baron, Samuel. 1978. "Ivan the Terrible, Giles Fletcher and the Muscovite Merchantry: A Reconsideration." *The Slavonic and East European Review* 56 (4). https://www.jstor.org/stable/4207722.

Barrionuevo, Alexei. 2006. "Enron Chiefs Guilty of Fraud and Conspiracy." *The New York Times*. https://www.nytimes.com/2006/05/25/business/25cnd-enron.html.

Barrionuevo, Alexei. 2011. "Inflation, an Old Scourge, Plagues Argentina Again." *The New York Times*. https://www.nytimes.com/2011/02/06/world/americas/06argentina.html.

Barua, Dipal Chandra. 2006. *Five Cents a Day: Innovative Programs for Reaching the Destitute with Microcredit, No-Interest Loans, and Other Instruments: The Experience of Grameen Bank*. https://web.archive.org/web/20080226233631/http://www.microcreditsummit.org/papers/Workshops/7_Barua.pdf.

Basin, David, Ralf Sasse, and Jorge Toro-Pozo. 2021. *The EMV Standard: Break, Fix, Verify*. 2021 IEEE Symposium on Security and Privacy. https://doi.org/10.1109/SP40001.2021.00037.

Bátiz-Lazo, Bernardo, and Gustavo A. Del Angel. 2016. *The Dawn of the Plastic Jungle: The Introduction of the Credit Card in Europe and North America, 1950-1975*. Economics Working Paper No. 16107. Hoover Institution. https://www.hoover.org/sites/default/files/research/docs/16107_-_dawn_of_the_plastic_jungle_-_batiz-lazo_and_del_angel.pdf.

Bátiz-Lazo, Bernardo, and Robert J.K. Reid. 2008. *Evidence from the Patent Record on the Development of Cash Dispensing Technology*. No. 9461. MPRA Paper. https://mpra.ub.uni-muenchen.de/9461/.

Baxter, W. T. 1989. "Early Accounting: The Tally and Checkerboard." *The Accounting Historians Journal* 16 (2). https://www.jstor.org/stable/40697984.

BEA. 1929. "Brokers in Uproar As Market Boils." *Bureau of Economic Analysis Number = 23-33, Url = Https://Www.Bea.Gov/Sites/Default/Files/2023-07/Gdp2q23_adv.Pdf*, October 25, 3.

Bean, Simon C. 1994. "The Coinage of the Atrebates and Regni." PhD dissertation, University of Nottingham. http://eprints.nottingham.ac.uk/11944/1/262143.pdf.

Beck, Thorsten, Ross Levine, and Alexey Levkov. 2010. "Big Bad Banks? The Winners and Losers from Bank Deregulation in the United States." *The Journal of Finance* 65 (5). https://www.jstor.org/stable/40864982.

Bell, Adrian R., Chris Brooks, and Tony K. Moore. 2017. "The Non-Use of Money in the Middle Ages." In *Peter Spufford's Money and Its Use in Medieval Europe - Twenty-Five Years On*. Royal Numismatic Society Special Publication 52.

Bell, Elliott V. 1929. "'Crash': An Account of the Stock Market Crash of 1929." In *Freedom: A History of the US*. https://www.thirteen.org/wnet/historyofus/web12/features/source/docs/C01.pdf.

Bell, J. F. 1954. "The Dollar Gap." *Current History* 26 (149). https://www.jstor.org/stable/45308579.

Benediktsdóttir, Sigríður, Gauti B. Eggertsson, and Eggert Þórarinsson. 2017. "The Rise, Fall, and Resurrection of Iceland: A Postmortem Analysis of the 2008 Financial Crisis." *Brookings Papers on Economic Activity*. https://www.jstor.org/stable/90019458.

Benston, George. 2003. "The Quality of Corporate Financial Statements and Their Auditors before and after Enron." *Policy Analysis*, no. 497. https://web.archive.org/web/20100615092807/http://www.cato.org/pubs/pas/pa497.pdf.

Berg, Andrew. 1999. *The Asian Crisis: Causes, Policy Responses, and Outcomes*. Working Paper No. 99/139. International Monetary Fund. https://www.imf.org/external/pubs/ft/wp/1999/wp99138.pdf.

Berkowitz, Michael. 2012. "The Madoff Paradox: American Jewish Sage, Savior, and Thief." *Journal of American Studies* 46 (1). https://www.jstor.org/stable/41427319.

Bernard, Carole, and Phelim P. Boyle. forthcoming. "Mr. Madoff's Amazing Returns: An Analysis of the Split-Strike Conversion Strategy." *The Journal of Derivatives* 17 (1). https://www.sfu.ca/~poitras/JD_Madoff_09.pdf.

Bernard, Seth. 2016. "Debt, Land, and Labor in the Early Republican Economy." *Phoenix* 70 (3). https://doi.org/10.7834/phoenix.70.3-4.0317.

Bernard, Victor L., Robert C. Merton, and Krishna G. Palepu. 1995. "Mark-to-Market Accounting for Banks and Thrifts: Lessons from the Danish Experience." *Journal of Accounting Research* 33 (1). https://doi.org/10.2307/2491290.

Bernholz, Peter, and Peter Kugler. 2007. *The Price Revolution in the 16th Century*. Working Paper No. 12/07. WWZ. https://www.econstor.eu/bitstream/10419/123383/1/wp2007-12.pdf.

Bhatia, Rattan J. 1985. *The West African Monetary Union: An Analytical Review*. IMF.

Bian. 2012. "西汉萌芽的金融膨胀与应对之策." http://economy.guoxue.com/?p=7878.

Bilefsky, Dan, and Landon Thomas. 2010. "Greece Takes Its Bailout, but Doubts for the Region Persist." *The New York Times*. https://www.nytimes.com/2010/05/03/business/global/03drachma.html.

Bilgen, Can, Martin Dutto, and Tim Colberg. 2024. *Analyzing the CBDC Tree: The Case of the Bahamian Sand Dollar Using Three-Level Central Bank Digital Currency Design Framework*. https://www.researchgate.net/publication/379227178_Analyzing_the_CBDC_Tree_The_Case_of_the_Bahamian_Sand_Dollar_Using_Three-Level_Central_Bank_Digital_Currency_Design_Framework.

"Bill Clinton on Free Trade and Financial Deregulation (1993-2000)." n.d. https://www.americanyawp.com/reader/30-the-recent-past/bill-clinton-on-free-trade-and-financial-deregulation-1993-2000/.

Birtles, Sara. 1999. "Common Land, Poor Relief and Enclosure: The Use of Manorial Resources in Fulfilling Parish Obligations 1601-1834." *Past & Present*, no. 165.

Blakley, E. R. (Jim), and Karen Barnette. 1985. *Historical Overview of Los Padres National Forest*.

Board of Governors of the Federal Reserve System. 1943. *Banking and Monetary Statistics, 1914-1941, Part I*. St. Louis Federal Reserve.

Board of Governors of the Federal Reserve System. 1976. *Banking and Monetary Statistics, 1941-1970*. St. Louis Federal Reserve.

Bodde, Derk. 1946. "Henry A. Wallace and the Ever-Normal Granary." *The Far Eastern Quarterly* 5 (4). https://doi.org/10.2307/2049789.

Bogle, John. 1997. "The First Index Mutual Fund." Bogle Center. https://boglecenter.net/wp-content/uploads/JCB_first_index_mf.pdf.

Bold, Tuvshintulga. 2004. *Explaining Rise of Barter in Russia: Virtual Economy vs. Monetary Issues*. M.S. Research Paper. https://economics.ecu.edu/wp-content/pv-uploads/sites/165/2019/04/TuvshintulgaBold.pdf.

Bordo, Michael D., and Barry Eichengreen. 1993. *A Retrospective on the Bretton Woods System: Lessons for International Monetary Reform*. University of Chicago Press.

Bordo, Michael, Eric Monnet, and Alain Naef. 2017. *The Gold Pool (1961-1968) and the Fall of the Bretton Woods System. Lessons for Central Bank Cooperation*. Working Paper No. 24016. National Bureau of Economic Research. https://doi.org/10.3386/w24016.

Bordo, Michael, and Anna Schwartz. 1987. *The ECU – an Imaginary or Embryonic Form of Money: What Can We Learn from History?* Working Paper No. 2345. National Bureau of Economic Research. https://www.nber.org/system/files/working_papers/w2345/w2345.pdf.

Borowiecki, Karol Jan, Michał Dzieliński, and Alexander Tepper. 2022. *The Great Margin Call: The Role of Leverage in the 1929 Stock Market Crash.* Discussion Paper No. 1/2022. University of Southern Denmark.

Borowiecki, Karol Jan, Michał Dzieliński, and Alexander Tepper. 2023. "The Great Margin Call: The Role of Leverage in the 1929 Wall Street Crash." *The Economic History Review* 76 (3).

Borrell, H. P. 1839. "An Inquiry into the Early Lydian Money, and an Attempt to Fix the Classification of Certain Coins to Croesus." *The Numismatic Chronicle (1838-1842)* 2 (June). https://www.jstor.org/stable/42681074.

Bowman, Cynthia Paez. 2022. "The Surprising History of Credit Cards: How This Tech Has Evolved and Where It's Headed." *CNET*. https://www.cnet.com/personal-finance/credit-cards/features/the-history-of-credit-cards/.

Boxer, C. R. 1969. "Brazilian Gold and British Traders in the First Half of the Eighteenth Century." *The Hispanic American Historical Review* 49 (3). https://doi.org/10.2307/2511780.

Bradford, Terri. 2007. "The Evolution of the ACH." *Kansas City Fed*. https://www.kansascityfed.org/Payments%20Systems%20Research%20Briefings/documents/723/briefings-psr-briefingdec07.pdf.

Brady, Peter, and Sarah Holden. 2009. "The U.S. Retirement Market, 2008." *Research Fundamentals* 18 (5). https://www.ici.org/doc-server/pdf%3Afm-v18n5.pdf.

Bromberg, Benjamin. 1940. "Temple Banking in Rome." *The Economic History Review* 10 (2). https://doi.org/10.2307/2590789.

Brooke, C. G. 1931. *The Medevil Moneyers.* https://www.britnumsoc.org/publications/

Digital%20BNJ/pdfs/1931_BNJ_21_4.pdf.

Brown, Charles. 1988. "Minimum Wage Laws: Are They Overrated?" *The Journal of Economic Perspectives* 2 (3).

Browning, Andrews. 1966. *English Historical Documents: 1660 to 1714.* Eyre & Spottiswoode.

Broz, Lawrence. 2001. "Paying for the Privilege of Bank of England Charters, 1694-1843." *WCFIA Publications*. https://wcfia.harvard.edu/publications/paying-privilege-bank-england-charters-1694-1843.

Bruno, Alexander. 2019. "What Really Is the American Dream?" *APSA Preprints*, ahead of print. https://doi.org/10.33774/apsa-2020-6wqmc.

Bryan, Micheal. 2013. "The Great Inflation." https://www.federalreservehistory.org/essays/great-inflation.

Buenker, John D. 1981. "The Ratification of the Federal Income Tax Amendment." *Cato Journal* 1 (1). https://web.archive.org/web/20120114120602/http://www.cato.org/pubs/journal/cj1n1/cj1n1-10.pdf.

Bureau of Labor Statistics. 2024a. *Consumer Price Index – October 2024.* https://www.bls.gov/news.release/pdf/cpi.pdf.

Bureau of Labor Statistics. 2024b. *The Employment Situation — October 2024.* https://www.bls.gov/news.release/pdf/empsit.pdf.

Burnet, Gilbert. 1823. *Bishop Burnet's History of His Own Time.* Oxford Clarendon Press.

Burnett, A. M. 1977. "The Authority to Coin in the Late Republic and Early Empire." *The Numismatic Chronicle (1966-)*, Seventh Series, vol. 17 (137). https://www.jstor.org/stable/42666582.

Bussing-Burkes, Marie. 2003. *Influential Economists.* The Oliver Press, Inc.

Caley, E. R., and L. W. Shank. 1966. "Composition of Two Manillas." *The Numismatic Chronicle (1966-)*, Seventh Series, vol. 6. https://www.jstor.org/stable/42665091.

Calomiris, Charles W., and Larry Schweikart. 1991. "The Panic of 1857: Origins, Transmission, and Containment." *The Journal of Economic History* 51 (4).

Cannadine, David. 1998. *Beyond Class? Social*

Structures and Social Perceptions in Modern England. The British Academy. https://www.thebritishacademy.ac.uk/documents/2459/97p095.pdf.

Cano Borrego, Pedro Damián. 2023. *Spanish Dollar: The First Global Currency.* Lulu.

Carcasson, Martin. 1998. "Herbert Hoover and the Presidential Campaign of 1932: The Failure of Apologia." *Presidential Studies Quarterly* 28 (2).

Card, David. 2011. "Origins of the Unemployment Rate: The Lasting Legacy of Measurement without Theory." *The American Economic Review* 101 (3).

Cardozo, Manoel. 1946. "The Brazilian Gold Rush." *The Americas* 3 (2). https://doi.org/10.2307/978703.

Carlson, Mark. 2006. "A Brief History of the 1987 Stock Market Crash." *Finance and Economics Discussion Series* 2007 (13). https://www.federalreserve.gov/Pubs/feds/2007/200713/200713pap.pdf.

Case No. OIG-509: Investigation of Failure of the SEC To Uncover Bernard Madoff's Ponzi Scheme. 2009. Securities and Exchange Commission. https://www.sec.gov/files/oig-509-exec-summary.pdf.

Casella, Alessandra, and Barry Eichengreen. 1991. *Halting Inflation in Italy and France after World War II.* Working Paper No. 3852. National Bureau of Economic Research. https://www.nber.org/system/files/working_papers/w3852/w3852.pdf.

Cazel, Fred A. 1989. "Financing the Crusades." In *A History of the Crusades: Volume 6.*

Centonze, Arthur. 2011. "Case Study: Iceland's Financial Meltdown." *Journal of Financial Education* 37 (1).

Challis, C. E. 1967. "The Debasement of the Coinage: 1542-1551." *The Economic History Review*, New Series, vol. 20 (3).

Chan, Wellington. 1975. "Merchant Organizations in Late Imperial China: Patterns of Change and Development." *Journal of the Hong Kong Branch of They Royal Asiatic Society* 15. https://www.jstor.org/stable/23881621.

"Charles Ponzi: A Pyramid of Postage." 1986. *The New York Times.*

"Chase Bank Swift Code in the United States." n.d. https://wise.com/us/swift-codes/countries/united-states/chase-swift-code.

Chen, James. 2022. "Consolidated Tape: What It Is, How It Works." https://www.investopedia.com/terms/c/consolidated-tape.asp.

Chen, Jerome. 1958. "The Hsian-Feng Inflation." *Bulletin of the School of Oriental and African Studies, University of London* 21 (1). https://doi.org/10.2307/2751407.

Chen, Ting, and James Kai-Sing Kung. 2023. "Commercial Revolution in Medieval China." *SSRN*, ahead of print. https://doi.org/10.2139/ssrn.3960074.

Cheng, Linsun. 2003. *Banking in Modern China.* Cambridge University Press.

Chernow, Ron. 1990. *The House of Morgan: An American Banking Dynasty and the Rise of Modern Finance.* Atlantic Monthly Press.

Chiu, Becky, and Mervyn Lewis. 2006. *Reforming China's State-Owned Enterprises and Banks.* Edward Elgar Publishing.

Cho, Jang-Ok. 2017. "거시경제학의 눈으로 본 식민지 근대화론, Macroeconomic Assessment of Colonial Development in Korea." 경제학연구 65 (1).

Cipolla, Carlo. 1964. "The Economic Depression of the Renaissance?" *The Economic History Review*, New Series, vol. 16 (3). https://doi.org/10.2307/2592852.

Cipolla, Carlo. 1967. *Money, Prices, and Civilization in the Mediterranean World, Fifth to Seventeenth Century.* Gordian Press.

Clapman, J. H. 1945. *The Bank of England: A History.* Cambridge University Press.

Clapp, Newell. 1962. "Trading Stamps." *Ohio State Law Journal* 23 (1). https://kb.osu.edu/server/api/core/bitstreams/455d8955-c508-5c56-bf0d-a272c15f16fe/content.

Clark, Robert L., Lee A. Craig, and Jack W. Wilson. 2003. *A History of Public Sector Pensions in the United States.* University of Pennsylvania Press.

Clarke, Hermann F. 1937. "John Hull: Mint Master." *The New England Quarterly* 10 (4). https://doi.org/10.2307/359931.

Clemens, Michael A., and Michael Kremer. 2016. "The New Role for the World

Bank." *Journal of Economic Perspectives* 30 (1). https://pubs.aeaweb.org/doi/pdfplus/10.1257/jep.30.1.53.

Clinton, Bill. 1999. "Statement on Signing the Gramm-Leach-Bliley Act." The American Presidency Project. https://web.archive.org/web/20181007121619/http://www.presidency.ucsb.edu:80/ws/?pid=56922.

"Coal Production for France." n.d. FRED. https://fred.stlouisfed.org/series/A01214FRA422NNBR.

Cohen, Edward. 1992. *Athenian Economy and Society: A Banking Perspective*. Princeton University Press.

Cohen, Luc, and Jody Godoy. 2023. "Sam Bankman-Fried Convicted of Multi-Billion Dollar FTX Fraud." *Reuters*. https://www.reuters.com/legal/ftx-founder-sam-bankman-fried-thought-rules-did-not-apply-him-prosecutor-says-2023-11-02/.

"Coin Reform of Charlemagne (Münzreform Karls Des Großen)." n.d. https://web.archive.org/web/20161203183114/http://www.geschichte.uni-wuerzburg.de/institut/abteilungen/fraenkische_landesgeschichte/personal/leng/denar_karls_des_grossen/muenzreform_karls_des_grossen/.

Coletta, Paolo Enrico. 1973. *The Presidency of William Howard Taft*. University Press of Kansas.

Collard, Fabrice, and Harris Dellas. 2007. "The Great Inflation of the 1970s." *Journal of Money, Credit and Banking* 39 (2).

Collins, Andrew, and John Walsh. 2014. "Fractional Reserve Banking in the Roman Republic and Empire." *Ancient Society* 44. https://www.jstor.org/stable/44079991.

Committee for the Study of Economic, and Monetary Union. 1989. *Report on Economic and Monetary Union in the European Community*. https://ec.europa.eu/economy_finance/publications/pages/publication6161_en.pdf.

Comstock, Alzada. 1920. "British Income Tax Reform." *The American Economic Review* 10 (3). https://www.jstor.org/stable/1809046.

Comstock, Alzada. 1953. "Inflation: Greenbackism and Free Silver." *Current History* 24 (141).

Constitution Annotated. n.d. "ArtI.S8.C5.1 Congress's Coinage Power." https://constitution.congress.gov/browse/essay/artI-S8-C5-1/ALDE_00001066/.

"Consumer Price Index, 1913-." n.d. Mineapolis Fed. https://www.minneapolisfed.org/about-us/monetary-policy/inflation-calculator/consumer-price-index-1913-.

"Consumer Price Index: History." 2014. https://www.bls.gov/opub/hom/cpi/history.htm.

"Continental Illinois: A Bank That Was Too Big to Fail." 2023. https://www.federalreservehistory.org/essays/continental-illinois.

Cooper, Michael, and Louise Story. 2011. "Q. and A. on the Debt Ceiling." *The New York Times*.

Corkery, Michael. 2016. "Wells Fargo Offers Regrets, but Doesn't Admit Misconduct." *The New York Times*. https://www.nytimes.com/2016/09/10/business/dealbook/wells-fargo-apologizes-but-doesnt-admit-misconduct.html.

"Court Rejects H.K. Residents' Claims on Military Yen." 1999. *Kyodo News International*. https://www.thefreelibrary.com/Court+rejects+H.K.+residents'+claims+on+military+yen.-a054973168.

Cowen, David. 2000. "The First Bank of the United States and the Securities Market Crash of 1792." *The Journal of Economic History* 60 (4).

Crabbe, Leland. 1989. "The International Gold Standard and U.S. Monetary Policy from World War I to the New Deal." *Federal Reserve Bulletin*, June. https://fraser.stlouisfed.org/files/docs/meltzer/craint89.pdf.

Craig, Ben R., and Sara E. Millington. 2017. "The Federal Funds Market since the Financial Crisis." *Economic Commentary, Federal Reserve Bank of Cleveland*, ahead of print. https://doi.org/10.26509/frbc-ec-201707.

Craig, Valentine. 2001. "Merchant Banking: Past and Present." *FDIC Banking Review*, September. https://web.archive.org/web/20080911094848/http://www.fdic.gov/bank/analytical/banking/2001sep/br2001v14n1art2.pdf.

Crain, Matthew. 2021. *Profit over Privacy:*

How Surveillance Advertising Conquered the Internet. University of Minnesota Press.

Cribb, Joe, Catherine Eagleton, Elizabeth Errington, and Dr. Jonathan Williams. 2007. *Money: A History.* Firefly Book.

Cronin, Mary J. 1998. *Banking and Finance on the Internet.* John Wiley & Sons.

"Crowds See Market History Made." 1929. *New York Times*, October 30, 3.

Curtis, Michael. 1961. *The Great Political Theories.* HarperPerennial.

Daggett, Stephen. 2008. *Costs of Major US Wars.* CRS Report for Congress. https://apps.dtic.mil/sti/tr/pdf/ADA484276.pdf.

Dale, Richard S., Johnnie E. V. Johnson, and Leilei Tang. 2005. "Financial Markets Can Go Mad: Evidence of Irrational Behaviour during the South Sea Bubble." *The Economic History Review*, New Series, vol. 58 (2). https://www.jstor.org/stable/3698692.

Dangerfield, George. 1952. *The Era of Good Feelings.* Harcourt.

Danziger, Sheldon. 2013. "Introduction: Evaluating the Effects of the Great Recession." *The Annals of the American Academy of Political and Social Science* 650. https://www.jstor.org/stable/24541674.

Das, Santosh Kumar. 1925. *The Economic History of Ancient India.* Mitra Press: Calcutta.

Davidson, Adam. 2016. "How Regulation Failed with Wells Fargo." *The New Yorker.* https://www.newyorker.com/business/currency/the-record-fine-against-wells-fargo-points-to-the-failure-of-regulation.

Davies, Glyn. 1997. *History of Money.*

Davis, E. Philip. 2003. "Comparing Bear Markets – 1973 and 2000." *National Institute Economic Review*, no. 183. https://doi.org/10.1177/0027950103183001464.

Day, John. 1978. "The Great Bullion Famine." *Past & Present*, no. 79.

De La Torre, Augusto, Eduardo Levy Yeyati, Sergio L. Schmukler, Alberto Ades, and Graciela Kaminsky. 2003. "Living and Dying with Hard Pegs: The Rise and Fall of Argentina's Currency Board [with Comments]." *Economía* 3 (2). https://www.jstor.org/stable/20065441.

De Roover, Raymond. 1946a. "The Medici Bank: Financial and Commercial Operations." *The Journal of Economic History* 6 (2). https://www.jstor.org/stable/2113081.

De Roover, Raymond. 1946b. "The Medici Bank: Organization and Management." *The Journal of Economic History* 6 (1). https://www.jstor.org/stable/2112995.

De Roover, Raymond. 1947. "The Decline of the Medici Bank." *The Journal of Economic History* 7 (1).

De Roover, Raymond. 1963. *The Rise and Decline of the Medici Bank.* Harvard University Press.

De Roover, Raymond. 1999. *Money, Banking and Credit in Medieval Bruges: Italian Merchant-Bankers, Lombards, and Money-Changers: A Study in the Origins of Banking.* Routledge/Thoemmes Press.

"Delinquency Rate on Single-Family Residential Mortgages, Booked in Domestic Offices, All Commercial Banks." n.d. FRED. https://fred.stlouisfed.org/series/DRSFRMACBS.

Delivorias, Angelos. 2016. *Argentina's Debt Restructuring and Economy Ahead of the 2023 Elections.* PE 753.938. European Parliamentary Research Service. https://www.europarl.europa.eu/RegData/etudes/BRIE/2023/753938/EPRS_BRI(2023)753938_EN.pdf.

DeLong, J. Bradford, and Konstantin Magin. 2006. *A Short Note on the Size of the Dot-Com Bubble.* Working Paper No. 12011. National Bureau of Economic Research.

"Depression Cuts Divorce Rate." 1933. *New York Times*, January 1, E6.

"Depression Hits Marriage Rate." 1933. *New York Times* E8 (January).

Derman, Emanuel. 2015. "'The Age of Cryptocurrency,' by Paul Vigna and Michael J. Casey." *New York Times.* https://www.nytimes.com/2015/03/22/books/review/the-age-of-cryptocurrency-by-paul-vigna-and-michael-j-casey.html.

Dickinson, Elizabeth. 2011. "GDP: A Brief History." *Foreign Policy.* https://web.archive.org/web/20140828030822/http://www.foreignpolicy.com/articles/2011/01/02/gdp_a_brief_history.

Dickson, Peter R., and Philippa K. Wells. 2001. "The Dubious Origins of the Sherman Antitrust Act: The Mouse That Roared." *Journal of Public Policy & Mar-*

keting, Competition Policy and Antitrust Law, vol. 20 (1). https://www.jstor.org/stable/30000640.

Dilke, Oswald A. W. 1987. *Mathematics and Measurement*. University of California Press, Berkeley.

Dillenbeck, Richard. 1962. "The European Investment Bank." *The Business Lawyer* 17 (3).

"Diners | Cards." n.d. https://www.about-payments.com/knowledge-base/method/diners-club.

Dolley, R. H. M. 1962. *Anglo-Saxon Coins*. Taylor and Francis.

Dominguez, Kathryn M. E. 2006. "The European Central Bank, the Euro, and Global Financial Markets." *The Journal of Economic Perspectives* 20 (4). https://www.jstor.org/stable/30033684.

Dornbusch, Rudiger. 1985. *Purchasing Power Parity*. Working Paper No. 1591. National Bureau of Economic Research. https://www.nber.org/system/files/working_papers/w1591/w1591.pdf.

Dornbusch, Rudiger, and Stanley Fischer. 1981. *Macroeconomics, 2nd Ed.* McGraw-Hill.

Doti, Lynne Pierson. n.d. "Penn Square Bank." An Encyclopedia of Oklahoma History and Culture. https://www.okhistory.org/publications/enc/entry.php?entry=PE009.

Douglas, Justin. 2018. "Manufacturing Debt: A History of the Bank Credit Card Infrastructure." PhD Thesis, University of Toronto, Department of History.

Dow, J. B. 1971. "Early Actuarial Work in Eighteenth-Century Scotland [with Discussion]." *Transactions of the Faculty of Actuaries* 33 (240). https://www.jstor.org/stable/41218891.

"Dow-Jones Industrial Stock Price Index for United States." n.d. FRED.

Dray, Sacha, Camille Landais, and Stefanie Stantcheva. 2023. *Wealth and Property Taxation in the United States*. Harvard University. https://scholar.harvard.edu/stantcheva/files/dray_landais_stantcheva_wealth_property_tax_us.pdf.

Drelichman, Mauricio, and Hans-Joachim Voth. 2011. "Lending to the Borrower from Hell: Debt and Default in the Age of Philip II." *The Economic Journal* 121 (557). https://www.jstor.org/stable/41301355.

Dubs, Homer H. 1940. "Wang Mang and His Economic Reforms." *T'oung Pao, Second Series* 35 (4). https://www.jstor.org/stable/4527181.

Dunbar, Willis F., and George S. May. 1995. *Michigan: A History of the Wolverine State*. Wm. B. Eerdmans Publishing.

Dunnan, Nancy. 1985. "BANKING LAW: The Wild World of Interstate Banking." *ABA Journal* 71 (11). https://www.jstor.org/stable/20758436.

Dunnan, Nancy. 1989. "Mortgage-Backed Securities." *ABA Journal* 75 (4). https://www.jstor.org/stable/20760449.

Dwyer, Gerald. 1996. "Wildcat Banking, Banking Panics and Free Banking in the United States." *Federal Reserve Bank of Atlanta Economic Review* 81. https://web.archive.org/web/20150907080558/https://www.frbatlanta.org/-/media/Documents/filelegacydocs/ACFCE.pdf.

Eads, Linda. 1991. "From Capone to Boesky: Tax Evasion, Insider Trading, and Problems of Proof." *California Law Review* 79 (6).

Eagle, James. 2021. "Here's How Reserve Currencies Have Evolved over the Past 120 Years." https://www.visualcapitalist.com/cp/how-reserve-currencies-evolved-over-120-years/.

Ebrey, Patricia, Anne Walthall, and James Palais. 2006. *East Asia: A Cultural, Social, and Political History*. Houghton Mifflin.

"Economic and Monetary Union – A Timeline." n.d. https://europe.unc.edu/wp-content/uploads/sites/314/2017/05/1005Edwards_EMU_timeline.pdf.

"Economic Report of the President (2021)." 2021. https://www.whitehouse.gov/wp-content/uploads/2022/04/ERP-2022.pdf.

Economopoulos, Andrew, and Heather O'Neill. 1995. "Bank Entry during the Antebellum Period." *Journal of Money, Credit and Banking* 27 (4). https://doi.org/10.2307/2077790.

Editor, Moneyzine. 2022. "Super Display Book." *Moneyzine*. https://moneyzine.com/investments/super-display-book/.

Edling, Max. 2007. "'So Immense a Power in the Affairs of War': Alexander Hamilton and the Restoration of Public Credit." *The William and Mary Quarterly*, Third Series, vol. 64 (2).

Edmonds, Tim. 2018. *Money Laundering Law*. Briefing Paper No. 2592. House of Commons Library. https://research-briefings.files.parliament.uk/documents/SN02592/SN02592.pdf.

Ehrenberg, Victor. 1964. "Caesar's Final Aims." *Harvard Studies in Classical Philology* 68. https://doi.org/10.2307/310803.

"EIB – Promoting EU Standards Globally." 2017. *The European Investment Bank: An Overlooked (f)Actor in EU External Action?* https://www.jstor.org/stable/resrep06674.8.

Eichengreen, Barry. 2012. *Exorbitant Privilege: The Rise and Fall of the Dollar and the Future of the International Monetary System*. Oxford.

Eichengreen, Barry J. 2008. *Globalizing Capital: A History of the International Monetary System*.

Einaudi, Luca L. 2000. "From the Franc to the 'Europe': The Attempted Transformation of the Latin Monetary Union into a European Monetary Union, 1865-1873." *The Economic History Review*, New Series, vol. 53 (2).

"Elements of Stagflation Theory." 1976. *Zeitschrift Für Nationalökonomie / Journal of Economics* 36 (1/2). https://www.jstor.org/stable/41797816.

Elliot, Colin. 2018. "The Role of Money in the Economies of Ancient Greece and Rome." In *Handbook of the History of Money and Currency*. https://www.academia.edu/41258142/The_Role_of_Money_in_the_Economies_of_Ancient_Greece_and_Rome.

Elliott, Larry. 2012. "No EU Bailout for Greece as PM Promises to 'Put House in Order.'" *The Guardian*. https://www.theguardian.com/business/2010/jan/28/greece-papandreou-eurozone.

Elton, Edwin J., and Martin J. Gruber. 1997. "Modern Portfolio Theory, 1950 to Date." *Journal of Banking & Finance* 21 (11–12). https://www.sciencedirect.com/science/article/pii/S0378426697000484.

Elwell, Craig K. 2011. *Brief History of the Gold Standard in the United States*. Congressional Research Service. https://sgp.fas.org/crs/misc/R41887.pdf.

"Emergence of Chinese Charms: Symbols Begin to Appear on Chinese Coins." n.d. https://primaltrek.com/charmcoins.html.

EMVco. 2022. "EMV Chip At-a-Glance." EMVco. https://www.emvco.com/wp-content/uploads/2022/09/EMV%C2%AE-Chip-At-A-Glance-EMVCo-eBook.pdf.

Encyclopedia Britannica. 2023. "J. P. Morgan." https://www.britannica.com/biography/J-P-Morgan.

Encyclopedia Britannica. 2023. "Lydia." https://www.britannica.com/place/Lydia-ancient-region-Anatolia.

Encyclopedia Britannica. n.d. "As | Roman unit of weight." https://www.britannica.com/topic/as.

Encyclopedia Britannica. n.d. "Senate." https://www.britannica.com/topic/Senate-Roman-history.

Encyclopedia of Korean Culture. n.d. "조선은행." https://encykorea.aks.ac.kr/Article/E0052168.

Ernst, Joseph Albert. 1965. "Genesis of the Currency Act of 1764: Virginia Paper Money and the Protection of British Investments." *The William and Mary Quarterly* 22 (1). https://doi.org/10.2307/1920767.

Ery, William, Christopher Tse, David Scheuermann, and Patrick Heusser. 2022. *The Collapse of FTX: A Post Mortem Report*. Crypto Finance AG. https://www.crypto-finance.com/wp-content/uploads/FINAL-VERSION_THE-COLLAPSE-OF-FTX-A-POST-MORTEM-REPORT-16.11.pdf.

European Court of Auditors. 2019. "Audit Preview: Control of State Aid to Banks." European Court of Auditors. https://www.eca.europa.eu/lists/ecadocuments/ap19_05/ap_state_aid_en.pdf.

European Financial Stability Facility. 2016. ESM Europa. https://www.esm.europa.eu/sites/default/files/2016_02_01_efsf_faq_archived.pdf.

Evans, David S., and Richard L. Schmalensee. 2005. *Paying with Plastic: The Digital*

Revolution in Buying and Borrowing. MIT Press.

Evans-Pritchard, Ambrose. 2008. "European Recession Looms as Spain Crumbles." *The Telegraph.* https://web.archive.org/web/20080719113018/http://www.telegraph.co.uk/money/main.jhtml?xml=/money/2008/07/15/ccspain115.xml.

Fateh, Mostafa Khan. 1928. "Taxation in Persia: 'A Synopsis from the Early Times to the Conquest of the Mongols.'" *Bulletin of the School of Oriental Studies, University of London* 4 (4). https://www.jstor.org/stable/607253.

Faure, Alexander Pierre. 2013a. "Money Creation: Genesis 1." In *SSRN Electronic Journal.* http://dx.doi.org/10.2139/ssrn.2244998.

Faure, Alexander Pierre. 2013b. "Money Creation: Genesis 3." In *SSRN Electronic Journal.* http://dx.doi.org/10.2139/ssrn.2245041.

Faverio, Michelle. 2022. "More Americans Are Joining the 'Cashless' Economy." https://www.pewresearch.org/short-reads/2022/10/05/more-americans-are-joining-the-cashless-economy/.

Fawcett, Peter. 2016. "'When I Squeeze You with Eisphorai': Taxes and Tax Policy in Classical Athens." *Hesperia: The Journal of the American School of Classical Studies at Athens* 85 (1). https://doi.org/10.2972/hesperia.85.1.0153.

Fay, C. R. 1935. "Newton and the Gold Standard." *The Cambridge Historical Journal* 5 (1).

FDIC. 1998. *A Brief History of Deposit Insurance.*

Feavearyear, A. E. 1963. *The Pound Sterling: A History of English Money.* Oxford at the Clarendon.

"Fed Slashes Interest Rates To All-Time Low." 2008. *CBS News.* https://www.cbsnews.com/news/fed-slashes-interest-rates-to-all-time-low/.

Federal Deposit Insurance Corporation. 1984. *Federal Deposit and Insurance Corporation: The First Fifty Years: A History of the FDIC 1933-1983.* FDIC.

Federal Deposit Insurance Corporation. 1997. *History of the Eighties, Lessons for the Future, Vol. 1.* Federal Deposit Insurance Corporation.

Federal Reserve Committee. 1930. *Branch Banking in the United States.* Federal Reserve Committee. https://fraser.stlouisfed.org/files/docs/historical/federal%20reserve%20history/frcom_br_gp_ch_banking/branch_banking_us.pdf.

"Fedwire Funds Service - Annual Statistics." 2023. https://www.frbservices.org/resources/financial-services/wires/volume-value-stats/annual-stats.html.

Feinman, Joshua. 1993. "Reserve Requirements: History, Current Practice, and Potential Reform." *Federal Reserve Bulletin.* https://www.federalreserve.gov/monetary-policy/0693lead.pdf.

Fendel, Ralf, and David Maurer. 2015. "Does European History Repeat Itself?" *Journal of Economic Integration* 30 (1).

Ferguson, Niall. 2008. *The Ascent of Money.* Penguin.

Fernihough, Alan, and Kevin Hjortshøj O'Rourke. 2021. "Coal and the European Industrial Revolution." *The Economic Journal* 131 (635). https://doi.org/10.1093/ej/ueaa117.

"FINAL VOTE RESULTS FOR ROLL CALL 674." 2008. https://clerk.house.gov/evs/2008/roll674.xml.

"Financial Markets: Panicky Liquidation on Stock Exchange Partly Checked." 1929. *New York Times* 41 (October).

"Financiers Ease Tension: Five Wall Street Bankers Hold Two Meetings at Morgan Office." 1929. *New York Times.* https://timesmachine.nytimes.com/timesmachine/1929/10/25/96006629.pdf.

First Republic Bank. 2022. "Accounting 101: Debit and Credit." https://www.firstrepublic.com/insights-education/debit-and-credit-in-accounting.

Fisher, Douglas. 1989. "The Price Revolution: A Monetary Interpretation." *The Journal of Economic History* 49 (4).

Fisher, Jonas, and Andreas Hornstein. 2001. *The Role of Real Wages, Productivity, and Fiscal Policy in Germany's Great Depression 1928-37.* Working Paper Nos. 01–07. Federal Reserve Bank of Richmond. https://www.richmondfed.org/-/media/richmondfedorg/publications/research/working_papers/2001/pdf/wp01-7.pdf.

Fleckner, Andreas Martin. 2014. *Roman Business Associations*. https://extranet.sioe.org/uploads/isnie2014/fleckner.pdf.

Flugge, Barbara. 2017. *Smart Mobility – Connecting Everyone: Trends, Concepts and Best Practices*. Springer.

Foot, Sarah. 2011. *Aethelstan: The First King of England*. Yale University Press.

Forgang, Greg. 2019. "Money Laundering Through Cryptocurrency." La Salle University Digital Commons.

Forum, EMV Migration. 2015. "Understanding the 2015 U.S. Fraud Liability Shifts." https://web.archive.org/web/20150919095559/http://www.emv-connection.com/downloads/2015/05/EMF-Liability-Shift-Document-FINAL5-052715.pdf.

Foundation, Constitutional Rights. 2012. *J. P. Morgan, the Panic of 1907, & the Federal Reserve Act*. https://teachdemocracy.org/images/pdf/jpmorgan.pdf.

"France Loses AAA Rating as Euro Governments Downgraded." 2012. *BBC News*. https://www.bbc.com/news/business-16552623.

Frank, Tenney. 1919. "Rome's First Coinage." *Classical Philology* 14 (4). https://www.jstor.org/stable/263497.

Frank, Tenney. 1935. "The Financial Crisis of 33 AD." *The American Journal of Philology* 56 (4). https://doi.org/10.2307/289972.

Frankel, Jeffrey. 2015. *The Plaza Accord, 30 Years Later*. Working Paper No. 21813. National Bureau of Economic Research. https://www.nber.org/system/files/working_papers/w21813/w21813.pdf.

Friedman, Milton. 1990. "The Crime of 1873." *Journal of Political Economy* 98 (6).

Friedman, Milton. 1997. "John Maynard Keynes." *Federal Reserve Bank of Richmond Economic Quarterly* 83 (2). https://www.richmondfed.org/-/media/richmondfedorg/publications/research/economic_quarterly/1997/spring/pdf/friedman.pdf.

Friedman, Milton, and Anna Schwartz. 1980. *From New Deal Banking Reform to World War II Inflation*. Princeton University Press.

Frisby, Dominic. 2016. "Zimbabwe's Trillion-Dollar Note: From Worthless Paper to Hot Investment." *The Guardian*. https://www.theguardian.com/money/2016/may/14/zimbabwe-trillion-dollar-note-hyerinflation-investment.

Fritz, Sven. 2003. "The Riksbank up to the 20th Century." https://web.archive.org/web/20061230115428/http://www.riksbank.com/templates/Page.aspx?id=8184.

Frydman, Carola, and Eric Hilt. 2017. "Investment Banks as Corporate Monitors in the Early Twentieth Century United States." *The American Economic Review* 107 (7).

Fu, Zhufu. 1981. "The Economic History of China: Some Special Problems." *Modern China* 7 (1). https://www.jstor.org/stable/188871.

Fulfer, Johnny. 2022. "Panic of 1857." https://economic-historian.com/2020/07/panic-of-1857/.

Fund, International Monetary. 1996. *The International Monetary Fund 1966-1971: The System under Stress Volume I: Narrative*. International Monetary Fund.

Furness, Eric L. 1975. *Money and Credit in Developing Africa*.

Gallow, Nick. 2023. "Robinhood and the Gamification of Investing." https://finmasters.com/gamification-of-investing/.

Garbade, Kenneth D., and William L. Silber. 1978. "Technology, Communication, and the Performance of Financial Markets: 1840-1975." *The Journal of Finance* 33. https://doi.org/10.2307/2326479.

Garber, Peter. 1989. "Tulipmania." *Journal of Political Economy* 97 (3). https://www.jstor.org/stable/1830454.

Garbutt, Douglas. 1984. "The Significance of Ancient Mesopotamia in Accounting History." *The Accounting Historians Journal* 11 (1). https://www.jstor.org/stable/40697796.

Garfinkle, Steven J. 2004. "Shepherds, Merchants, and Credit: Some Observations on Lending Practices in Ur III Mesopotamia." *Journal of Economic and Social History of the Orient* 47 (1). https://www.jstor.org/stable/25165020.

Garnett, Porter. 1917. "The History of the Trade Dollar." *The American Economic Review* 7 (1).

Garraty, John A. 1973. "The New Deal, National Socialism, and the Great Depression." *The American Historical Review* 78 (4).

Garvy, George. 1977. *Money, Financial Flows, and Credit in the Soviet Union.* National Bureau of Economic Research.

Gastineau, Gary L. 1991. "A Short History of Program Trading." *Financial Analysts Journal* 47 (5). https://www.jstor.org/stable/4479463.

Gavin, Michael, and Dani Rodrik. 1995. "The World Bank in Historical Perspective." *The American Economic Review* 85 (2).

Gelderblom, Oscar, Abe de Jong, and Joost Jonker. 2013. "The Formative Years of the Modern Corporation: The Dutch East India Company VOC, 1602–1623." *The Journal of Economic History* 73 (4). https://doi.org/10.1017/S0022050713000879.

Gemery, H. A., and J. S. Hogendorn. 1988. "Continuity in West African Monetary History? An Outline of Monetary Development." *African Economic History*, no. 17. https://doi.org/10.2307/3601337.

Gershon, Livia. 2021. "World's Oldest Known Coin Mint Found in China." *Smithsonian Magazine.* https://www.smithsonianmag.com/smart-news/worlds-oldest-known-coin-mint-found-china-180978394/.

"Getting to Know the World Bank." 2012. https://www.worldbank.org/en/news/feature/2012/07/26/getting_to_know_the_worldbank.

Ghizoni, Sandra. 2013. "Creation of the Bretton Woods System." https://www.federalreservehistory.org/essays/bretton-woods-created.

Ghosh, D. N. 2006. "Genesis of High Finance: Case of Medici Bank." *Economic and Political Weekly* 41 (7). https://www.jstor.org/stable/4417808.

Gilbert, Adam M., Dara Hunt, and Kenneth C. Winch. 1997. "Creating an Integrated Payment System: The Evolution of Fedwire." *FRBNY Economic Policy Review.* https://www.newyorkfed.org/medialibrary/media/research/epr/97v03n2/9707gilb.pdf.

Gilmore, Oisín. 2007. "A Critique of John Locke and the Value of Money." *Student Economic Review* 21. https://www.tcd.ie/Economics/assets/pdf/SER/2007/Ois%EDn_Gilmore.pdf.

Glahn, Richard von. 2023. *Fountain of Fortune: Money and Monetary Policy in China, 1000-1700.* University of California Press.

Glasner, David. 1997. *Business Cycles and Depressions: An Encyclopedia.* Routledge.

Glitnir. 2008. *Condensed Consolidated Interim Financial Statements.* Glitnir Bank. https://web.archive.org/web/20090205091126/http://www.glitnirbank.com/servlet/file/2quarter_2008.pdf?ITEM_ENT_ID=11447&COLLSPEC_ENT_ID=156.

Godley, Wynne. 1992. "Maastricht and All That." *London Review of Books* 14 (19). https://www.lrb.co.uk/the-paper/v14/n19/wynne-godley/maastricht-and-all-that.

Goetzmann, William N., and K. Geert Rouwenhorst. 2005. *The Origins of Value: The Financial Innovations That Created Modern Capital Markets.* Oxford University Press.

Goetzmann, William, and K Rowenhorst. 2005. *The Origins of Value: The Financial Innovations That Created Modern Capital Markets.* Oxford University Press.

Goldberg, Dror. 2009. "The Massachusetts Paper Money of 1690." *The Journal of Economic History* 69 (4). https://www.jstor.org/stable/25654034.

Goldstein, Jacob. 2014. "The Invention Of 'The Economy.'" *NPR.* https://www.npr.org/sections/money/2014/02/28/283477546/the-invention-of-the-economy.

Golembe, Carter H. 1955. "Origins of Deposit Insurance in the Middle West, 1834-1866." *Indiana Magazine of History* 51 (2). https://www.jstor.org/stable/27788262.

Gomber, Peter, Björn Arndt, Marco Lutat, and Tim Uhle. 2011. *High-Frequency Trading.* Deutsche Börse Group. https://www.deutsche-boerse.com/resource/blob/69642/6bbb6205e-6651101288c2a0bfc668c45/data/high-frequency-trading_en.pdf.

Gompers, Paul, and Josh Lerner. 2001. "The Venture Capital Revolution." *The Journal of Economic Perspectives* 15 (2).

Goodrich, L. C. 1969. *A Short History of the Chinese People.* Harper.

Gordon, Barry. 1961. "Aristotle, Schumpeter, and the Metalist Tradition." *The Quarterly Journal of Economics* 75 (4). https://doi.org/10.2307/1884321.

Gordon, Cecil. 1939. "Old English Silver." *World Affairs* 102 (3).

Gorton, Gary. 2015. *The Maze of Banking.* Oxford University Press.

Gould, J. D. 1964. "The Price Revolution Reconsidered." *The Economic History Review*, New Series, vol. 17 (2).

Gould, J. D. 1970. *The Great Debasement: Currency and the Economy in Mid-Tudor England.* Oxford University Press.

Gourdin, Theodore S. 1855. *Historical Sketch of the Order of Knights Templar.* Walker & Evans Printers.

Graeber, David. 2011. *Debt: The First 5000 Years.*

Grameen Bank. 2021. *Annual Report 2021.* Grameen Bank. https://web.archive.org/web/20230906190504/https://grameen-bank.org/public/assets/archive/annual_report/Annual_Report_2021.pdf.

Granados, Jose A. Tapia, and Ana V. Diez Roux. 2009. "Life and Death During the Great Depression." *PNAS* 106 (41). https://www.pnas.org/doi/pdf/10.1073/pnas.0904491106.

Greene, Jack P., and Richard M. Jellison. 1961. "The Currency Act of 1764 in Imperial-Colonial Relations, 1764-1776." *The William and Mary Quarterly* 18 (4). https://doi.org/10.2307/1921098.

Greenwald, Bruce, and Jeremy Stein. 1988. "The Task Force Report: The Reasoning Behind the Recommendations." *The Journal of Economic Perspectives* 2 (3). https://www.jstor.org/stable/1942811.

Grimes, Paul. 1981. "PRACTICAL TRAVELER: COUPONS AND OTHER BONUSES FOR THE AIRBORNE." *New York Times.*

"Gross Domestic Product." n.d. GDPA. FRED. https://fred.stlouisfed.org/series/GDPA.

"Gross National Product." n.d. GNPA. FRED. https://fred.stlouisfed.org/series/GNPA.

Grossman, Richard S. 2010. "US Banking History, Civil War to World War II." Economic History Association. https://web.archive.org/web/20120905180528/http://eh.net/encyclopedia/article/grossman.banking.history.us.civil.war.wwii.

Gruben, William, and Sherry Kiser. 1999. "Beyond the Border - Brazil: The First Financial Crisis of 1999." *Southwest Economy*, no. 2. https://www.dallasfed.org/~/media/documents/research/swe/1999/swe9902c.pdf.

Grytten, Ola Honningdal. 2020. *Is There Really a Relationship Between Protestantism and Economic Growth?* Discussion Paper. Norwegian School of Economics. https://www.researchgate.net/publication/355032436_Is_There_Really_a_Relationship_Between_Protestantism_and_Economic_Growth.

Gu, Ban. 1950. *Food and Money in Ancient China.* Translated by Nancy Lee Swann. Princeton University Press.

Guan, Hanhui, Nuno Palma, and Meng Wu. 2022. "The Rise and Fall of Paper Money in Yuan China, 1260-1368." *University of Manchester Economics Discussion Paper Series*, no. EDP-2207. https://hummedia.manchester.ac.uk/schools/soss/economics/discussionpapers/EDP-2207.pdf.

Guarino, Arthur. 2015. "Philadelphia Stock Exchange." https://philadelphiaencyclopedia.org/essays/philadelphia-stock-exchange/.

Guinnane, Timothy W., and Jochen Streb. 2021. "The Introduction of Bismarck's Social Security System and Its Effects on Marriage and Fertility in Prussia." *Ruhr Economic Papers*, no. 901. http://dx.doi.org/10.4419/96973042.

Guo, Daoyang. 1989. "Historical Contributions of Chinese Accounting (or R-P=E-B)." *Accounting Historians Notebook* 12 (2). https://egrove.olemiss.edu/cgi/viewcontent.cgi?article=1261&context=aah_notebook.

Guo, Xiaowei. 2008. "The Fall of Long-Term Capital Management." *Lingnan Journal of Banking, Finance and Economics* 1. https://commons.ln.edu.hk/cgi/viewcontent.cgi?referer=&httpsredir=1&article=1001&context=ljbfe.

Guzman, Martin. 2016. *An Analysis of Argentina's 2001 Default Resolution.* CiGI Papers, no. 110. https://www.cigionline.org/

static/documents/documents/CIGI%20 Paper%20No.110WEB_0.pdf.

Hammond, Bray. 1947. "Jackson, Biddle, and the Bank of the United States." *The Journal of Economic History* 7 (1). https://www.jstor.org/stable/2113597.

Hammond, Bray. 1953. "The Second Bank of the United States." *Transactions of the American Philosophical Society* 43 (1). https://doi.org/10.2307/1005664.

Handel, John. 2022. "The Material Politics of Finance: The Ticker Tape and the London Stock Exchange, 1860s–1890s." *Enterprise & Society* 23 (3). 10.1017/eso.2021.3.

Hanke, Steve. 2002. "Currency Boards." *Annals, AAPSS* 579. https://www.cato.org/sites/cato.org/files/articles/steve-hanke-annals.pdf.

Hanke, Steve H., and Alex K. F. Kwok. 2009. "On the Measurement of Zimbabwe's Hyperinflation." *Cato Journal* 29 (2). https://www.cato.org/sites/cato.org/files/serials/files/cato-journal/2009/5/cj29n2-8.pdf.

Hanley, Ryan, and Maria Paganelli. 2014. *Adam Smith on Money, Mercantilism and the System of Natural Liberty.* https://digitalcommons.trinity.edu/cgi/viewcontent.cgi?article=1023&context=econ_faculty.

Harper, Robert Francis. 1904. *The Code of Hammurabi.*

Harris, Everette. 1970. "History of the Chicago Mercantile Exchange." Chicago Mercantile Exchange. https://legacy.farmdoc.illinois.edu/irwin/archive/books/Futrs_Tradng_in_Livestck/Futures_Trading_in_%20Livestock_Part%20I_2.pdf.

Harris, Kevin. 2007. "Was the Inca Empire A Socialist State? A Historical Discussion." *Historia* 16. https://www.eiu.edu/historia/Harris.pdf.

"Harry Markowitz." n.d. https://rady.ucsd.edu/faculty-research/faculty/emeriti-faculty/harry-markowitz.html.

Haselgrove, Colin, and Stefan Krmnicek. 2012. "The Archaeology of Money." *Annual Review of Anthropology* 41. https://www.jstor.org/stable/23270709.

Hass, Matthew. 2013. "Goldman Sachs: The Greek Situation." https://business.uccs.edu/sites/g/files/kjihxj2561/files/inline-files/Goldman%20Sachs_0.pdf.

Hauser, Christine. 2011. "U.S. Stocks Return to Pre-Downgrade Level." *New York Times.*

Hawkland, William. 1966. "American Travelers Checks." *Buffalo Law Review* 15 (3). https://digitalcommons.law.buffalo.edu/cgi/viewcontent.cgi?article=2578&context=buffalolawreview.

Hawtrey, R. G. 1918. "The Collapse of the French Assignats." *The Economic Journal* 28 (111). https://doi.org/10.2307/2222796.

Hayward, Justin. 2023. "How American Airlines' AAdvantage Program Became The World's First Frequent Flyer Scheme." https://simpleflying.com/american-airlines-aadvantage-origin-story/.

Heakal, Reem. 2023. "Glass-Steagall Act of 1933: Definition, Effects, and Repeal." https://www.investopedia.com/articles/03/071603.asp.

Healy, Paul M., and Krishna G. Palepu. 2003. "The Fall of Enron." *Journal of Economic Perspectives* 17 (2). https://websites.umich.edu/~kathrynd/JEP.FallofEnron.pdf.

Heilbroner, Robert L. 1953. *The Worldly Philosophers.*

Heldring, Leander, James A. Robinson, and Sebastian Vollmer. 2021. "The Long-Run Impact of the Dissolution of the English Monasteries." *NBER Working Papers,* no. 21450. http://www.nber.org/papers/w21450.

Henriques, Diana. 2011. *The Wizard of Lies: Bernie Madoff and the Death of Trust.* St. Martin's Griffin.

Henriques, Diana B., and Alex Berenson. 2008. "The 17th Floor, Where Wealth Went to Vanish." *New York Times.* https://graphics8.nytimes.com/packages/other/times-premier/madoff.pdf.

Herszenhorn, David M. 2008. "Bailout Plan Wins Approval; Democrats Vow Tighter Rules." *New York Times.* https://www.nytimes.com/2008/10/04/business/economy/04bailout.html.

Hill, Fiona, and Pamela Jewett. 1994. *Back in the USSR: Russia's Intervention in the Internal Affairs of the Former Soviet Republics and the Implications for United States Policy Toward Russia.* Ethnic Conflict Project. https://www.brookings.edu/wp-content/uploads/2016/06/back-in-the-ussr-1994.

pdf.

Hill, Joseph. 1894. "The Civil War Income Tax." *The Quarterly Journal of Economics* 8 (4). https://doi.org/10.2307/1885003.

Hirschey, Mark. 1998. "How Much Is a Tulip Worth?" *Financial Analysts Journal* 54 (4). https://www.jstor.org/stable/4480088.

Hirt, Geoffery. n.d. "World's Oldest Coin Mint Is Discovered in China." https://www.mheducation.com/highered/ideas/articles/the-world-s-oldest-coin-mint-is-discovered-in-china.

"Historical Coal Data: Coal Production, Availability and Consumption 1853 to 2022." 2013. Department for Energy Security and Net Zero and Department for Business, Energy & Industrial Strategy. https://www.gov.uk/government/statistical-data-sets/historical-coal-data-coal-production-availability-and-consumption.

"History of Anti-Money Laundering Laws." n.d. https://www.fincen.gov/history-anti-money-laundering-laws.

Hobler, Francis. 1839. "Salt Money of Ethiopia." *The Numismatic Chronicle* 2. https://www.jstor.org/stable/42681065.

Hodge, Helen Henry. 1904. "The Repeal of the Stamp Act." *Political Science Quarterly* 19 (2). https://doi.org/10.2307/2140283.

Holcombe, Charles. 2001. *The Genesis of East Asia, 221 B.C.-A.D. 907*. University of Hawaii Press.

Holzer, H. Peter, and Hanns-Martin Schonfeld. 1963. "The German Solution of the Post-War Price Level Problem." *The Accounting Review* 38 (2). https://www.jstor.org/stable/242929.

"Homeowner Vacancy Rate in the United States." n.d. FRED. https://fred.stlouisfed.org/series/RHVRUSQ156N.

Hong, Euny. 2014. *The Birth of Korean Cool*. Picador.

Hopkins, Keith. 1980. "Taxes and Trade in the Roman Empire (200 B.C.-A.D. 400)." *The Journal of Roman Studies* 70. https://doi.org/10.2307/299558.

Hoppit, Julian. 2002. "The Myths of the South Sea Bubble." *Transactions of the Royal Historical Society* 12. https://www.jstor.org/stable/3679343.

Horesh, Niv, and M. J. Jones. 2018. "Domesday Book: An Early Fiscal, Accounting Narrative." *Provincial China* 50 (3). https://research-information.bris.ac.uk/ws/portalfiles/portal/132980427/Domesday_book_2017.pdf.

Horioka, Charles Yuji. 2006. *The Causes of Japan's 'Lost Decade': The Role of Household Consumption*. Working Paper No. 12142. NBER. https://www.nber.org/system/files/working_papers/w12142/w12142.pdf.

Horsefield, J. Keith. n.d. "Why a Central Bank?" *Finance and Development*. https://www.elibrary.imf.org/downloadpdf/journals/022/0002/003/article-A005-en.pdf.

Houck, Davis W. 2000. "Rhetoric as Currency: Herbert Hoover and the 1929 Stock Market Crash." *Rhetoric and Public Affairs* 3 (2).

House, Xinhua Publishing. 2018. *History of Chinese Currency: 16th Century BC-20th Century AD*. Xinhua Publishing House.

Howe, Frederic C. 1916. "Dollar Diplomacy and Financial Imperialism under the Wilson Administration." *The Annals of the American Academy of Political and Social Science* 68.

Hsiao, Katherine Huang. 1971. *Money and Monetary Policy in Communist China*. Columbia University Press.

Hudson, Micheal. n.d. "Reconstructing the Origins of Interest-Bearing Debt."

Hulse, Carl, and Helene Cooper. 2011. "Obama and Leaders Reach Debt Deal." *New York Times*.

Hulsmann, J. G. 2003. "Has Fractional-Reserve Banking Really Passed the Market Test?" *The Independent Review* 7 (3). https://www.jstor.org/stable/24562451.

Hunt, Edward S. 1990. "A New Look at the Dealings of the Bardi and Peruzzi with Edward III." *The Journal of Economic History* 50 (1). https://www.jstor.org/stable/2123442.

Hunt, Edwin, and James Murray. 1999. *A History of Business in Medieval Europe, 1200-1550*. Cambridge University Press.

Hussain, Mumtaz, Asghar Shahmoradi, and Rima Turk. 2015. "An Overview of Islamic Finance." https://www.imf.org/external/pubs/ft/wp/2015/wp15120.pdf.

I. M. F. Staff. 1998. "The Asian Crisis: Causes and Cures." *Finance & Development* 35 (2). https://www.imf.org/external/pubs/ft/

fandd/1998/06/pdf/imfstaff.pdf.

Ialongo, Nicola, and Giancarlo Lago. 2021. "A Small Change Revolution. Weight Systems and the Emergence of the First Pan-European Money." *Journal of Archaeological Science* 129. https://doi. org/10.1016/j.jas.2021.105379.

IMF. 2013. *Press Release: Statement by the IMF Executive Board on Argentina.* IMF Press Release 13/33. IMF. https://www.imf. org/en/News/Articles/2015/09/14/01/49/ pr1333.

"Information Guide - European Central Bank." n.d. https://aei.pitt.edu/74892/1/ European_Central_Bank.pdf.

Ingersoll, Ernest. 1883. "Wampum." *American Journal of Numismatics, and Bulletin of the American Numismatic and Archaeological Society* 18 (2). https://www.jstor.org/ stable/43585204.

Inman, Phillip. 2012. "Black Wednesday 20 Years on: How the Day Unfolded." *The Guardian.* https://www.theguardian.com/ business/2012/sep/13/black-wednesday-20-years-pound-erm.

Institute, Moscow Financial. 1966. *Soviet Financial System.* Progress Publishers.

"Irish Republic 85bn Euro Bail-out Agreed." 2010. *BBC.* https://www.bbc.com/news/ world-europe-11855990.

Isidore, Chris. 2008. "Fed Slashes Key Rate to near Zero." *CNN Money.* https://money. cnn.com/2008/12/16/news/economy/ fed_decision/index.htm.

"Italy's Sovereign Debt Rating Cut by S&P on Growth Fear." 2012. *BBC News.* https://www.bbc.com/news/business-14981718.

Jacob, Charles. 1985. "Reaganomics: The Revolution in American Political Economy." *Law and Contemporary Problems* 48 (4). https://scholarship.law.duke.edu/cgi/ viewcontent.cgi?article=3812&context=lcp.

Jacobsen, Lyle. forthcoming. "The Ancient Inca Empire of Peru and the Double Entry Accounting Concept." *Journal of Accounting Research* 2 (2). https://www. jstor.org/stable/2490002.

Jahan, Sarwat, Ahmed Saber Mahmud, and Chris Papageorgiou. 2014. *What Is Keynesian Economics?* https://www.imf.

org/external/pubs/ft/fandd/2014/09/pdf/ basics.pdf.

James, Edwin. 1920. "France Wants Gold of Soviets Seized." *New York Times.* https:// www.nytimes.com/1920/06/11/archives/ france-wants-gold-of-soviets-seized-will-ask-britain-to-hold-up-all.html.

James, Harold. 1984. "The Causes of the German Banking Crisis of 1931." *The Economic History Review* 37 (1). https://doi. org/10.2307/2596832.

James, Harold. 2010. "1929: The New York Stock Market Crash." *Representations* 110 (1). https://doi.org/10.1525/ rep.2010.110.1.129.

James, Harold. 2020. *Making a Modern Central Bank: The Bank of England 1979–2003.* Cambridge University Press.

Japan, Bank of. n.d. "The History of Japanese Currency." https://www.imes.boj.or.jp/ cm/english/history/content/.

Jarus, Owen. 2015. "Ancient Receipt Proves Egyptian Taxes Were Worse Than Yours." *Live Science.* https://www.livescience. com/50139-ancient-egyptian-tax-receipt. html.

Jedwab, Remi, Noel Johnson, and Mark Koyama. 2020. "The Economic Impact of the Black Death." https://www2.gwu. edu/~iiep/assets/docs/papers/2020WP/ JedwabIIEP2020-14.pdf.

Jeffries, Adrianne. 2014. "Apple Pay Allows You to Pay at the Counter with Your iPhone 6." *The Verge.* https://www.theverge. com/2014/9/9/6084211/apple-pay-iphone-6-nfc-mobile-payment.

Jensen, Nathan M. 2004. "Crisis, Conditions, and Capital: The Effect of International Monetary Fund Agreements on Foreign Direct Investment Inflows." *The Journal of Conflict Resolution* 48 (2).

Jickling, Mark. 1999. *Systemic Risk And The Long-Term Capital Management Rescue.* Congressional Research Service. https:// crsreports.congress.gov/product/pdf/RL/ RL30232/3.

Johnson, Ben. n.d. "Decimalization in Britain." https://www.historic-uk.com/ HistoryUK/HistoryofBritain/Decimalisation-in-Britain/.

Johnson, Roger. 2010. *Historical Beginnings... The Federal Reserve.* Federal Reserve

Bank of Boston. https://web.archive.org/web/20130828150502/http://www.bos.frb.org/about/pubs/begin.pdf.

Kagan, Julia. 2023. "Mortgage-Backed Securities (MBS) Definition: Types of Investment." https://www.investopedia.com/terms/m/mbs.asp.

Kallet, Lisa, and John H. Kroll. 2020. *The Athenian Empire: Using Coins as Sources.* Cambridge University Press.

Kanas, Angelos. 2005. "Pure Contagion Effects in International Banking: The Case of BCCI's Failure." *Journal of Applied Economics* 8 (1).

Kaupthing Bank. 2008. *Condensed Consolidated Interim Financial Statements.* Kaupthing Bank. https://web.archive.org/web/20081114164038/http://www.kaupthing.com/lisalib/getfile.aspx?itemid=17006.

Kedar, Benjamin Z. 1974. "The General Tax of 1183 in the Crusading Kingdom of Jerusalem: Innovation or Adaptation?" *The English Historical Review* 89 (351).

Kennedy, Devin. 2017. "The Machine in the Market: Computers and the Infrastructure of Price at the New York Stock Exchange, 1965–1975." *Social Studies of Science* 47 (6). https://www.jstor.org/stable/48568900.

Kent, Roland G. 1920. "The Edict Diocletian Fixing Maximum Prices." *University of Pennsylvania Law Review and American Law Register* 69 (1). https://doi.org/10.2307/3314009.

Kenton, Will. 2021. "Designated Order Turnaround (DOT (SuperDOT))." https://www.investopedia.com/terms/d/dot.asp.

Kenton, Will. 2022. "New York Stock Exchange (NYSE): Definition, How It Works, History." https://www.investopedia.com/terms/n/nyse.asp.

Khan, B. Zorina. 2011. "Antitrust and Innovation before the Sherman Act." *Antitrust Law Journal* 77 (3). https://www.jstor.org/stable/23075633.

Khandker, Shahidur R., M. A. Baqui Khalily, and Zahed H. Khan. 1995. *Grameen Bank: Performance and Sustainability, Parts 63-306.* World Bank Publications.

Khanna, Manish, and Saurabh Kaushal.

2014. "Growth of Banking Sector in India: A Collective Study of History and Its Operations." *Asian Journal of Advanced Basic Sciences.* https://www.ajabs.org/articles/growth-of-banking-sector-in-india-a-collective-study-of-history-and-its-operations.pdf.

Killawala, Alpana. 2016. "Withdrawal of Legal Tender Status for ₹ 500 and ₹ 1000 Notes: RBI Notice." Reserve Bank of India. https://rbi.org.in/Scripts/BS_PressReleaseDisplay.aspx?prid=38520.

Kim, Keunsoo. 2013. "Chaebols and Their Effect on Economic Growth in South Korea." *Korean Social Sciences Review* 3 (2). https://s-space.snu.ac.kr/bitstream/10371/91035/1/01_Kim%20Keunsoo.pdf.

Kindleberger, Charles. 1991. "The Economic Crisis of 1619 to 1623." *The Journal of Economic History* 51 (1). https://www.jstor.org/stable/2123055.

Kindleberger, Charles, and Robert Aliber. 2005. *Manias, Panics, and Crashes.* Wiley.

King, Betty. 1975. "Japanese Colonialism and Korean Economic Development, 1910-1945." *Asian Studies: Journal of Critical Perspectives on Asia* 13 (3). https://www.asj.upd.edu.ph/mediabox/archive/ASJ-13-03-1975/king-japanese-colonialism-korean-economic-development.pdf.

King, Frank H. H. 2014. *Money and Monetary Policy in China.*

King, L. W. n.d. "The Code of Hammurabi." https://avalon.law.yale.edu/ancient/hamframe.asp.

King, W. T. C. 1945. "The Bank of England." *The Economic History Review* 15 (1/2). https://doi.org/10.2307/2590313.

Kirby, William C. 1995. "China Unincorporated: Company Law and Business Enterprise in Twentieth-Century China." *The Journal of Asian Studies* 54 (1). https://doi.org/10.2307/2058950.

Kirilenko, Andrei, Albert S. Kyle, Mehrdad Samadi, and Tugkan Tuzun. 2014. *The Flash Crash: The Impact of High Frequency Trading on an Electronic Market.* https://www.cftc.gov/sites/default/files/idc/groups/public/@economicanalysis/documents/file/oce_flashcrash0314.

pdf.

Kirkpatrick, Charles D. II, and Julie R. Dahlquist. 2010. *Technical Analysis: The Complete Resource for Financial Market Technicians*. FT Press.

Klaffke, Pamela. 2003. *Spree: A Cultural History of Shopping*. Arsenal Pulp Press.

Klein, Maury. 1929. *Rainbow's End: The Crash of 1929*. Oxford University Press.

Kleit, Andrew N. 2018. *Modern Energy Market Manipulation*. Emerald Group Publishing.

Knodell, Jane. 2006. "Rethinking the Jacksonian Economy: The Impact of the 1832 Bank Veto on Commercial Banking." *The Journal of Economic History* 66 (3). https://www.jstor.org/stable/3874852.

Kopf, Edwin W. 1927. *The Early History of the Annuity*. L. W. Lawrence.

Korea, Visual. 2020. "한국은 어떻게 전세계를 바꾸어왔을까?" https://brunch.co.kr/@visualisingkor/6.

Kosmetatos, Paul. 2014. *Financial Contagion and Market Intervention in the 1772-3 Credit Crisis*. Working Paper Nos. 21–2014. Cambridge. https://www.econsoc.hist.cam.ac.uk/docs/CWPESH-number21October2014.pdf.

Kozo, Yamamura. 1973. "The Development of the Za in Medieval Japan." *The Business History Review* 47 (4). https://www.jstor.org/stable/pdf/3113366.pdf.

Krauss, Clifford. 2001. "ARGENTINE LEADER DECLARES DEFAULT ON BILLIONS IN DEBT." *New York Times* A1 (December).

Kruse, Susan E. 1988. "Ingots and Weight Units in Viking Age Silver Hoards." *World Archaeology* 20 (2). https://www.jstor.org/stable/124476.

Kuehn, Daniel. 2012. "A Note on America's 1920–21 Depression as an Argument for Austerity." *Cambridge Journal of Economics* 36 (1). https://www.jstor.org/stable/24232385.

Kunze, Neil L. 1971. "The Origins of Modern Social Legislation: The Henrician Poor Law of 1536." *Albion: A Quarterly Journal Concerned with British Studies* 3 (1).

Kuznets, Simon. 1934. "National Income, 1929-32, Senate Document No. 124, 73rd Congress." https://fraser.stlouisfed.

org/title/971?start_page=3.

Kynaston, David. 2017. *Till Time's Last Sand: A History of the Bank of England 1694-2013*. Bloomsbury Publishing.

Lacapra, Emi. 2023. "What Is Robinhood, and How Does It Work." https://cointelegraph.com/explained/what-is-robinhood-and-how-does-it-work.

Laffey, Des. 2004. "The Rise and Fall of the Dot Com Enterprises." *International Journal of Entrepreneurship Education* 2 (2).

Lahaye, Laura. n.d. "Mercantilism." In *The Concise Encyclopedia of Economics*. https://www.econlib.org/library/Enc1/Mercantilism.html.

Lamim-Guedes, Valdir. 2012. "Colher o Fruto Sem Plantar a Árvore." CIÊNCIAHOJE. https://web.archive.org/web/20160310184656/http://cienciahoje.uol.com.br/revista-ch/2012/292/pdf_aberto/opiniao292.pdf/at_download/file.

Landsbanki. 2008. *Condensed Consolidated Interim Financial Statements*. Landsbanki. https://web.archive.org/web/20081206081632/http://www.landsbanki.is/Uploads/Documents/ArsskyrslurOgUppgjor/landsbanki_consolidated_interim_financial_statements_30-jun-2008.pdf.

Lane, Kris. 2011. "Potosi." In *New World Objects of Knowledge: A Cabinet of Curiosities*, edited by Mark Thurner and Juan Pimentel. University of London Press.

Lange, Ann-Christina. 2017. "The Noisy Motions of Instruments: The Performative Space of High-Frequency Trading." In *Performing the Digital: Performance Studies and Performances in Digital Cultures*, edited by Martina Leeker, Imanuel Schipper, and Timon Beyes. Transcript Verlag.

Larkin, Charles. n.d. *The Great Recoinage of 1696*. https://www.researchgate.net/publication/256037493_The_Great_Recoinage_of_1696_Charles_Davenant's_Developments_in_Monetary_Theory.

"Lateran III Complete." n.d. https://web.archive.org/web/20131006143907/http://faculty.cua.edu/pennington/Medieval%20Papacy/Lateran%20III%20Complete.pdf.

Lattman, Peter. 2010. "Wall St. Programmer Guilty of Code Theft." *New York Times*.

Laumakis, Paul. 2003. "Designing a 401(k):

A Case Study." *SIAM Review* 45 (4).

Lawson, Nigel. 2006. *Big Bang 20 Years On*. City of London Centre for Policy Studies.

Lazar, Marianna. 2022. "Ancient Coins of Japan." *Journal of East Asian Culture* 14 (1). https://doi.org/10.38144/TKT.2022.1.4.

Le Goff, Jacques. 2012. *Money and the Middle Ages*. Polity.

Le Maux, Laurent. 2020. "Central Banking and Finance: The Bank of England and the Bank Act of 1844." https://hal.science/hal-02854521/document.

Lee, Phil-Sang. 2000. "Economic Crisis and Chaebol Reform in Korea." https://business.columbia.edu/sites/default/files-efs/imce-uploads/PFS/APEC_New/PSLee.PDF.

Leightner, Johnathan. 2007. "Thailand's Financial Crisis: Its Causes, Consequences, and Implications." *Journal of Economic Issues* 41 (1).

Leitgeb, E., C. Patauner, H. Witschnig, D. Rinner, A. Maier, and E. Merlin. 2007. *High Speed RFID/NFC at the Frequency of 13.56 MHz*. Institute of Broadband Communications. https://www.researchgate.net/publication/240631530_High_Speed_RFIDNFC_at_the_Frequency_of_1356_MHz.

Leonard, Thomas. 2005. "Eugenics and Economics in the Progressive Era." *Journal of Economic Perspectives* 19 (4). https://www.princeton.edu/~tleonard/papers/retrospectives.pdf.

Levi, Michael. 2002. "Money Laundering and Its Regulation." *The Annals of the American Academy of Political and Social Science* 582.

Levin-Waldman, Oren. 2015. *Minimum Wage: A Reference Handbook*. ABC-CLIO.

Lewis, Michael. 2010a. "Betting on the Blind Side." *Vanity Fair*. https://www.vanityfair.com/news/2010/04/wall-street-excerpt-201004.

Lewis, Michael. 2010b. *The Big Short: Inside the Doomsday Machine*. W. W. Norton & Company.

Li, Ling-Fan. 2009. *After the Great Debasement, 1544-51: Did Gresham's Law Apply?* Working Paper No. 126/09. London School of Economics. https://www.lse.ac.uk/Economic-History/Assets/Documents/WorkingPapers/Economic-History/2009/WP126.pdf.

Li, Yun. 2020. "NYSE to Temporarily Close Floor, Move to Electronic Trading after Positive Coronavirus Tests." *CNBC*. https://www.cnbc.com/2020/03/18/nyse-to-temporarily-close-trading-floor-move-to-electronic-trading-because-of-coronavirus.html.

Liberto, Danial. 2021. "What Is the European Monetary System (EMS)? Definition, History." https://www.investopedia.com/terms/e/ems.asp.

Library of Congress. n.d. "Wall Street and the Stock Exchanges: Historical Research." https://guides.loc.gov/wall-street-history/exchanges.

Ligt, Luuk de. 2007. "Roman Law and the Roman Economy: Three Case Studies." *Latomus* 66 (1). https://www.jstor.org/stable/41545348.

Lin, Connie. 2020. "Why an Empty Floor at the New York Stock Exchange Will Have Little Impact on Trading." *Fast Company*. https://www.fastcompany.com/90480818/why-an-empty-floor-at-the-new-york-stock-exchange-will-have-little-impact-on-trading.

Lioudis, Nick. 2023. "What Is the Gold Standard? Advantages, Alternatives, and History." https://www.investopedia.com/ask/answers/09/gold-standard.asp#toc-the-fall-of-the-gold-standard.

Lissardy, Zelmar. 1989. "ARGENTINA RUNS SHORT OF CURRENCY GOVERNMENT DECLARES BANK HOLIDAY WHILE MORE AUSTRALS PRINTED." *Washington Post*. https://www.washingtonpost.com/archive/business/1989/04/29/argentina-runs-short-of-currency-government-declares-bank-holiday-while-more-australs-printed/c26c170d-657e-42cc-8e12-ac46616b26b1/.

Littleton, A. C. 1926. "Evolution of the Ledger Account." *The Accounting Review* 1 (4).

Littleton, A. C. 1927. "The Antecedents of Double-Entry." *The Accounting Review* 2 (2).

Littleton, A. C., and B. S. Yamey. 1952. "A Short History of Tallies." *Accounting Re-*

search 3 (3). https://www.mgh-bibliothek. de/dokumente/a/a146433.pdf.

Liu, Zongyuan Zoe. 2023. *Sovereign Funds: How the Communist Party of China Finances Its Global Ambitions.* Harvard University Press.

Lockard, Craig. 2020. *Societies, Networks, and Transitions: A Global History.* Cengage Learning.

Loomis, Carol J. 1966. "The Jones Nobody Keeps up With." *Fortune.* https://tilson-funds.com/TheJones.pdf.

Lopez, Jose A. 2018. *Uncertainty and Hyperinflation: European Inflation Dynamics after World War I.* Working Paper Nos. 2018–06. Federal Reserve Bank of San Francisco. https://doi.org/10.24148/ wp2018-06.

Lopez, R. S., and H. A. Miskimin. 1962. "The Economic Depression of the Renaissance." *The Economic History Review, New Series* 14 (3). https://doi. org/10.2307/2591885.

Lopez, Robert Sabatino. 2001. *Medieval Trade in the Mediterranean World: Illustrative Documents.* Columbia University Press.

Luce, T. J. 1968. "Political Propaganda on Roman Republican Coins: Circa 92-82 B.C." *American Journal of Archaeology.* https://doi.org/10.2307/501820.

Lydon, Gislaine. 2009. *On Trans-Saharan Trails: Islamic Law, Trade Networks, and Cross-Cultural Exchange in Nineteenth-Century Western Africa.* Cambridge University Press.

Ma, Debin. 2012. *Money and Monetary System in China in the 19th-20th Century: An Overview.* Working Papers No. 159/12. https://eprints.lse.ac.uk/41940/1/WP159. pdf.

MacDonald, James. 2015. "Tax Day in Ancient Egypt." *JSTOR Daily.* https://daily. jstor.org/tax-day-ancient-egypt/.

Mackintosh, Phil. 2021. "Nasdaq: 50 Years of Market Innovation." https://www.nasdaq. com/articles/nasdaq%3A-50-years-of-market-innovation-2021-02-11.

Maginn, John L., Donald L. Tuttle, Dennis W. McLeavey, and Jerald E. Pinto. 2010. *Managing Investment Portfolios: A Dynamic Process.* John Wiley & Sons.

"Magnetic Stripe Technology." n.d. https://

www.ibm.com/ibm/history/ibm100/us/ en/icons/magnetic/.

Makin, John. 2008. "Japan's Lost Decade: Lessons for the United States in 2008." *American Enterprise Institute for Public Policy Research.* https://www.aei.org/wp-content/uploads/2011/10/20080225_22772EO-March_g.pdf.

Malepati, Venkataramanaiah. 2015. *The Profile of Bombay Stock Exchange Limited.* https://www.researchgate.net/publication/289504506_The_Profile_of_the_ Bombay_Stock_Exchange_Limited.

Mall, Scott. 2021. "FreightWaves Classics/ Leaders: J.P. Morgan Controlled US Railroads and Industry Policies." https://www. freightwaves.com/news/freightwaves-classicsleaders-jp-morgan-greatly-influenced-us-railroads-in-the-late-19th-century.

Manly, Ronan. 2021. "British Requests for $3 Billion in US Treasury Gold – The Trigger That Closed the Gold Window." https:// www.bullionstar.com/blogs/ronan-manly/ british-requests-for-3-billion-in-us-treasury-gold-the-trigger-that-closed-the-gold-window/.

Marcias, Amanda. 2022. "EU, UK, Canada, US Pledge to Remove Selected Russian Banks from Interbank Messaging System SWIFT." *CNBC.* https://www. cnbc.com/2022/02/26/eu-uk-canada-us-pledge-to-remove-selected-russian-banks-from-swift.html.

Mark, Joshua J. 2017. "Ancient Egyptian Taxes & the Cattle Count." *World History Encyclopedia.* https://www.worldhistory. org/article/1012/ancient-egyptian-taxes--the-cattle-count/.

"Market Capitalization of Listed Domestic Companies (% of GDP) - United States." n.d. World Bank. https://data. worldbank.org/indicator/CM.MKT. LCAP.GD.ZS?end=2022&locations=US&skipRedirection=true&start=1 975&view=chart.

"Market Capitalization of Listed Domestic Companies (Current US$) - United States." n.d. World Bank. https://data.worldbank.org/indicator/ CM.MKT.LCAP.CD?end=2022&locations=US&skipRedirection=true&start=1

975&view=chart.

Marmefelt, Thomas. 2018. *The History of Money and Monetary Arrangements: Insights from the Baltic and North Seas Region*. Routledge.

Marshall, John M. 1976. "Moral Hazard." *The American Economic Review* 66 (5). https://www.jstor.org/stable/1827499.

Martin, Thomas R. 1996. "Why Did the Greek 'Polis' Need Coins?" *Historia: Zeitschrift Für Alte Geschichte* 45 (3). https://www.jstor.org/stable/4436427.

Marx, Karl, and Friedrich Engels. 1888. *The Communist Manifesto*.

Mason, Edward, and Robert Asher. 1973. *The World Bank since Bretton Woods*. The Brookings Institution.

Mattingly, H. 1945. "The First Age of Roman Coinage." *The Journal of Roman Studies* 35 (1/2). https://doi.org/10.2307/297279.

Mazur, Mieszko, Man Dang, and Miguel Vega. 2021. "COVID-19 and the March 2020 Stock Market Crash: Evidence from S&P1500." *Finance Research Letters* 38. https://www.ncbi.nlm.nih.gov/pmc/articles/PMC7343658/.

McAndrews, James. 1994. "The Automated Clearing House System: Moving towards Electronic Payment." *Philadelphia Fed Business Review*. https://www.philadelphiafed.org/-/media/frbp/assets/economy/articles/business-review/1994/brja94jm.pdf.

McCrank, John. 2022. "Visa, Mastercard Suspend Operations in Russia over Ukraine Invasion." *Reuters*. https://www.reuters.com/business/finance/visa-suspends-operations-russia-over-ukraine-invasion-2022-03-05/.

McEvedy, Collin, and Richard Jones. 1978. *Atlas of World Population History*. Harmondsworth.

McGabe, Patrick. 2008. "The Economics of the Mutual Fund Trading Scandal."

McGowan, Micheal. 2010. "The Rise of Computerized High-Frequency Trading." *Duke Law and Technology Review*, no. 16. https://scholarship.law.duke.edu/dltr/vol9/iss1/15/.

McGuire, John. 2004. "The Rise and Fall of the Oriental Bank in the Nineteenth Century." *15th Biennial Conference of the Asian Studies Association of Australia*. https://web.archive.org/web/20131024070303/http://coombs.anu.edu.au/SpecialProj/ASAA/biennial-conference/2004/McGuire-J-ASAA2004.pdf.

Meadows, Andrew, and Kirsty Shipton. 2001. *Money and Its Uses in the Ancient Greek World*.

Meggs, Philip B., and Alston W. Purvis. 2006. *Meggs' History of Graphic Design*. John Wiley.

Meikle, Scott. 1994. "Aristotle on Money." *Phronesis* 39 (1). https://www.jstor.org/stable/4182455.

Merced, Michael J. 2008. "Effort Under Way to Sell Madoff Unit." *New York Times*. https://www.nytimes.com/2008/12/25/business/25madoff.html.

Metcalf, William E. 2012. *The Oxford Handbook of Greek and Roman Coinage*. Oxford University Press.

Metrick, Andrew. 2024. "The Failure of Silicon Valley Bank and the Panic of 2023." *The Journal of Economic Perspectives* 38 (1). https://doi.org/10.1257/jep.38.1.133.

"Michael Milken's Guilt." 1990. *New York Times*.

Michener, Ron. n.d. "Money in the American Colonies." https://eh.net/encyclopedia/money-in-the-american-colonies/.

Middelkoop, Willem. 2016. *The Big Reset: War on Gold and the Financial Endgame*. Amsterdam University Press.

Milevsky, Moshe. 2017. "The (Early) History of (Bond) Finance." https://www.palgrave.com/gp/blogs/business-economics-finance-management/exploring-economic-history/the-early-history-of-bond-finance.

Million, John Wilson. 1894. "The Debate on the National Bank Act of 1863." *Journal of Political Economy* 2 (2). https://www.jstor.org/stable/1819470.

Miskimin, Harry A. 1967. "Two Reforms of Charlemagne? Weights and Measures in the Middle Ages." *The Economic History Review* 20 (1).

Mitchell, W. C. 1898. "The Value of the 'Greenbacks' During the Civil War." *Journal of Political Economy* 6 (2).

Mitchell, W. C. 1903. *A History of the Greenbacks: With Special Reference to the Economic Consequences of Their Issue,*

1862-65. University of Chicago Press.

Mizrach, Bruce, and Christopher J. Neely. 2006. "The Transition to Electronic Communications Networks in the Secondary Treasury Market." *Federal Reserve Bank of St. Louis Review* 88 (6). https://files.stlouisfed.org/files/htdocs/publications/review/06/11/Mizrach.pdf.

Mockford, Jack. 2014. "'They Are Exactly as Banknotes Are': Perceptions and Technologies of Bank Note Forgery during the Bank Restriction Period, 1797-1821." PhD Thesis, University of Hertfordshire.

Moen, Jon. 2001. "The Panic of 1907." https://eh.net/encyclopedia/the-panic-of-1907/.

Moll-Murata, Christine. 2008. "Chinese Guilds from the Seventeenth to the Twentieth Centuries: An Overview." *International Review of Social History* 53 (S16). https://doi.org/10.1017/S0020859008003672.

Moncarz, Elisa S., Raúl Moncarz, Alejandra Cabello, and Benjamin Moncarz. 2006. "The Rise and Collapse of Enron: Financial Innovation, Errors and Lessons." In *Contaduría y Administración.* no. 218. https://www.redalyc.org/pdf/395/39521802.pdf.

Money Gallery, From Prehistory to the Present Day. n.d. British Museum. https://www.britishmuseum.org/sites/default/files/2021-05/Money_Gallery_LPG_2020_Room_68.pdf.

"Money Laundering." n.d. https://www.unodc.org/unodc/en/money-laundering/overview.html.

Money Laundering and Financial Crimes. 2002. U.S. Securities and Exchange Commission. https://2009-2017.state.gov/documents/organization/8703.pdf.

Morgan, Wayne H. 1956. "The Origins and Establishment of the First Bank of the United States." *The Business History Review* 30 (4). https://doi.org/10.2307/3111717.

Morgenson, Gretchen. 2023. "Phony Bank Accounts Resurface at Wells Fargo, with a Twist." *NBC News.* https://www.nbcnews.com/news/investigations/phony-bank-accounts-resurface-wells-fargo-twist-rc-na98005.

Morio, Seno'o. 1996. *Yamada Hagaki and the History of Paper Currency in Japan.* https://www.imes.boj.or.jp/research/papers/english/96-E-25.pdf.

Mork, Randal, and Fan Yang. 2010. *The Shanxi Banks.* Working Paper No. 15884. NBER. https://www.nber.org/system/files/working_papers/w15884/w15884.pdf.

Mørkholm, Otto. 1991. *Early Hellenistic Coinage from the Accession of Alexander to the Peace of Apamaea (336-188 BC).* Cambridge University Press.

Morris-Cotterill, Nigel. 2001. "Money Laundering." In *Foreign Policy.* no. 124.

Morrison, Ashley James. 2016. "Shocking Intellectual Austerity: The Role of Ideas in the Demise of the Gold Standard in Britain." *International Organization* 70 (1). https://www.jstor.org/stable/24758289.

Morrissey, Daniel J. 2016. *Book Review: "JP Madoff: The Unholy Alliance Between America's Biggest Bank and America's Biggest Crook."* nos. 2016–4. Gonzaga University School of Law. https://dx.doi.org/10.2139/ssrn.2779750.

Morton, Scott. 1995. *China: Its History and Culture.* McGraw-Hill.

Moshenskyi, Sergii. 2008. *History of the Weksel: Bill of Exchange and Promissory Note.* Xlibris.

Moss, David, and Eugene Kintgen. 2010. "The Dojima Rice Market and the Origins of Futures Trading." https://edisciplinas.usp.br/pluginfile.php/151297/mod_resource/content/2/Dojima_Rice_Market_Case.pdf.

Muhs, Brian. 2016. *The Ancient Egyptian Economy.* Cambridge University Press.

Müller, Leonie. 2021. "Understanding Paper: Structures, Watermarks, and a Conservator's Passion." https://harvardartmuseums.org/article/understanding-paper-structures-watermarks-and-a-conservator-s-passion.

Mundell, Robert A. 2002. *The Birth of Coinage.* Nos. 0102–08. Discussion Paper Series. Columbia University Department of Economics. https://doi.org/10.7916/D8Q531TK.

Munro, George E. 1997. "Finance and Credit in the Eighteenth-Century Russian Economy." *Jahrbücher Für Geschichte Osteuropas, Neue Folge* 45 (4). https://www.jstor.

org/stable/41049998.

Munro, John H. 2003. "The Medieval Origins of the Financial Revolution: Usury, Rentes, and Negotiability." *The International History Review* 25 (3).

Munro, John H. 2008. "Some Basic Principles of Marxian Economics." Economics 301Y and 303Y. University of Toronto Department of Economics. https://www.economics.utoronto.ca/munro5/MARXECON.pdf.

Murray, Gilbert. 1908. *The Frogs. Translated into English Rhyming Verse.* George Allen & Sons.

N. P. R. Staff. 2015. "When The World Bank Does More Harm Than Good." *NPR*. https://www.npr.org/sections/goatsandsoda/2015/04/17/399816448/when-the-world-bank-does-more-harm-than-good.

Naef, Alain. 2022. *An Exchange Rate History of the United Kingdom, 1945–1992*. Cambridge University Press.

Nair, Anjana. 2019. *Muhammad Tughlaq's Token Currency*. https://www.academia.edu/39326109/Muhammad_Tughlaqs_Token_Currency.

Nakamoto, Satoshi. 2008. *Bitcoin: A Peer-to-Peer Electronic Cash System*. https://bitcoin.org/bitcoin.pdf.

"Nasdaq Composite Index." n.d. Wall Street Journal. https://www.wsj.com/market-data/quotes/index/COMP/historical-prices.

n.d. n.d. "Wedge Shaped Writing." https://www.canterbury.ac.nz/exhibition/ancient-writing/cuneiform/index.shtml.

Nelson, Rebecca. 2017. *The Greek Debt Crisis: Overview and Implications for the United States*. No. R44155. Congressional Research Service. https://crsreports.congress.gov/product/pdf/R/R44155/5.

"New York Stock Exchange (NYSE): Definition, How It Works, History." 2023. https://www.britannica.com/money/topic/New-York-Stock-Exchange.

New York Times. 1869. "The Gold Excitement." September 25. https://timesmachine.nytimes.com/timesmachine/1869/09/25/79820520.html.

New York Times. 1929. "Ticker Prints Last Quotation 4 Hours 8 1/2 Minutes Late." October 25. https://timesmachine.nytimes.com/timesma-

chine/1929/10/25/79820520.html.

Newlyn, W. T. 1954. *Money and Banking in British Colonial Africa*. Oxford University Press, London.

Newman, Eric. 2008. *The Early Paper Money of America*. Krause Publications.

News, Qilu Evening. 2013. "王莽与他的经济改革." *Qilu Evening News*. https://sjb.qlwb.com.cn/qlwb/content/20131108/ArticelE15002FM.htm.

Nezhad, Zarra M. 2004. "A Brief History of Money in Islam and Estimating the Value of Dirham and Dinar." *Review of Islamic Economics* 8 (2).

Nichols, Glenn. 1971. "English Government Borrowing, 1660-1688." *Journal of British Studies* 10 (2). https://www.jstor.org/stable/175350.

Nielsen, Eric. 2005. "Monetary Policy in the Confederacy." *Richmond Federal Reserve*. https://www.richmondfed.org/-/media/richmondfedorg/publications/research/econ_focus/2005/fall/pdf/economic_history.pdf.

"Nikkei Stock Average." n.d. FRED. https://fred.stlouisfed.org/series/NIKKEI225.

Niskanen, William A. 1988. "Reaganomics." https://www.econlib.org/library/Enc1/Reaganomics.html.

Nitschke, Christoph. 2018. "Theory and History of Financial Crises: Explaining the Panic of 1873." *The Journal of the Gilded Age and Progressive Era* 17 (2).

"Nominal GDP for China." n.d. No. MKTGDPCNA646NWDB. FRED.

Norman, Laurence. 2020. "EU Ramps Up Trade System With Iran Despite U.S. Threats." *Wall Street Journal*.

North, Douglass C., and Robert Paul Thomas. 1971. "The Rise and Fall of the Manorial System: A Theoretical Model." *The Journal of Economic History* 31 (4).

Nygaard, Kaleb. 2020. "The Federal Reserve's Response to the 1987 Market Crash." *Journal of Financial Crises* 2 (3). https://elischolar.library.yale.edu/journal-of-financial-crises/vol2/iss3/4.

Odling-Smee, John, and Gonzalo Pastor. 2001. *The IMF and the Ruble Area, 1991-93*. No. 01/101. IMF Working Paper. International Monetary Fund. https://www.imf.org/external/pubs/ft/wp/2001/

wp01101.pdf.

Office, Congressional Budget. 1992. *The Economic Effects of the Savings and Loan Crisis*. Congressional Budget Office. https://www.cbo.gov/sites/default/files/102nd-congress-1991-1992/reports/1992_01_theeconeffectsofthesavings.pdf.

Office, United States General Accounting. 1988. *Preliminary Observations on the October 1987 Crash*. Report to Congressional Requesters. http://archive.gao.gov/d30t5/134907.pdf.

Officer, Lawrence H. 1981. "The Floating Dollar in the Greenback Period: A Test of Theories of Exchange-Rate Determination." *The Journal of Economic History* 41 (3).

"Official Bank Rate History Data from 1694." n.d. Bank of England. https://www.bankofengland.co.uk/-/media/boe/files/monetary-policy/baserate.xls.

Okina, Kunio, Masaaki Shirakawa, and Shigenori Shiratsuka. 2000. *The Asset Price Bubble and Monetary Policy: Japan's Experience in the Late 1980s and the Lessons*. Institute for Monetary and Economic Studies, BOJ. https://www.imes.boj.or.jp/research/papers/english/00-E-12.pdf.

Okina, Kunio, Masaaki Shirakawa, and Shigenori Shiratsuka. 2001. *The Asset Price Bubble and Monetary Policy: Japan's Experience in the Late 1980s and the Lessons*. Monetary and Economic Studies (Special Edition). Institute for Monetary and Economic Studies, BOJ. https://www.imes.boj.or.jp/research/papers/english/me19-s1-14.pdf.

Oldroyd, David. 1995. "Role of Accounting in Public Expenditure and Monetary Policy in the First Century AD Roman Empire." *Accounting Historians Journal* 22 (2). https://core.ac.uk/reader/288025130.

Oliker, Olga, and Tanya Charlick-Paley. 2002. *Assessing Russia's Decline: Trends and Implications for the United States and the U.S. Air Force*. RAND Corporation.

Oner, Ceyda. n.d. "Inflation: Prices on the Rise." *Finance and Development*. https://www.imf.org/-/media/Files/Publications/Fandd/Back-to-Basics/oner-inflation.ashx.

Onge, Peter. 2017. "How Paper Money Led to the Mongol Conquest: Money and the Collapse of Song China." *The Independent Review* 22 (2).

Op den Kamp, Claudy, and Dan Hunter. 2019. *A History of Intellectual Property in 50 Objects*. Cambridge University Press.

OpenStax. 2022. *Principles of Macroeconomics 3e*. OpenStax. https://openstax.org/details/books/principles-macroeconomics-3e.

Oshiro, Carl. 1990. "Partners in Crime: California's Role in the $335 Billion Savings and Loan Heist." *The California Regulatory Law Reporter* 10 (4). https://digital.sandiego.edu/cgi/viewcontent.cgi?article=2330&context=crlr.

Ovunda, Adum Smith. 2015. "Luca Pacioli's Double-Entry System of Accounting: A Critique." *Research Journal of Finance and Accounting* 6 (18). https://core.ac.uk/download/pdf/234631058.pdf.

Painter, David. 2014. "Oil and Geopolitics: The Oil Crises of the 1970s and the Cold War." *Historical Social Research* 39 (4). https://doi.org/10.12759/hsr.39.2014.4.186-208.

Pakonen, R. Rodney. 1969. *Branch versus Unit Banking: A Survey of the Literature*. State of Minnesota House of Representatives. https://researchdatabase.minneapolisfed.org/downloads/m326m1871.

Pamuk, Sevket. 2000. *A Monetary History of the Ottoman Empire*. Cambridge University Press.

Pani, Marco. 2017. *Crisis and Reform: The 1893 Demise of Banca Romana*. Working Paper. IMF. https://www.elibrary.imf.org/view/journals/001/2017/274/article-A001-en.xml.

Pankenier, David W. 1998. "The Mandate of Heaven." *Archeology* 51 (2). https://www.jstor.org/stable/41771361.

Passant, John. 2016. "Tax and the Forgotten Classes: Magna Carta to English Revolution." *Australasian Accounting, Business and Finance Journal* 10 (3). https://ro.uow.edu.au/cgi/viewcontent.cgi?referer=&httpsredir=1&article=1708&context=aabfj.

Passas, Nikos. 1996. "The Genesis of the BCCI Scandal." *Journal of Law and Society* 23 (1). https://doi.org/10.2307/1410467.

Pasvolsky, Leo. 1933. "The Gold Standard before and after the War." *The Annals of the American Academy of Political and Social Science* 165.

Pasvolsky, Leo, and Harold Glenn Moulton. 1924. *Russian Debts and Russian Reconstruction*. McGraw-Hill.

Pauletto, Christian. 2012. "The History of Derivatives: A Few Milestones." Seminar on Regulation of Derivatives Markets. http://dx.doi.org/10.13140/RG.2.2.13901.15844.

Paybarah, Azi. 2022. "Mastercard and Visa Suspend Operations in Russia." *New York Times*. https://www.nytimes.com/2022/03/05/world/europe/mastercard-visa-suspend-operations-russia.html.

Pechter, Kerry. 2008. *Annuities for Dummies*. Wiley.

Peterson, Bruce. 1961. "The Danegeld and Its Effect on the Development of Property Law." *Dickinson Law Review* 66 (4). https://ideas.dickinsonlaw.psu.edu/cgi/viewcontent.cgi?article=2307&context=dlra.

Petram, L. O. 2011. "The World's First Stock Exchange: How the Amsterdam Market for Dutch East India Company Shares Became a Modern Securities Market, 1602-1700." PhD Thesis, Universiteit van Amsterdam.

"Petty Impressive." 2013. *The Economist*. https://www.economist.com/finance-and-economics/2013/12/21/petty-impressive.

Pezzolo, Luciano. 2005. "Bonds and Government Debt in Italian City-States, 1250-1650." In *The Origins of Value: The Financial Innovations That Created Modern Capital Markets*. Oxford University Press.

Philips, Mathew. 2008. "How Credit Default Swaps Became a Timebomb." *Newsweek*. https://www.newsweek.com/how-credit-default-swaps-became-timebomb-89291.

Phillips, Charles. 2019. *Kings & Queens of Britain*. Anness Publishing.

Pickering, John. 1844. "The History of Paper Money in China." *Journal of the American Oriental Society* 1 (1). https://doi.org/10.2307/3217743.

"Plea Allocution of Bernard L Madoff." n.d. In *Wall Street Journal*. https://www.wsj.com/public/resources/documents/20090315madoffall.pdf.

Plender, John. 1986. "London's Big Bang in International Context." *International Affairs* 63 (1). https://doi.org/10.2307/2620231.

Pohl, Manfred. 1994. *Handbook on the History of European Banks*. Edward Elgar Publishing.

Poitras, Geoffrey. 2009. "The Early History of Option Contracts." In *Vinzenz Bronzin's Option Pricing Models*. Springer.

Poole, A. L. 1955. *From Domesday Book to Magna Carta, Second Edition*. Oxford University Press.

Popper, Nathaniel. 2015. "Decoding the Enigma of Satoshi Nakamoto and the Birth of Bitcoin." *New York Times*. https://www.nytimes.com/2015/05/17/business/decoding-the-enigma-of-satoshi-nakamoto-and-the-birth-of-bitcoin.html.

Porteous, John. 1969. *Coins in History*. Putnam.

"Portugal's 78bn Euro Bail-out Is Formally Approved." 2011. In *BBC*. https://www.bbc.co.uk/news/business-13408497.

Post, Bullion by. n.d. "UK Coins." https://www.bullionbypost.co.uk/index/collectible-coins/uk-coins/.

Poterba, James. 1997. *The History of Annuities in the United States*. Working Paper No. 6001. National Bureau of Economic Research. https://www.nber.org/system/files/working_papers/w6001/w6001.pdf.

Potter, Lee Ann, Karen Needles, and Marisa Wilairat. 2003. "The Purchase of the Louisiana Territory." *Social Education* 67 (2). https://www.socialstudies.org/system/files/publications/articles/se_6702100.pdf.

Powell, James. 2005. *A History of the Canadian Dollar*. Bank of Canada.

Powell, Marvin A. 1996. "Money in Mesopotamia." *Journal of Economic and Social History of the Orient* 39 (3). https://www.jstor.org/stable/3632646.

Pozsar, Zoltan, Tobias Adrian, Adam Ashcraft, and Hayley Boesky. 2010. *Shadow Banking*. Staff Report No. 458. Federal Reserve Bank of New York. https://www.newyorkfed.org/medialibrary/media/research/staff_reports/sr458.pdf.

Prendergast, John, and Jamal Jafari. 2004.

"Zimbabwe on the Brink." *Georgetown Journal of International Affairs* 5 (1). https://www.jstor.org/stable/43133600.

Prestwich, Michael. 2005. *Plantagenet England, 1225-1360.* Clarendon Press.

Pryor, John H. 1977. "The Origins of the Commenda Contract." *Speculum* 52 (1). https://doi.org/10.2307/2856894.

Pujo, Arsene. 1913. *Report of the Committee Appointed Pursuant to House Resolutions 429 and 504 to Investigate the Concentration of Control of Money and Credit.* United States Congress.

Pujol, Nicolas, and Vadim Rossman. 2011. "The Well-Field System: How China Pioneered Open Source 30 Centuries Ago." *SSRN*, ahead of print. https://dx.doi.org/10.2139/ssrn.1958693.

Pulliam, Roscoe. 1924. "Taxation in the Roman State." *The Classical Journal* 19 (9).

Punyaratabandhu, Suchitra. 1998. "Thailand in 1997: Financial Crisis and Constitutional Reform." *Asian Survey* 38 (2). https://doi.org/10.2307/2645674.

Pusey, Allen. 2019. "A Tale of Two Silver Markets—and Two Disasters." *ABA Journal* 105 (1). https://www.jstor.org/stable/26913076.

Quinn, Stephen, and William Roberds. 2005. *The Big Problem of Large Bills: The Bank of Amsterdam and the Origins of Central Banking.* Working Paper Nos. 2005–16. Federal Reserve Bank of Atlanta. https://www.atlantafed.org/-/media/Documents/research/publications/wp/2005/wp0516.pdf?la=en.

Quinn, Stephen, and William Roberds. 2015. "Responding to a Shadow Banking Crisis: The Lessons of 1763." *Journal of Money, Credit and Banking* 47 (6).

Rae, John. 1895. *Life of Adam Smith.* Macmillan & Co.

Rajisha, T. 2019. "History of Banking in India and Emergence of New Generation Banks." *International Journal of Research in Social Sciences* 9 (2). https://www.ijmra.us/project%20doc/2019/IJRSS_JULY2019/IJMRA-15886.pdf.

Rajput, Prashant Singh. 2018. "Evolution of Banking System in India." *Journal on Contemporary Issues of Law* 4 (3). https://jcil.lsyndicate.com/wp-content/uploads/2023/06/Evolution-of-Banking-System-in-India-Prashant-Singh-Rajput-4.pdf.

Ramma, Hussain G. 2003. "Mudaraba in Islamic Finance: Principles and Application." *Business Journal for Entrepreneurs* 16 (4). https://www.researchgate.net/publication/256002436_Mudaraba_in_Islamic_Finance_Principles_and_Application.

Ramsden, Henry A. 2011. *Chinese Paper Money.* Harvard University.

Ray, Sanjana. 2016. "25 QUOTES FROM BANKING LEGEND JP MORGAN TO INSPIRE THE VISIONARY IN YOU." https://yourstory.com/2016/12/jp-morgan-famous-quotes.

Record, The. 1840. "The South Sea Bubble." *Recordnet*, August 22. https://www.jstor.org/stable/60211031.

"Reflections of the 1837 Panic." 1933. *Bulletin of the Business Historical Society* 7 (4). https://doi.org/10.2307/3110974.

Renger, Johannes. 1994. "On Economic Structures in Ancient Mesopotamia: Part One." *Orientalia* 63 (3). https://www.jstor.org/stable/43076166.

Reserve, Federal. 2021. *The FED Explained: What the Central Bank Does.* Federal Reserve Public Education & Outreach.

Reuters. 1997. "Antwerp Bourse—World's Oldest—Closes." *Los Angeles Times.* https://www.latimes.com/archives/la-xpm-1997-dec-31-fi-3623-story.html.

Reuters. 2011. "Fitch Says AAA Rating For U.S. Will Stand." *New York Times.*

Reuters Staff. 2018. "Iran Switches from Dollar to Euro for Official Reporting Currency." *Reuters.*

Revill, John. 2023. "Swiss Have Frozen $8.8 Billion of Russian Assets." *Reuters.* https://www.reuters.com/world/europe/swiss-have-frozen-88-bilion-russian-assets-2023-12-01/.

Rezneck, Samuel. 1935. "The Social History of an American Depression, 1837-1843." *The American Historical Review* 40 (4). https://doi.org/10.2307/1842418.

RFE/RL. 2022. "EU Cuts Seven Russian Banks From SWIFT, Bans RT And Sputnik." *Radio Free Europe Radio Liberty.* https://www.rferl.org/a/eu-swift-russian-banks/31732511.html.

Richards, R. D. 1930. "The 'Stop of the Exchequer.'" *Economic History* 2 (5). https://www.jstor.org/stable/45366411.

Richardson, Gary. n.d. "Medieval Guilds." EH.Net.

Richmond, Federal Reserve Bank of. 1975. "The Classic Concept of the Lender of Last Resort." *Economic Review (Richmond Fed)* 61 (1). https://www.richmondfed.org/~/media/richmondfedorg/publications/research/economic_review/1975/pdf/er610101.pdf.

Riksbank. 2009. "Stockholms Banco." https://www.riksbank.se/globalassets/media/riksbanken-350-ar/tidslinjen/stockholm-banco/24-45-stockholms-banco_eng.pdf.

Rippy, Darren. 2014. "The First Hundred Years of the Consumer Price Index: A Methodological and Political History." *U.S. Bureau of Labor Statistics Monthly Labor Review.* https://doi.org/10.21916/mlr.2014.13.

Roach, Stephen. 2022. *Accidental Conflict: America, China, and the Clash of False Narratives.* Yale University Press.

Roberds, William, and François R. Velde. 2014. *Early Public Banks.* Working Paper Nos. 2014–9. Federal Reserve Bank of Atlanta. https://www.atlantafed.org/~/media/Documents/research/publications/wp/2014/wp1409.pdf.

Robson, Eleanor. 1998. "Counting in Cuneiform." *Mathematics in School* 27 (4). https://www.jstor.org/stable/30211866.

Rockoff, Hugh. 2009. *Upon Daedalian Wings of Paper Money: Adam Smith and the Crisis of 1772.* Working Paper No. 15594. NBER. https://www.nber.org/papers/w15594.

Romer, Christina. 1986. "Spurious Volatility in Historical Unemployment Data." *Journal of Political Economy* 94 (1). https://www.jstor.org/stable/1831958.

Romer, Christina D. 1990. "The Great Crash and the Onset of the Great Depression." *The Quarterly Journal of Economics* 105 (3). https://doi.org/10.2307/2937892.

Rothman, Lily. 2014. "How We Underestimated the 'Black Tuesday' Stock Market Crash." *Time.* https://time.com/3544350/black-tuesday-1929/.

Rothschild, Emma. 1994. "Adam Smith and the Invisible Hand." *The American Economic Review* 84 (2).

Routt, David. 2008. "The Economic Impact of the Black Death." https://eh.net/encyclopedia/the-economic-impact-of-the-black-death/.

Rouwenhorst, K. Geert. 2004. *The Origins of Mutual Funds.* Working Paper No. 10539. NBER. https://www.nber.org/papers/w10539.

Rovekamp, Frank. 2020. *The Evolution of the European Stability Mechanism: Lessons for Asian Integration.* Working Paper No. 1173. Asian Development Bank Institute (ADBI). https://www.adb.org/sites/default/files/publication/634726/adbi-wp1173.pdf.

Rovelli, Alessia. 2018. "From the Fall of Rome to Charlemagne (c.400–800)." In *Money and Coinage in the Middle Ages.* Brill.

Rowell, David, and Luke B. Connelly. 2012. "The History of the Term 'Moral Hazard.'" *The Journal of Risk and Insurance* 79 (4). https://www.jstor.org/stable/23354958.

Saikia, Bijoy Sankar. 2016. "Demonetisation May Drag India behind China in GDP Growth, Rob Fastest-Growing Economy Tag." *The Economic Times.* https://economictimes.indiatimes.com/markets/stocks/news/demonetisation-to-drag-india-behind-china-in-gdp-growth-rob-fastest-growing-economy-tag/articleshow/55492970.cms.

Sakuraki, Shin'ichi, Helen Wang, Peter Kornicki, Nobuhisa Furuta, Timon Screech, and Joe Cribb. 2010. *Catalogue of the Japanese Coins Collection (Pre-Meiji) at the British Museum.* The British Museum.

"Samsung Announces Launch Dates for Groundbreaking Mobile Payment Service: Samsung Pay." 2015. https://news.samsung.com/global/samsung-announces-launch-dates-for-groundbreaking-mobile-payment-service-samsung-pay.

Sanders, E. P. 1993. *The Historical Figure of Jesus.* Historicity.

Sándor, István. 2016. "Antecedents of the Company in Ancient Laws." *LR Legal Roots.* https://www.academia.

edu/38530381/Antecedents_of_the_Company_in_Ancient_Laws.

"Savings and Loan Crisis." 2013. https://www.federalreservehistory.org/essays/savings-and-loan-crisis.

Saxton, Jim. 2003. *Argentina's Economic Crisis: Causes and Cures.* Joint Economic Committee United States Congress. https://www.jec.senate.gov/public/_cache/files/5fbf2f91-6cdf-4e70-8ff2-620ba901fc4c/argentina-s-economic-crisis---06-13-03.pdf.

"Say Money Trust Is Now Disclosed." 1913. *New York Times.* https://timesmachine.nytimes.com/timesmachine/1913/01/12/100604553.pdf.

Schaps, David. 2007. "The Invention of Coinage in Lydia, in India, and in China." *Bulletin Du Cercle d'Etudes Numismatiques* 44 (1). https://www.academia.edu/11080934/The_Invention_of_Coinage_in_Lydia_in_India_and_in_China.

Schcenk, Catherine R. 2009. *The Retirement of Sterling as a Reserve Currency After 1945: Lessons for the US Dollar?* https://www.cirje.e.u-tokyo.ac.jp/research/workshops/history/history_paper2009/history1109.pdf.

Scheidel, Walter. 2006. "The Divergent Evolution of Coinage in Eastern and Western Eurasia." *Princeton/Stanford Working Papers in Classics.* https://citeseerx.ist.psu.edu/document?repid=rep1&type=pdf&doi=288a121edac53d4945d445055318b-b39938984c7.

Scheller, Hanspeter K. 2004. *The European Central Bank: History, Role and Functions.* European Central Bank.

Schnabel, Isabel. 2004. "The German Twin Crisis of 1931." *The Journal of Economic History* 64 (3).

Schnabel, Isabel, and Hyun Song Shin. 2003. *Lessons from the Seven Years War.* CentrePiece. https://cep.lse.ac.uk/pubs/download/CP150.pdf.

Schnabel, Isabel, and Hyun Song Shin. 2004. "Liquidity and Contagion: The Crisis of 1763." *Journal of the European Economic Association* 2 (6).

Schrager, Allison. 2018. "Why Dutch and Danish Retirees Sleep Well at Night." *Quartz.* https://qz.com/1436159/the-se-cret-to-a-happy-retirement.

Schweitzer, Arthur. 1947. "On Depression and War: Nazi Phase." *Political Science Quarterly* 62 (3). https://doi.org/10.2307/2144293.

Scott, Susan V., and Markos Zachariadis. 2009. *Origins and Development of SWIFT, 1973–2009.* London School of Economics. https://eprints.lse.ac.uk/46490/1/Origins%20and%20Development%20of.pdf.

Seburn, Patrick. 1991. "Evolution of Employer-Provided Defined Benefit Pensions." *Monthly Labor Review.* https://www.bls.gov/mlr/1991/12/art3full.pdf.

SEC. 2008. *Report and Recommendations Pursuant to Section 133 of the Emergency Economic Stabilization Act of 2008: Study on Mark-To-Market Accounting.* SEC. https://www.sec.gov/files/marktomarket123008.pdf.

Selgin, George. 2010. "Gresham's Law." https://web.archive.org/web/20130317073119/http://eh.net/encyclopedia/article/selgin.gresham.law.

Selgin, George. 2012. *The Rise and Fall of the Gold Standard in the United States.* https://www.hillsdale.edu/wp-content/uploads/2016/02/FMF-2012-The-Rise-and-Fall-of-the-Gold-Standard.pdf.

Seligman, Joel. 1982. *The Transformation of Wall Street: A History of the Securities and Exchange Commission and Modern Corporate Finance.* Houghton Mifflin.

Service, Congressional Research. 2009. "American Recovery and Reinvestment Act of 2009 (P.L. 111-5): Summary and Legislative History." Congressional Research Service. https://crsreports.congress.gov/product/pdf/R/R40537.

Seth, Rama, Asani Sakar, and Sunil Mohanty. n.d. *Loan Flows, Contagion Effects, and East Asian Crisis.* New York Fed. https://www.newyorkfed.org/medialibrary/media/research/economists/sarkar/contagion.pdf.

Setton, Kenneth. 1969. *A History of the Crusades: Volume 6.* University of Wisconsin Press.

Sevilla, Christina R. 1995. *Explaining the September 1992 ERM Crisis: The Maastricht Bargain and Domestic Politics in Germany, France, and Britain.* European Community Studies Association, Fourth Biennial

International Conference. https://aei.pitt.
edu/7014/1/sevilla_christina.pdf.

Sharma, Shalendra. 2001. "The Missed
Lessons of the Mexican Peso Crisis."
Challenge 44 (1). https://www.jstor.org/
stable/40722054.

Shaw, William Arthur. 1896. *The History of
Currency, 1252 to 1894*. Putnam.

Sheridan, Richard B. 1960. "The British
Credit Crisis of 1772 and the American Colonies." *The Journal of Economic
History* 20 (2). https://www.jstor.org/sta-
ble/2114853.

"Sherman Anti-Trust Act." 2022. https://
www.archives.gov/milestone-documents/
sherman-anti-trust-act.

Shirras, G. Findlay, and J. H. Craig. 1945.
"Sir Isaac Newton and the Currency." *The
Economic Journal* 55 (218/219). https://
www.jstor.org/stable/pdf/2226082.pdf.

Sieber, Arlyn G. 2012. *U.S. Coins & Currency*.

Sigler, Laurence. 2012. *Fibonacci's Liber Abaci*. Springer New York.

Signe, Landry. 2019. "How the France-
Backed African CFA Franc Works as an
Enabler and Barrier to Development."
Brookings. https://www.brookings.edu/
articles/how-the-france-backed-african-
cfa-franc-works-as-an-enabler-and-barrier-
to-development/.

Silber, William L. 2009. "Why Did
FDR's Bank Holiday Succeed?" *FRB-
NY Economic Policy Review* 15 (1).
https://www.newyorkfed.org/research/
epr/09v15n1/0907silb.html.

Siles, William H., Henry W. Jones, and Asa
S. Shipman. 1986. "Quiet Desperation: A
Personal View of the Panic of 1837." *New
York History* 67 (1).

Simard, Dominique, Michael Bordo, and
Eugene White. 1994. "France and the
Breakdown of the Bretton Woods Inter-
national Monetary System." *International
Monetary Fund* 1994 (128). https://doi.
org/10.5089/9781451935363.001.

"Sing a Song of Six Pence." n.d. https://
allnurseryrhymes.com/sing-a-song-of-six-
pence/.

Skultety, Steven C. 2006. "Currency, Trade,
and Commerce in Plato's 'Laws.'" *History
of Political Thought* 27 (2).

"'Slave Trade' Bracelets." n.d. https://web.
archive.org/web/20070707114118/http://
www.calgarycoin.com/primitive1.htm.

Slivinski, Stephen. 2009. "Too Interconnected to Fail?" *Richmond Federal Reserve*.
https://www.richmondfed.org/-/media/
richmondfedorg/publications/research/
econ_focus/2009/summer/pdf/econom-
ic_history.pdf.

Smiley, Gene. 2004. "US Economy in the
1920s." https://eh.net/encyclopedia/the-u-
s-economy-in-the-1920s/.

Smiley, Gene, and Richard H. Keehn. 1988.
"Margin Purchases, Brokers' Loans, and
the Bull Market of the Twenties." *Business
and Economic History* 17.

Smith, Courtney Weiss. 2012. "A 'Foundation in Nature': New Economic Criticism
and the Problem of Money in 1690s
England." *The Eighteenth Century* 53 (2).
https://www.jstor.org/stable/41468178.

Smith, Helena. 2010. "Greece Erupts in Violent Protest as Citizens Face a Future of
Harsh Austerity." *The Guardian*. https://
www.theguardian.com/world/2010/
may/02/greece-violence-bailout-imf-euro.

Socolofsky, Homer Edward. 1987. *The Presidency of Benjamin Harrison*. University
Press of Kansas.

Sodhi, Rajber Singh. 2020. *Self Learning
Material*. Directorate of Distance Education, University of Jammu. https://www.
distanceeducationju.in/pdf/BA%20Part-
II%20History.pdf.

Southern, David B. 1979. "The Revaluation
Question in the Weimar Republic." *The
Journal of Modern History* 51 (1). https://
www.jstor.org/stable/1878444.

Southern, Pat. 2007. *The Roman Army: A
Social and Institutional History*. Oxford
University Press.

Speer, Emory. 1906. "Alexander Hamilton."
The Yale Law Journal 16 (2). https://doi.
org/10.2307/785473.

Spitzer, Eliot. 2003. "State of New York vs.
CANARY CAPITAL PARTNERS, LLC,
CANARY INVESTMENT MANAGE-
MENT, LLC, CANARY CAPITAL
PARTNERS, LTD and EDWARD J.
STERN." Supreme Court of the State of
New York County of New York. https://
web.archive.org/web/20051027042809/

http://www.oag.state.ny.us/press/2003/sep/canary_complaint.pdf.

Sprague, O. M. W. 1908. "The American Crisis of 1907." *The Economic Journal* 18 (71). https://doi.org/10.2307/2221551.

Springer, Gary L., and Jorge L. Molina. 1995. "The Mexican Financial Crisis: Genesis, Impact, and Implications." *Journal of Interamerican Studies and World Affairs* 37 (2). https://doi.org/10.2307/166271.

Spufford, Peter. 1988. *Money and Its Use in Medieval Europe.* Cambridge University Press.

"Standard & Poor's Downgrades EU Bailout Fund EFSF." 2012. *BBC News.* https://www.bbc.com/news/business-16586807.

Starr, Chester. 1977. *The Economic and Social Growth of Early Greece, 800-500 B.C.*

Statista Research Department. 2023. "Largest Stock Exchange Operators Worldwide as of May 2023, by Market Capitalization of Listed Companies." https://www.statista.com/statistics/270126/largest-stock-exchange-operators-by-market-capitalization-of-listed-companies/.

Stax. n.d. "The Impact of EMV Technology on Payment Transactions." https://stax-payments.com/blog/emv-technology-impact-on-transactions/.

Stearns, David. 2011. *Electronic Value Exchange: Origins of the VISA Electronic Payment System.* Springer Science & Business Media.

Stein, Robert, and Brian S. Wesbury. 2009. "Why Mark-To-Market Accounting Rules Must Die." *Forbes.* https://www.forbes.com/2009/02/23/mark-to-market-opinions-columnists_recovery_stimulus.html.

Stempel, Jonathan. 2019. "Former Goldman Programmer Fails, Again, to Toss Theft Conviction." *Reuters.* https://www.reuters.com/article/idUSKBN1WN2AQ/.

Stephens Jr., W. Richard. 1982. "The Fall of Rome Reconsidered: A Synthesis of Manpower and Taxation Arguments." *Mid-American Review of Sociology* 7 (2).

Stepien, Marek. 2009. *From the History of State System in Mesopotamia - The Kingdom of the Third Dynasty of Ur.*

Stevens, Matt, and Matthew Haag. 2019. "Jeffrey Skilling, Former Enron Chief, Released After 12 Years in Prison." *New York Times.* https://www.nytimes.com/2019/02/22/business/enron-ceo-skilling-scandal.html.

Stith, Griffin. 1894. "The Stamp Act." *The William and Mary College Quarterly Historical Papers* 2 (4). https://doi.org/10.2307/1915409.

Stowell, Theresa L. n.d. "Trading Stamps." https://web.archive.org/web/20160105175953/http://ebusinessinusa.com/2767-trading-stamps.html.

Straus, Ilana E. 2016. "The Myth of the Barter Economy." *The Atlantic.* https://www.theatlantic.com/business/archive/2016/02/barter-society-myth/471051/.

Strouse, Jean. 2000. "J. Pierpont Morgan: Financier and Collector." *The Metropolitan Museum of Art Bulletin* 57 (3). https://doi.org/10.2307/3258853.

Stukenbrock, Kai. 2004. *The Stability of Currency Boards.* Peter Lang AG.

Sučić, Marko. 2011. "Greece Debt Crisis and Wall Street Role Behind It." *SSRN.* https://papers.ssrn.com/sol3/papers.cfm?abstract_id=2085430.

Suplee, Curt. 2000. "The History of Zero." *Washington Post.* https://www.washingtonpost.com/archive/2000/01/12/the-history-of-zero/36a6a2fd-9e18-484d-ae6f-450af0340830/.

Sussman, Nathan. 1998. "The Late Medieval Bullion Famine Reconsidered." *The Journal of Economic History* 58 (1). https://www.jstor.org/stable/2566256.

Svizzero, Serge, and Clement Tisdell. 2019. "Barter and the Origin of Money and Some Insights from the Ancient Palatial Economies of Mesopotamia and Egypt." *HAL.* https://hal.science/hal-02274856/document.

Swary, Itzhak. 1986. "Stock Market Reaction to Regulatory Action in the Continental Illinois Crisis." *The Journal of Business* 59 (3). https://www.jstor.org/stable/2352713.

"Swift History." n.d. https://www.swift.com/about-us/history.

Sydenham, E. A. 1918. "THE ROMAN MONETARY SYSTEM. Part I." *The Numismatic Chronicle and Journal of the Royal Numismatic Society, Fourth Series* 18. https://www.jstor.org/stable/42678509.

Sydenham, E. M. 1919. "THE ROMAN MONETARY SYSTEM: Part II." *The Numismatic Chronicle and Journal of the Royal Numismatic Society, Fourth Series* 19. https://www.jstor.org/stable/42663761.

Sylla, Richard, Robert E. Wright, and David J. Cowen. 2006. *The U.S. Panic of 1792: Financial Crisis Management and the Lender of Last Resort.* NBER DAE Summer Institute. https://web.archive.org/web/20210422193313/http://public.econ.duke.edu/~staff/wrkshop_papers/2006-07Papers/Sylla.pdf.

Sylla, Richard, Robert E. Wright, and David J. Cowen. 2009. "Alexander Hamilton, Central Banker." *The Business History Review* 83 (1).

Synderman, George S. 1954. "The Function of Wampum." *Proceedings of the American Philosophical Society* 98 (6). https://www.jstor.org/stable/3143870.

Taagepera, Rein. 1979. "Size and Duration of Empires: Growth-Decline Curves, 600 B.C. to 600 A.D." *Social Science History* 3 (3/4). https://doi.org/10.2307/1170959.

Tagaris, Karolina. 2012. "Biggest Greek Bank Warns of Dire Euro Exit Fallout." *Reuters.* https://www.reuters.com/article/greece-euro-idUSL5E8GTI5320120529/.

Tan, Mei Ah. 2017. "Monetary Policy as Key to State Authority and Income in Tang China." *Journal of Chinese Studies*, no. 64. https://www.cuhk.edu.hk/ics/journal/articles/v64p035.pdf.

Tanner, Norman P. n.d. "Third Lateran Council – 1179 A.D." https://www.papalencyclicals.net/councils/ecum11.htm.

"Taxes in the Ancient World." 2002. *University of Pennsylvania Almanac* 48 (28). https://almanac.upenn.edu/archive/v48/n28/AncientTaxes.html#egypt.

Taylor, Ian. 2019. "France à Fric: The CFA Zone in Africa and Neocolonialism." *Third World Quarterly* 40 (6). https://doi.org/10.1080/01436597.2019.1585183.

Teall, John. n.d. "Chapter 2: A History of Merchant, Central and Investment Banking." https://www.jteall.com/cib02.pdf.

Teitelbaum, Richard. 2008. "The Code Breaker." *Bloomberg Markets.* https://math.berkeley.edu/~berlek/pubs/bloomberg.pdf.

Tempkin, Adam. 2013. "1977: US$100m Deal for Bank of America: The First Private-Label MBS." *International Financing Review*, no. 2000. https://www.ifre.com/story/1291711/1977-us100m-deal-for-bank-of-america-the-first-private-label-mbs-1jmn8r7fh9.

"The Assumption Bill." n.d. Democracy Project, University of Delaware. https://www.bidenschool.udel.edu/ipa/content-sub-site/Documents/Democracy-Project/handout6-3.doc.

The Bank of England: History and Functions. 1970. Bank of England.

"The Bank of England Note - a Short History." 1969. *Bank of England Quarterly Bulletin*, no. 2. https://www.bankofengland.co.uk/-/media/boe/files/quarterly-bulletin/1969/the-boe-note-a-short-history.pdf.

The Cost of Black Wednesday Reconsidered. 1997. The National Archives. https://webarchive.nationalarchives.gov.uk/ukgwa/20130403000951/http://www.hm-treasury.gov.uk/d/Cost_Black_Weds_reconsidered.pdf.

"The EU Bank at a Glance." n.d. European Investment Bank. https://web.archive.org/web/20230729011820/https://www.eib.org/attachments/60-anniversary-eib-infographic-en.pdf.

The Fedwire Funds Service: Assessment of Compliance with the Core Principles for Systemically Important Payment Systems. 2014. Federal Reserve. https://www.federalreserve.gov/paymentsystems/files/fedfunds_coreprinciples.pdf.

The Financial Crisis Inquiry Commission. 2011a. *The Financial Crisis Inquiry Report.* The Financial Crisis Inquiry Commission.

The Financial Crisis Inquiry Commission. 2011b. *The Financial Crisis Inquiry Report.* The Financial Crisis Inquiry Commission. https://www.govinfo.gov/content/pkg/GPO-FCIC/pdf/GPO-FCIC.pdf.

"The First Bank of the United States." 2015. https://www.federalreservehistory.org/essays/first-bank-of-the-us#:~:text=President%20Washington%20signed%20the%20bill,with%20a%20twenty%2D-year%20charter.

"THE FTC DURING THE ADMINISTRATIONS OF FRANKLIN D.

ROOSEVELT (1933-45) AND HARRY S. TRUMAN." n.d. https://www.ftc.gov/reports/ftc100-bibliography/1933-1953.

"The History of NYSE." n.d. https://www.nyse.com/history-of-nyse.

"The Madoff Files: Bernie's Billions." 2009. *London Independent*. https://www.independent.co.uk/news/business/analysis-and-features/the-madoff-files-bernie-s-billions-1518939.html.

"The Meiji Restoration and Modernization." n.d. http://afe.easia.columbia.edu/special/japan_1750_meiji.htm.

"The 'Money Trust.'" 1911. *New York Times*.

"The Royal Exchange." n.d. https://www.walklondon.com/london-attractions/royal-exchange.htm.

"The Stock Market." 1929. *New York Times*, October 30.

"The Travels of Marco Polo." n.d. https://en.unesco.org/silkroad/publications/travels-marco-polo.

The U.S. Dollar as the World's Dominant Reserve Currency. 2022. Congressional Research Service. https://crsreports.congress.gov/product/pdf/IF/IF11707.

Thompson, Christine M., and Sheldon Skaggs. 2013. "King Solomon's Silver? Southern Phoenician Hacksilber Hoards and the Location of Tarshish." *Internet Archaeology* 35. https://doi.org/10.11141/ia.35.6.

Thompson, Earl. 2007. "Tulip Mania: Fact or Artifact?" *Public Choice* 130 (1). https://www.jstor.org/stable/27698044.

Thornton, M. K., and R. L. Thornton. 1990. "The Financial Crisis of 33 AD: A Keynesian Depression?" *The Journal of Economic History* 50 (3). https://www.jstor.org/stable/2122822.

Timberlake, Richard H. Jr. 1964. "Ideological Factors in Specie Resumption and Treasury Policy." *The Journal of Economic History* 24 (1).

"Timeline of the Debt Negotiations." 2011. *New York Times*. https://archive.nytimes.com/www.nytimes.com/interactive/2011/07/31/us/politics/timeline-of-the-debt-ceiling-negotiations.html?searchResultPosition=6.

Toepke, Utz P. 1981. "The European Economic Community – A Profile." *Northwestern Journal of International Law and Business* 3 (2). https://scholarlycommons.law.northwestern.edu/cgi/viewcontent.cgi?article=1108&context=njilb.

Tomkiw, Lydia. 2024. "Jim Simons, Pioneering Quant and Founder of Renaissance Technologies, Dies at 86." *Pensions & Investment*. https://www.pionline.com/memoriam/jim-simons-pioneering-quant-and-founder-renaissance-technologies-dies-86.

"Topics in Wall Street." 1929. *New York Times*, October 22.

Toussaint, Eric. 2022. "Russia: Origin and Consequences of the Debt Repudiation of February 10, 1918." https://www.cadtm.org/Russia-Origin-and-consequences-of-the-debt-repudiation-of-February-10-1918.

Trade, United Nations Conference on and Development. 1998. *The Russian Crisis*. United Nations Conference for Trade and Development. https://unctad.org/system/files/official-document/poirrsd002.en.pdf.

"Trading Analysis of October 27 and 28, 1997." 1998. https://web.archive.org/web/20230219001726/https://www.sec.gov/news/studies/tradrep.htm.

Triennial Central Bank Survey: Foreign Exchange Turnover in April 2013: Preliminary Global Results. 2013. Bank for International Settlements. https://www.bis.org/publ/rpfx13fx.pdf.

"Troubled Asset Relief Program (TARP)." n.d. https://home.treasury.gov/data/troubled-asset-relief-program.

Tuovila, Alicia. 2022. "Mark to Market." https://www.investopedia.com/terms/m/marktomarket.asp.

Turgeon, Nicole. 2020. *Money, Manipulation, & Madoff: What Are Ponzi Schemes and How to Avoid Becoming a Fraud Victim*. https://digitalcommons.assumption.edu/cgi/viewcontent.cgi?article=1071&context=honorstheses.

Turner, Grant, Nicholas Tan, and Dena Sadeghian. 2012. "The Chinese Banking System." *Reserve Bank of Australia Bulletin*. https://www.rba.gov.au/publications/bulletin/2012/sep/7.html.

Twight, Charlotte. 2015. "Dodd–Frank: Accretion of Power, Illusion of Reform."

The Independent Review 20 (2).

Twin, Alexandra. 2023. "Antitrust Laws: What Are They, How They Work, Major Examples." https://www.investopedia.com/terms/a/antitrust.asp.

Twitchett, D. C. 1970. *Financial Administration under the Tang Dynasty*. Cambridge University Press.

"United States of America Long-Term Rating Lowered To 'AA+' Due To Political Risks, Rising Debt Burden; Outlook Negative." 2011. https://web.archive.org/web/20140310053618/http://www.standardandpoors.com/ratings/articles/en/us/?assetID=1245316529563.

"U.S. Equity Market Resiliency during Times of Extreme Volatility." n.d. https://www.nyse.com/network/article/nyse-increases-resiliancy-during-extreme-volatility.

Van Dillen, J.G., Geoffrey Poitras, and Asha Majithia. 2006. "Isaac Le Maire and the Early Trading in Dutch East India Company Shares." In *Pioneers of Financial Economics: Volume 1*.

Vaughn, Karen. 1978. "JOHN LOCKE AND THE LABOR THEORY OF VALUE." *Journal of Libertarian Studies* 2 (4). https://cdn.mises.org/2_4_3_0.pdf.

Velde, François R. 2007. "John Law's System." *The American Economic Review* 97 (2). https://www.jstor.org/stable/30034460.

Venable, James. 2016. *Wells Fargo: Where Did They Go Wrong?* Harvard Scholar. https://scholar.harvard.edu/files/jtv/files/wells_fargo_where_did_they_go_wrong_by_james_venable_pdf_02.pdf.

Verboven, Koenraad. 2011. "INTRODUCTION: PROFESSIONAL COLLEGIA: GUILDS OR SOCIAL CLUBS?" *Ancient Society* 41. https://www.jstor.org/stable/44079950.

"Viking Weights and Measures." n.d. https://web.archive.org/web/20110215005124/http://www.hunterian.gla.ac.uk/archive/vikings/weights.html.

Vila, Sol Trumbo. 2017. "The Bailout Business in the EU." *Euractiv*. https://www.euractiv.com/section/economy-jobs/opinion/the-bailout-business-in-the-eu/.

Vishnia, Rachel Feig. 2012. *State, Society and Popular Leaders in Mid-Republican Rome 241-167 B.C.* Routledge.

Vitiello, Domenic, and George E. Thomas. 2010. *The Philadelphia Stock Exchange and the City It Made*. University of Pennsylvania Press.

Walker, W. Christopher. 1998. *CONTAGION: How the Asian Crisis Spread*. EDRC Briefing Notes No. 3. Asian Development Bank. https://aric.adb.org/pdf/edrcbn/edrcbn03.pdf.

Wang, Yu-Chuan. 1951. "Early Chinese Coinage." *Numismatic Notes and Monographs*, no. 122.

Ward-Perkins, C. N. 1950. "The Commercial Crisis of 1847." *Oxford Economic Papers, New Series* 2 (1). https://www.jstor.org/stable/2661749.

Wassink, Alfred. 1991. "Inflation and Fiscal Policy under the Roman Empire to the Price Edict of 301 AD." *Historia: Zeitschrift Für Alte Geschichte* 40 (4). https://www.jstor.org/stable/4436215.

Waxman, Olivia. 2017. "How a Financial Panic Helped Launch the New York Stock Exchange." *Time Magazine*. https://time.com/4777959/buttonwood-agreement-stock-exchange/.

Weale, Martin. 2000. "1300 Years of Pound Sterling." *National Institute Economic Review*, no. 172. https://www.jstor.org/stable/23872674.

Wearden, Graeme. 2011. "Portugal Bailout Details Boost Euro and Bond Markets." *The Guardian*. https://www.theguardian.com/business/2011/may/04/portugal-bailout-euro-rises-bond-markets.

Webel, Baird, and Edward Murphy. 2008. *The Emergency Economic Stabilization Act and Current Financial Turmoil: Issues and Analysis*. CRS Report. https://sgp.fas.org/crs/misc/RL34730.pdf.

Weck, Hannelore, and Bruno S. Frey. 1983. "A Statistical Study of the Effect of the Great Depression on Elections: The Weimar Republic, 1930-1933." *Political Behavior* 5 (4).

Weinberg, Ari. 2015. "Should You Fear the ETF?" *Wall Street Journal*. https://www.wsj.com/articles/should-you-fear-the-etf-1449457201.

Weiner, Eric. 2007. *What Goes up: The Uncensored History of Modern Wall Street as Told by the Bankers, Brokers, CEOs, and Scoundrels Who Made It Happen*. Little, Brown.

Weisbrot, Mark, and Luis Sandoval. 2007. *Argentina's Economic Recovery: Policy Choices and Implications*. CEPR. https://www.cepr.net/documents/publications/argentina_recovery_2007_10.pdf.

Wells, O. V. 1937. "The Depression of 1873-79." *Agricultural History* 11 (3).

White, Eugene. 1990. "The Stock Market Boom and Crash of 1929 Revisited." *Journal of Economic Perspectives* 4 (2).

White, Eugene N. 2018. "Censored Success: How to Prevent a Banking Panic, the Barings Crisis of 1890 Revisited." *Rutgers University and NBER*. https://economics.rutgers.edu/downloads-hidden-menu/news-and-events/workshops/macroeconomic-theory/1747-eugenewhitefeb12/file.

White, Eugene Nelson. 1995. "The French Revolution and the Politics of Government Finance, 1770-1815." *The Journal of Economic History* 55 (2).

"Why Are Chip Cards More Secure Than Swiping?" 2023. https://www.tdecu.org/blog/why-are-chip-cards-more-secure-than-swiping.

Wilentz, Sean. 2005. *The Rise of American Democracy: Jefferson to Lincoln*. WW Norton & Company.

Willan, T. S. 1954. "The Muscovy Merchants of 1555." *The Economic Journal* 64 (255). https://doi.org/10.2307/2227766.

"William Hague: Euro Is a Burning Building." 2011. *BBC News*. https://www.bbc.com/news/uk-politics-15098567.

Williamson, John. 1985. "On the System in Bretton Woods." *The American Economic Review* 75 (2). https://www.jstor.org/stable/1805574.

Williamson, John. 2009. "Understanding Special Drawing Rights (SDRs)." *Peterson Institute for International Economics*, nos. PB09-11. https://web.archive.org/web/20100622191605/http://www.iie.com/publications/pb/pb09-11.pdf.

Wilson, C. H. 1939. "The Economic Decline of the Netherlands." *The Economic History Review* 9 (2). https://doi.org/10.2307/2590218.

Wilson, Charles. 1941. *Anglo-Dutch Commerce & Finance in the Eighteenth Century*. Cambridge University Press.

Witten, David. 2001. "The Depression of 1893." https://web.archive.org/web/20090427161827/http://eh.net/encyclopedia/article/whitten.panic.1893.

Woods, Andrew R. 2018. "From Charlemagne to the Commercial Revolution (c.800–1150)." In *Money and Coinage in the Middle Ages*. Brill.

"World's Earliest Coin Workshop Found in Central China's Henan." 2021. *Shine. Cn*. https://www.shine.cn/news/nation/2108093337/.

Wright, R. N. J. 1976. "The Silver Dragon Coinage of the Chinese Provinces, 1888-1949." *The Numismatic Chronicle (1966-)*, Seventh Series, vol. 16 (136). https://www.jstor.org/stable/42664795.

Wroughton, Lesley. 2013. "IMF Reprimands Argentina for Inaccurate Economic Data." *Reuters*. https://www.reuters.com/article/idUSBRE91019A/.

Wunsch, Cornelia. 2007. "The Egibi Family." In *The Babylonian World*. Routledge.

Xu, Chengzi. 2022. "Reshaping Global Trade: The Immediate and Long-Run Effects of Bank Failures." *The Quarterly Journal of Economics* 137 (4). https://doi.org/10.1093/qje/qjac016.

Xu, Yan. 2017. "The State Salt Monopoly in China: Ancient Origins and Modern Implications." Sec. 18. *Studies in the History of Law* 8. https://www.researchgate.net/publication/340442948_The_State_Salt_Monopoly_in_China_Ancient_Origins_and_Modern_Implications.

Yang, Bin. 2011. "The Rise and Fall of Cowrie Shells: The Asian Story." *Journal of World History* 22 (1). https://www.jstor.org/stable/23011676.

Yu, Liuliang, and Hong Yu. 2004. *Chinese Coins: Money in History and Society*.

Zhang, Wei-Bin. 2006. *Confucianism and Industrialization*. https://www.apu.ac.jp/rcaps/uploads/fckeditor/publications/journal/RJAPS_V2_Zhang.pdf.

Zheng, Bao-Hong. 2012. 圖片香港貨幣. 三聯書店(香港)有限公司.

Zhou, Sheng. 2014. "Bitcoin Laundromats for Dirty Money: The Bank Secrecy Act's

(BSA) Inadequacies in Regulating and Enforcing Money Laundering Laws over Virtual Currencies and the Internet." *Journal of Law & Cyber Warfare* 3 (1).

"中国货币史." 2022. https://crchat.crc.com.cn/258A/2022-09-26/232669.html.

"北魏至唐中葉期間均田制發展與政治興衰的關係." n.d. Education Bureau of Hong Kong. https://www.edb.gov.hk/attachment/tc/curriculum-development/kla/pshe/references-and-resources/chinese-history/module4_2.pdf.

甘露 (Gan, Lu). 2006. "论'交子'作为纸币的法律特征." 金融法苑 71. https://www.finlaw.pku.edu.cn/jrfy/gk/2006_jrfy/2006nzd71j/240178.htm.

"银行发展史." 2022. https://winfo.crc.com.cn/crc_mobile/crc/magazine/258/202205/t20220530_609233.htm.

Image Credits

Photos are listed by their associated event number.

2: Gokhan Dogan/Shutterstock

9: Dima Moroz/Shutterstock

13: Vvoe/Shutterstock

17: Classical Numismatic Group, Inc. http://www.cngcoins.com - This file is licensed under the Creative Commons Attribution-Share Alike 3.0 Unported license

19: David L. Tranbarger rare coins

28: Enez35/Flickr - Licensed under the Creative Commons Attribution 2.0 Generic license

37: http://ark.bnf.fr/ark:/12148/cb419723645, CC0, via Wikimedia Commons - Creative Commons CCO 1.0 public domain

52: Classical Numismatic Group, Inc. http://www.cngcoins.com - Creative Commons Attribution-Share Alike 2.5 Generic license

54: Israel Silvestre/public domain

58: Wikimedia Commons/Public domain

64: Wikimedia Commons/Public domain

67: Jean-Michel Moullec/Flicker & Wikimedia Commons - Creative Commons 2.0

72: PHGCOM/Wikimedia - Creative Commons Attribution-Share Alike 3.0

80: Tsien Tsuen-Hsun *Science and Civilization in China*: Volume 5, Part 1, Paper and Printing/Wikimedia Commons - Public domain

83: http://www.domesdaymap.co.uk/book/devon/01/ "Open Domesday" / Wikimedia Commons - Public domain

84: John C. Cobden/Wikimedia Commons

89: Hampshire Museums/Wikimedia Commons

114: Wikimedia Commons/Public domain

122: Wikimedia Commons/Public Domain

123: Wikimedia Commons/Public Domain

126: Wikimedia Commons - Creative Commons Attribution-Share Alike 4.0 International

130: De Agostini/Getty, Public domain, via Wikimedia Commons

136: The Portable Antiquities Scheme/ The Trustees of the British Museum, CC BY-SA 4.0 <https://creativecommons.org/licenses/by-sa/4.0>, via Wikimedia Commons

139: Joan Nieuhof/Wikimedia Commons

151: The Portable Antiquities Scheme/ The Trustees of the British Museum, Public domain, via Wikimedia Commons

153: Wikimedia Commons/Public domain

164: Bank of England/Public Domain

170: ごーちゃん, CC BY-SA 4.0 <https://creativecommons.org/licenses/by-sa/4.0>, via Wikimedia Commons

176: Julie Ceccaldi, CC0, via Wikimedia Commons

194: Wikimedia Commons: Public Domain

198: Public Domain

200: Public Domain

212: Public Domain

222: Wikimedia Commons/Public Domain

227: The Ministry of Revenue of the Manchu Qing Dynasty., Public domain, via Wikimedia Commons

228: Wikimedia Commons/Public Domain

230: Wikimedia Commons/Public Domain

236: H. Zimmer, CC BY 3.0 <https://creativecommons.org/licenses/by/3.0>, via Wikimedia Commons

241: Public Domain

248: Public Domain

250: Wikimedia Commons/Public Domain

251: Wikimedia Commons/Public Domain

259: Public Domain

263: Public Domain

266: Public Domain

269: Wikimedia Commons/Public Domain

270: Public Domain

281: Wikimedia Commons/Public Domain

286: Wikimedia Commons/Public Domain

288: Richard from USA, CC BY 2.0 <https://creativecommons.org/licenses/by/2.0>, via Wikimedia Commons

289: Associated Press, Public domain, via Wikimedia Commons

294: Seattle Municipal Archives, CC BY 2.0 <https://creativecommons.org/licenses/by/2.0>, via Wikimedia Commons

297: Dorothea Lange, Public domain, via Wikimedia Commons

300: Arquivo Nacional Collection/Public

domain

304: David Low, Public domain, via Wikimedia Commons

317: FORTEPAN / Teller Ferenc, CC BY-SA 3.0 <https://creativecommons.org/licenses/by-sa/3.0>, via Wikimedia Commons

321: Max12Max, CC BY-SA 4.0 <https://creativecommons.org/licenses/by-sa/4.0>, via Wikimedia Commons

328: Pancho Medrano Papers, CC BY 4.0 <https://creativecommons.org/licenses/by/4.0>, via Wikimedia Commons

337: Alisdare Hickson from Woolwich, United Kingdom, CC BY-SA 2.0 <https://creativecommons.org/licenses/by-sa/2.0>, via Wikimedia Commons

343: Arthahn, CC BY-SA 3.0 <https://creativecommons.org/licenses/by-sa/3.0>, via Wikimedia Commons

347: Ganesh Dhamodkar, CC BY 4.0 <https://creativecommons.org/licenses/by/4.0>, via Wikimedia Commons

356: Jeff Keyzer from Austin, TX, USA, CC BY-SA 2.0 <https://creativecommons.org/licenses/by-sa/2.0>, via Wikimedia Commons

359: The Central Intelligence Agency, Public domain, via Wikimedia Commons

366: juggadery, CC BY-SA 2.0 <https://creativecommons.org/licenses/by-sa/2.0>, via Wikimedia Commons

374: Series: Reagan White House Photographs, 1/20/1981 - 1/20/1989Collection: White House Photographic Collection, 1/20/1981 - 1/20/1989, Public domain, via Wikimedia Commons

377: Mike Mozart from Funny YouTube, USA, CC BY 2.0 <https://creativecommons.org/licenses/by/2.0>, via Wikimedia Commons

378: jailbird, CC BY-SA 3.0 DE <https://creativecommons.org/licenses/by-sa/3.0/de/deed.en>, via Wikimedia Commons

385: Txllxt TxllxT, CC BY-SA 4.0 <https://creativecommons.org/licenses/by-sa/4.0>, via Wikimedia Commons

390: Идеологист, CC BY-SA 4.0 <https://creativecommons.org/licenses/by-sa/4.0>, via Wikimedia Commons

397: Maksym Kozlenko, CC BY-SA 4.0 <https://creativecommons.org/licenses/by-sa/4.0>, via Wikimedia Commons

404: Bautsch, CC0, via Wikimedia Commons

409: Oisacc, CC BY-SA 4.0 <https://creativecommons.org/licenses/by-sa/4.0>, via Wikimedia Commons

411: Adam Moreira (AEMoreira042281), CC BY-SA 4.0 <https://creativecommons.org/licenses/by-sa/4.0>, via Wikimedia Commons

418: 김둥둥, CC BY 4.0 <https://creativecommons.org/licenses/by/4.0>, via Wikimedia Commons

423: Usuario:Barcex, CC BY-SA 3.0 <http://creativecommons.org/licenses/by-sa/3.0/>, via Wikimedia Commons

441: Percival Kestreltail, CC BY-SA 3.0 <https://creativecommons.org/licenses/by-sa/3.0>, via Wikimedia Commons

448: OddurBen, CC BY-SA 3.0 <https://creativecommons.org/licenses/by-sa/3.0>, via Wikimedia Commons

453: Public Domain

460: Gruntzooki, CC BY-SA 2.0 <https://creativecommons.org/licenses/by-sa/2.0>, via Wikimedia Commons

462: Raul Lanus, CC BY-SA 4.0 <https://creativecommons.org/licenses/by-sa/4.0>, via Wikimedia Commons

466: Joanna, CC BY 2.0 <https://creativecommons.org/licenses/by/2.0>, via Wikimedia Commons

472: The White House from Washington, DC, Public domain, via Wikimedia Commons

478: Tomek Grabarczyk, CC BY 3.0 <https://creativecommons.org/licenses/by/3.0>, via Wikimedia Commons

481: Used under fair use for educational purposes

486: Ggia, CC BY-SA 4.0 <https://creativecommons.org/licenses/by-sa/4.0>, via Wikimedia Commons

487: Indurema, CC BY-SA 4.0 <https://creativecommons.org/licenses/by-sa/4.0>, via Wikimedia Commons

492: Metropolitan Transportation Authority of the State of New York from United States of America, CC BY 2.0 <https://creativecommons.org/licenses/by/2.0>, via Wikimedia Commons

498: Minh Nguyen, CC BY-SA 4.0 <https://creativecommons.org/licenses/by-sa/4.0>,

via Wikimedia Commons
500: Zzyzx, CC BY 3.0 <https://creativecommons.org/licenses/by/3.0>, via Wikimedia Commons